CUTTING EDGE

CUTTING EDGE

*Gillette's
Journey to
Global
Leadership*

GORDON MCKIBBEN

Harvard Business School Press
Boston, Massachusetts

Printed in the United States of America

01 00 99 98 97 5 4 3 2 1

McKibben, Gordon C., 1930–
 Cutting edge : Gillette's journey to global leadership / Gordon C. McKibben.
  p. cm.
 Includes bibliographical references and index.
 ISBN 0-87584-725-0 (alk. paper)
 1. Gillette Company. 2. Razor industry—United States. 3. Consolidation and merger of corporations—United States. I. Title.
HD9999.R34G556 1998
338.7'6885—dc21   97-25517
                                                                  CIP

The paper used in this publication meets the requirements of the American National Standard for Permanence of Paper for Printed Library Materials Z39.49-1984

For Peggy

CONTENTS

———

———

PREFACE

———

AMERICAN SAFETY RAZOR Company was founded in 1901 over a fish market on the Boston waterfront by King Camp Gillette and a few friends and risk takers who hoped to grow rich on Gillette's invention of a new razor. A smart move by those friends and risk takers! American Safety Razor Co., which soon changed its name first to Gillette Safety Razor Co., and then later to The Gillette Company, defined and dominated the world shaving industry from its early days.

It was not easy. In its first few years there were financial, patent, and personality crises. Mismanagement brought on by reckless growth in the late 1920s forced the company to merge with the much smaller AutoStrop Safety Razor Company in 1930 on AutoStrop's terms, but Gillette survived as a company and moved on to better days. After World War II, Gillette began manufacturing men's and women's toiletries. Today it is the world leader in sales of some important consumer product groups, including razors, blades, electric shavers, pens, toothbrushes, and alkaline batteries.

Thanks to the vision of its founder, the company has retained a global mindset from its earliest days, and pushed into every corner of the earth, usually ahead of its competitors. Just prior to

---

the 1996 acquisition of Duracell International, Inc., 70 percent of total sales and 72 percent of total profits came from Gillette's operations outside the United States. More than 80 percent of the company's employees work abroad. In its continuing process of taking on the world, Gillette has developed a breed of global manager, has created global mechanisms, and has evolved a global strategy that sets it apart from most other international business operations.

Much of the historical detail in the first three chapters of this book, covering the period up to 1975, was first published in *King C. Gillette: the Man and His Wonderful Shaving Device,* by Russell Adams (Boston, Mass.: Little, Brown, 1978). I owe much to Adams' good work.

This book focuses on Gillette's modern years that began around 1975, when Colman M. Mockler, Jr., took over as chairman. Mockler's era included possibly the greatest crisis in the company's history, the threat to Gillette's independent existence from hostile takeover attacks by Wall Street raiders, followed closely by a bitterly contested proxy fight for control of the company. The raiders had one thing right: they recognized great value in Gillette. The momentum of Gillette's global growth, and the consequent increase in shareholder value since the 1988 proxy fight ended, would astonish even King C. Gillette, that utopian socialist, traveling salesman, and entrepreneurial inventor who started it all in the first place.

The final four chapters of *Cutting Edge* examine how Gillette has developed mechanisms over the years to translate its global mindset into a business reality—for example, how it manufactures overseas, how it manages foreign currency flows from a Boston "war room," and how it builds and executes a one-world marketing strategy. Chapters fifteen and sixteen examine how Gillette's global culture and mechanisms work in Latin America, Russia, and certain other Eastern European and Asian markets that, until recently, were closed to American companies. Much of the source information used in these chapters was obtained by the author during trips to Gillette outposts in Europe, including Russia and Poland, and to Brazil and Argentina. A final chapter examines how

Gillette converted Braun AG, which it acquired in 1967, from a parochial German manufacturer to a major global enterprise.

More than 60 Gillette executives on three continents were interviewed for this book, as were many lawyers, investment bankers, and other outsiders involved in Gillette's history since 1975. This book was commissioned by Gillette. Chairman Alfred M. Zeien and others at Gillette agreed not to impose conditions on the content or the author's interpretation of events, and all were true to their word.

I

THE STAGE
IS SET

1

A
GLOBAL
HERITAGE

As KING C. GILLETTE *boarded ship in Liverpool for the ten-day trip to New York and Boston that day in August 1904, he was outraged. Had this man John J. Joyce no vision? True, he had saved the infant Gillette Safety Razor Company from liquidation or bankruptcy in 1902, when King Gillette had coaxed him to invest $60,000 in the year-old company. But now Joyce, the company's largest shareholder, was poised to sacrifice King Gillette's clear vision of a global company selling blades and razors all over the world. In need of money to move beyond token production, Joyce proposed to sell off foreign rights to the Gillette safety razor to investors from Chicago for $100,000 cash and royalties on foreign sales. Unthinkable! He must stop Joyce.*

So King Gillette, an unpaid director of the tiny Boston company that he founded and that bore his name, abandoned his full-time job as the Baltimore-based Crown Cork & Seal Co.'s sales representative in England and sailed to Boston to plead with Joyce not to give up Gillette Safety Razor's global future. As King Gillette saw it, the razor he had invented was a universal product. There were almost no cultural or ethnic barriers to shaving. It would be folly to give up worldwide control and accept paltry royalty payments on Gillette blades and razors that he felt sure would one day be sold by the millions in every corner of the planet.

He arrived in Boston just in time to persuade his fellow directors to pull back from the foreign royalties deal, which had been agreed to in preliminary form by the directors while Gillette was still aboard ship, powerless to intervene. He had been sure that once in Boston he could sell his global vision anew to Joyce and block the deal. King C. Gillette was a great salesman—everybody gave him that—and he succeeded. At the very next directors' meeting in October, this time with Gillette in attendance, a one-sentence entry from the handwritten minutes of the meeting understates the drama of a pivotal decision in the company's history: "Mr. Holloway [W. B. Holloway, another director] reported the agreement as to the foreign end of the business would not be entered into at present, it being deemed for the best interests of the company to make no arrangements at this time."

In retrospect, King C. Gillette's timely trip to block the royalty scheme probably ranks as the single most important contribution he made for the company beyond his invention. He did no less than preserve the tiny company's global heritage and make it possible for him and succeeding generations of Gillette managers to build the worldwide enterprise that has emerged ready to take on all challengers in the global economy of the late twentieth century. Had the deal gone through, The Gillette Company, if it had survived at all, today would have been just another big American company with a flow of foreign royalties to spice up its earnings. Instead, it found another way to finance its start-up production and steadily moved beyond America to Europe and then to the rest of the world, becoming the dominant global manufacturer and marketer of blades and razors and, much later, other consumer products like toothbrushes and small batteries, in demand almost everywhere.

King C. Gillette had it right when he boarded that ship to block Joyce's move.

THE EARLY YEARS

The earliest days of Gillette have become the stuff of legend. At once a first-rate traveling salesman and a utopian dreamer who wanted to construct a socialist paradise on earth, King C. Gillette had a startling vision one morning in 1895 as he struggled to shave at his Brookline, Massachusetts, home. His razor was too dull to cut his whiskers, and the edge was too far gone for him to strop it at home. The razor would have to be sent out to a barber or cutler for sharpening. There must be some better way to shave, he thought; the idea of a separate razor handle with a disposable blade then came to him "more with the rapidity of a dream than by the slow process of reasoning." He recounted the moment more than twenty years later to the editors of the Gillette *Blade*, the company house organ: "As I stood there with my razor in hand, my eyes resting on it lightly as a bird settling down on its nest, the Gillette razor was born. I saw it all in a moment. . . . I could see the way the blade could be held in a holder; then came the idea of sharpening the two opposite edges on the thin piece of steel that was uniform in thickness throughout, thus doubling its services; and following in sequence came the clamping plates for the blade and a handle equally disposed between the two edges of the blade."

There are other claimants to an earlier "safety razor." It is generally agreed that the first two-piece safety razor was the single-edge Star, patented in 1876 by the brothers Frederick and Otto Kampfe of Brooklyn, New York, which was used and praised by such luminaries as Oliver Wendell Holmes. The Star was followed by look-alike models named Fox, Gem, and Ever-Ready.[1] Safety for the shaver, compared with potentially lethal straight razors, marked the shared bond of these two-piece razors, not disposability or economy. Indeed, the Star basically was a small piece of a straight razor clamped to a handle, with its sharp edge exposed. The user had to remove the cumbersome blade before each shave to place it in a special holder for stropping on a heavy leather belt and then had to reinsert the blade into the handle, a process that no doubt accounted for many accidental cuts to the hand if not the face. After a time, the blade had to be sent to a cutler for honing.

King Gillette's concept of a permanent handle holding an inexpensive double-edge blade to be thrown away after a few shaves differed fundamentally from Star-type safety razors, which were essentially two-piece variations of the much more common single-edge straight razors. From his comments, it is evident that Gillette was thinking primarily of the convenience and the attractive economics of a refillable razor and blade system, and not just safety, when he invented what the U.S. Patent Office labeled the K. C. Gillette Razor but which became known and was promoted by the company as a safety razor.

As one version has it, Gillette rushed out to a Boston hardware store the same day he had his vision and bought some steel ribbon used for clock springs and some bits of brass. Then he returned home to his office and workshop and made the first Gillette safety razor—a crude likeness to be sure. No computers, no R & D project teams, no million dollar budgets—just a bottle cap salesman tinkering in his spare moments. He wrote to his wife, who was away in Ohio visiting relatives, "I have got it; our fortune is made."

Well, not at once. It took six years to go from idea in his head to a working model and drawings that could be submitted to the Patent Office. He had to convince friends to support him. He needed to find a metallurgist or engineer who could figure how to stamp out a wafer-thin blade from sheet steel and then harden it so that the blade could hold a sharp edge—technical work well beyond his capabilities. Gillette was an able tinkerer but no mechanical genius. He was a concept man, a big idea visionary, and in the end his big idea hatched from a bad shave was vindicated. Patent number 775134 for "razor," filed December 3, 1901, clearly was a representation of his first "eureka" vision of a two-piece shaving system—a thin sharpened blade clamped firmly to a permanent razor handle. It was a shaving *system*, as opposed to the conventional one-piece straight razor.

Gillette's business genius was to grasp the idea of a true mass market where none existed. As he saw it, those skinny blades that somehow or other would be inexpensively stamped from sheet steel would be used for a few shaves and then thrown away when dulled to the point at which they could no longer scrape off more hair without undue bloodletting. Then the shaver would buy another Gillette blade, and another, with profits to be reaped from repeat sales. Detractors scoffed at the very idea. Conventional wisdom ruled that the ideal razor should last a lifetime if its edge was properly stropped and honed, and should be priced accordingly for a market of professional barbers and sure-handed gentlemen adept at home shaving. Razor makers at the great European cutlery centers around Solingen, Germany, and Sheffield, England, were dedicated to this notion. An inexpensive blade, crudely mass produced and designed to be thrown away after a few shaves! A preposterous scheme, they told each other and any who would listen.

So much for conventional wisdom.

Born to Invent

Given his family background and the entrepreneurial and inventive zest of America in the late nineteenth century, it is not surprising that young King Camp Gillette grew up to challenge the status quo. He was born into a Wisconsin family of middle-class achievers, his unusual first and middle names honoring a family friend, Judge King, and his mother's family name, Camp. When he was four, the family moved to Chicago, where his father ran a successful hardware business and worked as a patent agent promoting a new type of shingle-making machine. The elder Gillette was an inventive man with several patents to his name, and he passed on his love of tinkering to King Camp and his brothers. His mother raised him and his four siblings and published bestselling cookbooks. After his father's business was wiped out by the Chicago Fire of 1871, King Camp was forced to forgo further schooling and, at the age of seventeen, took a job as a hardware salesman. He was good at his work. In 1895, he was forty years old, and he was established as a star salesman for Crown Cork & Seal, peddling the company's patented bottle cap to industrial customers, including brewers and bottlers in his New England territory.

He had already been granted patents for several of his inventions, none of which had been a money-maker. His mentor at Crown Cork, William Painter, had invented the corked bottle cap, which was his company's prime source of profit. At one point, he chided Gillette about wasting time on inventions that failed to show commercial promise: "King, you're always thinking and inventing: why don't you try to invent something like the 'Crown Cork' which, when used once, is thrown away and the customer comes back for more, and with every additional customer you get, you are building a permanent foundation for profit?" Gillette later claimed that Painter's idea became an obsession with him and eventually led to his invention of the safety razor and blades as a "bottles and bottle caps" invention with the profit potential of repeat sales of throwaway parts.

King C. Gillette was more than a first-rate salesman and insightful inventor. Today he would be regarded as a Renaissance man or more likely a headstrong visionary, in deference to the radical social engineering schemes he espoused. In the 1890s he worked countless hours promoting his remarkably specific vision of a social utopia even as he sold bottle caps to support his family and struggled to translate his idea for a new razor into a working model that could be patented. Just how his unusual social philosophy evolved is unknown. There is no record from his youth to suggest anger at an unjust society. As a family man with a wife, a child, a nice house, and for those days, a good salary, he appeared outwardly more Babbitt than Marx.

In 1894, he published *The Human Drift*, which described a vast metropolis near Niagara Falls where tens of millions would live in a classless society. Electricity from Niagara Falls would supply power to immense glass-domed, circular apartment towers wherein the inhabitants would happily pursue personal interests, since work would be secondary to uplifting activities. Competition would be banished and "rotten" capitalism ended. Gillette the utopian thinker had earnest backers at this time who attempted to raise money so that he could quit his business duties and become the full-time leader and promoter of a fledgling company, Twentieth Century Corporation. After publication of *The Human Drift*, he published a thirty-four-page follow-up tract in 1897. The corporation never came into being, but Gillette did not give up. He published a second book, *World Corporation*, in 1908, when he was deeply involved in Gillette Safety Razor Company's successful takeoff. He established a World Corporation headquarters at 6 Beacon Street in Boston and publicly offered the presidency of the company to Theodore Roosevelt, explaining that World Corporation would displace all governments in the world and thus be a greater job than the one T. R. had just finished as president of the United States. Roosevelt declined the offer. In 1924, by now a rich and famous business leader, Gillette published another utopian book, *The People's Corporation*. This unusual man was equally at ease in the worlds of business and radical social philosophy. When he died in 1932—the year Franklin D. Roosevelt defeated Herbert Hoover for the U.S. presidency, Gillette was a registered Republican.

FROM VISION TO PRODUCT

Gillette had many real-world problems to overcome as he fought to make his vision of a two-piece razor a commercial reality at the turn of the century. These included technical problems far beyond his ken. The world's cutlery experts believed that only forged steel could hold the keen edges needed for shaving. Gillette's razor would work only if blades made from thin sheet steel could be hardened and tempered and made to hold a sharp edge. But this was impossible, Gillette was told by cutlers and machinists throughout New England and the East, and by metallurgists at prestigious Massachusetts Institute of Technology (MIT). His friends took to scoffing at his determined pursuit of a newfangled razor with remarks like "Well, Gillette, how's the razor?" followed by winks and smirks.

Not knowing enough to quit, as he put it later, Gillette finally found his man—William E. Nickerson, surely to this day the most important recruit enlisted by the Gillette enterprise. Nickerson was the indispensable link between vision and reality. He was a sixth-generation Cape Codder, having been born at Provincetown, Massachusetts, in 1853. The family name is given to the large state park on the upper Cape. Nickerson graduated from MIT with a chemistry degree, worked for a while in the tanning industry, and then moved into mechanical fields, starting with the development of patented safety devices for elevators that were prompted by a fatal elevator crash in Boston. Among his seven elevator patents are a push-button system that stops elevators at the desired floor and the device that prevents elevator shaft doors from opening until the car arrives. These seemingly impressive advances, alas, brought him no financial gain.

Nickerson was recruited to the safety razor cause by his friend Henry Sachs, a Boston lamp maker and stockbroker, and by Sachs's son-in-law Jacob Heilborn, an industrial promoter. The three men had been involved in a venture to build a new type of lightbulb using air-pump technology that Nickerson had perfected; the venture had failed when a Boston judge ruled that Edison Company patents had been infringed, but the men remained friends. Sachs showed one of Gillette's crude working models to Nickerson one evening when the inventor dropped by his Brookline home. Nickerson was not impressed. Also, he was busy with another, more promising venture—an automatic weighing machine he had invented and nursed to the point of commercial success. The financially inept inventor did not know it at the time, but he was about to lose control of the weighing machine venture to backers he had trusted. Months later, now with time on his hands, Nickerson finally gave in to Heilborn, who had practically begged him to take the Gillette razor seriously. Reluctantly, he agreed to think about it for thirty days and then render his judgment.

Nickerson liked it! He wrote to Heilborn, "It is my confident opinion that not only can a successful razor be made on the principles of the Gillette patent, but that if the blades are made by the proper methods a result in advance of anything known can be reached." Nickerson's reply went to the heart of the matter: "In my opinion the success of the razor depends very largely, if not wholly, on the production at a low price of a substantially perfect blade . . . [that] should combine extreme keenness with a hardness and toughness sufficient to stand using several times without much deterioration."

Nickerson had given much thought to how such a blade could be manufactured in mass quantities and was confident that he could design the necessary production equipment to ensure a successful outcome. He estimated that it would cost $4,850 to set up manufacturing on a commercial basis. "So thoroughly am I satisfied that I can perfect machinery . . . which will be patentable, that I am ready to accept for my compensation stock in a Company which I understand you propose forming," his letter concluded.

Nickerson was introduced to King C. Gillette for the first time at Heilborn's office. The inventor was impressed with Nickerson and agreed to entrust his razor concept to the Yankee engineer, even swallowing his pride when Nickerson suggested that it would be inappropriate to name the proposed company just for the inventor. The American Safety Razor Company was chartered on September 28, 1901, with King C. Gillette as president. It was capitalized at $500,000, which was divided into 50,000 shares priced at $10. The founders awarded 30,000 shares to themselves as directors, split 17,500 to King C. Gillette and 12,500 to Heilborn, Sachs, Nickerson, and Edward Stewart, a mutual friend of the others. In addition, 20,000 treasury shares were split into blocks of 500 shares, discounted to $250 for the block, and put up for sale to investors. These 20 blocks had to be sold to raise the $5,000 that Nickerson thought sufficient to start production.

Having assigned all rights to his inventions to the company in return for $40 a week in salary, Nickerson got to work at once at a rented workshop set up over a fish shop at 424 Atlantic Avenue in Boston. It was next to a dock where garbage was loaded onto scows, creating a certain "perfume," as Nickerson called the stench. Heilborn set out to sell shares of stock to investors. Gillette was president in name but of necessity remained a full-time salesman for Crown Cork. The fundraising proved difficult, with only thirteen blocks of stock sold by the end of the year. The remaining seven were bought by Henry Sachs in order to bring the full $5,000 into the treasury.

Nickerson had no problem determining the size and shape of the blade, but how to harden the sheet steel proved more difficult. As he later told it, the idea came to him as he sat in a rocking chair at his Cambridge, Massachusetts, house one night in March 1902. There were no computers, no project teams, just a pragmatic engineer rocking in his chair, thinking. Solving the tempering process came more easily. By the end of May, he announced that manufacturing could begin as soon as more funds could be raised.

Of course, it was not quite that easy. Nickerson, with a crew of up to six, had already gone through the original $5,000 and had to borrow from Sachs to meet the payroll. The company had to have more capital. Nickerson's erstwhile weighing machine partners in New York offered to supply $150,000—but demanded 51 percent control of the company, which the Boston group wisely refused. Shares of the company, now known as Gillette Safety Razor Company, to the delight of the founder, could be bought for twenty-five cents a share. There was very little interest from investors, even at this discounted price, and suppliers were not enthused at the idea of accepting the stock in lieu of cash. Gillette's great razor project stalled for lack of capital.

For a year or so, the company's fate hung in the balance as efforts to raise money faltered. The situation was so desperate that the discouraged directors, meeting at Sachs's downtown office, agreed to consider liquidation. Leaving the meeting, Gillette by chance encountered his old friend and brewer client, John Joyce, at Young's Hotel, a popular downtown lunch place for Boston businesspeople. Joyce, an Irish immigrant who had risen from poverty to wealth in the beer business and later through electric utility investments, knew Gillette from the days when Gillette sold him bottle caps by the carload. Acting on Gillette's advice, Joyce had some years earlier invested $20,000 in New Era Carbonator Co., a start-up company that Gillette had promoted for an inventor-friend. New Era had collapsed and Joyce lost his $20,000, which presumably explained why Gillette had not approached him earlier to invest in the razor company. Still on good terms nonetheless, the two men sat down to lunch. Talk turned quickly to the razor venture which, Gillette noted sadly, was on the verge of failing for lack of capital, unless. . . . King Gillette the salesman moved in for the kill, and by the end of lunch a rough understanding was in the works.

Having been burned once, Joyce drove a tough bargain. He said he would buy up to $100,000 worth of 8 percent bonds but at sixty cents on the dollar, and with each bond he bought, he demanded an equivalent amount of company stock. The company directors accepted the deal, and Joyce promptly put $9,500 into Gillette. Nickerson started up his "line," consisting of a single sharpening machine and allied equipment, and slowly, very slowly, prototype razors and blades began to appear. They were suitable for testing and showing to the trade, but that was not enough for Joyce, who wanted full-scale production. He could order his brewmasters to produce more beer when thirsty New Englanders demanded it. Why couldn't Nickerson turn up the volume of razors he produced like his breweries could turn up the flow of suds when weather turned hot? Nickerson bristled at his new boss's impatience and made his case once again for more funds to increase production capacity. Joyce came up with another $8,500 for a second sharpening machine. Word began to spread as sample razor systems began to circulate.

With Joyce now in control, the directors turned to the critical issue of pricing for the blades and razors. They agreed on $1 for a pack of twenty blades, which were to be wrapped in green paper with the clean-shaven face of the founder on the front. Most of the directors wanted the razor to sell for $3 or less, but Joyce demanded a $5 price, and that was that. In a tip-off of Gillette strategic priorities to come, the company's first advertisement appeared in a business journal, *System*, in fall 1903 under a headline that proclaimed "We Offer a New Razor," with pictures of the razor and blade. The ad copy promised, a bit expansively, a new kind of razor and a thin blade "that will hold its edge for 20 or 30 shaves . . . and is so tightly held it could not possibly hurt you."

Included was a coupon to send along with $5 for a silver razor and a two-year supply of twenty blades, or $12 for a gold razor. At year's end, Gillette's first annual sales report was in: 51 razors and 168 blades had been sold in 1903.

It was time to start a real business, with offices and salespeople. For King Gillette, the start-up was bittersweet. Crown Cork had been eager to send him to England to oversee sales there and offered to boost his salary to $6,000 annually. With no other means of support, Gillette could not put Crown Cork off for much longer. In what would seem a reasonable request, he asked Joyce to pay him a salary so that he could remain in Boston. Gillette was, after all, the founder and president and second-largest shareholder. Joyce turned him down, and there was nothing for Gillette to do but sail off for London with his wife and son. He resigned as president but remained a director.

After just seven months, he was back from London on his emergency mission to block the deal to sell off foreign patent rights. Autumn 1904 was a critical period for the fledgling company. William Nickerson came through just in time with the invention of a new blade-grinding machine that unplugged the production bottleneck that had so disturbed Joyce. By year's end, sales increased to 90,884 razors and 123,648 blades, and a much happier Joyce credited Nickerson with "saving the company." (Nickerson did it again in 1914 with automatic honing machines, which greatly increased productivity and again earned Joyce's praise.) Moreover, the crucial U.S. patent on the Gillette safety razor was granted on November 15, 1904, giving the company seventeen years to make the best of its new product without significant competition—an assurance that helped the company raise money from investors.

As sales began to take off, King Gillette again implored Joyce to pay him a salary so that he could take part in business affairs, as befit the company's founder. Joyce gave in, and Gillette was accorded an $18,000 annual salary and made a vice president. Gillette returned to London to pick up his wife and son, King Gaines. Soon he was on the job in Boston. But it was an uneasy situation. Joyce and Gillette, both strong-willed entrepreneurs, had had a falling-out after Gillette blocked Joyce's proposal to sell foreign rights to the razor. The jousting grew nasty. Joyce put an end to secretive efforts by Gillette to move the company to Newark, New Jersey. Gillette threatened to walk away from the enterprise unless he was reappointed president. To keep the peace, Joyce agreed to bestow the title but ceded no power.

There was agreement on one point. From the start, once the foreign royalties question was settled, The Gillette Company held to its conviction that its products should be sold and manufactured abroad at the earliest practicable moment. Moving quickly into new geographic markets, often in the face of significant business or political risks, is a hallmark of Gillette's strategy to this day. The first sales office was opened in London in 1905, the same year a blade-making plant was started in one corner of a maker of bicycle seats in Paris. By 1906, Gillette was operating a blade plant in Canada as well, and a European distribution network was established in Germany, with sales reported in many nations, including Russia. A Mexican sales operation also started up that year. The small company thought big and moved fast.

Joyce Wins Out

Back in Boston, the clash of egos between King C. Gillette and John J. Joyce became intolerable. The two men quarreled and struggled for control of the company until 1910, when Joyce made a decisive move. He bought out most of the stock owned by Gillette and some of his loyalists on the board. That made Gillette a millionaire at last. It also gave John Joyce unchallenged control of the company, which he held until 1916, when in declining health, he retired to California. He died a few months later.

Shortly after Joyce bought his stock, Gillette moved to southern California to grow oranges, dates, and figs and live the life of a gentleman rancher, world traveler, and part-time social dreamer, but he kept in close touch with the company he founded. He was seldom without an opinion about what the company should do, and his ideas appear to have been welcomed by many of his former colleagues, who kept up a steady correspondence with him. He remained an influential and outspoken director and retained his honorary title as president until shortly before he died in 1932, at the age of seventy-eight.

When Joyce gained control, management moved beyond the entrepreneurial jealousies that marked its first decade, and the company became more professionally managed. Frank J. Fahey and Thomas W. Pelham were at the top. Fahey had been with Gillette since 1906 and as vice president had proved himself an able general manager. It did not hurt his prospects that he had married Joyce's daughter. Even after the marriage broke up, the father of the bride gave his full professional support to Fahey.

Thomas Pelham was a New York lawyer who became a Gillette enthusiast when he first shaved with a Gillette razor in 1903 and found it cut his shaving time with an old straight razor from twenty minutes to five. Within a short time, he joined the company and became a member of Joyce's inner circle as sales director. For more than two decades, Pelham was the company's sales and marketing director and an important legal voice. By dint of personality and energy, he was probably the company's most visible officer, apart from the founder. He was a tireless world traveler and motivator, with an indomitable urge to spread the gospel of the Gillette razor to all corners of the earth. He was a marketing innovator who broke new ground, as in 1915, when the company shocked conventional thinkers by introducing a woman's razor named MiLady Décolleté. An advertising campaign advised women that "it was the safest and most sanitary method of acquiring a smooth underarm." The word "shave," however, was banned as unfeminine.

Pelham and Fahey were both enthusiastic internationalists who spent much time abroad. They encouraged Gillette's nascent globalism as World War I loomed and then started, and the United States finally was pulled in, with great consequences for Gillette, as it turned out.

Shortly after Joyce died in 1916, the controlling shares held in his estate were sold to John E. Aldred of New York, an old banking associate of his from the brewery days and later a partner with him in Shawinigan Water & Power Co. Aldred, working through a syndicate of New York bankers under the name Aldred & Co., reorganized the company as a Delaware corporation, and the New Yorker assumed control. He made a point of assuring Fahey and Pelham that they were still the top managers and seems to have impressed them mightily. Pelham called Aldred's purchase "the most important day in Gillette's history." Frank Fahey exulted that the purchase date, September 20, 1917, was a "red letter day in Gillette history." Years later, he wrote that he was with fellow director King C. Gillette, in Boston for the event, as the final papers were signed. Gillette, he reported, "tore off the date sheet from a wall calendar and handed it to him, remarking 'Frank, have this framed; it marks an epoch in this company's history.'" Fahey had the calendar page framed, and it hung in his South Boston office for the next several years.

William Nickerson stayed on in active service. He served as vice president and director of manufacturing until he retired in 1928, proudly reminding friends that he was Gillette's first sala-ried employee, at $40 a week. He was an educational philanthro-pist, giving his time and large sums of money to his alma mater, MIT, and to Boston University, whose large outdoor stadium, Nickerson Field, is named for him. He died in 1931.

WORLD WAR I AND THE 1920S

Until America entered World War I, it still was not a sure thing—this notion of a mass market for razors and throwaway blades to satisfy the habit of shaving at home. Gillette's unit sales of razors and blades overall grew at a modest pace from 1908 until 1916, though producing steadily greater profits, thanks to John Joyce's insistence on a $5 razor and premium-priced blades. But it was not inclusive growth, not a true mass market. Barbers still did a brisk shaving business, and many men continued to take pride in their skill with the straight razor, or "cut-throat razor," as the company called it. Perhaps not in parlors and boardrooms, but among the general population, a two-day stubble was acceptable or at least was overlooked without too much comment.

Interestingly, barbers in the United States did not offer much resistance to the notion of home shaving, which of course cut into their core "shave and a haircut" business, whether it was six bits, or in World War I days, closer to two bits. In its first decade Gillette's advertisements attacked barbers with exaggerated disdain. An ad in 1906 declared "if the time, money, energy and brainpower wasted in the barbershops of America were applied to direct effort, the Panama Canal would be dug in four hours." An ad in 1910 implied home shaving with a Gillette razor was more manly than "the ladylike massage finish of the tonsorial artist" and the "reek of violet water."[2] But Gillette soon changed course and cut back on attack ads. Instead, the company shrewdly made barber shops a key part of its distribution strategy, giving barbers a small percentage from the sale of each blade and razor sold to customers. This probably explained the general lack of resistance by barbers to home shaving.

From the Middle Ages on, barbers have had to be entrepreneurial. Well into the eighteenth century, many barbers called themselves barber-surgeons and supplemented their hair cutting and shaving income by using their expertise to perform surgeries. Some also practiced dentistry. The New York City barber and historian of the tonsorial arts, Charles de Zemler, estimated that shaving revenue for barbers dropped from 50 percent around the time of the Spanish-American War to 10 percent by 1939 because of the invention of the safety razor and electric razor. According to Zemler, haircuts provided 40 percent of average revenue, with other services like massages, facials, and allied special services making up the remaining 50 percent. He advised young barbers to branch out into "hair saving programs" for the growing number of prematurely bald men he detected in the late 1930s.

From the company's first days, Gillette advertisements have emphasized the manliness and sexiness of the smooth-shaven man, and that has not changed in nine decades. But as has been noted, it took World War I to erase any doubt about the arrival of the home-shaving mass market. In 1917—the year President Woodrow Wilson declared war on the Central Powers—Gillette sold

1.1 million razors. Military regulations at first required every soldier to provide himself with a shaving kit, and Gillette's compact $5 kit with disposable blades far outsold competitors like AutoStrop and Eversharp, which had cumbersome stropping attachments. Gillette displayed a deft marketing touch by designing a military-only case decorated with army and navy insignia. In 1918, taking a cue from the example of British and French officers, who encouraged their troops engaged in trench warfare to keep

---

SHAVING LORE

The history of shaving the male face goes back to the days of cavemen, when individual men presumably "home shaved" with sharpened shell edges or the like. At any given time in history, some men have cut the hair from their faces and some have not. In ancient days, soldiers like the Macedonian troops commanded by Alexander the Great shaved to prevent enemies from grabbing their beards in hand-to-hand combat. Sometimes clean-shaven faces have been a matter of social status, as in the royal courts of Europe in the seventeenth century. In America, full beards enjoyed status as late as the Civil War years, when Abe Lincoln went from being clean-shaven to full-bearded. The leaders and soldiers of both North and South generally were bearded.

This was the Roman poet Ovid's advice to lovelorn males some two thousand years ago, in a poem entitled "Lover's Handbook":

> Let exercise your body brown:
> Don't slobber: see your teeth are clean:
> Your hair well cut and brushed quite down:
> Your cheeks close shaved with razor keen:
> Your toga spotless, and neat:
> Your sandals fitting to your feet.[3]

---

clean-shaven, to maintain health and morale, the U.S. military started issuing Gillette shaving kits to every U.S. serviceman. Gillette sales quadrupled: the company sold 3.5 million razors and 32 million blades that were stuffed into canvas kits and metal boxes. Gillette discounted the price on this huge sale to the War Department, of course, but still made money on the deal.

But what was far more important than a one-year sales spurt was that the enforced habit of shaving acquired by millions of young males in barracks and on ships broke down any remaining resistance to self-shaving. When the soldiers came home from Europe to America's cities and towns and farms, Gillette ads in newspapers and magazines reinforced the shaving habit servicemen had acquired at war. Gillette's advertising after the war emphasized the brand name, making sure that shaving and Gillette were perceived as one and the same. There was no time to be lost, because the seventeen years' protection ensured by Gillette's original patent was to run out on November 15, 1921, and a host of competitors would be hawking cut-rate imitations that would fit on Gillette handles just as well as Gillette blades, even if they were of inferior quality. It was rumored that tens of thousands of Japanese-made blades and razors were stacked in a Chicago warehouse awaiting the patent expiration.

Gillette had a plan, however. With great fanfare, the company introduced the New Improved Gillette Safety Razor in spring 1921, six months before the patent expiration. It was so good, Nickerson solemnly assured salesmen at the product's lavish introduction, that the new razor may have reached the limits of improveability. The effusive Pelham extolled it as near perfect and declared that his salesmen showed "unbounded enthusiasm." It was a better razor. But what was just as important as quality was that the introduction of the New Improved Razor showed off the marketing and pricing shrewdness that has been a hallmark for most, if not all, of Gillette shaving product introductions through the years. In 1921 the idea was to develop a pricing strategy that would outflank all the low-cost competitors eager to jump into the shaving market and dethrone King C. Gillette. The New Improved Razor, heavily advertised, was packaged in a handsome box and sold at the familiar $5 price that had served the company so well in its noncompetitive years. In addition, Gillette continued to sell its original razors, officially labeled "Old Type" as opposed to "New Improved." Many Old Type razors were inexpensively packaged in three-blade packs and sold under the name Brownies for the unheard-of low price of $1. Other Old Type blades were packaged more handsomely, with more blades, and were priced variously, with $3.50 the average. Rather than wait for cheaper imitations to make inroads, Gillette itself introduced the price competition it knew was coming.

The American public went for all this in a big way, especially the Brownies. In New York, a police officer had to be summoned to restore law and order when a mob of eager customers crowded one store. Gillette's pricing policy had converted a product that was still something of a luxury at $5 to an everyman product at $1 and in so doing vastly increased the market for its blades. By 1925, Gillette sales were up tenfold in unit terms from 1917, and Gillette had been transformed from a modest niche company into a fast-growth performer with unlimited prospects.

And it was not just Americans who had caught the shaving habit. Gillette's tireless internationalism was paying off. Immediately after World War I ended, Gillette expanded its European operations. A new manufacturing plant was built at Slough, near London, to turn out the New Improved Razor. It started production barely in time to satisfy British patent law that would have let other manufacturers copy the new system without penalty. Pelham opened dozens of offices and subsidiary operations in Europe and in other parts of the world, trying to lessen dependence on jobbers who were not exclusive Gillette agents. By the company's twenty-fifth anniversary in 1926, Gillette's global character was much commented upon, though the term *globalism* was not at the time applied to businesses, nor were such latter-day business school terms as *multinational* and *transnational*. Chairman J. R. Aldred thought he knew why Gillette was gaining a reputation for foreign business at the same time many New England companies had fallen behind competitors: "The Gillette company has been fortunate in being able to bring home to its operations the experience and opinion of men who have gone out to all parts of the world and brought home to Boston . . . the lessons they have learned," he told a group of business leaders. Aldred's observation may have been the first recognition of one of modern Gillette's great strengths—its corps of experienced global managers.

Aldred surely must have been thinking in particular of Pelham, who regularly reported his rich experiences in foreign markets to home office managers, and King Gillette, who served as a sort of goodwill ambassador for his namesake company around the globe. In the silver anniversary issue of the *Blade*, the seldom-humble King Gillette noted that his invention had not only revolutionized the shaving industry but to some degree had altered the habits of mankind: "In my travels, I have found it [the Gillette razor and blades] in the most northern town of Norway and in the heart of the Saharan desert where no white man lives." Not to be outdone, *Blade* editors claimed that "it is impossible to name any other manufactured commodity with distribution as great and widespread as Gillette. . . . In every town and city in the world Gillette razors and blades may be purchased! . . . The message of Gillette razors and blades was carried to each race in its own language on terms which people would understand and in a manner that would induce purchasing." An unnamed Gillette chronicler wrote that foreigners told him the three best-known American products abroad were the Ford motor car, the Singer sewing machine, and the Gillette razor.

Gillette advertising tried to keep up with the company's impressive distribution system. Although a spokesman reckoned that only 8 percent or 25 million of India's "teeming millions" were literate in the mid-1920s, Gillette nevertheless produced advertising extolling its razors in Marathi, Gujarathi, Telugu, Burmese, Hindu, Urdu, and Bengali dialects, as well as in English. With alliterative flair, Vice President and Treasurer Frank Fahey, whose importance to the company exceeded his titles, boasted that "the name of Gillette is as well known in Bombay as in Boston."

One thing remained the same regardless of geography: every pack of blades sold—and they were in the hundreds of millions by the mid-1920s—was adorned with a green wrapper showing the face of the unsmiling, mustachioed founder. King C. Gillette's original notion that it made great sense to establish a trademark "as internationally recognizable as a U.S. one dollar bill"—his own image, of course—was coming true.

2

Sudden Decline,
Slow Recovery

COMPANY REPORTS TOLD of ever-increasing growth throughout most of the 1920s, with no hint of problems. In the United States, variations of the Old Type and New Improved razors, like the $1 gold plated razor of 1923, were offered at regular intervals. A 1926 ad trumpeted that "629 out of 761 Railroad Men agreed on one razor—Gillette." It showcased the Bostonian, selling for $5 in silver plate and $6 in gold, advising that railroad men and anyone else could obtain New Improved Gillette razors ranging in price from $5 to $75. The Big Fellow, a model with an extra large handle, was a fast seller for a while, though the $1 Brownie was the company's biggest seller.

Giveaway promotions proliferated. Banks bought great quantities of blades at discounted prices and ran shave and save campaigns to attract new depositors, offering razors free to customers who started new deposits with $5 or $10. Razors were given away with Wrigley's gum and with packets of tea, coffee, spices, and marshmallows. All of this meant more business for Gillette, around the world as well as at home.

Gillette boasted that it sold more blades than all its world competitors put together. Frank Fahey claimed that the foreign growth came the honest way, "by intelligent application of the management to the principle of an excellent product, good advertising and sound merchandising," as opposed to buying out the many small competitors who had copied Gillette's shaving systems. One major exception was the German company Roth-Büchner, which alarmed Gillette by its success in selling inexpensive blades to European shavers who did not want to pay the Gillette premium for the real thing. Gillette bought controlling interest in Roth-Büchner's European business in 1926. In a few years, the newly acquired Berlin manufacturing plant was producing blades bearing no less than 250 private labels and had captured the lion's share of the low-end blade market in Europe. The policy worked so well that Gillette, not for the last time, imported to the United States an idea already proven successful on foreign shores. South Boston blade rejects—blades that were not good enough for the familiar green King Gillette packaging but were better than nearly all imitations and were too good to throw away—were packaged under the Rubie name and sold at cut-rate prices in the United States by Gillette salespeople. A small factory bearing the Rubie name opened for a time in New York, churning out private-label blades for such national chains as Woolworth's, R. H. Macy, Montgomery Ward, and Sears, Roebuck.

The company stayed alert to publicity opportunities calculated to promote Gillette blades. A yellowed clip from the *Boston Evening American*, May 25, 1927, headlined "Lindbergh Shaves with Razor from the Hub," quoted Frank Fahey: "Reports that Lindbergh carried a razor on his flight are incorrect. He arrived in Paris badly in need of a shave so our Paris manager supplied him with a Gillette gold traveling set."

Writing to King Gillette, Fahey crowed that the German-inspired strategy of dominating both the high end and the low end of the blade market was making inroads around the world. Fahey, who continued the founder's tradition of mixing business with outspoken comment on social and political matters, re-marked that European business was extremely gratifying and looked better to him during a 1927 tour than it had eighteen months earlier. He did not much like a bullfight he attended in Madrid but noted Germany "hard at work." He also mentioned approvingly Gillette's Near East headquarters office in Vienna, where, he said, Gillette men covered Bulgaria, Romania, Hungary, Turkey, Yugo Slavia (sic), Czecho Slovakia (sic), Poland, Finland, Albania, Greece, and the Baltic states—"countries that bid fair to rival Western neighbors as markets for Gillette goods." A traveler who appreciated trains that ran on time, Fahey reserved his high-est praise for Mussolini's Italy, where he attended the fifth-anni-versary celebration of the Fascist takeover in Rome and reported

THE MUSSOLINI CLAIM

In the 1920s, of course, Mussolini used a carbon steel blade, the only kind available, though his vanity may have lent a touch of exaggera-tion to his remarks about the number of shaves to be gotten from a blade. It is estimated that most carbon blade customers shaved at least a half-dozen times before replacing blades. Seventy years later, it is estimated by Gillette researchers that a man changes his Sensor car-tridge with twin stainless steel blades every ten or twelve shaves to maintain closeness and comfort.

It is unrecorded whether Mussolini's colleague of later years, Adolf Hitler, shaved with Gillette blades when they were available to him. But according to one biographer of Nazi leader Hermann Göring, Hitler's sycophant assured his Führer that American planes and tanks being sent to North Africa to engage Erwin Rommel's Desert Korps were not up to snuff in comparison with German equipment. About all that Americans made better than Germans were refrigerators and razor blades, he scoffed.

For the record, Gillette researchers say that beard hair is like copper wire of the same thickness, so it is important prior to shaving to soak the beard with warm water to expand the hair and make it softer and easier to cut.

that with the threat of bolshevism ended, "everyone seems happy, contented and industrious and the name of Mussolini is spoken with reverence and awe." As it happened, the clean-shaven Italian dictator, who had officially proclaimed that Italy was "anti-whiskers," was a public advocate of Gillette blades, having declared them in newspaper articles as equal to the task of shaving his supposedly extra-tough beard—a fact the company's alert sales department was quick to exploit. The vain Mussolini added a new twist to the continuing argument of how many shaves a man could get from a single blade when he told a United Press reporter that his beard was so tough, even the remarkable Gillette blade was good for only one shave of his manly whiskers.

By any measure, Gillette was growing fast in the roaring twenties, especially as compared with the slower years before the first world war. Pelham summed it up well when he noted that razor sales had increased from 51 units in 1903 to nearly 15 million in 1925, and blades from 168 units to 636 million. There was no hint of trouble in the self-congratulatory messages of the silver anniversary year of 1926. Around the world, but especially in the United States, high-volume retailers like the United Cigar Store Corporation were offered large discounts to buy more razors and blades. Faster and faster growth was the goal. The growth continued into 1927, but a close watcher of the company might have detected cause for concern. Domestic sales of blades actually slipped that year by 15 percent as a swarm of competitors cut into Gillette's once-impregnable market share, several with good-quality products and advertisements and pricing schemes designed to persuade Gillette customers to switch. Only fast-increasing overseas sales kept Gillette's total growth moving ahead.

Gillette fought back. It tried to capitalize on its skill in laying keen edges on hard metal by developing nonshaving cutting tools. Rug cutting tools, twine cutters, paper knives, chiropody chisels, and surgeon's scalpels—all made to accept replaceable blades— were put on the market, but they never amounted to much and gradually were withdrawn. These tools were difficult and costly to make, and there were special problems in honing the edges.

In what proved to be a costly blunder, the company decided

in 1928 to develop for the market a new blade that had been under development for some time. The Kroman blade, so-called because it was made with chromium and manganese alloyed with the usual carbon steel, was scheduled to sell for $1.50 for a package of ten, up from the usual $1 a pack, and to be wrapped in orange paper to distinguish it from the traditional package in green. King Gillette thought the idea was farfetched and did not hesitate to say so, sarcastically suggesting to Fahey that the blade ought to be gold-plated to justify its high price and the cost of making it. The Kroman blade was difficult to produce, and though it lasted longer than blades made from carbon steel, it proved less comfortable for users and did not give as smooth a shave as its lesser-priced cousins. Not long after its introduction, the Kroman was withdrawn from the market.

THE AUTOSTROP CHALLENGE

Henry J. Gaisman, the inventor of a restroppable razor system and the founder of AutoStrop Safety Razor Company, had been among the most persistent of the small American competitors who had hung in against dominant Gillette since the early days. Gaisman's original razor held a single-edge blade and employed a built-in stropping device. It was dismissed as more nuisance than threat, but nonetheless, Gaisman had been badgering the Gillette company since 1907 to buy him out. Although Gaisman lost a patent suit in the courts contesting Gillette's claim to a clamping mechanism, that did not stop him.

Now Gaisman was back, and this time he represented more serious trouble to Gillette. Pelham and Fahey were forced to listen. He had invented a new, double-edged, more flexible blade, Gaisman said, softer in the middle and less likely to crack in two than Gillette's stiffer blades. He proposed to manufacture his new Probak blade on the strip steel continuous production equipment that he and several competitors had been using for many years while Gillette clung to its slower blade-by-blade stamping machines. The new Probaks would have H-shaped perforations rather than the round holes of the Gillette blade and would fit on Gillette razors, though conversely, Gillette blades would not fit on a new razor he had designed. He thought Gillette might be interested in joining forces with him in some way. Gillette demurred, but Gaisman had the company's attention.

More than a year passed, and then at dinner one evening in 1928, at New York's Belmont Hotel, Gaisman told Pelham he had patented his new blade and razor. Was Gillette interested in buying him out? He would consider a price in seven figures, he said, leaving plenty of room for negotiation. If Gillette was not interested, perhaps he would try to sell his invention to another razor company. Or perhaps he would produce the razor and blade himself and challenge Gillette head on.

Several months passed. The two men met again at Boston's Copley Plaza Hotel and Gaisman pressed for a response, this time saying he had something like $5 million in mind. Pelham flatly rejected the notion, to which Gaisman replied that although he disliked hurting a good company like Gillette, he had no choice left but to start manufacturing the new blade himself. Pelham did not say so to Gaisman, of course, but he must have left the hotel a worried man. The prospect of full-scale competition from an established competitor with a possibly superior product loomed for the first time in Gillette's history. Moreover, AutoStrop was a global competitor with a worldwide distribution system.

Gillette counterattacked at once. Forty-eight hours after the Copley Plaza lunch, Gillette designers were at work on a new razor and blade system to match what Gaisman had told Pelham about the proposed AutoStrop model. After about four months of feverish work, they came up with a round-cornered blade supposedly less susceptible to the breakage caused when razors with conventional square-cornered blades accidentally fell into bathroom sinks. The new blade originally was designed with diamond-shaped holes that would not fit the proposed Probak razor, but at the last minute Gillette's decision makers conferred with the designers and decided instead to build a new razor as well as a new blade. The blades would feature a horizontal slit that fit into a corresponding raised horizontal bar on the new razor but would also fit existing Gillette razors. The new Gillette razor,

Gillette strategists thought, would not accept the expected Probak blades nor would the new Gillette blades fit the Probak razor. Gaisman would be foiled. A clever defensive move—except that at almost the same time that Gillette decided on its new system, Gaisman's designers were adjusting the proposed AutoStrop system so that its new Probak blades were almost identical with the Gillette design. Moreover, AutoStrop got its Gillette-fitting Probak blades to market first and, crucially, established its patent before Gillette.

There were those at Gillette who insisted that AutoStrop had planted spies in Gillette's design departments and stole drawings and perhaps blade samples. And there were AutoStrop officials who let it be known that they were sure an unnamed Gillette official had infiltrated Probak's New York factory and returned hastily to Boston with the new blades in his pocket. At any rate, shrewdly or by chance, AutoStrop seemed to have anticipated Gillette's moves and to have outmaneuvered its bigger rival. By the start of 1930, fully patented slotted Probak blades that fit Gillette razors were on the market. What's more, the blades were tempered with a new process that appeared to give them a quality edge over Gillette's products.

Already burdened with turning out great quantities of its carbon steel blades on outmoded stamping equipment and having difficulties starting production of its new Kroman blades, Gillette lagged several months behind AutoStrop in starting production of its new slotted razor and blades. Fahey and Pelham remained confident that Gillette could outmaneuver Gaisman despite Gillette's late start, and a major ad campaign heralded the March 1930 introduction of the new Gillette razor and blade, which were said to solve two heretofore unmentioned problems—razor pull and messy clean up. The razor cost $1, and a package of ten of the new slotted blades also sold for $1. Both products were prominently marked "patents pending," as Gaisman delighted in pointing out. Gillette rashly and publicly dared Gaisman to sue, running a newspaper ad headlined "If anyone thinks our company has infringed his patent rights, we suggest he come into court." Four days after the dare, Henry Gaisman obliged.

Frank Fahey sent a curt reply rejecting AutoStrop's claims and, in a letter designed to reassure a major distributor, added an ugly aside that Gaisman's move was just a play by "the AutoStrop people with their Hebrew management." The battle shifted to the courtroom, where AutoStrop increased the stakes by demanding a royalty on each Gillette blade sold—a potentially staggering sum. The stock market seemed to be betting on AutoStrop as that firm's stock moved up while Gillette's went down, from $100 to about $60. Before the matter reached a judge, Gillette decided to settle, and Gaisman got what he wanted—a lucrative Gillette buyout. He agreed to sell his company to Gillette in exchange for 310,000 nonvoting shares, a costly good riddance deal for Gillette.

Before Gaisman could be bought out, Gillette absorbed a terrible blow of its own making. A routine auditor's report ordered by AutoStrop directors to protect shareholders against undisclosed problems revealed that Gillette had for several years been greatly overstating its sales and profits by reporting shipments to overseas subsidiaries as actual sales, whether or not the blades and razors had in fact been sold to dealers. Pelham, Fahey, and others had received large bonuses based on earnings that had been inflated by $12 million over a five-year period. Gaisman sized up the new situation for the potential legal disaster it presented for Gillette. Nevertheless, he said that despite the hurtful new revelations, he would still sell out, but he demanded a large block of preferred stock with voting rights that would give him control of the merged company. With the patent lawsuit about to begin and its lawyers deeply concerned about whether Gillette could win in court, Gillette directors caved in. On October 16, 1930, the merger of little AutoStrop with big Gillette was announced. Henry Gaisman was now in charge of the company that bore King C. Gillette's name.

To restore goodwill among employees, the directors of the new Gillette agreed to refund with interest money paid into an employee stock purchase plan. The plan dated to 1928, when hundreds of Gillette employees enthusiastically paid on an installment plan $100 for stock then worth $125. As the stock plummeted, eventually into the thirty-dollar range, the employees were stuck with installment payments far above the worth of the stock they had pledged to buy. A shareholder suit claiming financial misdeeds by management was settled for $400,000. Frank Fahey and some others who had received unearned bonuses returned the money; for Fahey, the sum was $53,518. It was an appalling fall from grace of a proud company, a fact made poignant by King C. Gillette's resignation from his largely honorary position as president—though he was reelected director—in April 1931, a few months following the installation of Gaisman as the new man in charge.

The old duo of Fahey and Pelham and other senior Gillette executives resigned from management. Five new vice presidents, all from AutoStrop, were installed. They had their hands full with Gillette's aging blade-by-blade manufacturing operations in South Boston, now considered obsolete against the much faster continuous strip method that AutoStrop routinely used for blade-making in factories as remote as Rio de Janeiro. Moreover, Gillette blade quality had slipped so obviously that a company accustomed to glowing testimonials from satisfied customers was hearing from angry customers who had purchased dull blades. At the same time, Gillette dealers like United Cigar were up in arms over what they considered the company's reneging on discount deals that had been promised them by the departed Pelham.

Taking their cue from Wall Street and particularly J. P. Morgan partner George B. Whitney, company directors asked Gerard B. Lambert, a millionaire socialite, horseman, and yachtsman, to take over as president and senior operating officer. Lambert had made a fortune with Listerine mouthwash, drumming the phrase "Your best friend won't tell you" about the "dread disease" halitosis into the public conscience. He had invested his money in 4 percent bonds just before the 1929 Wall Street crash, so his personal fortune was untouched by the Depression. As Lambert admitted in his breezy autobiography *All Out of Step*, he "didn't know a damn thing about razors."[1] But he did know a safe harbor when he saw it. It so happened that he and his wife had agreed to divorce, and under the laws of their home state, New Jersey, he needed to prove that he had deserted her for two years. He went straight from New York by train to Boston's South Station and took a cab to the

Ritz-Carlton, where he engaged a sitting room, bedroom, and bath, and this was his home for the next several years. When he reported to South Boston for duty in 1931, he announced with considerable understatement that "Gillette was in a pretty pickle."

THE TROUBLED THIRTIES

The 1930s were difficult for Gillette, as they were for most corporations and citizens, though at least razor blades were relatively depression-resistant. Advertisements suggested, none too subtly, that clean-shaven executives were less likely to be fired than equally qualified men who might be tempted to skip a day's shave or risk unsightly stubble by shaving with inferior, that is, non-Gillette blades. Few customers gave up their daily shaves, but sales indicated that they used each blade for more shaves. The company's once-huge slice of domestic market share slipped below 50 percent as many hard-pressed consumers ignored Gillette's warnings and chose cheap off-brands, some selling for as little as a penny a blade. Gillette's profits eroded as the company was forced to play down its quality-based premium pricing and compete on price, though the company never dipped to the penny-a-blade level.

Gillette's marketers had learned to exploit the hot new medium of radio. In many homes, a popular Friday night fixture on the National Broadcasting Company was a show featuring The Gillette Blades orchestra, along with a vocal group named the Gay Young Blades, which was accompanied by a two-piano team, The Original Double Blades. A five-minute sports summary featuring the famed broadcaster Graham McNamee apparently was Gillette's first use of sports broadcasting.

To the dismay of some old timers, Lambert concluded that the persistent problem of eroded blade quality must be met head on. It had become evident to both discerning customers and Gillette engineers that quality control had suffered in the rush to get the new razor and blade to market in 1930. Lambert decided that confession beat stonewalling, and he ordered an unusual ad that appeared throughout the United States and in other countries: "The Gillette Safety Razor Company in fairness to its millions of customers feels called upon to make a confession and a statement that are undoubtedly unique in the annals of American business. It is with deep regret and no little embarrassment that we do this in order to tell you frankly what actually happened when we introduced a new Gillette razor and blade." The ad went on to say that in its haste to get to market, the company had over-extended its production machinery and shipped poor-quality blades to markets.

The company coupled the ad with an outright withdrawal of the premium-priced Kroman blade. In its place, Gillette intro-duced in 1932 what became by any measure of sales volume or name recognition the most famous double-edge blade ever pro-duced—the Blue Blade, first called the "Blue Super Blade" until the marketing people wisely recognized that "Super" in the mid-dle made the name a tongue twister to pronounce. It was called the Blue Blade because of the blade's hue after it was dipped in a blue lacquer and for its blue wrapping, which replaced the old green. King C. Gillette's face was still on the wrapping; penitence knows its bounds, and this first blade from the new strip process did prove to be a quality product worthy of his name and face. Ironically, Gillette died in Los Angeles just before the Blue Blade reached the market, financially devastated by the Depression's impact on his many real estate investments in southern California.

Lambert walked away from the Gillette job in 1934, happy to return to his yachts and horses and no longer at the mercy of Victorian divorce laws. His services to Gillette were not compen-sated because of a gamble the wealthy executive had taken when he accepted the job. Rather than ask for money, Lambert had struck a deal whereby he would be paid off in stock from the company treasury if and when Gillette shares went above $5, with a sliding scale that could have yielded him stock worth $2 million if it had risen to the $50 level he had confidently predicted. Gillette stock never came close to $5, let alone $50, and Lambert, refusing offers by the directors for at least some remuneration, walked away without a penny or a grudge, having lost a gentleman's wager that he could easily afford. He was replaced by Samuel C. Stampleman, who had come over from AutoStrop, and who tried to hold things together for the next four years.

In a sign of a time to come when Gillette would become a toiletries and dry shaving giant, Gillette chemists developed a shaving preparation made from peanut oil called Brushless Shaving Cream. A dry shaver was later introduced. Electric shavers already on the market had met with minimal success. A Gillette official wrote to a concerned shareholder in 1929 that Gillette had "experimented with one fifteen years ago" and found it unworthy of marketing. He told the shareholder not to worry about a $5 shaver that was being offered by an unnamed competitor because Gillette did not consider it a serious threat. But the company was hedging its bets. As it turned out, Gillette's first dry shaver generated modest sales at best in the later years of the Depression, and it was soon withdrawn.

The wisdom of the company's aggressive moves to produce and market overseas became ever more obvious as earnings generated outside the United States began to surpass domestic profits.

Though strapped for cash, management played its international strengths for all they were worth. The AutoStrop strip-process blade factory in Brazil, which was the company's first blade plant outside North America and Europe, proved a good base for expansion into Latin America, where the company eventually became a major force. In England, the AutoStrop and Gillette operations were combined under the Gillette name, under the leadership of AutoStrop's Canadian-born Ernest Cooper, later to become Sir Ernest. Cooper would prove one of the company's most able managers and a dominant non-American executive, not to mention Gillette's only knighted executive. In 1937, Cooper oversaw the construction of the Isleworth plant in West London (pronounced with the "s" as in Eiselworth rather than without, as in Isle of Wight). The Isleworth plant remained Gillette's largest European blade plant in terms of unit production sixty years later. Opened by the Lord Mayor of London with considerable pomp, the facility survived wartime bombing and became the company's European administrative headquarters.

The Berlin subsidiary doing business as Roth-Büchner was a bright spot in Gillette's business. In 1937, Roth-Büchner manufactured 40 percent of Germany's 900 million blades and held 65–70 percent of the domestic German market, despite efforts by some two hundred manufacturers in Solingen to form a cartel to gain more business. Roth-Büchner moved into a newly built factory at Berlin-Templehof in 1937, an investment that Gillette regretted when the plant was expropriated by Hitler's economic command in 1941 without so much as a deutsche mark for Gillette.

More than half of the company's 1935 earnings came from overseas and two-thirds by 1937. In 1938, the worst of the Depression years for Gillette, nearly all the company's earnings of $2.9 million came from foreign operations. Gillette's U.S. market share of razors and blades sold in 1938 fell to about 18 percent, its lowest-ever level. Commenting with restraint, Sam Stampleman called the year's domestic results "disappointing."

There was one important though belated blade product introduction. Gillette introduced its two-for-a-nickel Thin Blade in 1938 with hopes of going all out for the "poor man's market" that, after seven years of the Depression, must have seemed more or less permanent. The Thin Blade literally was a thin blade, about half the weight of the standard five-cent Blue Blade, though it cost almost as much to manufacture. The move paid off, however, in 1939 and through the war years ahead, as the combination of high demand for low-cost products and a shortage of carbon steel catapulted Thin Blade sales ahead of Blue Blades for several years.

Stampleman had grown weary of the difficult day-to-day management chores that came with the president's job and gratefully moved to the less demanding chairman's job late in 1938, replacing Henry Gaisman. Gaisman lived another thirty-six years, dying at the age of 104. Also in 1938, John Aldred retired as director, having survived the financial scandals that pushed out his colleagues Frank Fahey and Thomas Pelham.

In a move that brought new energy and a shift in management styles to Gillette, Stampleman was replaced by Joseph Peter Spang, Jr., a Harvard-educated Bostonian who had gone west and risen from a job shaving pig bristles in a slaughterhouse to the top sales position at Swift & Company. Spang was a doer whose style was to delegate operations, though not policy, and to keep close tabs on performance by subordinates. He demanded results and rejected excuses. He immediately dumped the last vestiges of the complex rebate and discount program that had created more ill will than new sales during the Depression years. Within weeks, he had ordered a much-needed upgrading of Gillette's grinding, sharpening, and honing machines, based on Gillette's success with new equipment in England. The new production process allowed superior quality control and quickly paid off, lending the ring of truth to one of Gillette's most memorable ad claims: "The sharpest edges ever honed." A new and happier era at Gillette was soon to begin, amplified by the crack of a bat against horsehide, when radio sponsorship of baseball's World Series would help to create a remarkably fruitful relationship between Gillette and American men.

CAVALCADE OF SPORTS

America's attention in autumn 1939 was, as usual, focused on the annual ritual of baseball's World Series. The New York Yankees had won three years in a row and were aiming for their fourth-straight against the Cincinnati Reds. In September, Adolf Hitler's armies had invaded Poland, and follow-on blitzkrieg invasions soon conquered most of Europe. Britain and France formally declared war on Germany. But death and destruction in Europe did not dilute American interest in the World Series, and advertising surveys showed that nearly all American men paid at least some attention to baseball's great October show. That fact had caught the attention of Joe Spang, who determined when he became president to move quickly to reestablish Gillette's preeminence among shavers.

Spang had already made a bold move when, weeks after his arrival in Boston, he had ordered the 1939 advertising budget increased by 50 percent to about $1.5 million. He made another bold move in this period of Gillette's most dismal earnings performance when he heeded the advice of Gillette's advertising manager, A. Craig Smith, about the selling power of baseball and spent $100,000 for exclusive radio rights to the 1939 Series. In addition, he committed just over $100,000 for radio time and for promotion. These sums added up to almost 20 percent of the total advertising budget—a lot for those uneasy days, when cost-cutting had become the watchword at Gillette and caution had replaced aggressive marketing. The few old timers left in management after Spang had cleaned house muttered about money down the drain, citing the forgettable results of Gillette's earlier plunge into radio sponsorship of a single sports event with the Max Baer–Jim Braddock fight. (Gillette had, of course, tied its name to sports heroes numerous times in print ads with testimonials dating to 1910, when New York Giants manager John McGraw declared his admiration for the closeness of Gillette shaves.) The naysayers became even more convinced of Spang's folly when the 1939 Series was swept in four-straight by the Yankees, led by Joe DiMaggio, Bill Dickey, and Charlie "King Kong" Keller, cutting almost in half the air time that could have been used to plug Gillette products had the Series gone to seven games.

Then came the sales results and the convincing evidence that the sales pitches of announcers Red Barber and Bob Elson had been as much on target as the fastball pitches of star Yankee hurler Charles "Red" Ruffing. For its baseball promotion, which had been hastily developed in the month before the Series began, Gillette had packaged a large number of Tech razors with five Blue Blades, advertised on radio as the forty-nine-cent World Series Special. And when Red Barber drawled to tens of millions of radio listeners that Gillette was bringing them "a swell ball game, and if you pick up a Tech razor tonight with a Gillette Blue Blade, it will bring you a swell shave tomorrow morning and every morning," they believed him. Retailers could not keep up with demand. When the final count was in, about 2.5 million World Series Specials had been sold—more than double the company's expectations. Spang's faith in sports radio as a means of persuading American males to buy Gillette products had been vindicated.

If baseball worked, why not football? Spang and his agents

quickly snapped up the Orange Bowl and Sugar Bowl, later adding the Cotton Bowl and the biggest collegiate spectacle of all, the Rose Bowl. Next came the Kentucky Derby and, in late 1940, the professional football playoff game still remembered as the mismatch of all time—Chicago Bears 73, Washington Redskins 0.

Boxing, the so-called manly art, probably gave Gillette the most payback for its advertising dollar because it delivered an overwhelmingly male audience suited to Gillette's overwhelmingly male product line, and it was inexpensive to produce. Ad man Craig Smith wasted no time in going for a knockout blow to other consumer goods companies who were catching on to the sales impact of sports radio. He soon made boxing and the sound of the bell announcing the start of each round synonymous with Gillette. The company's first sponsorship of a prize fight on radio since the Max Baer–Jim Braddock contest was the classic heavyweight title bout between the great Joe Louis and challenger Billy Conn in summer 1941. Don Dunphy called the action from ringside that night and for most of the next 20 years he continued as the raspy and quite famous voice of the "Friday Night Fights," aka "Fight of the Week," "Monday Night Fights," and "Saturday Night Fights."

About the time of the Louis–Conn bout, some inspired soul at Gillette, or probably its advertising agency, came up with "Cavalcade of Sports" as Gillette's signature title for all of its exclusively sponsored sports events. Cavalcade of Sports presented nearly all the big national sports events of the next twenty-five years or so before television ad costs became too great for one sponsor. The Cavalcade signature was one of the most effective corporate themes ever developed for radio and TV sports. Most males in the 1940s and 1950s did not have to be told that the Cavalcade of Sports meant Gillette was sponsoring another ball game or horse race.

Television was so new in 1944 that not much note was made of Gillette's first Cavalcade broadcast, which featured a featherweight fight between Willie Pep and Chalky Wright. Only about 6,000–7,000 television sets within viewing range of the New York station broadcast the fight, so Pep's victory was witnessed by only a privileged few. Radio announcer Don Dunphy described the action for viewers peering at jumpy black and white images on their screen, just as he would in the ensuing years, when television pushed radio aside.

Gillette retained a special place in its heart and in its advertising budget for the World Series, which in those days delivered the biggest audiences of all for sports radio and television, until it was overtaken by pro football's Super Bowl. Moreover, baseball's fall classic was fortuitously timed for selling products. The series became the annual "Christmas in October" for Gillette. The company promoted the event heavily, introduced its most important new products, and generally opened its biggest sales season of the year with an estimated nine out of ten American males tuned in to at least some portion of each ball game.

WARTIME GILLETTE

America's entry into World War II cut into Gillette's blade and razor production at South Boston and also abroad, where great swaths of the prewar world market were closed off and Gillette plants and property had been expropriated by German and Japanese forces. The company's plants in South Boston and London were converted in part to weaponry production, turning out fuel control units for carburetors on military aircraft and classified devices for naval mines. In a bit of cloak and dagger work, a trusted elite group at South Boston produced perfect copies of German razor blades that were inserted into the toilet kits of secret agents parachuted behind German lines so that their American identity would not be given away by their shaving habits.

Another little-known fact about Gillette's covert involvement in World War II was revealed by ex-U.S. military intelligence operative Lloyd R. Shoemaker in his 1990 book *The Escape Factory.* According to Shoemaker, patriotic Gillette executives, contacted by his brigade, whose mission was to free Nazi POWs, followed intelligence directives and worked to secretly manufacture magnetized double-edge blades that imprisoned soldiers could use as a compass. The "G" of the familiar Gillette trademark would point north on each specially crafted blade. In addition, maps and money were loaded into the razor handles, and concealed lot numbers correlating to each POW camp were embedded over the company's name on the razor's box. All told, approximately five thousand of the magnetized razor sets were manufactured by the company, and about one thousand more contained the escape maps.

In 1942 the War Production Board ordered the company to dedicate its entire razor production and most blade production to the military. There was not much left over for civilians, so demand outstripped supply. Gillette began to run so-called educator ads advising men how to get the most from their blades (wash with water, never with a cloth). The best blades—top of the line Blue Blades—went to the military in kits. By the war's end, servicemen had been issued 12.5 million razors and more than 1.5 billion blades.

Back home, many of the blades available for sale to civilians were lower-priced Thin Blades that Gillette had put on the market in 1938 to counter competitors' low-priced blades. Despite the company's inability to meet demand because of wartime restrictions, Gillette advertised throughout the war in newspapers and magazines, as well as on its Cavalcade of Sports broadcasts. A typical print ad showed a smiling soldier carrying his GI bride across the threshold of their honeymoon house. Implausibly, he pauses to declare:

Of low price blades your surest bet
is keen long lasting Thin Gillette
You save real dough—look slick as well;
You shave with speed—your face feels swell!

In late 1944 restrictions on civilian output were lifted, and Gillette, its worker ranks depleted by the draft and enlistees, was hard pressed to catch up with demand. Men had money to spend from defense jobs, and they no longer needed to squeeze more shaves from aging blades. They snapped up the available blades. When the war ended in 1945, a new generation of servicemen who had learned to shave with Gillette razors and blades sailed home, many with their government-issue razors packed in their duffel bags. Spang made a distinction between the GI users of the two great wars: World War I taught soldiers the self-shaving habit, he said; World War II taught the daily shave habit. At any rate, the returning GI's wanted the best.

Joe Spang was able to report to the directors in 1946 that the ruinous era of the blade price wars was over and that Gillette was in a strong position to regain the dominant share of the shaving market it had lost during the Depression. Cheap blade imitators were gone or reduced to irrelevance, with the number of competitors narrowed to old rivals such as Eversharp Inc.'s Schick Safety Razor division; American Safety Razor Corp., which made Gem and Blue Star blades; and Pal Blades, maker of an array of both single and double-edge blades.

Overseas, Gillette reopened its Berlin plant adjacent to Templehof airport, conveniently inside the American zone, but not at once. When Spang arrived to inspect the plant in 1946, he found that the U.S. Army had temporarily taken it over, reporting that "the officers invited us to lunch in our own building, which was a rather novel experience." Since the Red Army had got to Berlin first, and much of the old blade-making equipment had been removed by the Soviets a few miles east to Poland, blade making would have been difficult for a while anyway. The U.S. Army returned the empty factory to Gillette in 1947, and a few pieces of equipment were returned by the Soviets before Cold War hostilities made such cooperative acts impossible.

Gillette had better luck in formerly German-occupied France, where its blade plant in the eastern district of Paris had been threatened by Nazi officials intent on removing usable equipment to Germany. The Gillette manager, M. Juge, was told by the company to do what he could to keep the idled equipment intact during the Occupation. When the German army stormed into Paris, a contingent of officers and men were sent to the plant with orders to confiscate equipment, but the plant appeared to them to be stripped of salvageable gear. The Germans left empty-handed. After the Allied Forces liberated Paris in 1944, Gillette officials were told by Juge not to worry, because he and some loyal employees had disassembled the blade-making machines, packed the parts in boxes, and hidden the boxes in the factory basement before the Germans arrived. As a result, Gillette was able to resume production shortly after the war. According to André Doucet, who later joined Gillette as manager of its French subsidiary, the company's ability to resume blade manufacturing expeditiously was a key to Gillette quickly gaining a leading share of the French market, which developed into one of Gillette's top markets worldwide.

The company moved rapidly to add production capacity and modernize its major razor and blade plants in the United States and England, and to add capacity to several foreign plants, including those in Canada, Brazil, and Argentina. A new Swiss facility was added to serve the devastated European continent; blade production started up in Mexico City. After the dismal 1930s and World War II, Gillette was on the move.

3

THE GOAL
IS
GROWTH

IN THE UNITED STATES the emphasis was on growth after the cost-cutting years of the Depression and the wartime restrictions, and that suited Gillette. President Joe Spang wanted more production, more sales—a lot more sales, like in the good old Thomas Pelham days in the 1920s minus Pelham's ruinous discounting. To do the job, he hired as vice president for sales a just-released army colonel and West Point graduate named Boone Gross, whose industrial experience had been in liquor sales. Gross was named for a direct ancestor, frontiersman Daniel Boone, and he had a commanding presence and booming voice that became legend around the Gillette world. Spang's orders to Gross were simple and direct: boost blade sales to an annual rate of 1 billion. Gross met the goal in 1947 and was on his way to the top. He reorganized Gillette's U.S. sales force into an effective organization of districts and territories, with the object of moving the decision level down the line to the personnel in the field and making them responsible for results.

One of Gross's early recruits to the sales battle was a returning soldier who had hired on at Gillette right out of high school in 1941 for $25 a week to answer consumer complaints. By the time he entered the armed forces, Stephen J. Griffin's salary had been raised to $30. The army sent him to Europe where, as a master sergeant, he was among the first wave of American soldiers to enter conquered Berlin in 1945. His Gillette instincts took over, and after inspecting the building that had housed Gillette's German subsidiary before expropriation, he sent back to South Boston the first report on its condition. The building seemed structurally sound, Griffin reported, though stripped of machinery.

A few months later, out of the army and newly married, he had visions of $50 a week as he faced Boone Gross to discuss job assignments. Gross got right to the point. He wanted Griffin to try his hand at sales and would raise him to $40 a week. Griffin gulped and accepted, but on the way out of the room he screwed up his courage to ask Gross if he couldn't manage another $5 or so. Gross, his famously loud voice rising, said "Steve, if you are as good a man as I think you are, you'll never have to ask for a raise again." As it turned out, of course, both the ex-colonel and the ex-sergeant in due time became presidents of Gillette, and before too long, Griffin had more than enough money to indulge his scholarly pursuit of collecting classic books.

His many years with Gross and the leaders who followed gave Griffin a front-row seat in the great postwar buildup of the company, which started as the V-J Day celebrations ended. Sales exceeded $50 million for the first time in 1946 and had doubled by 1950. These sales, moreover, had not been artificially pumped up by discount pricing—a major break from the Depression years. As a result, the once famously high Gillette profit margins returned.

Gillette wasted no time getting to market with a blade dispenser that had been developed during the war. The dispenser did away with wax-paper wrappers so that the user could load the blade into the razor without touching the sharp edge. It was aimed at Schick's very successful "push, pull, click, click" injector razor, which had given Gillette a run for its money for several years. The Gillette dispenser soon was augmented with a double-duty dispenser that had a compartment to hold used blades. In 1947 the Gillette Super Speed Razor was launched, the first new razor since the "revolutionary new three-piece Tech razor," so extolled by Red Barber during the 1939 World Series broadcast. Gillette was poised to dominate the blade market again; its share of the market passed 50 percent in 1950 and kept climbing. Spang began to heed a faction of management and directors led by Chairman William A. Barron, Jr., who had been urging him to diversify and lessen the company's dependence on one product.

Suddenly, an opportunity came up. The Toni Company was a small firm that had been launched in St. Paul, Minnesota, in 1944 by the Harris brothers: R. Neison or "Wishbone," as he liked to be called, who had the product idea; and Irving, who had advertising flair and came in as half owner at his brother's request. Their product was the Toni home permanent kit, which took over a lucrative niche market. The kits sold for fifty-nine cents to $2 to women who preferred to make their hair wavy in the privacy of their bathrooms rather than make costly repeat trips to beauty parlors for permanents. To finance growth, the Harris brothers decided to sell out rather than seek equity financing and agreed to a deal with Lever Bros., only to have the London headquarters turn down American president Charles Luckman's $7.5 million offer as too pricey. Next was Procter & Gamble, which made a complex offer worth $18 million over three years. The impatient Harrises disliked haggling with Procter & Gamble, which took its time, as very large companies often do. Enter Gillette's Joe Spang, who closed a $20.5 million deal in about three weeks. The Harris brothers were named Gillette directors and were left in charge of Toni operations, by now moved to Chicago. The Toni deal was the first step in the process that changed Gillette from a one-product specialty company to a broad-based manufacturer of hundreds of consumer products.

Spang was elated. "After 50 years of shaving hair we've started

waving it," he reportedly told puzzled colleagues. Most significantly, the acquisition brought a female grooming product to
Gillette's predominantly male grooming business, adding the
other half of the world's population as potential Gillette customers. The Toni kit was nothing more than a mix of low-cost ammo-
nium thioglycolate. If applied with plastic curlers and pins
according to the enclosed directions, the mix produced waves in
the customer's hair that would last for months, just like beauty
parlor permanents. The original home permanent business quickly
peaked, even as Gillette was buying Toni, and eventually became
largely a refill market for kits already sold in a highly competitive
market. Home perm sales plateaued, but the Harris brothers were
gifted entrepreneurs with other ideas for female grooming products. With Gillette's money and Spang's encouragement, they
proceeded to develop and market an impressive array of shampoos, hair lacquers, and curlers with names like Tame, Adorn, and
Bobbi, and even a lipstick, Viv.

Before Gillette bought Toni and before the era of television
dominance, Irving Harris had come up with the great advertising
line "Which Twin has the Toni?" Magazine ads dared women to
figure out which wavy-haired identical twin had spent $10 to $12
at the beauty parlor and which twin had transformed her straight
hair into curly waves at home, using perhaps fifty cents' worth of
materials and a half hour of her time for rinsing and pinning on
large pink curlers. Seeking to internationalize home perms, Toni
sent six sets of Toni Twins to England, Belgium, Scotland, Ireland,
and Holland to launch a "Which Twin has the Toni?" ad campaign
to European women. The product was well received in the United
Kingdom but died on the Continent, where the habit of weekly
trips to the beauty salon was well entrenched. A slanderous anti-
Toni campaign was launched in France that included angry testimony from a bald woman who claimed a faulty home perm kit
caused her hair to fall out. The next year, a smart young promoter
in Chicago named Daniel Edelman, just beginning a successful
public relations career, was hired by Toni to organize an American
tour for six sets of Toni Twins, supposedly in search of other Toni

Twins. It got off to a rocky start in Tulsa, where a local cosmetologist worried about the impact of home treatments on the beauty parlor business cited a city ordinance and had Alva and Alice Anderson arrested at their hotel by two apologetic cops—the same pair that had earlier given the twins a motorcycle escort into the city. Forty years later, appearing on NBC's Today show with Edelman, the Anderson twins recalled that they spent an hour in jail before a Toni official had them released. Edelman said the jailing of the innocent young twins provided a great publicity coup, yielding headlines across America next morning along the likes of "Outrage: Toni Twins Jailed." The rest of the tour was a great success, and Toni sales moved briskly.

GILLETTE REORGANIZES

Having tasted success with diversification to Toni products, Gillette wanted more. The company reorganized in 1952 as The Gillette Company, with three divisions: the Gillette Safety Razor Company, the Toni Company, and Eastern Hemisphere, a group run out of Gillette Industries, Ltd., which was Gillette's semi-autonomous London company. The Eastern Hemisphere's territory bore a remarkable resemblance to the old British Empire, Canada not included. Spang moved up to the presidency of the parent company, and top blade salesman Boone Gross was made president of the core Gillette Safety Razor (GSR) division.

At about this time, researchers and product developers at GSR developed a product that proved money could be made in markets for shaving products other than blades and razors. Foamy shaving cream, packaged in an aerosol can that released clouds of white lather at the press of a knob, was put on the market casually in 1953, when instant lathers were beginning to supplant older products, including Gillette Brushless Shave Cream. With minor ad support at the start, Foamy took off and became a big seller. It remained one of Gillette's best known product names decades later.

In 1955, Spang made a second decisive move into other fields when, at the urging of Wishbone Harris, he bought the Paper Mate Pen Company, another Chicago firm. Paper Mate was then the leading force in the fast-growing ballpoint pen market. Harris had befriended fellow entrepreneur and Paper Mate founder Patrick J. Frawley and was on the verge of quitting Gillette to join forces with the colorful, hard-drinking king of the ballpoint pen makers. He was persuaded by Vice President Carl Gilbert to wait until he could talk with Spang, who was in Europe on business. Perhaps Gillette would buy Paper Mate, and they could all work together, he suggested to Harris. Gilbert had Harris's ear because, as an outside lawyer from Boston, he had worked out the details of the Gillette-Toni deal, which had proved so lucrative to the brothers; Gilbert had joined Gillette right after the deal went through and was on a fast track to the top. As the story goes, Gilbert met Spang at dockside on his return and convinced him to buy Paper Mate at once to keep the company out of the hands of rival Eversharp. Spang quickly made a $15.5 million cash offer to Frawley, who just as quickly accepted. With that, Gillette was in the ballpoint pen business, which made strategic sense as well as helped to keep the peace in the Gillette family. Refillable pens shared the replacement market characteristics of razor blades, and even though distribution patterns differed, both shaving systems and inexpensive pens were products in demand by consumers everywhere.

An erratic man with a habit of mixing his business life with his outspoken political and social beliefs, Frawley was a mismatch for Gillette's conservative ways of doing business and its tightly structured organization. He lasted only three months as president of Paper Mate. When he resigned, his old pal Wishbone Harris took over the operation. Paper Mate, whose core factory was located at Santa Monica, California, became a thriving arm of the expanding Gillette Company. Frawley resurfaced as the president of Eversharp, the producer of Schick Injector razors and Schick blades. His first act was to unleash a major advertising campaign ridiculing Gillette's newly announced adjustable double-edge razors, a move that did nothing to repair strained relations.

TELEVISION'S CRITICAL ROLE AT GILLETTE

It is difficult to overstate the importance of television advertising to Gillette's postwar momentum. A former vice president for corporate planning, Paul Fruitt, characterized the postwar years up to about 1965 as a period when effective use of television marketing was a prime factor behind the company's rapid growth in North America. Starting in 1944 with the Willie Pep fight, when television was a flyspeck on the media wall, Gillette correctly sensed its astonishing selling power and stayed ahead of more cautious competitors. Only far larger Ford Motor Company came close to matching Gillette's TV sports spending, which peaked in the mid-1950s, when 85 percent of the company's ad budget was given over to the Cavalcade of Sports. For one year only— 1947, Ford and Gillette cosponsored the World Series television broadcast. In 1948 Gillette bid higher and regained exclusive sponsorship.

Craig Smith, who had become advertising vice president and a member of the board, ensured that Gillette's Christmas in October sales kickoff would continue when, in 1950, he bought for $6 million the exclusive television rights for the World Series for the next six years, with the All-Star game included. At the time, it was the highest price ever paid for athletic events—in 1996, $6 million bought about 20 thirty-second World Series spots averaging $225,000—but television was still in its infancy. Some thought that baseball commissioner Albert "Happy" Chandler, a folksy former Democratic senator from Kentucky, had taken Gillette to the cleaners. Others realized that actually Gillette had skinned Happy Chandler. Television audiences increased along with the value of television advertising time, and by 1956, Gillette had to spend more than $3 million a year for the next exclusive multiyear deal. By 1959, television costs were so high that Gillette had to sell off half of its World Series time to General Motors, although it was able to use its rousing Cavalcade of Sports theme for half of each game.

Interestingly, the most famous of all the company's television advertising themes had its origins in print, before the shift was made to radio and then television. In late 1945 an advertisement in a trade publication concluded with these lines: "There is a brand new Buy-line—look sharp, feel sharp, be sharp. Use Gillette Blue Blades with the sharpest edges ever honed." The author, according to some accounts, was none other than Craig Smith. The catchy words were set to music and were sung on radio and in animated television commercials by the Sportsmen Quartet.

The first year that national television was extended to California was in 1951, making it possible for viewers there to watch Gillette's telecast of the World Series between the New York Yankees and the New York Giants. The next World Series would bring another memorable first—the introduction of the lilting march version of Gillette's "Look Sharp" jingle, which instantly became one of the most effective television jingles of all time. As music blared, voices sang "To Look Sharp, ev'ry time you shave/To feel sharp, and be on the ball/To be sharp . . ." The march was composed by Mahlon Merrick, the musical director of Jack Benny's comedy program. "Look Sharp" took on a touch of class when it was scored for full symphony for a Gillette Christmas special on television. The "Look Sharp" march was performed frequently at Boston Pops concerts thereafter and also showed up in the half-time routine of college marching bands, to the delight of Gillette people, who realized that product jingles that become part of the folklore are rarities to be prized.

For that same 1952 World Series telecast Merrick also composed another ditty that was in the same league as "Look Sharp" for longevity and latter-day nostalgic recall. He composed the music for "How're Ya Fixed for Blades?," a jingle that often served as background in cartoons that featured a raucous parrot named Sharpie. The noisy bird constantly demanded "How're ya fixed for blades" of startled men in their undershirts caught in mid-shave, their faces lathered up and razor poised. The jingle grew out of a merchandising campaign to train store checkout clerks to remind customers to stock up on blades before they ran out. The ad campaign took on a life of its own, and Sharpie was almost as well known for a while as Donald Duck and Mickey Mouse.

In the innocent fifties, the great ballplayers of the day, from

Willie Mays of the Giants to Whitey Ford of the Yankees, were only too happy to shave in a studio setting to endorse Gillette razors and blades for $500 a turn, a sum unimaginable to the high salaried athletes and their agents of a later period. The collective impact of repeated endorsement of Gillette blades on sports television broadcasts by the baseball heroes of the fifties and sixties arguably had as much impact on Gillette sales as the 1990s endorsement of Nike shoes by basketball superstar Michael Jordan had on Nike sales.

Gillette did not spend millions on television advertising without assessing the new medium's effectiveness. After 1954, the company's negotiators were armed with market research data that conclusively showed television's ability to sell blades. Data gathered by Paul Fruitt correlated Nielsen audience data with blade sales in each of Gillette's eighteen sales districts in the United States for 1948 through 1953. In those years, television viewing spread across the country, from the East Coast to California and then up the Pacific Coast to the Northwest, its geographic range restrained by the need to install thousands of miles of coaxial cable across several time zones. The data showed that Gillette blade sales correlated almost perfectly with the arrival of television (and the Cavalcade of Sports) in each sales district. The survey results astonished the remaining television skeptics and made it easier for Craig Smith and other Gillette ad people to spend the company's cash for new television deals without second-guessing from those back at the office.

By the mid-1960s, baseball television rights had ballooned in value to the point that only the major networks could afford the hundreds of millions of dollars demanded by major league baseball for World Series rights. The winning network then sold costly thirty- and sixty-second spots to all comers, which forced Gillette to share its sponsorship of major sports events with a raft of brewers, car companies, shoemakers, and the like. Still, for many years the distinctive Cavalcade of Sports jingles and musical themes were so familiar to viewers that Gillette's ad people reckoned the company was getting far more value for the money on its short commercials than competitors who could not match Gillette's name recognition with sports fans.

SELLING TO THE FEMALE MARKET

Sports sells blades to men, but what about the women who were Toni's customers? Toni scored an early win by buying exclusive sponsorship of Arthur Godfrey's television series. The folksy God-frey, whose "ah shucks" style proved to have exceptional rapport with his women listeners, got a lot of mileage out of the "Which Twin has the Toni?" theme in his rambling product introductions. As Toni's product lines proliferated and sales grew much larger, the company searched for a signature event like the World Series that would have special appeal to women. They found it with exclusive sponsorship of the Miss America pageant, the annual must-see evening of television as Bert Parks crooned his familiar song, and beautiful girls chosen to represent their home states paraded along a runway in formal gowns and swimsuits.

It was knockout TV entertainment for many years, before a more cynical era arrived, and was watched by huge numbers of women in a mood to buy what made Miss America attractive. It was the perfect setting to promote the many products coming out of Toni's development labs. Miss America became a Gillette em-issary, traveling the nation to visit stores, make television appear-ances, and exude the fresh good spirits of young womanhood that, it was hoped, would translate into goodwill and sales of home perms and shampoos.

Adding new mileage to Irving Harris' "Which Twin has the Toni?" theme, advertising agencies hired by Gillette put the Toni Twins into TV's big leagues. Television screens were filled with images of the twins bouncing their clean, curly hair while extolling the virtues of Toni products.

THE GREAT SUCCESS OF THE SUPER BLUE

The 1960s started strong with the introduction of the Gillette Super Blue blade, the first coated-edge blade and the first major im-proved blade for Gillette since the Blue Blade of the 1930s. The

Right: Gillette's famous
diamond-and-arrow trademark,
unveiled in 1908, was usually accompanied
by the slogan, "Known the World Over."

Above: A dapper King C. Gillette, circa 1908,
wearing a Panama hat. This photo is said to
be the founder's favorite picture of
himself.

Right: A copy of the patent for "K.C. Gillette Razor," granted to Gillette on November 15, 1904.

Facing page: Engineer Frank Brown is pictured, in 1901, with the company's first grinding machine. Brown was an assistant to William E. Nickerson, who designed and built this and other crucial production machinery during Gillette's early decades.

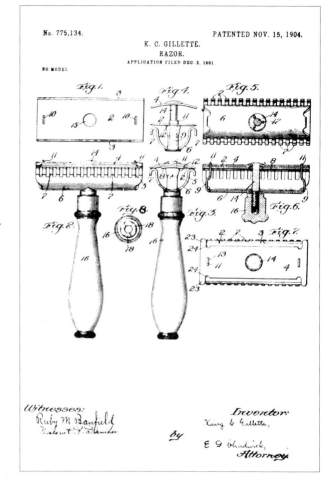

Above: Department heads of the Gillette Safety Razor Company, 1917.

Right: An early Gillette razor and blade.

Star Ball-Players of Both Big Leagues Thank the Gillette Safety Razor

for the clean, cool GILLETTE shave that kept their faces smooth and fit through the sun and wind of the season's race for the American and National Pennants. Sixty-three of them have written their appreciation of the GILLETTE. Four of these letters are reprinted below:

Hugh Jennings
Manager of the Detroit Team:

"Always a Gillette for mine. Nearly all of my team mates use the Gillette and are as highly pleased with it as I am."

John H. Wagner
Leading Batter of the Pittsburg Team:

"I shave with a Gillette. I know of nothing that could induce me to change the system."

Harry H. Davis
Philadelphia; Captain of the Leaders of American League:

"After trying every advertised safety razor I can truthfully say that none has given anywhere near the full measure of satisfaction as the Gillette."

John J. McGraw
Manager of the New York Giants:

"I wouldn't be without my Gillette, especially when I am on the road with the team. It makes shaving all to the merry."

Three million other alert, self-reliant men shave themselves with the GILLETTE Safety Razor. You will find GILLETTE enthusiasts in every community of America — in the hotel — in the sleeping car and on the steamer.

The GILLETTE is typical of the American spirit that thinks for itself, does for itself and insists on quick action and efficiency in everything.

Buy a GILLETTE and *use it*. The GILLETTE shave takes three minutes *or less*—it gives a tone and a brace that last all day. No stropping, no honing — and any man can shave with it the first time he tries.

Gillette Safety Razor, $5.00. Regular box of 12 Blades, $1.00; carton of 6 blades, 50c.

King C Gillette

New York, Times Building
Chicago, Stock Exchange Bldg.

GILLETTE SALES COMPANY
22 West Second Street, Boston

Factories: Boston, Montreal
Leicester, Berlin, Paris

Gillette Safety Razor, Ltd., London
Canadian Office: 63 St. Alexander St., Montreal   Eastern Office: Shanghai, China

Four baseball luminaries endorse the Gillette safety razor in a 1910 advertisement, an early hint of the company's enduring association with sports as the key to reaching the male market.

King C. Gillette estimated that, by 1926, the company's output of sharpened steel could encircle the globe at the equator.

A German advertisement for Gillette safety razors that predates World War I.

Above: Thomas W. Pelham, Gillette's tireless Director of Sales and world traveler, boards a plane in London bound for Paris in the 1920s.

Left: A Gillette delivery truck outside the company's blade factory in Slough, England, in 1920.

D.V. Muller (in pith hel-
met), president of Gillette's
Far East distributor, Muller
and Phipps (Asia) Limited,
is pictured selling Gillette
products to a bazaar
merchant in Baghdad in
1926.

Gillette U.S. Service Set
It Fits the Kit or the Pocket

HERE is how the Great War developed the most compact and efficient shaving outfit in the world. From the start, all the Allied Armies called for Gillette Razors—first by thousands, then by hundreds of thousands. All sorts of sets—leather, metal, Standard Sets and Pocket Editions. The demand finally centered on the Metal cases: they stood the racket. Suggestions came from every front.

A year ago our own boys were called to the Mexican Border: among them a young Officer from the Gillette organization. He came back with an idea—a soldier's idea of what the Gillette means to the fighting man—the best model to go in the soldier's Kit or the sailor's Ditty-box!

We went to work on a Service Model—sifted all the suggestions, all the ideas, and developed them. When Uncle Sam jumped into the Big War the Gillette was ready to do its bit.

So here is the new U. S. Service Set; a solid metal case, heavy nickel-plated and embossed with the Insignia of the U. S. Army and Navy. Strong, thin, compact: 1⅞ inches wide, 4 inches long, ⅝ inch thick. It fits the Kit or slips into the breast pocket of the shirt or coat. Contains a nickel-plated Gillette Safety Razor, Blades and Blade Box. Indestructible Trench Mirror inside the lid.

Price, $5

The U. S. Army Regulations call for a shaving outfit. Every man has to bring his own. Here is his favorite razor and the one that takes up the least room. You ought to see the boys reach for them! Every man in Khaki ought to have one.

If you're a friend of his give it to him, or get it to him. Most gifts he will have to leave behind. This is one he will carry with him and use every day.

No Strops or Hones. Nothing to carry but the compact little case, and new Blades can be had anywhere in France, England, Russia, and Italy.

The Gillette U. S. Service Set is a leading specialty with Gillette Dealers everywhere

Gillette Safety Razor Company
Boston, Mass., U. S. A.

Gillette Safety Razor Company of Canada, Ltd.,
73 St. Alexander Street, Montreal

If he has already gone, you can send him a Gillette U. S. Service Set by mail. If your dealer does not have this Set, send us $5 and your Sammie's address and we will make *free* delivery direct to his hands from our Paris Office or to any American Cantonment from our Boston Office.

A Gillette World War I advertisement selling $5 military kits to soldiers and sailors just before the U.S. War Department began providing Gillette kits as standard issue to every serviceman.

WE MADE A MISTAKE

—A STATEMENT BY THE GILLETTE SAFETY RAZOR COMPANY

THE Gillette Safety Razor Company feels called upon to make a confession and a statement that are undoubtedly unique in the annals of American business. It is with deep regret and no little embarrassment that we do this in order to tell you frankly what actually happened when we introduced a new Gillette razor and blade.

Soon after this was done, we found that, although the great majority was pleased, some users complained quality was not up to standard.

We learned why. Our equipment had not been equal to the task of producing millions of blades at high speed without a certain variation in quality that affected a small portion of our output. As a result some blades that left the factory were not as good as you had a right to expect. Immediately we directed our principal effort toward the achievement of uniformity. Everything within our power was done to end variation. More than this—impossible as it seemed of accomplishment at the time — we set out to develop or find a better production process, having as a major requirement the elimination of varying quality.

We discovered and purchased for our exclusive use and at the cost of millions of dollars a manufacturing process that was amazingly superior to our own.

By this method, modern and automatic, millions of blades can be made at top speed without variation in quality.

We incorporated refinements of our own invention and installed the new machinery, throwing out all of our old equipment.

Now we announce today's Gillette blades, made by the new management. The usual superlatives have no place in this sincere statement of ours, so we will let the quality of the blades speak for itself. The green Gillette package remains unchanged, but the blades are new in every respect, quality, performance, and method of manufacture.

You can try today's Gillette blades without risking a cent. If you don't agree they are superior, return the package and your dealer will refund your money. **Our reputation depends upon the proof of these claims. Being absolutely certain of the quality of these Gillette blades, we do not hesitate to make this statement over our signature.**

The Gillette Blue Super-Blade

The $2 Kroman De Luxe blade has been withdrawn from production. We offer the Blue Super-Blade as its successor. This sensational blade is far superior to the Kroman and costs considerably less. You pay only a few cents more than for the regular blade and get unmatched shaving comfort. **Its extraordinary shaving performance will convince you that the Blue Blade is the sharpest ever produced.** A blue color has been applied to the blade for easy identification. It is contained in a blue package, Cellophane wrapped.

GILLETTE SAFETY RAZOR CO.
BOSTON, MASSACHUSETTS

Confession advertising: In 1932, the company confessed to producing inferior blades unworthy of the Gillette name. This ad also introduced the "Gillette Blue Super-Blade," soon renamed Blue Blade, the company's largest-selling carbon steel blade for nearly 30 years.

Above: The manufacturing floor at Gillette's South Boston blade and razor plant, the world's largest, as it looked in the 1930s.

Left: Joseph Spang, Jr., who became president of Gillette in 1938, used all-out sports promotion, beginning with the 1939 World Series, to produce more and more growth for the company.

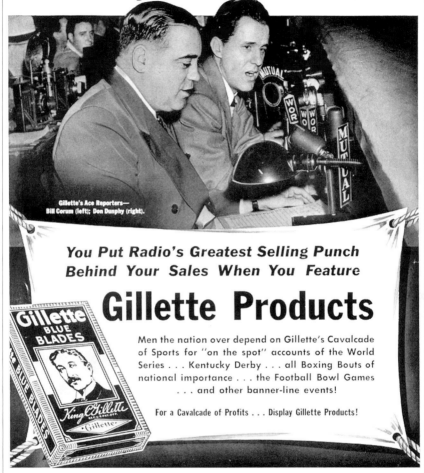

Gillette Cavalcade Of Sports Broadcasts Makes Money For You The Year Around

Gillette's Ace Reporters—
Bill Corum (left); Don Dunphy (right).

You Put Radio's Greatest Selling Punch Behind Your Sales When You Feature

Gillette Products

Men the nation over depend on Gillette's Cavalcade of Sports for "on the spot" accounts of the World Series . . . Kentucky Derby . . . all Boxing Bouts of national importance . . . the Football Bowl Games . . . and other banner-line events!

For a Cavalcade of Profits . . . Display Gillette Products!

The Gillette Cavalcade of Sports, begun in 1942, was America's premier vehicle for radio and television sports broadcasting for many years.

We Men and Women of Gillette Are Proud of Our Army-Navy "E"

—and are out to break the war-production record that won this award for us!

BILL BRONICK, Gillette Airplane Parts Division

DORIS HALLORAN, Gillette Naval Ordnance Department

QUOTED FROM OFFICIAL CITATION:
"The high accomplishment of you men and women of the Gillette Safety Razor Company is inspiring. Your record will be difficult to surpass, yet the Army and Navy have every confidence that it was made only to be broken."

ARMY · NAVY

GILLETTE SAFETY RAZOR COMPANY

More than seventy per cent of the Gillette Safety Razor Company's working hours are devoted to war production for which employees have been awarded the coveted Army-Navy "E". The advertisement shown above is appearing in 232 daily newspapers with a combined circulation of over 24,000,000. It indicates to civilian customers why you dealers occasionally are unable to satisfy their demands for Gillette products.

Gillette

For their efforts in war production, which included tens of thousands of fuel control units for combat aircraft, Gillette employees received two Army-Navy "E" (for excellence) awards during World War II.

Company officials visited
Berlin in 1946 to deliver
care packages to Gillette
employees in war-
devastated Germany.

WHICH TWIN HAS

THE *Toni?*

Lovely Consuelo O'Connor of New York, the Toni twin, says, "My twin sister, Gloria, had a beauty shop permanent— I had a Toni Home Permanent. And none of our friends could tell which had which—can you?" (See answer below.)

See how easy it is to give yourself a lovely TONI Home Permanent for your date tonight

Soft, smooth, natural-looking curls and waves. Yes a Toni is truly lovely. But, before you try Toni, you will want to know —

Will TONI work on my hair?
Yes, Toni waves any kind of hair that will take a permanent, including gray, dyed, bleached or baby-fine hair.

Is it easy to do?
Easy as rolling your hair up on curlers. That's why every hour of the day another thousand women use Toni.

Will TONI save me time?
Definitely. The actual waving time is only

2 to 3 hours. And during that time you are free to do whatever you want.

How long will my TONI wave last?
Your Toni wave is guaranteed to last just as long as a $15 beauty shop permanent — or your money back.

Why is TONI a creme?
Because Toni Creme Waving Lotion waves the hair gently — leaves it soft as silk with no frizziness, no dried-out brittleness even on the first day.

How much will I save with TONI?
The Toni Home Permanent Kit with reusable plastic curlers costs only $2 . . .

with handy fiber curlers only $1.25. The Toni Refill Kit complete except for curlers is just $1. (All prices plus tax. Prices slightly higher in Canada.)

Which is the TONI Twin?
Consuelo, at the left, has the Toni. Ask for Toni today. On sale at all drug, notions or cosmetic counters.

HOME PERMANENT
THE CREME COLD WAVE

This advertisement for Toni home permanents was published in 1947, a year before Gillette acquired Toni in its first major move away from male shaving products.

During the past year, there has been much speculation as to why we were not the first company to market a treated stainless steel blade, particularly since it was our own research which resulted in the discoveries that adherent coatings of certain materials on the cutting edges of razor blades, made either of carbon steel or of stainless steel, materially improved the shaving qualities of those blades.

Above: The 1952 World Series introduced the familiar jingle,"How're Ya Fixed for Blades?," starring Sharpie the parrot, one of the nation's most recognized cartoon characters of the 1950s.

Left: Gillette was embarrassed when Wilkinson was the first to market, in 1962, a stainless steel blade. This excerpt from the company's 1963 annual report tries to put the best face on Gillette's failure, which was soon forgotten when the company's own stainless steel blade blew its competitors out of the water.

Super Blue was a great success from the moment the first shipments hit the drugstores, supermarkets, and major chains like
Kresge, which were beginning to supplant the corner drugstore
as dominant retailers of Gillette products.

Gillette veterans like Steve Griffin cite the success of the coated
Super Blue as the start of a period when chemistry became as
important as metallurgy to Gillette's blade-making prowess. The
contribution of British scientists employed at Gillette's labs in
England was important at this stage and, indeed, for decades to
come; many years later, Griffin commented that the creativity of
Gillette's British scientists "gave us a lot of the 'R' in our most
important R & D projects." The breakthrough of the Super Blue
resulted from British-American teamwork in formulating and
learning to apply silicone to blade edges. In laboratory tests,
coated Blue Blades produced a far more comfortable shave than
uncoated Blues because the silicone-coated edges reduced the
adhesion of whiskers to the blade and produced closer shaves.
Technicians worked feverishly to devise mass production methods.

About the time Patrick Frawley was unleashing an attack ad
by Schick mocking Gillette adjustable razors and the company's
supposedly old fashioned Blue Blades, Carl Gilbert, who had
become chairman in 1958, was told that production lines were
ready to turn out coated blades. Boone Gross and Gillette Safety
Razor President Vincent C. Ziegler, Jr., and other senior managers
started to plan for the launching of the new blade, which was to
be the successor to the company's long-time breadwinner, the Blue
Blade. They decided to name the new product the Super Blue. The
price was set at seven cents, as a compromise between those who
wanted to make it a dime a blade and the cautious faction, which
thought that the Super Blue should carry the same nickel-a-blade
price the old uncoated Blue had carried for nearly thirty years.

Stymied over how to convince a jaded public that this blade
really *was* superior to older blades that had been advertised as the
best ever, Gillette's long-time ad company, Detroit-based Maxon
Inc., counseled low-key sincerity. When the Super Blue made its
debut in 1960, the advertisements said simply "Gillette Offers a

New Blade So Good It's Hard to Describe," though, of course, the copywriters did. Taking aim both at Schick's popular injector razors with single-edge blades and the rising number of men switching to dry shaving with electric razors, Gillette ads guaranteed the best shave ever, "regardless of what shaving method you have used in the past." Gillette offered two free blades to induce customers to try it and made sure that leaders and celebrities were sent Super Blues, hoping for many repeats of the coup achieved with an incidental but widely reported endorsement of the new blade by President Dwight D. Eisenhower at a White House breakfast with Speaker of the House Sam Rayburn.

Ziegler knew at once that GSR had a big winner. Despite its premium price, the Super Blue sold out regularly because consumers recognized its demonstrably superior comfort and quality. By the end of 1961, Gillette's share of the double-edge-blade market had climbed to 90 percent, and Gillette's share of the total blade market was more than 70 percent. Super Blues outsold the old Blue Blades and Thin Blades combined. It was product cannibalism, of course, but nobody in Boston was shedding tears as the higher margin Super Blue pushed aside the old standbys. Gillette's strengths in large volume manufacturing of high quality products, supported by matchless distribution channels, mowed down competitors with the ease of a Super Blue shaving off peach fuzz, as *Business Week* put it.

Total Gillette sales, which had declined in 1957 and 1958 after two decades of straight-up growth, took off once again, moving to $276 million in 1962, compared with $209 million in 1959, the final pre-Super Blue year. It was not just the Super Blue. Toni shampoos and hair sprays more than made up for declining home permanent revenues, and Paper Mate sales were climbing. To add to the good news, Gillette had successfully launched a major new product in 1960 with the introduction of Right Guard aerosol deodorant. Right Guard took more than a quarter of the total market for male underarm deodorants. It was advertised heavily on the Cavalcade of Sports as the deodorant that a man could just spray on. Gillette researchers refined aerosol valves supplied by vendors so that they produced an even spray application, helping to make Gillette the leading purveyor of aerosol spray products and giving the company a major sales boost: the combined sales of Right Guard, Foamy, and Adorn hair spray totaled 13 percent of Gillette's total sales in 1962.

Women's products beyond the Toni goods began to get advertising support. GSR had launched a Lady Gillette, though it was more or less the standard adjustable razor in pink and was hardly a breakthrough product. In a coup credited to Ziegler, the marketing of Right Guard was changed from a male-only spray to one for the whole family. Gillette flooded daytime television and a few prime-time entertainment shows with ads reminding women that Right Guard was a deodorant to be sprayed under the arm, unlike sticks and roll-ons—that is, competitive brands like Ban, Arrid, and Mennen. There was no need to make contact with underarm skin and hair. The general theme of the ads was, "Nothing touches you but the spray itself," which neatly hammered home the notion that Mom and Sis could use the same can of Right Guard that Dad did, or vice versa. Surveys showed that the television campaign worked, and for several profitable years, Right Guard ruled the market as America's leading family deodorant.

Company strategists took note of Right Guard's success and began to look more intensively beyond the world of blades and razors and male products for new companies or product lines. Joseph Turley, later to become president but working in a government liaison job in Washington at the time, recalled that Gillette had nearly acquired the pharmaceuticals and hospital equipment company Becton Dickinson, with a deal all but completed, when one of Becton's three principals refused to go along. Disappointed Gillette officials shifted ground and in August 1962 bought Sterilon Corp., a Buffalo manufacturer of disposable hospital supplies.

There were some misses. Just weeks before the Sterilon deal, Boone Gross had announced that Gillette was abandoning a brief effort to enter the proprietary pharmaceuticals field and was withdrawing several products, including a cough syrup and a cold pill manufactured by Gillette Laboratories. Gross explained that other fields appeared more attractive for the company's diversification efforts, which he said would continue apace. The Sterilon purchase did not work out any better than the pharmaceuticals venture, and the company was sold nine years after it was acquired. Gillette was learning the hard way about the risks of diversification, but in 1962 at least, there was not much concern as all that cash from Super Blues flowed in.

According to *Fortune* magazine, Gillette was the third most profitable company in America.[1]

THE WILKINSON SHOCK

Then came a shock that punctured Gillette's complacency. Tiny Wilkinson Sword, Ltd., of London, a cutlery company that had moved from making eighteenth-century combat swords used in the Napoleonic wars to straight razors and finally blades for safety razors introduced coated stainless steel blades to the market. The new stainless blades were good—excellent in fact, selling out at once in the few American stores that could get deliveries in mid-1962. Users claimed that they would get at least a dozen smooth shaves from each blade, compared with three or four shaves from the best carbon steel blades, including the Super Blue. A superior product based on a technology breakthrough had overnight challenged Gillette's unquestioned leadership in the blade market, just when Gillette was on top of the world with its fast-selling Super Blues. As Gillette struggled to respond, its smaller rivals, Schick and the American Safety Razor division of Philip Morris Co., came out with their own stainless steel blades.

Gillette technicians had long known that blades made from corrosion-resistant stainless steel would yield more shaves per blades than carbon steel blades and had produced the ill-fated stainless steel Kroman blade in the early 1930s. Since Gillette's experience with the Kroman, no blade maker, including Gillette, had figured out how to make stainless blades hold a keen edge.

The same R & D effort in chemistry that produced the silicone coating for the carbon steel Super Blue had also developed a coating that appeared to work with stainless steel blades, but efforts to develop it had been pushed aside in the rush to get the Super Blue on the market. Gillette officials later explained away their failure to beat Wilkinson in the race to introduce a stainless blade by claiming that certain metallurgy problems made large-scale production of such blades problematical. Boone Gross told security analysts that the company decided to continue searching for a superior stainless steel alloy while enjoying several years of high sales and high profits from the Super Blue, which seemed a reasonable approach given the Super Blue's unchallenged competitive edge. Wilkinson's product coup upset that complacent strategy. Ironically, it became apparent that Gillette had been ahead of Wilkinson in the race to develop a satisfactory coating for stainless steel: Gillette researchers had patented the same coating process used by Wilkinson before Wilkinson could obtain a patent, and so the English company was forced to pay a royalty to Gillette for each stainless blade it sold—on the very blades that presented the first serious challenge in decades to Gillette's leadership in the world blade market.

It was not easy for Gillette to abandon the Super Blue, which was providing such large profit margins. Even after the Wilkinson's stainless blade had been launched to unanimous praise, Gilbert and Boone Gross debated whether to stick with the Super Blue, whereas Ziegler was pushing for a shift to stainless. Steve Griffin, then vice president of GSR, recalled heated strategy sessions on how the company could defend the superiority of its carbon blades. Some thought it folly to abandon a winner for a new type of blade that would cost twice as much as a Super Blue but would produce three, perhaps four, or even five times as many shaves. What would that do to profit margins, they asked, although they knew the answer: It would hurt. At one point, just after Wilkinson's products had hit the American market, three senior Gillette executives traveled to New York and told investment analysts that stainless might not be the revolutionary change everyone seemed to assume and that Gillette, for one, had great hopes for developing coated carbon steel blades with qualities equal to stainless.

The trouble was, shavers loved the Wilkinson stainless, and

Gillette could hardly ignore its customers. The Wilkinson blades instantly became a status symbol. The *New York Times* reported that normally self-deprecating men took to bragging, perhaps with a touch of hyperbole, about getting fifteen to twenty shaves from stainless blades. Gillette officials resignedly faced the inevitable, and the company diverted millions from its Super Blue cash flow into a crash project starting in mid-1962 to get coated stainless blades on the market before more damage was done. It was largely a matter of gearing up production equipment to turn out high-quality blades by the hundreds of millions, Gillette officials explained to critics who asked why it took so long for Gillette to get stainless blades to market. At the time, one day's production output in the Boston plant was about 12 million carbon blades, according to Ziegler, compared with only 7 million stainless blades that Wilkinson exported to the United States in all of 1962.

About a year after the Wilkinson shock, Gillette's stainless steel blade made its debut in late August 1963, selling for just under fifteen cents a blade—priced slightly less than Wilkinson and American competitors. Manufacturing problems made it impossible for Wilkinson to distribute throughout the entire United States for many more months, by which time the Gillette stainless blade was entrenched and Gillette was on its way to resuming undoubted domination of the world blade market. Even in Europe, Wilkinson's home territory, Gillette stainless blades established market leadership. Still, the company's share of the worldwide double-edge market dropped from 90 percent to about 70 percent, and development costs and price competition eroded profit margins. It was hardly catastrophic, but it was humbling.

Two years after launching the Gillette Stainless blade, Gillette followed its tried and true strategy of incremental product improvement, introducing its Super Stainless blade in the United States, marketed as the Super Silver in Europe. The Super Stainless was made from an improved stainless alloy coated with a more durable chemical compound. With considerable fanfare, Gillette also introduced the Techmatic, a new razor that housed a coiled narrow band of the continuous stainless blade in a plastic cartridge, that advertisements suggested would advance the blade to a new cutting edge every week or so.

Carl Gilbert, taking his cue from the Wilkinson experience, increased spending on research and development facilities in the United States and championed the construction of a corporate research facility at Rockville, Maryland that combined R & D personnel from both the Toni Company and the safety razor operation. The Rockville facility was set up to coordinate the company's long-standing research on skin and hair, and to evaluate the company's products in light of new government regulatory concerns on safety and the environment. In addition, Gilbert encouraged the further buildup of R & D activities in England in response to promising developments underway there in basic research that would lead to a new type of blade system, one that would make stainless over carbon steel seem a relatively minor advance.

CHANGING THE GUARD

In a changing of the guard in 1965, Vincent Ziegler moved up from running the Gillette Products Group, the company's largest division, to become president of The Gillette Company, succeeding Boone Gross, who retired at sixty. It was a move that Ziegler precipitated by writing a famous memo to his boss, Carl Gilbert, declaring that if 5 percent annual growth defined a growth company, Gillette was no longer in that category and probably never would be if it depended on the razor and blade market. The company must restructure and "embark on a broad and studied program of diversification," he concluded in the unasked-for message to his boss. Rather than fire him, Gilbert instead considered the message and decided that Ziegler was right. The board elected Ziegler president, giving him full operational duties, and promoted Stuart Hensley from running the Toni and Paper Mate operations worldwide to an expanded executive vice president job that included responsibility for all Gillette shaving-grooming products through Latin America, Australia, and Asia.

Less than a year later, the board of directors, following the recommendations of a Booz·Allen & Hamilton reorganization study they had commissioned, elevated Ziegler to the dual roles of chairman and chief executive officer and promoted Hensley to president. The company was restructured on the basis of product lines rather than geography.

Hensley's tenure was brief but important. He had installed a brand management system at Toni, and it had produced results. During the stainless steel setback at the safety razor division, when a lot of money was being spent in the race to retool and catch up with Wilkinson, Toni for a year or so made a greater profit for Gillette than the blade and razor business.

Hensley, a decisive executive skilled in sales and advertising, proved too "Chicago blunt" for the collegial senior management ranks at Boston, where group decision making was more likely to be practiced. Given his strong personality and his subordinate role to Ziegler, it was no surprise when Hensley resigned his post at Gillette in 1967 to take the top job at Warner-Lambert Pharmaceuticals, which in 1970 became Gillette's arch rival when it acquired Eversharp, producer of Schick blades and razors. Ziegler, a self-made man and college dropout from Michigan and, like his mentor Boone Gross, a former liquor salesman and army ordnance officer, added "president" to his string of titles. There was no doubt whatsoever about who was running the show.

The Gillette that Ziegler inherited was changing fast. Already internal diversification had begun to take hold, and it was obvious that the new company was no longer blades and razors and not much else. Toiletry sales had moved up considerably by 1965, thanks to the success of the aerosol twins, Right Guard and Foamy. In nonshaving markets, the Toni division was giving Gillette a greater share of the female personal care market with aggressive new product launches. Paper Mate was providing steady though unspectacular progress in the stationery business. Total company sales grew, but profit margins fell, the inevitable result of lessening dependence on the high-margin blade business.

The mid-1960s marked a time when Gillette was catching the conglomerate fever then sweeping American industry. The idea was to add all sorts of product lines to a company's core business, to diversify in order to promote fast growth and avoid over-dependence on a single business. By 1970, company sales would double from 1965 and nearly half the sales volume would come from new products outside the traditional areas of shaving equipment, writing instruments, and home permanents.

RETURN OF THE GLOBAL MINDSET

The immediate postwar focus at Gillette had been domestic expansion to satisfy pent-up demand for blades and razors and, later, new nonshaving products most easily sold in the United States. The Americanization of Gillette peaked in 1965, when sales and earnings generated in the United States accounted for two-thirds of sales and earnings.

The global outlook that characterized Gillette before the postwar expansion had been subordinated during the postwar expansion, but it never came close to dying out. Right after World War II, Gillette expanded its shaving markets overseas, wherever it saw growth potential, giving new attention to Latin America and Asia. Investments in these lesser-developed regions of the world did not pay off at once but entrenched the company in fast-growth nations that later became major markets. Gillette usually was established before its consumer goods competitors, quietly paving the way for its global future.

Cold War realities closed off huge markets that Gillette otherwise would have entered in a moment in Russia, China, Eastern Europe, parts of Asia and the Middle East, and of course, in Cuba, where Fidel Castro seized the company's assets when he marched into Havana in 1959. The talkative Marxist confided in a 1977 interview with television reporter Barbara Walters that he had been a satisfied Gillette customer in his younger days; he grew his trademark beard only when his blade supply ran out while he was in hiding with his guerilla comrades in the Sierra Maestra mountains.

During the 1950s, several older European plants were updated and sometimes relocated, as in France, where near-continuous blade production in Paris since 1905 ended in 1952 with a shift to the picturesque Alpine setting of Annecy, near the Swiss border.

The move was supported by the French government, which wanted to promote industrial development in the southern provinces and offered Gillette attractive incentives to relocate its operations.

Gillette had made and sold blades in Europe since the earliest days of King C. Gillette and generally thrived there, but by 1965 its European operations were in the doldrums. Gillette Industries, Ltd., the largely autonomous London office that was in charge of Asian, African, and Middle Eastern markets as well as European, had run out of steam, and its senior management ranks were rife with ineffective executives. Gillette's share of the European shaving market had slumped to about 30 percent. Ziegler decided the time had come to press the company's British cousins to make some changes. With International Executive Vice President George O. Cutter leading the way, many of the older executives were replaced. The European sales operation was changed to resemble the American model, with marketing and sales decision-making power passed down to the field but with strategic decision-making strengthened at headquarters. European factories were modernized. Elsewhere in the world, particularly in Latin America, Gillette invested time and money in building manufacturing and distribution networks, recognizing that eventually freer markets and fewer nationalist restrictions would open the way for large-scale Gillette penetration.

Vincent Ziegler's nine years as Gillette's CEO, starting in 1966, are sometimes viewed by latter-day observers as focused on quirky domestic acquisitions and diversification into new product lines. But the record of the self-made salesman from the Midwest indicates that Ziegler was an internationalist whose biggest moves often were made outside North America.

In important ways, 1967 marked a milestone in Gillette's internationalism. It was the year that Gillette moved its world headquarters from the South Boston factory site to the 52-story Prudential Tower in Boston's Back Bay. The Pru overlooks Boston harbor and the city's Logan International Airport; the move seemed to many to make a symbolic statement that Gillette was more ready than ever to take on the world. In more substantive terms, 1967 was the year Gillette outbid U.S. and European rivals to acquire Braun AG, the German maker of electric shavers, small appliances, cameras, and audio equipment. The purchase of Braun had been a defensive move against the alarming possibility that electric or dry shaving would seriously challenge wet shaving throughout the world. The parochial company, which at first did not look much beyond its homeland market, was eventually integrated into the emerging Gillette style of global operations and became one of the company's most profitable enterprises (see Chapter 17).

Ziegler understood what others did not: that it takes an international organization to make a global operation work, as Steve Griffin said later. Griffin worked closely with Ziegler as his senior vice president for administration until 1970, when he became head of international operations, with a mandate to think of The Gillette Company as a worldwide operation. He credits Ziegler with starting an effective training and development program for international managers and for making it easier for able managers of any nationality to move to Gillette posts anywhere in the world as expatriates. Ziegler, he said, insisted that Gillette's Boston managers travel more frequently.

When Ziegler realized that Gillette needed to look for fast growth outside the United States and not just from product diversification, he reorganized the company in 1971 to move more decision-making power to the international units. This reorganization reflected, among other things, the lesson Ziegler had learned much earlier, when Gillette leaders were caught napping by Wilkinson Sword's introduction of stainless steel blades in England.

Ziegler encouraged a secretive effort by the newly energized London office to enter the Soviet Union's huge blade market—and this was in the early 1970s, a bleak period of Cold War nastiness. George H. J. Robinson, who had risen from the factory floor at Isleworth to become the managing director of Gillette Industries after the shakeup there, led negotiations that involved meetings at Moscow, Leningrad, London, and a retreat in Scotland between Gillette executives and Soviet engineers and industrial bureaucrats. Griffin said that negotiations went so far as to prepare a contract that protected Gillette patents and guaranteed some revenue in return for Gillette installing some machines in Russia and training Russian workers. When negotiations collapsed, Wilkinson moved in and struck a deal roughly along the lines that Gillette had proposed.

Adventures in Joint Ventures

By the late 1960s Gillette's proud and unbending "all or nothing" rule on ownership of foreign subsidiaries was impeding foreign growth and had to give way to political and economic realities. More and more countries demanded local ownership in any foreign enterprise as the price of entry or continued operation. The break with the historic policy first bore fruit in Malaysia, a fast-growing Asian nation that refused to let Gillette enter without local partners and, moreover, effectively blocked imports with a prohibitively high tariff. In 1968, Gillette bowed to the inevitable and scrapped its demand for 100 percent control. A 40 percent Gillette–60 percent Malaysian joint venture to manufacture blades using innovative mini-plant technology began operations in 1970 and quickly proved successful.

Gillette's willingness to take risks in pursuit of foreign business is well illustrated by the company's use of the joint venture mechanism to move into Iran when its profitable export business there was threatened. Gillette had done well in Iran from 1950 to 1969 by selling through an agent. Iran was its largest export market for blades sold through a third-party agent, as opposed to a Gillette-financed sales subsidiary, producing nearly $750,000 profit from sales of 157 million blades in 1969. It was a vestige of Gillette's London-run international export business that had flourished without much input from Boston for so many years. But the comfortable old ways of doing business proved less effective as anti-colonial nationalist governments took hold from India and the Far East through the Middle East and Africa, and Iran proved no exception. In 1965 some Iranian entrepreneurs had decided that the blade business was too good to leave to foreigners and applied to the Iranian government for permission to manufacture blades locally, which in practical terms meant licensing a foreign blade maker to set up a plant in the country.

Fearing that its profitable export business would be curtailed by the government to protect local manufacturers, Gillette started four years of on-again, off-again negotiations with the shah's byzantine bureaucracy in Teheran. Gillette's first approach was business as usual, demanding 100 percent of a proposed Iranian subsidiary. The agents of the ruling Pahlavi family in the Ministry of Economy turned Gillette down flat, and Gillette's chastened English emissaries retreated to Isleworth. At Ziegler's urging, they returned with a joint venture offer to the brothers Babayan, Victor and William, who held one of the government's two blade-making licenses. That also failed, as did a joint venture offer to another Teheran licenser. The Babayan brothers instead negotiated an 80 percent–20 percent deal with Permasharp of Scotland and began turning out blades under the Perma Iran label.

Gillette feared its lucrative market was lost, but Perma Iran ran into production problems, and nervous bankers in Teheran who had loaned $1 million to the Babayan brothers started talks with Gillette. The company dispatched Export Director Bernard Petre and financial and technical experts from London to explore the possibility of replacing Permasharp as a foreign licensee. Robert Hinman, a key player in the Boston financial management group, was sent by Ziegler and Colman M. Mockler, Jr., the company's top financial manager, to join Petre in Iran.

Hinman recalls "gaining some leverage with the English," referring to Gillette's English managers, when Mockler granted him permission to hire a new set of auditors, since Gillette's usual auditors lacked representation in Iran.[2] He signed up auditors recommended to him by a former colleague he looked up in Teheran, Mike Hawley, who had left Gillette shortly before and was working for Ralston Purina in Teheran, though he soon would return to Gillette.

Mockler had told Hinman that he could go as high as $1.7 million for the Babayan brothers' assets and machinery, and so when a deal seemed to be struck at $1.1 million, Hinman was delighted. "I remember the [Gillette] English guys wanted to do even better and kept arguing around the table, but the Babayan brothers and I thought it was time to wrap things up and go out for cocktails," he recalled.

The brothers were eager to get out and Gillette was eager to get in, and not a lot of time was spent worrying about Iran's political stability. A report on the meetings sent back to Steve Griffin mentioned only in passing "the possibility of political upheaval" but added that Iran had been stable for a decade. There were complications, such as the shaky status of a pending export contract from Russia for up to 80 million blades. Iran held 51 percent control but government officials, who had seen weak management ruin the first joint venture, did not blink when Hinman and Petre insisted on 100 percent management control and said that at least eight expatriate managers would have to be sent to Teheran to run things. There were concerns about hard currency and how to arrange barter payments and much more. But the fear of losing the Iranian market and the chance to establish and manage a large new plant outweighed these problems. The company pledged to put in equipment and expand facilities for a modern factory that would be capable of making 100 million stainless and carbon steel blades the first year and up to 400 million blades for domestic and export sales in four years. In a triumphant letter to a high official in the Ministry of Economy, Petre emphasized that if the 400-million-blade capacity was reached, as it was eventually, Gillette's Iranian plant would be one of the largest and most modern blade factories in the world.

For nearly ten years the Iranian plant indeed was a jewel in the Gillette empire, until the lightly taken possibility of violent political upheaval became reality. Gillette was forced to abandon its modern plant after Ayatollah Khomeini threw out the shah in 1979 and American businesses were targeted as enemies of the new order. Gillette hung in for a while, but new restrictions, especially involving currency transfers, made Iran a lost cause. The few Western executives from the London office working in Teheran had left on short notice, when zealous mobs and the Ayatollah's police made life unbearable. Local representatives of the company continued to negotiate terms of reparations with minimal success, under what Steve Griffin, who later became company president, called "worsening conditions." When Gillette finally closed out its business altogether, it appealed what it considered unlawful actions by Iran's government before the International Court of Justice at the Hague.

"I was upset and disappointed, but I remember Mockler saying, 'The day will come, Bob, when we'll be back,'" said Hinman.

Griffin said years later that the Iranian saga was consistent with Gillette's history of taking acceptable risks and accepting losses in the overall pursuit of global growth markets. Gillette gained valuable experience in the Middle East and sold a lot of blades and salvaged some of its assets, he noted. And the company's history suggests it will move back if or when Iran's rhetoric cools to the point that Western business can return.

TRAC II BREAKTHROUGH

The major product success during Ziegler's term was the twin-blade Trac II razor, an innovative shaving system that ended forever the primacy of King Gillette's double-edge blades. The story of Trac II began in the Reading laboratories in England in early 1964, when Dr. Norman C. Welsh, then a new employee, experimented with tandem blades, a type of razor head on which one blade followed another in a twin-blade configuration.

In a lengthy memorandum titled "Origins of Trac II," written to correct what he called folklore in press reports after the launch of Trac II in 1972, Welsh noted that in spring 1964 he had discovered the "hysteresis effect," that is, when a blade engages a whisker it extends the whisker in the hair follicle before cutting it, and there is a finite amount of time before the stubble fully retracts. It was a matter of deduction, he pointed out, that if a second blade reached the stubble before it retracted it would produce a closer shave. Contrary to press reports, Welsh said he had discovered hysteresis without the aid of high-powered microscopes or modern photographic techniques—with "nothing more sophisticated than an old-fashioned microscope and bleary eyes." By that he meant he had studied the interaction of blades with skin by squinting through the soap slots of a double-edge blade razor head mounted on a microscope.

For the next six years, Welsh and his colleagues worked on a practical means of capitalizing on the hysteresis effect, concentrating almost entirely on what became known as the Atra twin-blade system (no relation to the Atra pivoting-head shaving system launched in 1977). The first Atra razor featured two narrow blades set in a plastic cartridge with facing edges so that whiskers were cut on an up stroke as well as a down stroke, requiring a scrubbing motion by the shaver. The experimental tandem blade system, dubbed "Rex," did not require the user to shave with this unfamiliar motion. But there were many technical problems that bedeviled the tandem system. Serious work on it did not begin until 1967, when Edward E. "Ted" Pomfret was appointed to lead a group at Gillette's U.K. research lab, which had been assigned to the project. Ziegler kept close watch on the promising twin-blade projects, sitting with English technicians late into the evening when he traveled to Reading to encourage their efforts.

The Atra system was much farther along than the tandem blade of the Rex system and had proved itself in a series of consumer tests in Europe, Australia, and the United States by outperforming existing razor systems like the Gillette Techmatic. In early 1970, the Atra project went into crash mode to ensure the earliest possible introduction, motivated by the threat of a new innovation by Wilkinson—a bonded single-edge blade encased in a plastic cartridge. The Atra razor was so far along by mid-1970 that packaging and production machinery was nearly in place to support a full-scale market introduction. The only holdup was the real fear expressed by Gillette marketing executives that shavers would resist learning how to shave with an up-and-down scrubbing motion and would shun the Atra despite its demonstrably superior performance over double-edge razors.

The situation was perplexing because Gillette's researchers had tested the tandem blade Rex system and found that it produced equally close and virtually nick-free shaves with familiar shaving strokes, taking full advantage of the hysteresis effect. The problem was that major design problems remained, and time was running short. An all-out drive to develop the tandem model began in mid-1970. Three men solved different pieces of the puzzle and hold the basic patents for Trac II. Warren Nissen in Boston designed the overall product; Ted Pomfret at Reading figured out the crucial geometry needed to position the two blades; and Frank Dorion in Boston solved the final problem of how to clear out the debris of hair and lather that clogged experimental versions. Pomfret made the first of many trips to South Boston, where technicians were working on a design for the high-speed production equipment needed to turn out cartridges for the blades. The difficulty was that production required untested techniques for making plastic cartridges holding very narrow steel blades in precise configurations. "I became known as the trans-Atlantic midwife," Pomfret joked.

The midwifery worked. Plans for the up-and-down Atra razor were abandoned. Rex, renamed Trac II, was introduced in fall 1971 at the World Series, the usual Gillette product launch venue, where announcers accurately plugged "the most significant shaving discovery since King C. Gillette invented the safety razor 75 years ago." The launch took place in time to neutralize the Wilkinson bonded blade that had hit the U.S. market a few months earlier. The Trac II seized the bulk of the premium shaving market and spawned many imitators.

TROUBLES AT THE TOP

Gillette's blade and razor franchise was flourishing in the early 1970s on the strength of Trac II's success, but not all was well in the Gillette world as Ziegler neared retirement.

Ziegler had continued to load up on nonshaving products and small company acquisitions, and many of them failed to work out. Acquired companies that were held briefly but sold off or otherwise disposed of by Ziegler or his successor included a wig maker (North American Hair Goods), a maker of room air-fresheners

(Days-Ease Home Products Corp.), a service company for displaced suburbanites (Welcome Wagon), a maker of home plant care products (Hydroponic Chemical Co.), and a cosmetics company (Eve of Roma). The purchase of S. T. Dupont of France was a major deal that gave Gillette an important new product—the Cricket disposable cigarette lighter. The lighter meshed well with the company's manufacturing strengths and distribution system but eventually succumbed to price-cutting competitors. The acquisition in 1973 of Jafra Cosmetics, a small California direct sales cosmetics company, proved more successful and enduring. Jafra management recruited thousands of saleswomen who became a major force in Tupperware-style direct product sales of skin care products and lotions in a dozen countries, with a particularly strong presence in Mexico.

Against the advice of William G. Salatich, who had responsibility for Toni and Paper Mate, Ziegler insisted on moving headquarters personnel for both operations to Boston, a process that cost Gillette the services of many talented researchers and managers who refused to move. Robert J. Murray, a former Gillette executive vice president, called the move a mistake that cost the company dearly in loss of internal growth momentum in the 1970s, and in time and money expended to rebuild a credible presence in both female toiletries and writing instruments.

Several once-promising product lines failed in the early 1970s, including Nine Flags cologne, which never was able to penetrate the more expensive men's market niche. Efforts to manufacture and sell such consumer electronic products as hand-held calculators and digital watches were started on the premise that they would fit Gillette's distribution network. These consumer electronics products proved highly sensitive to technological changes and extreme price slashing. Gillette, so successful with blades and other consumer lines where it offered top quality products and controlled major market shares, was unable to compete with the mainly Japanese consumer electronics suppliers and eventually abandoned the field.

The sudden death of an executive vice president, Paul Cuenin, while on a trip to Braun facilities in Germany dashed Ziegler's plans for an orderly management succession. Cuenin, who was forty-seven when he died of a heart attack in 1970, had been the favorite to move up to the presidency and then replace Ziegler as CEO when the latter would turn sixty-five in 1975. Despite the availability of able Gillette veterans like Salatich and Steve Griffin, Ziegler surprised and dismayed many Gillette veterans when he shattered a tradition of generally promoting from within, though he could point to the historic precedent of Joe Spang, who was plucked from Swift & Co. in 1938 to head Gillette.

In 1972, Ziegler recruited to Gillette's board a highly regarded marketing innovator, Edward Gelsthorpe, who was president of California-based Hunt-Wesson Foods. Gelsthorpe was well known in Boston, where he had earned the nickname "Cranapple Ed" for his astute promotion of a cranberry-apple juice drink while head of Massachusetts-based Ocean Spray Cranberries Inc. Gelsthorpe quit Hunt-Wesson to join Gillette full-time as vice chairman for marketing; after a few months, in April 1973, he was named president and was the obvious choice to succeed Ziegler as CEO. He came in with the burden of being a highly touted outsider, a man under a spotlight who was expected to bring more excitement to Gillette's marketing efforts, which were perceived as a tad stodgy. His casual loose-tie style clashed with the highly structured and formal Gillette environment, where decades later senior executives and some juniors, too, donned jackets to go next door for a short meeting or to the company cafeteria. He was isolated in a sullen working environment and seemed unable to communicate his goals and gain the confidence of colleagues he would have to depend on.

"It just didn't work out," Ziegler told Gelsthorpe when he realized the extent of resentment toward Gelsthorpe, who took the cue and resigned in mid-1974 to accept a senior job at United Brands, the Chiquita banana company which also was located at the Prudential Tower. There were occasional awkward moments when Gelsthorpe bumped into Gillette executives in the Pru lobby.

Ziegler did not repeat the mistake of going outside. He passed over more senior officials to choose Colman Mockler, the forty-four-year-old financial whiz who had spent almost his entire working career at Gillette. Mockler's work was cut out for him. Despite Trac II's global success, Gillette's diversification campaign had caught up with the company, and a number of losers were diluting the bottom line. By the end of 1975, sales had quadrupled to $1.4 billion from the 1965 level, when Ziegler became president, but warning signals were flashing. Earnings were down, sales had slowed, and profit margins were declining. The problems were compounded by a shaky world economy upset by inflated energy prices caused by the OPEC cartel's cutback of oil production. Wall Street had become disenchanted with Gillette's sluggish growth, and conglomerates were out of favor. After a breaking-in period as president, Colman Mockler took over the reins from Ziegler on the first day of 1976, to head a company that had a proud heritage and a strong global presence but clearly needed to look, feel, and be sharper to fend off trouble as the decade of the Wall Street raiders loomed. Colman Mockler had been dealt a strong hand by his predecessors, but it was not invincible.

II

THE SEARCH
FOR BALANCE

4

THE
QUIET MAN FROM
FINANCE

WHEN PRESIDENT, CHIEF executive officer, and chief operating officer Colman Mockler took on the additional role of chairman on the first day of 1976, he found himself directing scores of executives both older than he and with greater line operating experience, though nobody at Gillette knew more about money and treasury matters than this quiet man. Prior to his abrupt promotion to replace Ed Gelsthorpe as president and COO, he had served almost exclusively in financial administration for seventeen years, most notably revamping the company's international accounting system. His selection over more widely experienced colleagues for the president's job signaled to Gillette's restless inner ranks as well as to the outside world that Ziegler, then almost sixty-four, had chosen his successor with an eye toward calming troubled waters after the tumultuous Gelsthorpe period. Even so, Mockler had to survive what amounted to a crash training program on how to run the company and at the same time prove his leadership skills in those few months before Ziegler stepped aside completely and left him on his own.

As a respected and accomplished insider with distaste for confrontation and a cautious manner, Mockler was cut more in the mold of the diplomatic Carl Gilbert than Vincent Ziegler, more consensus-minded manager than salesman and motivator, more Harvard intellectual than self-made go-getter. Whether he had the vision to move Gillette beyond a period of needed consolidation and reignite the engine of growth Ziegler had built up would be tested in the years ahead.

One of the new chairman's first tasks was to select a president, obviously someone at the company with operating experience to balance his own financial savvy.

He chose Stephen J. Griffin, bypassing William G. Salatich, an able and genial sales and marketing veteran who was president of Gillette North America—the traditional Gillette power position, which encompassed the core domestic razor and blade business plus most other product lines—and Thomas E. Singer, who headed the collection of nontraditional businesses grouped under Diversified Companies. Griffin was president of Gillette's fast-growing international division. Foreign sales (excluding Canada) overtook North American sales as a percentage of the Gillette total in 1974 and were gaining momentum. The selection of Griffin as president seemed to confirm that Mockler would continue the urgent priority Gillette had placed on geographic expansion during Ziegler's tenure. Salatich was bumped up to vice chairman with responsibilities for business strategy and new products but chose early retirement a short time later. Singer also took early retirement.

The Mockler-Griffin duo proved a durable partnership, with Griffin remaining in the post until he retired at age sixty-five in 1981. Griffin joined the company out of high school in 1941, when sales were $26 million. Mockler, forty-six, joined Gillette in 1957 from a research associate's job at Harvard Business School. Whereas Mockler had stayed in finance, Griffin had worked at many sales and administrative jobs within the safety razor division and at headquarters before heading Gillette's international business. The two men inherited a company that had posted record sales of $1.4 billion in 1975 but whose net earnings had been dropping since 1973.

Mockler took the view that the glass was half full, telling a reporter that "a period of difficulty offers opportunities." His strategy would be to pursue balanced growth between traditional markets and new products. He would "weed out marginal product lines and keep good product lines strong," he told *Wall Street Journal's* Neil Ulman.[1] He would pay particular attention to cutting costs. Mockler was no payroll slasher, however, and employee totals crept up to 34,100 by the end of 1980 from 33,500 at year-end 1975. This, after all, was before the 1990s, when it became fashionable to downsize, or, in plain English, to fire thousands of workers in one big cost-cutting move. And certainly, downsizing was not Colman Mockler's style. "There was one thing Colman was terrible at doing, and that was firing people," remarked one of his long-time aides, Robert Hinman, in a statement echoed by many Mockler associates when they were pressed to think about his managerial weaknesses.

Although Mockler may have been reluctant to cut loyal employees, it should be noted that he and his associates knew how to grow sales without adding manpower. By 1990, fifteen years after Mockler began his eventful tenure as chairman, Gillette's sales had grown three-fold to just over $4.3 billion, but worldwide employment actually was 3,000 fewer than in 1975.

An early Mockler move brought Alfred M. Zeien back to Boston from the top job at Braun in Germany to take the post of senior vice president for technical operations. Zeien oversaw the complete retooling of the big South Boston blade and razor plant. South Boston soon doubled output with the same number of workers, and each division in the company was ordered by Mockler to do much the same. A good part of the savings went into increased advertising. The logic seemed unassailable, at least in the case of blades and razors: More ads would translate to more sales, which would generate ever-greater cash flow for capital spending and new product development.

An Unshakable Sense of Ethics

Colman Michael Mockler, Jr., was born in St. Louis, Missouri, December 29, 1929, into a close knit Irish-American family, the son of Colman Michael and Veronica Mockler. His father worked for Shell Oil Company. The family moved to Scarsdale, New York, when Colman was about ten. His younger brother Robert, a professor of business administration at St. John's University in New York City for more than thirty years, believes the Irishness of the Mocklers tells a lot about his brother Colman's sense of values and how he applied these at Gillette. Robert Mockler recalled the family ethic of optimism. His parents did not tolerate complaints from him and his brother and their two sisters, and the children were encouraged to work hard to gain a position of strength and then to make the best of it while respecting other points of view. Colman attended Catholic schools, and after a short stint of army service and a year at Fordham University, he enrolled at Harvard, where he graduated both from the college (class of 1952) and from Harvard Business School. After a few months at General Electric, he came back to the Business School as a researcher, writing case studies, and in 1957 began his career at Gillette as staff assistant to the controller.

Mockler's paternal grandfather emigrated to the United States from Clonmel in county Wexler, where the parish of Mocklertown adjoins the parish of Colman, the names suggesting the importance of roots to the American family. Robert said the family often discussed values that were rooted in Catholicism but were applied in a broad context. When Colman became an evangelical Protestant during his years at Harvard Business School it was, according to Robert, a continuum of familiar Christian values learned at home and church. Colman described in a 1977 newspaper article his rebirth and his giving himself over to Christ as a gradual experience.[2] He and his second wife Joanna—a brief first marriage ended in divorce—worshipped for many years at a large evangelical church, Grace Chapel, in Lexington, Massachusetts. They lived a quiet and private life in the town of Wayland, Massachusetts, where they raised four children. Mockler once told an interviewer that "there's my private life and my company life . . . and I don't mix the two."[3] He made one exception, though he seldom talked about it: Mockler was a prime mover in a group of Boston business leaders that included his close friend Thomas Phillips, chairman and chief executive officer at Raytheon Company. The group met regularly for breakfast meetings that focused on the carryover of religious values to business life.

What others saw as shyness or caution in Colman's management style, Robert Mockler said he interpreted as respect and consideration; he said the two brothers joked about the outsider's perception of Colman Mockler as shy and quiet. As a business professor fascinated with management techniques, Robert Mockler kept in close touch with his older brother's professional life, and over many years he formed a strong picture of his brother's management style. Colman's style, he said, was not to intrude and push his own view but to listen and to focus on fundamentals; when it was appropriate, he would begin to talk and move conflicting points of view toward a resolution that was in line with his values. His brother's interpretation is supported by many of Colman Mockler's associates at Gillette.

"Vin Ziegler was a creative guy who would think nothing of interrupting an operating manager to say 'hey, I think it ought to be done this way,' which tends to produce a certain amount of respect for leadership," said Paul Fruitt, former vice president for corporate planning. But, he added, it also leads to reluctance by line managers to go out on a limb for an idea and breeds reliance on top management for better ideas. Fruitt thinks Mockler's approach of trying to outline a clear strategy—balanced growth—and then placing able managers in the field to run their operations with less interference from headquarters was well suited to the large company that Gillette had become during the Ziegler years.

Mockler's intellectual abilities were often remarked upon. Robert Murray, a former executive vice president, worked closely with Mockler on many levels. An outspoken senior manager unafraid to criticize his company and associates, Murray said flat out of Mockler, "He's the most brilliant man I ever met . . . and I don't think I am easily intimidated by many people intellectually." Mockler's colleagues never failed to comment on his remarkable facility with numbers and his ability to grasp a situation based on a few key statistics in a report or a conversation. Another strength of Mockler's universally cited by colleagues was his unshakable sense of ethics. A successor as chief financial officer, Thomas F. Skelly, recalled him as "so honest . . . with such integrity . . . just a nice man." Skelly said Mockler told him when he made him CFO, "I want you to know that I don't want you to do anything that is unethical or wrong." Skelly said he smiled and reminded Mockler that he had worked with him for ten years, and Mockler replied, "Yes, but I want you to get that message."

Aiming for Balanced Growth

The transition from Vincent Ziegler to Colman Mockler marked a shift in strategy to one of more balanced and selective growth, after the enthusiastic expansionist strategy of Ziegler, who "was always looking for the hot button" when it came to new growth possibilities, as Steve Griffin put it. Bob Murray worked under both men, and while noting their differences he emphasized their similarities. He said they shared a long-term vision of a very diversified Gillette, and not a narrow company confined to blades and razors. They believed that the steady cash flow generated by the high-margin blade and razor business should be used to diversify the company into other growth areas, rather than left to accumulate or used to buy back stock.

For the moment, however, Mockler needed to sort out winners from losers in the hodgepodge of companies and product lines outside the thriving worldwide blade and razor business. It was a prickly time for the young chief, who had leapfrogged over others and then had to get rid of companies and product lines that had entrenched champions at Gillette. As Griffin put it, Gillette had to spend a lot of time in the late 1970s getting rid of what it had spent a lot of time acquiring in the early 1970s. And there were many complicating external factors, including sustained inflation in much of the world and a difficult period for European currency values measured against the dollar, which cut into the dollar profits Gillette operations abroad were able to report back to Boston at year-end.

There was also the worrisome specter of serious competition from an inexpensive new type of throwaway razor and blade system that had been introduced in Europe by Société Bic in 1974. Gillette would have to respond with a competitive product and figure some way to blunt the impact of the Bic shaver on Gillette's blade business.

To help him get a handle on which companies and product lines fit the company's strategic needs, Mockler pulled into his inner circle an outspoken young executive named Robert Ray. Ray's major experience was in international marketing, where he had been assigned to help Gillette managers in Asia, the Middle East, and elsewhere to adopt marketing and advertising tactics that had worked well domestically. He was traveling in Europe— "glad to be away from the body slamming in the executive floors back at the Pru"—when he got a call from Mockler in spring 1975 asking to meet him in Paris to discuss a new assignment. The two men spent a long evening in a hotel room drinking a few glasses of whiskey and sorting out what Mockler wanted Ray to do, which was to analyze each of the company's product lines and recommend whether it should be kept or dropped. Ray recalled that Mockler was persuasive and made it sound like a good job, so he took it. Back in Boston, Ray adopted a management consultant's strategy popularized by Boston Consulting Group and analyzed Gillette product lines as to whether they were mature "cash cows," potential fast growth lines that needed investment, or "dogs" that had no future. Then he reported his recommendation to Mockler. It was, he said, the "hot-seat" job at Gillette and not a career-enhancer.

"I didn't exactly endear myself. There were some real shouting matches. I remember one executive who refused to let me in his office because I wanted to get rid of one of his favorites, and another who would not permit me to meet with his operating heads without his prior approval," recalls Ray. The blade business in particular was an enormous cash provider, but Ray found his share of dogs and also product lines that he felt needed new direction. He made enemies at the Diversified Companies division, the business group that oversaw Braun, and at several other smaller companies when he recommended that the Cricket cigarette lighter business be moved to Gillette's North American operation.

In addition to risking the wrath of sponsors of poor performers, Ray had to persuade Mockler to take action. Mockler agreed to some pruning, though more gradually than his critics wanted and not before hearing prolonged arguments from pro and con factions. Ray said that although Mockler generally supported his recommendations, "in truth, he was not overly supportive." Ray felt that Mockler's lack of operating experience made him indecisive at times and made it difficult for him to sort out good arguments from bad on buy and sell decisions. Others at Gillette during those years said that Mockler's insistence on quietly gathering evidence and opinions from all sides without intruding with his own views reflected his typically analytical approach to decision making. When the evidence was in and he had thought about it, Mockler was decisive and not one to second guess his decisions, one close associate said. Over Mockler's first five years, more than a dozen businesses and product areas equal to about 7 percent of Gillette's total sales volume were sold off or discontinued. These included an Italian chewing gum operation, the ventures to market electronic calculators and digital watches, the Welcome Wagon business, Buxton Inc., a fine-leather goods company, and several money-losing appliance lines made by Braun.

Even as he pruned, Mockler continued with mixed success to buy new companies and to introduce new products. Several of the new ventures involved products sold by catalog or other means of selling directly to consumers. A California maker of needlepoint kits and a Colorado maker of mail-order sewing kits were among small companies bought and soon disposed of when they proved a poor fit for Gillette. The Appliance Division, formed in 1973 to market devices like hair dryers and hair curlers, tried unsuccessfully to market Captain Kelly smoke detectors and a line of fire extinguishers.

Eventually, Bob Ray headed up a new business development

group that, along with Al Zeien and others, recommended one of the company's major acquisition success stories—Oral-B. In 1988 Ray left Gillette for a successful career as a consultant and promoter of innovative business programs for inner city entrepreneurs.

LIQUID PAPER PROVES A WINNER

One acquisition that proved a big success was the 1979 purchase of Liquid Paper Corporation, which gave a needed boost to the company's writing instruments and stationery operations grouped under the Paper Mate Division.

Liquid Paper correction fluid, at first named Mistake Out, had been invented in 1951 and was manufactured, promoted, and sold from the kitchen of a young Dallas divorcée, Bette Nesmith. She worked as executive secretary for the chairman of Texas Bank & Trust Company to support her nine-year-old son, Michael, who a decade later achieved brief stardom as one of the Monkees, in a TV sitcom about a rock group of the same name. At a time when typists everywhere were having trouble adjusting to electric typewriters, whose keys jumped when pressed too hard, Nesmith was embarrassed by her typewritten mistakes and upset because she could not erase errors without leaving telltale smudges on the new carbon ribbons that had replaced fabric varieties. A freelance graphic artist as well as secretary, she sat down at her kitchen table one evening and with a bit of mixing came up with a watery paint that she applied with a paintbrush to cover or "white out" her mistakes. Her boss could not spot the white outs, and she was not about to tell him.

For five years, Nesmith continued to use her home-made Mistake Out, gradually sharing her secret with fellow secretaries but reluctant to promote her discovery, because after all, she was correcting mistakes. Finally, the clamor from other secretaries who heard about Mistake Out became so great that an office products manager convinced her that she should market her invention. In 1956 she organized the Mistake Out Company and applied for a trademark for her product, to be named Liquid Paper. She enlisted the help of a high school chemistry teacher and a paint company worker and gradually improved the product, which she made in ever-larger batches in her kitchen and later in her garage, bottling the fluid in whatever happened to be around the house. Liquid Paper consumed most of her time but was not yet making her money. She continued to work as a secretary, by now at IBM, but from her home she sold as many as one hundred bottles and tubes a week as word spread. An ad in a trade magazine produced a response that almost overwhelmed her. Later, when a trade newspaper described Liquid Paper as "an answer to a secretary's prayer," she was swamped with orders.

After one all-night session of mixing and bottling and sorting out orders, she went to work even sleepier than usual. The next morning she signed an important letter dictated by her boss with the name "Mistake Out Company" rather than IBM and was fired on the spot. She took a part-time secretarial job elsewhere and kept on building her business with the help of her son and friends who pitched in part time. She scraped together $200 to pay a chemist to develop a faster-drying fluid with a solvent base to replace her original water-based product. In 1962, she married Bob Graham, a salesman who built up a network of dealers and office supply stores. The business took off, with sales surpassing $1 million in 1967. By the time Gillette bought Liquid Paper Corporation for $47 million in 1979, sales were $38 million a year, and it was the leader in the correction fluid market that Bette Nesmith had invented, as well as a major source of typewriter ribbons.

After the $47 million deal was reported in the *Wall Street Journal,* a Gillette executive was introduced to the president of a Texas paint company—the names of man and company are forgotten now—who told him this story: He said he had been a struggling chemistry student when Bette Nesmith asked him to help her develop a faster-drying, solvent-based fluid. She had offered him $200 cash or a sizable number of company shares, and he was so broke he took the cash. The chemist fortunately had become prosperous on his own and was able to laugh off his bad decision back in Bette Nesmith's kitchen.

Gillette bought the company primarily for its typewriter ribbon business. Few planners expected typewriter correction fluids to be a growth product in the looming era of computer-driven word processing, which allowed typists to correct mistakes electronically. Conversely, Gillette thought replacement ribbons for computer accessories would be a natural growth product line for the office supply stores serviced by Paper Mate dealers.

So much for planning. The ribbons didn't work out in part because computer makers dominated the distribution channels. But correction fluid sales started to grow rapidly in tandem with personal computer sales. Gillette liquidated the ribbon business, closed Liquid Paper's Texas plant, and moved fluids production to a Gillette plant at St. Paul, Minnesota. As expected, the Paper Mate distribution system was made to order for Liquid Paper: Gillette paid off its Liquid Paper investment in three years. Bette Nesmith Graham's high-margin product became a major money-maker for Gillette, with dry variations of the product introduced as time passed.

Graham had remained Liquid Paper's biggest shareholder, and the Gillette sale made her wealthy beyond her dreams. When she died in 1980, she left $25 million to her son, who had become a respected country singer and entertainment media executive. Michael also heads the Gihon Foundation in New Mexico, which was founded by his mother. A faithful Christian Scientist throughout her life, she named it for a river in the Book of Genesis. The foundation was formed to display the work of woman artists, reflecting the founder's feminist convictions and interest in painting. Under Michael's guidance, the foundation's major endeavor has become the Council on Ideas, a convocation of world leaders in art, academe, and politics who meet at Gihon to discuss important world issues—a concept that no doubt would have pleased that old utopian, King C. Gillette.

A TRADITION OF CORPORATE ACTIVISM

When Mockler became chairman in 1976 he inherited a major uncertainty: could Gillette continue to market Right Guard and other aerosol spray products that used chlorofluorocarbon (CFC) liquid propellants? Gillette was ready for the CFC crisis as well as any company could be, thanks in large part to a man whose title accurately described his life work. Dr. Robert Giovacchini was vice president for corporate product integrity and the expert on product safety. Giovacchini had played a central role in several product safety issues dating back to Carl Gilbert's final days at Gillette, and with the conspicuous support of top management for almost three decades, he was the man most responsible for the company's reputation for responsiveness to safety concerns and cooperation with regulators, a reputation Mockler was determined to enhance.

Giovacchini had left a teaching job at University of Nebraska to join Gillette's Toni division in Chicago as a toxicologist and in 1964 moved to Washington, D.C., to help establish the Gillette Medical Research Institute at nearby Rockville, Maryland, at the behest of Gilbert. A consumer advocacy movement spawned by the publication of Rachel Carson's *Silent Spring* in 1963 had caused government to greatly increase its regulatory purview over consumer products, and Gilbert thought the institute would help Gillette stay abreast of regulatory concerns. The institute's scientists performed biological and medical research on new and existing products, with special attention to toxicity, irritants to skin and eyes, and damage to lungs or other organs.

After the Rockville lab was up and running, the Food and Drug Administration chief, James L. Goddard, became concerned about the effects of dimethylsulfoxide, or DMSO, which was a chemical carrier of other chemicals through the skin. DMSO had displayed great potential for improving the performance of personal care products such as hair dyes, shaving creams, and various lotions, and Gillette, along with other manufacturers, started using the additive. Goddard became concerned about possible misuse of DMSO and without fanfare classified it as a new drug, which meant it had to be tested and absolved of problems before it could be used. His unpublicized reclassification of DMSO went unnoted by manufacturers, including Gillette, who kept using the chemical. In reviewing the list of manufacturers buying quantities of DMSO, Goddard found Gillette's name and sent a "you have broken the law and please explain why or you may be going to jail" letter to the desk of Carl Gilbert, demanding his presence in Washington to explain why Gillette had not complied with the reclassification of DMSO. Gilbert and Gillette's R & D chief, Milton Harris, met with Goddard, who demanded action. In an effort to exculpate the company, Gilbert promised that Gillette would devise a rigorous set of testing procedures to prevent such a thing from ever happening again. That same day he ordered Giovacchini and Peter Barton Hutt, a lawyer from the Washington law firm of Covington & Burling, to come up with a system to test and evaluate products for safety before the products were put on the market. They produced a detailed report, and with the support of Gilbert and his successor, Vincent Ziegler, Giovacchini launched his mission to make proactive concern about product safety an unquestioned part of the Gillette culture. The 1967 medical and legal procedures manual produced by Giovacchini and Hutt has stood the test of time.

The first of many preemptive moves by Giovacchini came when he decided that Gillette spray products should adopt warning labels to protect Gillette against a growing problem—kids sniffing aerosol spray fumes to induce giddiness or a "high," which too often led to sickness and even death. Hundreds of aerosol spray products subject to misuse were on market shelves, including Gillette's Right Guard and some hair sprays (though not aerosol shave creams such as Foamy, which used different propellants). Before Washington ordered it, and over the objections of some Gillette marketing people, who did not like seeing such words as "harmful" and "fatal" on packaging, Giovacchini convinced Chairman Ziegler to order labels for Right Guard and hair spray containers that warned users against inhaling fumes from the spray. The FDA was more than satisfied and ordered all manufacturers of aerosol products to employ the same warning that Gillette pioneered.

Giovacchini again spotted trouble when Rockville performed some rigorous lab tests with hexachlorophene, an aerosol disinfectant. Despite derision from many industry chemists and product safety officers, Giovacchini persuaded Gillette to stop its use immediately. About two years later, Washington caught up with

Gillette and banned its use, catching a lot of companies with unsalable products containing hexachlorophene.

Ziegler also supported Giovacchini's controversial recommendation to not use vinyl chloride propellants, which some competitive brands were using as an inexpensive alternative to alcohol in aerosol sprays. As part of an FDA-appointed review committee on ingredients, Giovacchini had learned through data presented to the committee that vinyl chloride aerosol sprays were linked to liver problems in laboratory animals. The company never used this chemical, which made it tougher for Gillette to compete against less scrupulous manufacturers in the United States and especially abroad, where no restrictions applied. Years later, the FDA banned the use of vinyl chloride in the United States.

Then Right Guard was back in the news with another, costlier problem. A class of new Right Guard and Soft & Dri antiperspirant products labeled "extra strength" passed a first round of new product tests at Rockville, including ninety-day inhalation tests performed on rabbits and rats. Production started and shipment to distribution centers began. A second batch was tested at Rockville, this time with monkeys, and to the dismay of evaluators, a few monkeys developed slight lung inflammations. Dr. Giovacchini spent a weekend at Rockville with his aides evaluating the lung tissue and traced the inflammation to the chemical zirconium, which was the ingredient that provided the product's "extra strength." He concluded that zirconium in aerosol form posed a possible long-term hazard for humans, one that might not show up for five or ten years.

He immediately sent a memo to Boston recommending a halt to production, plus the drastic step of recalling zirconium products that had moved to market. A hasty meeting was called, and Giovacchini presented his case before Ziegler, Salatich, and about twenty other managers at what Ziegler called a "sweaty meeting during which a lot of people blew off their steam." With Ziegler's support, Giovacchini had the last word. At a cost of $2 million— even before the FDA was aware of the problem—Gillette pulled nearly 4 million Right Guard cans out of warehouses where they were awaiting shipment to stores. Giovacchini's clout and

Ziegler's determination not to risk the good reputation of the powerful Right Guard brand name carried the day.

Competitors complained about what they thought was Gillette's overly sensitive aversion to perceived risks. Procter & Gamble, maker of Sure, and Carter-Wallace, which sold Arrid Extra-Dry, declared the Gillette test inconclusive and kept selling zirconium sprays. Two years later, Gillette was vindicated when the FDA banned all zirconium sprays.

The CFC Dilemma

Mockler inherited this background of corporate activism just as the dilemma over CFC use was nearing a climax in 1976. CFC propellants had been used routinely in Right Guard and in thousands of other aerosol spray and refrigerant products since 1961. That changed in 1973, when scientists identified CFCs as a probable cause in the alarming degradation of the earth's protective ozone layer, which resulted in seasonal holes in the atmosphere over the poles and raised fears of global warming and an increased incidence of skin cancer. Overnight, CFC sprays became suspected hazards.

This time, Giovacchini moved more slowly. He was confident that aerosol sprays containing CFCs were safe for human use because of Gillette's exhaustive testing procedures. He had access to U.S. naval tests that showed no problems with sailors confined to submarines air-conditioned with fluorocarbon formulations. And CFCs were inexpensive and efficient propellants. Giovacchini was skeptical of arguments made by scientists based on computer models, but he realized that atmospheric ozone depletion was a type of safety hazard that was beyond the capabilities of product testing in a laboratory. He set to work testing the safety of a somewhat less efficient hydrocarbon (water-based) pump spray that could be used as an alternative for CFC propellants.

In the meantime Mockler restated the company's policy declared by his predecessor Ziegler, which was to keep selling Right Guard, Soft & Dri, and hair sprays made with CFCs during the two-year government test period then underway, tempered with

---

a pledge to stop using chlorofluorocarbons if scientific studies presented credible evidence linking CFCs with depletion of the ozone layer. In 1977, the government study was in, and the news was bad, indicting chlorofluorocarbon sprays. Government officials made ready to take action to ban CFC aerosols. Gillette did not wait for the order. Ready with the alternative water-based propellant, Mockler immediately stopped production of CFC-based spray products in the United States. In terms of product positioning, the decision was painful because Gillette was a leading seller of aerosol spray products of many kinds, and now all were under a cloud of suspicion.

Along with user-abuse issues raised in the 1980s by Liquid Paper solvents, on which Gillette was ahead of competitors in adding warning labels and in reformulating the product with foul-smelling oil of mustard to discourage abuse, the banning of CFCs probably was the biggest product safety issue Mockler faced. Over the past decade, regulatory restrictions involving Gillette products have diminished, which Giovacchini credits to the company's product integrity system, designed to look for problems before they happen and take care of them before they escalate. The proactive attitude would not have held for more than thirty years, he said, without unquestioned support from Gillette CEOs, ranging from Carl Gilbert to Alfred Zeien, who ignored the occasional comparisons to Ian Fleming's Dr. No or Cassandra (after the Greek seer who rejected Apollo's love and was punished by his decree that no one should believe her prophecies). Giovacchini said he recalled Vincent Ziegler turning back critics at one point by declaring "Well, we'll sell less antiperspirant, but we're going to sell safe antiperspirant."

In the long run, Giovacchini argued, the proactive attitude paid off hugely. He cited another company that made an aerosol food product without a warning label about sniffing hazards. That company fought and lost about ten lawsuits brought by families of those who had been injured or killed by abusing the product, and eventually gave up fighting and made costly out-of-court settlements.

Gillette's liability claims process, retooled under the direction of Gillette's legal chief, Joseph E. Mullaney, is an innovative component of the company's safety assurance program. During the late 1970s, Mullaney took a close look at the company's relationship with its insurers, who generally preferred to settle nuisance claims rather than defend the company through costly litigation. Although Gillette had never been hit with any major product liability claims, Mullaney was alarmed by some very large judgments against consumer products companies in California and New York, and he decided to take preventive action. He fired the company's insurance carrier and hired Cigna, which worked with Gillette to revamp product liability policy. Coordination and control was brought into Gillette's legal department. An outside counsel, J. Warren Jackman of Pray, Walker, Jackman, Williamson & Marlar in Tulsa, Oklahoma, was given the authority to hire firms in local states to provide vigorous defense. The initiative involved a significant commitment of time and money, but fighting frivolous suits rather than settling out of court seems to have worked. By contrast, rival Bic paid out large sums to settle suits from consumers claiming they were burned by faulty disposable lighter claims of the sort Gillette defended. Gillette gained a reputation among trial lawyers as a company that could not be bullied and as an industry leader in managing liability issues.

In addition to overseeing product safety, Giovacchini also was in charge of product quality for many years, having responsibility for a Boston-based laboratory that subjects new products and packaging to rigorous tests before they are certified market-ready. His jurisdiction included veto power over labeling and advertising claims that he felt were inappropriate or insupportable by scientific evidence. Giovacchini believed that Gillette's reputation as a company that made product safety, product quality, and advertising truthfulness a priority cannot be measured in dollars alone. His point was made by the well-known consumer activist Ralph Nader (not one given to casual praise), who wrote approvingly in *Taming the Giant Corporation* of Giovacchini's "authority to recall any Gillette product, quash any advertising claim, or order any packaging change he feels is necessary to protect the company's consumers."

Environmental Concerns

Another of Giovacchini's legacies at Gillette was a proactive stance to keep Gillette from being the target of environmental lawsuits involving hazardous waste disposal, as were W. R. Grace & Company and Beatrice Foods, in an enormously expensive and tragic case vividly described by Jonathan Haar in his 1995 bestseller *A Civil Action*. Gillette routinely checks for environmental problems that may not be obvious when it acquires a company. That is standard procedure for companies that want to avoid legal headaches and protect their reputation as a good corporate citizen, but Giovacchini often went further and set an exacting standard for Gillette. For example, in the course of an environmental audit at the Liquid Paper Corporation's factory site in Greenville, Texas, that was triggered by Gillette's acquisition, Giovacchini's inspectors discovered evidence of a chemical spill that had not been disclosed to Texas regulators. Gillette at once informed the state authorities, who otherwise would not have known about it. Then bulldozers moved in, and Gillette went through with a $2 million cleanup of the spill site, without being ordered to do so.

A decade later, Gillette spent about $25 million for an environmental audit and follow-through performed as part of the process of buying Parker Pen from English owners. One morning Parker employees at Janesville, Wisconsin, were surprised to see a crew hired by Gillette boring holes at the location of a chemical spill that, in this case, had been duly reported to state authorities when it had occurred. Giovacchini had uncovered the spill report in his audit and wanted to know more. A Parker official conceded that there had been a bit of trichloroethylene spilled. How much? Well, maybe five hundred gallons—someone had forgotten to turn a shut-off valve on a Friday night, and over the weekend the tank had leaked dry. Giovacchini decided it was important to quantify the extent of the spill and so ordered the borings, which satisfied him that the chemicals had migrated safely to a nearby river, dissipating untraceably without polluting local water supplies. He reported his findings to state regulators, who accepted Gillette's evidence and thanked the company for caring enough to follow up with a detailed report.

Gillette safety engineers investigated a similar but smaller chemical spill at the factory adjacent to Parker Pen's headquarters at Newhaven on the south coast of England. The company's insistence on making exploratory borings astonished local officials, who thought it was bizarre for the Yanks to reinvestigate a problem that had already been reported and resolved to the satisfaction of English authorities. Again, Giovacchini said he wanted to quantify the spill and guard against a possible unhappy surprise. Gillette's stance is that a global company should strive for uniform standards throughout the world, regardless of local laws: If a product or a factory is not considered safe by U.S. standards, it is not safe anywhere. In some cases but not often other nations have had stiffer safety and health regulations than those put forth in Washington. When the noise-level limit in Europe was found to be eighty-five decibels for production machinery compared with ninety in the United States, Gillette adopted the higher standard for its Boston-made blade making equipment.

The position of vice president of corporate product integrity, which includes broad powers to investigate and correct environmental hazards, was created by Ziegler for Giovacchini in 1974. The job survived his retirement in 1994, which would have pleased Ziegler, who once said that a great deal of thought went into the creation of a title that could not be diluted over the years and conveys a sense of manufacturing honesty and purpose.

TOILETRIES BECOME UNISEX

The company's 1978 annual report noted cautiously that sales and profits of Gillette toiletries and grooming aids had advanced moderately after several years of little growth. In the United States and Canada, Gillette's sales were virtually unchanged, and profits declined; abroad, sales were up and the line had gone from red ink to profitability. Picking out a bright spot, the report included the optimistic comment that a return to curlier hair styles in the United States had contributed to sharply higher sales of Toni home permanents. This cultural-commercial trend unfortunately was short lived, though Gillette to this day sells home-permanent kits to a faithful market of mostly older women living in the Midwest and South, some of whom were likely influenced by the Toni Twins to give it a try. But the report's comment about home perms and other women's products underscored that Gillette had moved a long way from its almost exclusively male product lines in the pre-Toni days.

When Joseph F. Turley was moved by Mockler from the Safety Razor Division to head Gillette North America in 1976, he reached to Canada and brought Derwyn F. Phillips to Boston to head up the Toiletries Division, the repository of predominately male product lines like Foamy or family products like Right Guard. Phillips was an aggressive Canadian marketing expert who had run Gillette Canada for several good years. A year later, at his urging, Toiletries was merged with the female-oriented Personal Care Division, which was largely the old Toni operation, to form a new, unisex division for personal care products. Separate R & D and marketing groups were merged, and results began to show in higher sales as well as in lower costs. Some things stayed the same: Miss America promoted female products, and baseball players extolled Foamy for the gents.

A strikingly new type of hair conditioner, Silkience, came on the market early in 1981, the result of a push by Gillette managers to break from the pack with an important new women's product that would dominate an emerging niche market called "post-shampoos." Brand manager Sandra Bartolini Lawrence was charged with launching Silkience in two years rather than the usual three years from concept to market.

Market research studies had convinced Lawrence that the product should be targeted as a self-adjusting conditioner, to be applied only where the user's hair needed it. Gillette scientists knew how to formulate the product, and Lawrence was persuaded by market research that a need and a demand existed for such a post-shampoo, though the concept was not easily explainable to consumers, and clever advertising would be critical. The research scientists on Lawrence's product team knew that human hair contains positive and negative electric charges. They suggested a conditioner specially formulated with an abundance of positive charges that would, like a magnet, attract hair damaged during shampoos, because damaged hair has an abundance of negative charges. Lawrence saw that the new product got top priority and good funding. The division's ad agency, Advertising to Women, prepared an award-winning campaign that used scanner photography to show the magnetic attraction.

Silkience scored well with women from its first day on the market, having been positioned as a sophisticated product that could be sold at a relatively high price because it offered a demonstrably superior approach to hair conditioning. Silkience kept its dominant market position for almost a decade, until upscale entries like Helene Curtis' Finesse and others flooded the market. An effort to reposition the brand in 1989 under a patented formula proven to "keep hair cleaner longer" proved a bust. "We went from nothing to a $100 million business virtually overnight and chased that success like the Holy Grail for the next ten years," John Darman, a Gillette marketing executive, said years later. The product was de-emphasized when it became apparent that it would cost too much to revive, with no certainty of success.

Lawrence won great credit from company and industry colleagues for guiding Silkience to the top. She later joined Polaroid Corporation in a senior management position.

White Rain hair care products proved a less flashy but more enduring success in the female personal grooming market. The bellwether White Rain shampoo was introduced in 1951 and died out during the 1970s, but it was revived in 1980 to counter Clairol's Condition shampoo. Revitalized again in the 1990s, the line was extended to fruit-fragranced shampoos, named White Rain Essentials, to counter competitors like strawberry-flavored Suave. Green Apple, Pink Grapefruit, Peach, and Coconut—Essentials had a shampoo with fragrance for every taste. Their success inspired another White Rain sub-brand, White Rain Exotics, which borrowed advanced technology used by fine perfumers to incorporate fragrances from living flowers rather than cut flowers.

THE MIXED MESSAGE OF DISPOSABLE RAZORS

At one level, the Gillette blade and razor business for men was in great shape as the 1980s began. When Mockler and Griffin assumed command in 1976, the company's razor and blade sales were greater than the combined total of competitors in most world markets. The high-margin profits these sales generated accounted for more than two-thirds of total Gillette profits on about 30 percent of total sales. These percentages were roughly the same at the end of 1980, and in dollar terms, Gillette blades were outselling all competitors combined, nearly everywhere.

New product launches did well. The pivoting-head Atra twin blade razor introduced in 1977 was touted as the system that would carry forward the innovative tradition. Compared to its double-edge predecessors, it may not have been a revolutionary new product in the sense the twin-blade Trac II was, but Atra's tilting head provided a visible improvement that shavers could understand and experience each morning. For advertising's creative minds, the Atra was a natural. There followed from Madison Avenue pithy words, diagrams, and tremendously enlarged slow-motion pictures on television of a man shaving his curved face. To the viewer, it suggested a smooth-running machine reaping wheat cleanly from a rolling field. "You've never shaved so close with so much comfort before" became the advertising slogan, a ten-word phrase that included two of the most critical words of the shaving ritual—"close" and "comfort."

In its first year on the market, Atra became the best-selling razor in the United States and before long would take over market leadership in Europe under the name Contour. In most other international markets, less expensive double-edge blades were outselling higher-priced twin-blade cartridges on a unit basis. Blue Blades, sold in packages with King C. Gillette's familiar face on them, remained the quality blade of choice in parts of Asia. In one form or another, Gillette blades were being sold virtually every-where, even behind the Iron Curtain, in small quantities. Gillette blades, like Coca-Cola, were universal products, available almost anywhere.

Still, anyone who followed Gillette closely realized that all was not well in blades and razors. Despite continuing growth in total sales and profits, words like "moderate" and "modest" started showing up in annual report summaries toward the end of the 1970s to describe the *rate* of growth in blade profits. The company's extraordinary profit margins (operating profits as a percentage of total sales) were about 18 percent in 1970 but slipped to 12 percent in 1979. The blame lay with reduced profit margins in blade sales, and it was painfully easy to pinpoint the reason—competition from makers of cheap disposable razors, primarily France's Bic. For the first time since the end of the war, Gillette was being forced into a blade price war with a formidable competitor in order to maintain dominant market share, and the price competition was beginning to affect profits. Soon there would be pitched battles fought within Gillette over fundamental strategies for combating disposables.

The trouble had started in Greece, of all places. Baron Marcel Bich, the Italian-born founder of the French company Société Bic SA, had worked with a Greek blade manufacturer to design and mass produce an inexpensive plastic razor with a single-edge blade embedded at the top. It was billed as the world's first disposable razor—not a disposable blade but a razor handle and single-edge blade molded into one throwaway razor made of cheap plastic. The idea was for a customer to buy a package of five or ten throwaway razors, instead of a pack of throwaway blades, for a price just a little more than the blades alone. The Bic shavers did not have the quality of a good blade and razor system, but the Bic shaver sold well nonetheless when launched in Greece in 1974. It then was launched in Italy and some other European markets. Steve Griffin and others realized that they faced a radical challenge to the company's seventy-five-year-old strategy of selling disposable blades to fit a permanent handle.

Gillette's first response was to design a high-quality disposable razor of its own and get it on the U.S. market before the Bic razor made it across the Atlantic. There was little time to waste. In an impressively fast turnaround, the Safety Razor Division's best people got the job done, designing both disposable razor and mass production machinery needed to turn out millions of good-quality throwaways. A single-edge model like the Bic shaver was designed but soon junked. Gillette's ace in the hole was a twin-blade disposable that was basically a Trac II cartridge molded into a blue plastic handle. It shaved smoothly and closely, and was a higher-quality product than Bic's throwaway. The Gillette twin-blade disposable was dubbed Good News, and the company fervently hoped it would be bad news for Bic when it was launched in 1976, about a year before the Bic shaver arrived in the United States.

When the Bic shaver did hit U.S. shores, it came with a $9 million promotion budget that included a giveaway of 40 million samples. Gillette responded by tying in with McDonald's to give away 20 million Good News along with its Big Macs, a gesture that possibly puzzled some adolescent customers of preshaving age. Reluctantly, Gillette priced Good News below the prevailing prices for Trac II cartridges. Gillette's move was hardly a recipe for superior profits, especially since it cost a penny or two more to manufacture each disposable razor as compared with a blade cartridge, and those pennies added up to many, many million dollars of lost profit, given the high level of production. The strategy worked in that it kept Bic at bay. Good News never lost market leadership in the United States as disposable sales for all razor makers took off. Under various names, Good News caught up with and surpassed the Bic shaver in much of Europe, and Gillette swiftly moved the product into important Bic-less areas of the world, such as Latin America.

The competition between Gillette and Bic for the worldwide disposable market might have been even more formidable if Bic had been successful in its bid to acquire the American Safety Razor (ASR) division of Philip Morris, whose Gem and Personna blades held 13 percent of the U.S. razor market. With this deal, Bic would have added major twin-blade capacity to its product line, but the $20 million sale was rejected by the Federal Trade Commission in 1977. The FTC focused on the then relatively small disposables segment of the market and concluded the purchase of ASR would give Bic unfair competitive advantages. Philip Morris, whose focus was on beer and cigarettes, decided to get out of the business all together when the Bic deal fell through. The ASR unit was sold to a management group that lacked the financial and marketing muscle of Philip Morris, and Gillette dodged a bullet.

In a way, Gillette was disappointed to see Good News do so well. Officials at first hoped disposable razors would take no more than 10 percent of the total razor and blade market—a manageable level that would not seriously disrupt the higher-margin systems market. But that was not to be, for the convenient disposable caught on, and by 1980, disposables accounted in units for more than 27 percent of the world shaving market, by some estimates. What's more, Bic refused to go away. Nobody knew better than Bic how to make money by manufacturing and selling inexpensive consumer products to the masses, something Gillette knew all too well. The throwaway razor battle was not the first time Marcel Bich had crossed swords with the company.

THE STICK PEN WARS

The first time Gillette encountered Baron Bich was in the writing instruments market. The Italian-born Bich was only thirty-six in 1949, an entrepreneur looking for an exciting new product, when he discovered a newfangled type of pen that did not leak (at least not usually)—the ballpoint pen. He bought a small pen company in France that same year and named it Bic rather than Bich because he thought consumers would recall the sharp three-letter word more easily than the family name. By 1953, his factory in the Paris suburb of Clichy was producing a quarter million pens a day.

In 1958, for only 5 million French francs (then worth about U.S. $10,000), he bought Waterman USA in the hopes of cracking the American market. It did not work out. After spending several million dollars with no payback, Bich sold Waterman USA to Francine Gomez in 1971 for $80,000—about the price of eight dozen top-of-the-line Waterman pens today.

By the mid-1950s Gillette had entered the ballpoint pen business with the acquisition of Paper Mate, and the battle had been joined. For decades, Bic and Gillette's Paper Mate battled for leadership of various segments of the market. By and large, Paper Mate did well in mid-priced pen markets, but Bic owned the stick pen (no-refill disposables) low end of the market. In the early 1970s Paper Mate decided to take on Bic with its own stick pen and launched Write Bros. (The packaging had a photo of an airplane with two flyers to underscore the pun for literal-minded or history-challenged customers.) Some at Gillette did not want the Paper Mate name on the packaging because they thought the name should be preserved as a middle- to upper-level market brand. Write Bros. barely got off the ground, with sales of less than 20 million pens annually in the early 1970s, which was far under the company's projected demand and plant capacity for 60 million. The line was resuscitated by shifting the sales emphasis from retail stores to large commercial office accounts, and by 1976 the sales goal and plant-capacity level of 60 million units was reached.

At the time, Bob Murray was heading commercial sales, and he was convinced that Paper Mate had the products and the marketing ability to challenge Bic's overall dominance of the stick

No Contact

There is no recorded contact between senior Gillette officials and Baron Marcel Bich, despite the decades-long competition between the two companies in pens and later cigarette lighters and razors. Bich did make one effort to meet Colman Mockler.

An avid and accomplished sailor, Bich competed twice in the America's Cup races. During one race week at Newport, Rhode Island, an hour's drive from Gillette's Boston headquarters, the baron called Colman Mockler and invited him to come down for a sail on his yacht. Gillette's general counsel, Joe Mullaney, worried about the propriety of a Mockler-Bich sail, given tough U.S. antitrust laws, and advised Mockler to decline. Baron Bich told Mockler that he understood and that perhaps the two men could get together someday in France, which has fewer anti-trust constraints.

pen market. Mockler gave the costly project his support. Over the next few years, Write Bros. gained market share rapidly and battled neck and neck with Bic for leadership. Unfortunately for Gillette, its product line was seldom much over break-even because the price competition was so intense.

Paper Mate had other, more profitable product lines during the 1980s, including the heavily advertised porous-tip Flair marker pens, various Liquid Paper products, and Eraser Mate, the first ballpoint pen with erasable ink. And the sales success of Write Bros. at least gave Paper Mate bragging rights in the increasingly global battle with Bic over which company could sell the most stick pens, even if the product made little or no money. Write Bros. remained a major product line for decades, selling more than half a billion pens annually in the mid-1990s.

THE SAD TALE OF CRICKET

Gillette's second competitive encounter with Bic was in the worldwide market for cigarette lighters and, in the end, turned out worse. It all started with another Frenchman, Bernard Dupont, an executive at S. T. Dupont. The family business had been making and selling expensive leather goods and high-priced, carefully crafted metal gift items for the carriage trade since the Franco-Prussian War. After World War II, S. T. Dupont became a leading maker of luxury cigarette lighters that became status symbols for Europe's postwar upper and middle classes. The metal lighters required replacement cartridges when fuel ran out, and Dupont had such a cartridge in his hand one day when he was struck by an idea. Why not put a simple striking mechanism on the cartridge, add a bit of plastic cover, and sell the unit as a cheap lighter to be thrown away when the fuel ran out? All those smokers out there! Dupont put his creation on the market in 1961 and, according to a Gillette fact sheet published in 1984, called it the Cricket to rhyme with *briquet,* the French word for lighter.[4]

Sales took off in France, and underfinanced S. T. Dupont had trouble keeping up with orders. An early attempt by S. T. Dupont to market Crickets in the United States failed; most Americans collected free matchbooks. A Gillette research study concluded that lighters were a passing fad in North America. But the fad would not fade, and disposable cigarette lighters began to sell briskly in the United States. Gillette, at the height of its grow-by-acquisition period, decided to buy its way into the emerging mass market. It purchased 48 percent of S. T. Dupont in 1971 (the French government would not allow a majority interest until a few years later), thus acquiring the underfinanced Cricket as its own. Gillette modernized the hand-assembly lighter line at Dupont's French plant, which by chance was near Gillette's blade factory at Annecy. In 1973, Gillette's Safety Razor Division started selling Crickets in the United States, and new facilities to manufacture Cricket were opened in Brazil, Mexico, and Puerto Rico as Gillette rapidly expanded Cricket marketing to smokers around the world.

Enter Marcel Bich. He had noted the Cricket's rise in his native France, and when Gillette bought out S. T. Dupont he decided it was time for him to move. A few months after Gillette began sales in the United States, Bic was in North America too, with product shipped by air from a French contract manufacturer. After that, it seemed, wherever Cricket went so did Bic, and often the Scripto lighter made by the company of the same name. Gillette never flinched. "After all," Gillette North America president Joseph Turley said, "Gillette practically created this market with Cricket." The chirpy green bug of the Gillette ads faced the brassy "Flick my Bic" competition of the Bic lighter in a costly fight. By 1977, the world market for lighters had grown six times the 1971 level to 350 million units, with Gillette and Bic close to even at 120 million apiece. It was a profitless prosperity, yet Gillette refused to blink.

Year after year, the story was the same. Sales were up in unit terms but off in dollar terms, and overall, the lighter business for Gillette was unprofitable. The pressure to meet demand was so strong that Gillette did not have time to retool its plants to reduce unit costs. Gillette paid dearly for this inability to match manufacturing costs against Bic, the master at producing low-cost goods for very high volume markets. It was not for lack of trying.

Fashion Crickets and Super Crickets were introduced. Advertising budgets were generous. Cricket quality was high, regularly rated by consumer agencies as the best-performing cigarette lighter. Cricket giveaways and promotions became routine. And always, the price went down. When Cricket was introduced in 1972, it sold for $1.49. By 1983, after years of severe inflation, the Cricket sold for seventy cents—and the Bic's price was sixty-nine cents or two for ninety-nine cents. Cricket's U.S. market share fell to 16 percent, as compared with 53 percent for Bic and 24 percent for Scripto. Gillette gave up and sold the Cricket business to the fourth player in the market, Swedish Match Company.

So Gillette knew all about Bic by the time the rival mass marketers squared off in the disposable razor market in the mid-1970s and knew it was in for a fight where it would hurt the most—in its hugely profitable blade and razor business. Gillette employed its technological and marketing muscle to catch up quickly with Bic in Europe and stay ahead in the U.S. market. Almost everywhere the Bic razor competed with Good News, Gillette was the market leader. Good News made a profit for Gillette but not as much per unit as Atra or Trac II, and the more disposables that were sold, the more Gillette's accustomed high margins in the total blade market eroded. Some at Gillette argued that disposables would be able to capture more than 50 percent of the total blade and razor market because that was what shavers wanted, and there was nothing to do but make sure Gillette stayed on top by aggressive marketing and advertising support, at whatever the cost to the traditional systems business.

Not that Gillette was in desperate shape as the decade ended. Sales had increased 65 percent, and profits were up 55 percent from 1975 to 1980. Mockler was firmly in charge and no longer prefaced his comments about new product plans with the remark "I'm not a marketing man." He understood the challenge to total blade profits posed by increasing sales of Good News disposables, and he was among those at the company who refused to accept the view that it was all over, that disposables were the wave of the future.

As it happened, an Englishman working in Europe for Gillette first went to the barricades against the French foe Bic, with a strategy designed to blunt the inroads made by plastic disposables and ensure that two-piece metal blade and razor systems remained the choice of shavers around the world. John Symons loomed larger than life at Gillette for the next decade, first at Gillette's European headquarters in London and later at Boston, where his challenge, "Are you a steel man or a plastic man?" was the only issue that mattered to a generation of blade and razor strategists.

5

ARE YOU A STEEL MAN

OR A

PLASTIC MAN?

FEW MEN HAD more impact on the direction of Gillette's core blade and razor business in the 1980s than John W. Symons.

Symons was born in 1930 in London's East End—the working-class Cockney district of the great city on the Thames—just at the time of the Great Depression, which made life marginal for many in the crowded neighborhoods. When war came in 1939 and the Luftwaffe attacked the city night after night, Symons was evacuated along with countless other children to the leafier and safer surroundings of rural England. During his first year away from home, his parents separated, and he never talked with his mother again. He finished his schooling and was drafted at once into the armed forces, where he served two years. Upon mustering out in 1950, he joined the ranks of the London police, became a bobby walking a beat on city streets for almost five years. He quit when friends persuaded him that if he went into sales he might be lucky and get a company car to drive. He was dazzled by the prospect of having a motorcar—if not his own, at least one that would be his to drive. He started selling for a pet food subsidiary of Mars, the big food and candy company, and soon switched to Nestlé, where he did indeed get a "little black Ford with 60,000 miles on it, and I thought I was the King of England."

To his great disappointment, most of his work career at Nestlé's was inner-city merchandising, a job that required walking from one store to another with no chance to use the company Ford. But he learned about his work and progressed steadily, and in 1965, he joined Gillette Industries Limited as a sales manager in northern England.

"I was thirty-five and I thought it was about time to get serious," Symons recalled thirty years later during a long talk in the suite of a high-rise hotel in London's Knightsbridge district. "I used to walk the streets down there as a cop," he mused, pointing in the general direction of Harrod's. Symons joined Gillette shortly after the Wilkinson stainless blade introduction had ended a long period of hefty profits for the U.K. company and Boston had begun to pay more attention to Europe. After a short period of carrying a sample bag from store to store, the sales work that starts many a Gillette career, Symons began to take on marketing jobs. All this time, Symons said, he was coming to grips with the basic rule of business, which, he says, shaped his future in senior management: the only thing that counts is the gap between what it costs to make a product and the price at which it is sold.

After six years in England, he got the promotion he was looking for and was posted to Switzerland as regional general manager, which also put him in charge of a Gillette veteran who was the company's long-time man in Austria. "That's where I learned that management is about motivating others, and I had a job to do with the Austrian," he recalled.

From Switzerland, he returned to Isleworth for two years as materials manager for the extensive U.K. manufacturing operation. Then he was off to South Africa, arriving six weeks before the violent Soweto riots of 1976 that shocked the country's white leadership and mobilized people around the world against apartheid. As general manager, Symons had a Gillette blade factory to manage in the racially charged environment. He also inherited a plastic bag company that his predecessor had persuaded the company to buy just before Symons arrived. Jiffy Plastic had labor problems, its production equipment was antiquated, and nobody had figured out how Gillette was to go about selling plastic bags.

Years later, Symons said he was appalled by the apparent senselessness of a blade and razor giant moving into the plastic bags business just because a predecessor local manager in South Africa thought it a good move or into chewing gum because an Italian general manager thought it was a good idea, to cite a couple of ventures that were spawned by European general managers and were encouraged by London and Boston. (The Italian venture was more than a passing fancy. Gillette President Stephen Griffin once informally explored whether his friend, chewing gum titan Philip Wrigley, would consider a venture with Gillette, but Wrigley expressed no interest.)

Such ideas generally were seen as synergistic—sell gum along with blades at adjacent displays at grocery or drugstore checkouts—but in practice, it was more like chaos, to Symons' view. Worst of all, he said, Gillette managers from Boston to Johannesburg were diverted from the greatly profitable blade and razor business, which he believed had suffered as management became preoccupied with diversification and lost faith in the ability of blades and razors to continue as a strong growth, high-profit business. "I thought management was starting to think of blades as just another commodity product," he said.

Symons shortly discovered how apartheid impeded normal business practices. When he arrived, he found that an expansion had begun at the company's blade assembly plant in the Johannesburg suburb of Springs, Transvaal. The new space was to house the Jiffy plastic bag operation, the idea being to cut costs by consolidating bag and blade production under one roof. There was one flaw in the idea. Of the 150 black workers at the Jiffy plant near Soweto, only 29 said they could shift to the new plant, which was outside the Johannesburg city limits. Symons asked why. Apartheid restrictions, he was told by workers. If we take a job outside the city, we lose permission to live there and lose access to the city's job market.

The Soweto riots had spawned militant student-worker black opposition to white rule. As the police and army cracked down throughout South Africa, opposition to South Africa's apartheid erupted in the United States and Europe. The very presence of American corporations doing business in South Africa, already a matter of controversy, became a great business and society issue of the time, and Gillette was caught in the middle. South African black employees wanted the company to stay on. The mainstream black political opposition in South Africa argued that staying on lent credibility to the apartheid government. In the United States, many religious and political groups agreed, contending that Gillette's presence helped sustain the white supremacy system the company deplored publicly. On several occasions, starting in 1974, shareholder resolutions calling for Gillette to get out were formally presented and voted upon at annual meetings, losing by wide margins.

EXIT SOUTH AFRICA

Through most of the 1980s, Gillette continued to maintain its presence, arguing that the company could be an agent for positive change in South Africa. James L. Clark, Symons' successor as general manager in South Africa, was a prime mover, along with strong support from top legal officer Joseph Mullaney, in establishing South Africa's first legal aid clinic.

Critics in the United States and Europe raised the stakes as the black political movement gained strength in South Africa in the mid-1980s and tensions escalated after a savage crackdown by the white government under the guise of a five-year state of emergency decree. Sanctions were imposed by the U.S. government, and political pressure on corporations to get out intensified. There were a spate of stockholder proposals sponsored by church groups in the late 1980s after Reverend Sullivan became embittered by the South African government's repeated roadblocks that made compliance with the Sullivan Principles impossible and by what he saw as a lack of will by Sullivan signatories to challenge the government. He abandoned the code of conduct effort and formed a new group that urged corporate withdrawal.

Gillette worked with groups like the Interfaith Council on Corporate Responsibility, which submitted resolutions demanding changes in South African business practices at many corporations, including Gillette. Mockler and his aides cooperated with the Interfaith group in the production of a detailed report that laid out Gillette's position supporting its continued presence.

In 1977, a year after the arrival of Symons, Gillette became one of the first of several American corporations to sign on to the so-called Sullivan Principles, as the code of conduct for American companies in South Africa became known. They were named for Leon Sullivan, a Philadelphia minister and community activist who served as a director of General Motors and, in the course of events, became a leading black spokesman on the issue of doing business in South Africa. Informed by what he saw at the General

---

Gillette sold its nonblade businesses and manufacturing operation in Springs, Transvaal, in fall 1989 to Twins Pharmaceuticals Ltd., an affiliate of a South African firm. The Gillette blade plant was closed in 1989, as part of the company's ongoing worldwide restructuring program, which had closed or consolidated manufacturing operations in Argentina, Brazil, the United States, Britain, France, Australia, and Canada. The sale of the nonblade operation was hailed by a mainly black South African trade union that said it should serve as a model for foreign companies pulling out of the country. Actually, the sale would have been difficult to complete without the support of the influential Chemical Worker's Industrial Union, which was demanding that foreign firms cut all ties with South Africa and had called strikes against Eastman Kodak's Sterling Drug subsidiary, among others. Twins Pharmaceuticals agreed to keep all staff who wanted to remain, guaranteed current conditions for eighteen months, recognized the union, and pledged to honor existing agreements.

Finally, in 1990, the government of F. W. de Klerk ordered the release from prison of the African National Congress' most important leader and symbol of black resistance, Nelson Mandela. De Klerk also began to ease some of the most onerous apartheid laws. In 1994, the African National Congress, led by Mandela, defeated de Klerk's government in national elections and assumed power. Apartheid was dead at last.

———

Motors operation there, he was critical of the business as usual attitude and challenged GM and other businesses to help South African blacks trapped by apartheid.

Administered by the Arthur D. Little Company, the code required the American signatories to adhere to six major pledges. These were to provide integrated eating, comfort, and work facilities; ensure equal and fair employment practices for all, regardless of race; ensure equal pay for employees doing equal work; initiate training to prepare blacks and other nonwhites for substantial numbers of supervisory, administrative, clerical, and technical jobs; increase the number of blacks and other nonwhites in management and supervisory jobs; and improve the quality of employees' lives outside work in such areas as housing, transportation, schooling, recreation, and access to health facilities. Each general principle was backed up by detailed examples of what was expected, including an admonition to each company to support the repeal of all apartheid laws.

Arthur D. Little personnel monitored the process, pored over required periodic reports, and gave out grades for performance and compliance. Gillette consistently scored well.

"I remember once I had the Reverend [Sullivan] coming down here to tell me about his principles," recalled Symons. Symons said he had an advantage over South African citizens who headed some American subsidiaries because he was outside the local cultural and political environment and could make things happen without worrying what colleagues would say when he returned home from work each day. There were three canteens (cafeterias) when Symons arrived, for blacks, whites, and mixed race or "coloreds," and he merged them into one canteen for all employees. For a few weeks, he and the company's finance officer were the only whites who would eat there. He said he sometimes spent more time dealing with complaints about common lavatories than increasing blade sales. The company Christmas party was integrated, which was no small matter. "This whole experience shaped me, I think. I felt as if I were alone in another part of another universe," Symons said.

EUROPEAN SHAKEUP

After his years in South Africa, John Symons returned to London in 1979 in charge of the European Sales Group, which comprised a collection of ten small nations: Sweden, Norway, Denmark, Finland, Luxembourg, Belgium, Holland, Austria, Switzerland, and Portugal. There was a problem with the Group, he was informed by Walter Hunnewell, executive vice president of Gillette International. Profit margins were suddenly falling at a rapid rate. He was told to do something. Symons came to grips quickly with one problem. The ten small nations, of course, represented multiple cultures, languages, and mindsets, and they were each going their own way without much direction from London. Symons set about to create a standard way of selling blades and other Gillette goods that cut across national lines, to have one marketing and manufacturing strategy instead of ten. It was, he said, his chance to apply at Gillette a transnational approach to selling products, a test of global strategies to come.

One of the first problems he tackled was advertising—always a major factor in the Gillette scheme of things. He inherited thirty-five advertising agencies, each going pretty much its own way and following the ideas of ten Gillette country managers who had diverse ideas on how and even what to sell. Symons hired a single agency to replace the thirty-five. It was a controversial proposition at the time, especially among the various country managers, who could not imagine how an agency in London could replace local knowledge and come up with an effective ad for their particular market. Symons ignored the clamor and hired Batton, Barton, Durstine & Osborne's (BBDO) London office, already doing some work for him, to take on the job. BBDO created television film for the entire group, leaving each country manager to provide the appropriate voice-over language. No longer were the ten country managers marketing strategizers and idea sources for ad agencies; now they basically were salesmen. Symons said the system sharply pared costs of advertising, but what was more important, it freed the country managers to focus on what they were equipped by local knowledge to do best, and that was to sell goods.

The consolidation of advertising and the centralization of other functions saved Gillette a great deal of money, but Symons was certain that the fundamental problem diluting profits was blade pricing. To meet the challenge of Bic's disposable razors, Gillette managers had dropped prices so low that not much profit was left. Symons knew it was serious when he looked at his old territory in Austria and saw that a profitable market had become a money loser in a matter of a couple of years. The market share had held steady—the Gillette mandate had been to hold on to market share in blades at any cost—but the Austrian manager, like his peers all over Europe, had held share against the Bic disposables only by slashing prices. He had increased advertising and that, too, cut into margins. Symons said it was completely obvious to him that playing the game Bic's way would be disastrous unless there were major cuts in overhead. He sent a loyal staffer to Vienna, and before long, 60 percent of the staff was terminated.

Symons said it was fundamental—"If you can't increase the price and can't make the product cheaper, then there's nothing left but to cut overhead"—but it was a tough lesson for Gillette managers to learn because the blade business always had been a high-margin operation. "This experience with the smaller nations taught me almost before anyone else at Gillette that if you try to outsell Bic in disposables, watch out, because Bic is very good at low-margin sales and he [sic] could beat you at it," Symons commented.

Over the next two years, Symons continued to cut overhead, reduce advertising for disposables, and centralize decision making in London. Profit margins turned sharply higher. By 1981, according to Symons, his group was reporting profits superior to those from Gillette France, Gillette Germany, and other large national markets reporting, as Symons did, to David Stone, general manager of Gillette Europe. Symons was not shy in telling others how he did it and in the process made a few enemies among his colleagues. Now over fifty, he began to wonder if his career, like

---

NON À GILLETTE!

Symons could not get it all done as fast as he wanted. The French government blocked Gillette from closing its Annecy plant for years, and anyway, it was not that easy to abandon an efficient plant in a country that was among Gillette's top five markets. With time out for wars, Gillette had made blades in France from 1905 on, first in Paris and then in Annecy, within sight of Europe's highest peak, the 15,781-foot Mont Blanc. But the market for double-edge blades made at Annecy had dwindled, and by the mid-1980s Gillette was consolidating such operations around the globe.

Bernard Bosson was both the mayor of Annecy and the minister for European affairs in the French Cabinet, a formidable presence who at one point subjected Colman Mockler to a lecture on the duty of overseas manufacturers. He offered Gillette an array of incentives to entice the company to abandon Berlin in favor of a big new plant at Annecy. When that failed, the powerful union at the plant played heavily on Gillette's moral obligation. But rather than strike, the union members decided to work so efficiently that Gillette would be shamed into staying. Newspaper and television ads alternately threatened and pleaded with Gillette. France's minister of industry, Roger Fauroux, called in half a dozen Gillette officials and informed them that he had instructed Gillette's best customers to lobby Gillette or face various problems with permits to do business. He threatened a government-sponsored boycott of Gillette products.

Gillette officials turned to Washington higher-ups, who ordered the American ambassador to France, William Rogers, to instruct Fauroux to withdraw the threats or face retaliation against French products sold in the United States. A very tense luncheon ensued in Paris, and a compromise was worked out whereby Gillette stayed put for a year, found a buyer for the factory, placed some of its workers in other plants, and provided a generous severance package for others. All was forgiven at the end, except by a mountain-climbing union leader who with friends had scaled Mont Blanc and planted a banner proclaiming "Non à Gillette" in letters so large they could be read by airline passengers in planes passing overhead.

those of other senior managers he knew at Gillette Europe, would end with early retirement at fifty-five or younger.

But retirement would wait for Symons. David Stone, an active Mormon layman who was well regarded at Gillette, unexpectedly left the company in 1983 to become assistant treasurer of the Church of Jesus Christ Latter-Day Saints in Salt Lake City; several years later, he took a senior management job at Black & Decker. Colman Mockler consulted with others about Stone's replacement and cast his vote for the self-described "arrogant SOB" from London who was shaking things up over there. Symons now had the top job in Europe, with Mockler's direct endorsement.

One Big Europe

Based on his success in consolidating ten small national markets into one, Symons determined to make Gillette Europe a pan-European company. He would treat Europe, with its ancient cultures and rivalries and its slew of different languages, currencies, and economic policies, as one big United States of Europe, a single market. The formation of the European Economic Community (EEC), with its relatively tariff-free common market, was still a decade away at the time, but Gillette would not wait.

"I saw no reason I could not run the fifteen national markets of Western Europe as one, based on the success I had with the smaller nations," Symons said. He now had the power to make things happen. He controlled the factories in England, Germany, France, and Spain. He noted that Boston's one factory supplied the entire United States, while it took four plants in Europe to make the same number of blades. At the completion of his five years as top man in London, Symons had begun a process that would consolidate European blade making at Isleworth and Berlin.

Symons gave BBDO the advertising account for all fifteen nations, a lucrative contract for a market of 360 million. He unsettled headquarters management staff at Isleworth by democratizing the canteen, just as he had done in South Africa. England being England, there had always been a separate room for managers, who were served by waitresses. Down came the wall, and if they wanted to eat, managers and blade sharpeners alike had to take a tray and go through the line. Joel Davis, who had been sent to London as European marketing manager and worked with Symons during his stint as head of the ten-nation unit, said that some oldtimers steeped in the English class system never again ate in the cafeteria, apparently favoring luncheon outside or starvation to picking up a tray and joining the hoi polloi.

"I thought it was a good example of John saying 'that's it, there's no more of the Old Boy, class system stuff here,'" said Davis. Symons, he noted, had made a point of refusing to eat in the managers' room even before he had the chance to tear it down.

War on Disposables

Market share was not the problem dragging down European profit. Gillette enjoyed a greater share of the total European blade and razor market—70 percent—than in the United States. Despite those strong sales, cash flow was declining when Symons took over. The cutting of overhead, efficiency improvements in factory operations, and other streamlining operations he put in place would help turn that around. But Symons wanted to take aim at what he saw as the heart of the matter: too much time, money, and attention spent on outselling Bic in disposables at the expense of Gillette's hugely profitable blade and razor systems. Gillette might win a battle by holding market share against Bic, but it would lose the war if, in the process, it gave up on its historic blade and razor systems franchise and settled for being the leading seller of cheap throwaway razors made of plastic. The very idea angered him.

Symons cut back and, in some cases, eliminated advertising for disposables. When sales managers asked why, he answered that it was self-defeating, even deceitful, for Gillette to suddenly inform loyal systems users there was a new and better way to shave, and that was with a hollow plastic throwaway. Better to redirect the advertising millions not spent on disposables to boost sales of the high-margin blade cartridges for Contour and other systems. He wanted to drum home a message of quality and manliness.

He wanted BBDO to produce ads that made men feel that it was important, a matter of pride, to achieve the closest, most comfortable, most satisfying shaving experience possible and that that was what they would get with a Gillette Contour or other sturdy blade and razor system.

There was strong market research from Boston's corporate headquarters that encouraged Symons. In fall 1979, Corporate Planning's Paul Fruitt spelled out in a confidential report what he considered to be desirable objectives for Gillette with regard to disposable razors. These objectives included trying to limit the growth of the disposable segment of the shaving market and so encourage Bic and other competitors to increase the price of their disposable razors. Fruitt laid out a series of pricing and advertising strategies and their likely consequences. The strategies ranged from heavy advertising of a high-priced disposable to no advertising of a reduced-priced disposable and variations in between. The report showed, for example, that raising prices and eliminating advertising for Gillette disposables would slow growth of the disposable segment, might encourage some competitive price increases, and would boost short-term Gillette profitability, though cutting market share.

The report followed up on a 1977 analysis by Gillette business researcher Carl Hoefel that compared the quality of shaving standards in national markets (low in Greece, where shavers still used a lot of carbon steel blades, and high in Austria and Belgium, where twin-blade cartridges had gained substantial market share), the relative price of Bic versus other blades, the level of advertising, and distribution. The Hoefel study concluded that quality standards and relative price were the most important factors affecting disposable growth. The Bic disposable shaver was a high-quality product by Greek standards and sold well, despite its relatively high price as compared with its low-grade competitors. In Austria and Italy, quality markets where Bic's relative price was markedly lower against competing products, the Bic still did well against Gillette, indicating that shaving customers could be lured to the new disposables by price alone, especially if heavy advertising outlays encouraged them to switch.

Other Gillette managers may have pondered the alternatives, but Symons knew what he wanted and moved fast. Throughout Europe he cut advertising for disposables to the bone and generally held the line on price. It did not take long to see the results. In several of the fifteen European nations, the total disposable market leveled off at about 40 percent in the early to mid-1980s, with the Gillette and Bic shares not changing much. At the same time, Gillette was flooding Europe with ads extolling the Contour system that had the same message in each market, and Gillette's high-margin blade sales improved. It did not take long for the combination of cost cutting, factory consolidation, and advertising focus on high-margin system sales to turn the ship around. Operating profits in Europe moved up from about $77 million in 1983 to about $96 million in 1985.

That got the attention of Boston, where U.S. blade profits had failed to show a comparable pickup despite very strong sales of the Good News disposables. Maybe the wild man in London who was shaking things up was on to something. In October 1985, a high-level delegation of Colman Mockler, Joe Turley, who had succeeded Steve Griffin as president in 1981, and senior legal officer Joe Mullaney came to Isleworth and sat around the boardroom table to review European results and talk about Gillette strategic planning. Years later, as he described what he remembered about the "famous Isleworth meeting," Symons said he picked up a plastic razor, looked at Mockler, and said something fairly polite like, "Is The Gillette Company going to be a plastics company or are we going to be a high quality metals business?" That was the origin, Symons recalled, of the sassier question that for the next several years symbolized his challenge to his colleagues: "Are you a steel man or a plastic man?" Symons did not recall whether the words came out that abruptly at the Isleworth meeting, but he said they might have because "I talked a lot and my hormones were jumping." Joe Mullaney recalled that Symons hurled a plastic Blue II disposable against a wall at one point.

Symons said he was secure in pushing his "steel man" views because he sensed that he had won Mockler over at the Isleworth meeting. "He was a man my age brought up on Glenn Miller and that sort of stuff, just like me. I think I caught his imagination at that meeting, and he began to wonder, for the first time, if he was going to preside over a company that was going to commoditize its famous blade and razor business." Mockler did not tip his hand at once but, in his usual polite manner, thanked Symons after the meeting. When weeks went by and no cease and desist orders were heard, Symons was sure he had made a convert.

GILLETTE GROWTH STALLS

While Symons was energizing blade and razor profits in Europe, Mockler's balanced growth strategy for the company as a whole was in trouble. Sales surged past $2 billion for the first time in 1980 and ended the year at $2.3 billion. But then sales stalled for five years, ending 1985 at $2.4 billion—basically no gain. The sluggish sales reflected in part the divestiture or de-emphasis of several marginal operations and a simultaneous economic recession in many worldwide markets. Exchange rate weakness cut into profits that were reported from Europe but expressed in U.S. dollars.

As price competition with Bic and other makers of disposables took its toll, the proportion of total profits generated by blades and razors fell from 71 percent in 1979 to 66 percent in 1985. The aging Atra was superseded by Atra Plus in 1985, the "plus" being a lubricating strip added to the pivoting Atra cartridge head. It gave marketers an enhanced product to tout. A Good News Plus with lubricating strip was close behind. Blade margins were noticeably stronger in Europe, as noted, and in Latin American markets, where disposables were sold as high-quality, high-margin products in a Bic-less environment.

The International Division under Rodney S. Mills—like Phillips, a Canadian—made major moves during the period. An important joint venture blade factory was launched in China in 1983, long before most American companies got started in the world's most populous nation, and Gillette expanded operations in the world's second largest blade market—India, and started operations in Thailand and Egypt. These were important positioning moves for later years but added little to immediate growth.

A note of political alarm in the 1983 annual report signaled Gillette's special concern, as a budding global company, for a world economic system free of protectionist distortions. Chairman Mockler and President Joe Turley warned in their yearly summary of events that worldwide recession and high unemployment had increased pressure in many nations for protectionist schemes that threatened the growth of an international trading system. The Gillette leaders might have added, "and could delay Gillette's march toward a global style of business operations." By the end of 1983, the company had forty-nine factories in twenty-four countries and was selling its goods in more than two hundred countries. Fifty-eight percent of its sales were generated outside the United States.

More dependent on U.S. sales than the company as a whole, the Paper Mate group was only marginally profitable during the first half of the 1980s. Sales and profits slumped when the high interest rate policy of Federal Reserve Board Chairman Paul Volcker triggered a sharp recession that knocked out the commercial office market. The highly profitable Eraser Mate refillable pen, the first pen with erasable ink, enjoyed only a few years of unchallenged success before it fell victim to a price war. According to former Paper Mate President Bob Murray the division survived being sold off only because Mockler made it clear to important executives within Gillette and their Wall Street allies that it would not be sold.

Although Paper Mate was safe, Mockler and his managers continued to sell off companies that lacked strong growth potential and outright misfits that had been acquired during the earlier rush to diversification. By the end of 1981, more than a dozen businesses and product lines had been sold, accounting for annual sales of $170 million, which was equivalent to 7 percent of Gillette's total sales volume. By 1984, companies or businesses accounting for another $100 million in sales had been divested. The once-major but now dwindling Cricket disposable lighter business was sold to Swedish Match, and a Puerto Rican lighter factory closed. Gone was the Italian chewing gum maker, and more importantly, gone were the elegant but unprofitable hi-fi's and cameras that Braun had been unable to sell in the face of largely Japanese competition.

Still these were cautious moves as opposed to wholesale housecleaning, and critics among institutional investors and a few insiders complained that Mockler could get a lot more value for shareholders if he would just get rid of the losers and middling performers and focus on blades.

ACQUISITION SPREE, ROUND TWO

Even as Mockler cautiously dispensed with the losers, the urge to diversify was still strong in Boston. The temptation was great to use Gillette's strong cash flow to acquire small companies perceived as having a chance to hit it big for what amounted to corporate pocket change. To the dismay of some observers, including the Wall Street investment houses that questioned Gillette's slow pace of sell-offs, a second round of unrelated acquisitions—initiated by top executives at Gillette North America Derwyn Phillips and his boss, Joe Turley—began in the early 1980s. It was characterized by Phillips as selective diversification and by unsympathetic colleagues as round two of the conglomerate craze. Phillips defended the buying program as designed to encourage sustained profitable growth through business expansion as well as the ongoing program to control costs. He claimed that there was a difference from the 1965–75 buildup at Gillette. This time, the companies acquired generally were very small and were often built around marketing concepts. The focus was on acquiring promising ventures that did not make a dent in the company treasury and thus were relatively free of financial risk.

In round two, Gillette acquisitions included a majority interest in a Boston-based group of franchised skin care salons, Elizabeth Grady Face First International Corporation. Next, Gillette invested in another consumer marketing concept, Noelle Day Spas, whereby women would pay $250 for a day of beauty treatment at a one-stop salon that offered hair styling, skin care, nail care, massage, and image consulting services. There were only three salons, but the vision was for dozens more to spring up across the nation and, later, the world. These ventures proved a poor fit for Gillette, whose management was better suited to mass marketing products with technical superiority. Both businesses were sold within a few years of their acquisition.

Phillips continued to defend his program of buying potentially high-growth entrepreneurial ventures as a low-risk strategy. Gillette tested the concept of selling eyewear through dedicated superstores, along the lines of Lenscrafters. The company also acquired Misco, a New Jersey company that sold computer accessories and supplies by catalog. Both were sold off after a few years.

Oral-B

By far, the largest acquisition of the period drew criticism at the time but proved to be a major long-term winner for Gillette. The acquisition of Oral-B Laboratories was negotiated in 1984 by Al Zeien, who had been elected vice chairman for technical operations and new business development in 1981. It proved the wisdom of staying alert for companies and product lines that met a more demanding set of Gillette acquisition criteria. Gillette bought Oral-B for $188.5 million in cash from Cooper Laboratories, a holding company headed by Parker C. Montgomery, Jr., a New England blueblood who was a nephew of Carl Gilbert, the former Gillette chairman. Oral-B was the leading marketer of toothbrushes in the United States.

Perhaps feeling the sting of critics who charged that the company's acquisition policy lacked a sense of vision and long-range planning, Gillette had prepared a new acquisitions checklist just prior to the Oral-B deal:

1. Must be a consumer product.

2. Should have potential to be a $200 million worldwide business.

3. Should offer potential to be a leader in its business segment.

4. Should have high re-purchase frequency (three or four times a year).

5. Must have proprietary element, such as a patented position or unique market niche.

6. Should provide an opportunity for Gillette to add value and improve performance.

7. Should be in a growth category in unit terms.

Oral-B met each of these guidelines, and as events would prove, this seemingly costly deal turned out to be a bargain for Gillette and served as a successful model for future acquisitions.

The Oral-B toothbrush had been invented in 1950 by a young California doctor who designed it with soft bristles and rounded ends suitable for cleaning teeth and massaging gums. He named it Oral-B, "Oral" because it was for the whole mouth and not just the teeth, and the "B" was for brush, that is, an "oral brush" as opposed to a toothbrush. The product's marketers dropped that awkward terminology and promoted it as a high-quality toothbrush that was good for gums as well as teeth. Cooper acquired the company in 1971.

The Gillette deal in 1984 was well timed for Parker Montgomery, because he soon would need the money. In 1986, arbitrageur Ivan Boesky bought a large block of one of the remaining Cooper Laboratory companies but abruptly dumped 400,000 shares about the time he confessed insider trading schemes and prepared to go to jail. Cooper stock took a huge hit at a difficult time for Montgomery and his concept of a holding company for venture enterprises.

About a year and a half after Oral-B was acquired, Jacques Lagarde was working as head of Gillette France at his desk at company headquarters in tranquil Annecy. The phone rang, and Gillette president Joe Turley got right to the point: Can you come to California as head of the Oral-B operation, and by the way, next week would be ideal? Lagarde reminded Turley that he had a wife and five children and would like some time for the move. Turley relented—a little—and gave him two weeks to move to Redwood City, California, which is about thirty miles south of San Francisco.

Lagarde arrived on schedule and met with the holdover managers and employees in a classic "new boss meets the troops" setting familiar to any worker for a small enterprise who has been on the scene when a big company takes over. Lagarde was an erudite Frenchman with an academic background replacing an aggressive American manager attuned to short-term goals. His new employees discovered at once that Lagarde was no less aggressive but was much more attuned to long-term growth.

For Lagarde the move to San Francisco was almost seamless, personally speaking, but managing Oral-B was more difficult. Lagarde kept most of the former managers for a few months as he immersed himself in understanding what it was that Gillette had bought, what parts of the Oral-B product line and corporate culture should be kept intact, which should be changed, what Gillette could bring to the new acquisition. Lagarde recognized that there had to be some major changes to make the deal work for Gillette.

He decided that Gillette should nurture the positive culture within Oral-B that had spawned the company's "let dentists do the selling" marketing approach. Oral-B had spent virtually no money in retail advertising but rather concentrated on promoting the product with dentists as a brush with bristles suitable for cleaning and massaging teeth and gums. The company counted on dentists to promote Oral-B products to their patients, who, they knew, would be exceptionally responsive during checkups to suggestions about better preventive care. At the time of the Gillette purchase, Oral-B toothbrushes claimed a 27 percent U.S. market share in dollar terms, and nine out of ten pharmacies stocked its toothbrushes.

A less attractive part of the Oral-B culture reflected the Cooper goal of building up companies for sale to the highest bidder—a sort of short-term cash management approach that held no brief for investment in supposed frills like R & D and manufacturing efficiency. A change in attitude and management personnel was required to adjust to Gillette's more patient, long-term outlook. Lagarde's first step, which was not unusual at Gillette, was to upgrade manufacturing technology.

He brought in a German technical operations manager from

Braun—Bernhard Wild, a manager with a reputation as one of the best technicians in German manufacturing. The Franco-German executive team at Oral-B decided that they had to get rid of the obsolete equipment in the company's main factory in Iowa City and start over. It took thirty trucks to haul away the old machinery, Lagarde recalled. Installation of state-of-the-art toothbrush production machines sent a message to Oral-B employees that Gillette was in this for the long run with a high-tech, lean management approach.

Then Lagarde turned to the nonexistent R & D and created a department charged with coming up with innovative, improved products. The Oral-B toothbrush on the market in 1985 was still the 1950 nylon bristle toothbrush, with minor changes. The original design had proved so enduring that the Oral-B was still the industry leader after thirty-five years, but as Lagarde had discovered, the toothbrush industry was not exactly high-tech heaven. Lagarde wanted work to start at once on a next-generation Oral-B and other dental products. Through the years, a stream of new products emerged, with everything from blue-colored indicator bristles that signaled the need for replacement to rubberized handles fitted for children, bearing such names as Squish Grip.

Oral-B in California and Braun in Germany jointly developed a Braun Oral-B motorized plaque remover toothbrush that became a market leader. Oral-B researchers designed the replaceable bristle head that fits in a Braun-designed handle with a miniature electric motor. The end product has clear parallels with King C. Gillette's safety razor, that is, a permanent handle with a replaceable bristle head that proved to be a big repeat sales item, like blades for a razor.

In addition, the geographic market expansion made possible by Gillette's global reach put Oral-B in markets it could not easily have entered on its own. Oral-B products, from floss to plaque removers, moved eventually into more than one hundred markets worldwide and were often sold by the same Gillette salesperson responsible for blades. The oft-cited but seldom achieved process of synergy worked in the case of toothbrushes and blades. Through internal accounting systems, a very high profit margin provided a powerful incentive to blade salespeople in the field to sell brushes as well as the familiar bread and butter blades line. The same accounting logic worked for Oral-B salespeople visiting drugstores and pharmacies, giving them added incentive to sell blades. The system was possible only because computerized techniques made complex accounting exercises manageable worldwide.

A CALL TO RETURN HOME

Colman Mockler traveled to New Delhi in fall 1986 to participate in ceremonies at the opening of a newly built blade plant in Bhiwadi, India. Since 1945, in protectionist India, there had been obstacles to direct foreign investment that had kept Gillette's presence minimal, but the obstacles were fading and this was something to celebrate. It seemed like a good occasion for Mockler to take a short break from pressures in the United States, where the Wall Street rumor mill was working overtime and more frequently linked Gillette, as a target, with various takeover and merger schemes.

Gillette had the profile the Wall Street raiders liked: its blade and razor business generated copious amounts of cash. The company listed little debt. Its stock was out of favor, which made it vulnerable to raiders. Critics charged that Mockler was not managing for maximum shareholder value and demanded more emphasis on short-term profits. Despite some signs of renewed growth and Mockler's optimism about long-term results, Wall Street activity signaled that something was about to happen. So it was not a complete surprise for Mockler when the phone rang at his New Delhi hotel and Al Zeien came on the line, urging him to get back home fast. Zeien told him that takeover rumors had reached a high pitch, fed by extremely heavy trading in Gillette shares that indicated a raider or raiders were accumulating shares prior to an attack. The chief was needed back home. Very soon, Gillette's comfortable world would change forever.

6

STORM
WARNINGS

FROM THE VANTAGE of hindsight, it seems apparent that Gillette had become too comfortable with slow growth in the 1980s and had set itself up for the turmoil about to erupt. Some observers traced the seeds of the trouble back to Vincent Ziegler and his early conviction that the blade business was mature, a reliable source of superior profit, and a prolific cash producer, but not an engine for the sort of long-term growth Gillette needed. Rapid diversification was his answer. When that failed to produce consistent results, Gillette reigned in and Colman Mockler sought more balanced growth, keeping winners, pruning losers, and cutting costs. It was a gradualist approach.

Mockler believed the blade business would soon enjoy major new growth keyed to geographic expansion and an exciting new blade and razor system then in development. But the new product was still a few years away from being ready, and some big institutional shareholders were growing impatient. They charged that

Gillette had become satisfied in the 1980s with yearly profit growth that barely kept up with the U.S. economy's annual gains of Gross Domestic Product plus inflation. In 1985, Gillette's profits were absolutely flat, having failed to meet even the GDP standard. Sales hardly increased at all from 1980 to 1985.

There seemed to be little sense of urgency at the company to stretch, set tough goals, and make strong moves to reassure restless shareholders and keep predators at bay. Very soon there would be no choice, because the luxury of time was running out and the option of gradualism had ended. Events would prove that the men and women of Gillette were capable of managing fast, profitable growth to maximize shareholder value, but it took a threat from outside the Gillette world to make it happen.

Storm warning flags were flying straight out at Gillette's headquarters thirty-nine floors up Boston's Prudential Tower in late autumn 1986 as Mockler hurried back to Boston from India. The approaching hurricane was direct from Wall Street. Fall 1986 marked a peak of the 1980s takeover frenzy, fueled by easily available junk bond financing from the likes of Drexel Burnham Lambert, the home base of billionaire junk-bond king Michael Milken. Corporate raiders like T. Boone Pickens, Carl Icahn, and the Bass brothers from Texas were riding high. Ivan Boesky was the most visible and cocksure among the many arbitrageurs, or "arbs," who were scoring massive profits, scandalous even to many Wall Streeters, by buying up stock of companies targeted for takeovers in anticipation that raiders would drive prices up.

As September moved into October and then November, Gillette's name was increasingly mentioned as a likely takeover or merger target. The company was rumored to be in the sights of individual corporate raiders and such corporations as Unilever NV, Colgate-Palmolive, Seagrams, RJR Nabisco, Philip Morris, Hanson Trust, CPC International, and more than once, Revlon Group Inc. Revlon itself had been taken over in November 1985 after a bruising, four-month hostile raid by Ronald O. Perelman, a relative newcomer to the ranks of big league raidership.

Rumors that CPC would seek merger with Gillette died out November 4—and Revlon loomed much larger—when it was disclosed that the big grocery products and corn processing company had bought back from Perelman about 8 percent of the company's shares that Perelman had acquired through a third party. Perelman made an estimated $50 million profit or greenmail on the buyback. As its stock price dropped like a rock, and arbs stuck with high-priced shares screamed foul, CPC announced further plans to buy back its stock, and the company launched a major restructuring. That ended speculation that CPC would go after Gillette. But with a new cash hoard on his hands and new proof of his relentless drive to play with the fattest of the fat cats, Perelman became an even greater threat to watch, though he was still just one of many possibilities.

Gillette's consistent response to rumors was "no comment." Of course, Gillette's "no comment" did not stop the rumors. News reporters and savvy investors focused on the heavy trading in Gillette and correctly sensed that something out of the ordinary was going on. Writers for mainstream newspapers and stock market tip sheets fed the rumor mill by obligingly running stories planted with them by arbitrageurs who stood to gain from the run-up of Gillette share prices. As the rumors picked up, so did the pace of trading.

Tape watchers had noted a pickup in Gillette trading dating back to early October. On October 7, 1986, a total of 160,000 shares traded, and the stock closed at $37 7/8. Trading increased steadily all month, with volume occasionally topping half a million shares. Then, on November 4, any doubts about unusual activity burst as a total of 2,334,600 shares traded; GS, Gillette's ticker symbol at the time, closed at $52 1/2, up 4 3/8. For the October 7 to November 4 period, Gillette's market capitalization increased $1 billion or 40 percent to $3.5 billion, gaining in twenty-nine days what it had previously taken seven years (from 1977 to 1984) to accomplish. November 4 was the first of sixteen consecutive days, with one exception, when more than a million shares traded. As the month progressed, the share price moved into the high 50s.

No one at Gillette knew who was behind all the buying. Gillette hired New York's Georgeson Company, experts in tracking stock trading and counting proxy votes, but Georgeson and other pros

---

in the business could not get beyond the obvious conclusion that arbitrageurs were loading up on Gillette. Ernst & Company, which did business with well-known arbs, was identified as a buyer of Gillette. That didn't help answer the real questions, however: Who was accumulating all that Gillette stock, and why?

Joe Mullaney recognized the financial storm signs as clearly as if they were sudden thunderclouds portending violent squalls off Cape Cod. As senior legal officer at Gillette, Mullaney had long ago started to worry about the growing strength of Wall Street raiders and the relative vulnerability of Gillette with its undervalued stock and strong cash flow. In the late 1970s, he made one of Gillette's first moves to shore up defenses against an unwanted suitor. After clearing it with Chairman Colman Mockler, he retained the legendary Wall Street takeover lawyer, Joseph Flom, of Skadden, Arps, Slate, Meagher & Flom. Joe Flom was paid about $40,000 a year to stand by, and to advise management and directors how to start thinking about the unthinkable. In the next half dozen years, Gillette took several actions suggested by Flom aimed at making it more difficult for hostile raiders to succeed. These moves included a 1985 poison pill measure that encouraged shareholders to purchase shares at a discounted price during a hostile takeover attempt, thereby creating a large number of new shares and raising the takeover price. Long after, Flom said it had been crucial for him to get on the job well before raiders actually hit because several years of exposure to Gillette enabled him to learn about the company and think about how to defend it before an attack was launched. "It was important to establish confidence with senior management and to get to know directors and to do some pre-planning so we could all react quickly," Flom said.

CRISIS PLANNING BEGINS

With Gillette stock being bought up by persons unknown and speculation rampant, Mullaney realized that the time for "what if" planning was rapidly running out and the company would be put to the test. So did Al Zeien, vice chairman, and in effect

Mockler's chief of staff and the company's contact man with Wall Street investment bankers. It became clear to Zeien from all he heard and saw that the Street's powerful arbitrageurs were buying up Gillette stock, and something would have to give immediately. Zeien decided to alert Mockler in New Delhi.

"I told him, 'Colman, something is going to happen here and you should return as soon as possible,'" Zeien recalled. Mockler checked out of the Taj Palace hotel and flew directly home.

In Boston, Zeien told the company's long-time investment banker, Morgan Stanley & Company, to start drafting a detailed takeover defense plan so that Gillette would be ready to act if a raider struck. A meeting to hear the Morgan Stanley defense team was duly held in Boston on November 6. It was attended by the just-returned Mockler, Zeien, Mullaney, CFO Tom Skelly, and other senior managers. What they heard was profoundly disturbing. Morgan's Peter Kellner told the restless Gillette managers that the Wall Street climate was totally favorable to raiders. He said, one participant recalls, that the Street was "awash in cash," with copious junk bond financing available to support inflated takeover prices. He left the clear impression that Gillette would find it impossible to defeat a determined raider and might have to start looking for a friendly buyer—a "white knight" in raider-talk—and forget about remaining independent. The tone seemed defeatist. There was no strategy suggested for fighting back.

The Morgan Stanley crew left the room but the Gillette executives remained, milling about, unhappy about what they considered an unimpressive performance by an inexperienced young man who did not recognize Gillette's determination to stay independent and was counseling surrender before the fight had even begun. One executive there remembers thinking, "Nice kid, the kind of guy you'd want your daughter to marry . . . but we wanted somebody mean." Mockler was particularly upset. Characteristically delegating what was sure to be an unpleasant call, he instructed Zeien to call Morgan Stanley bosses in New York to complain. Zeien told the Morgan chiefs that Gillette was prepared to shop for a second investment banker, which would mean splitting fees. That produced results. Eric Gleacher, the bank's merger and acquisition chief, was dispatched to Boston to work directly with Zeien. Gleacher was an ex-Marine who had made a name for himself as an imaginative attacker or stout defender in some of the era's biggest takeover battles, depending on which side of the street he was working. Gleacher had represented Texaco, for example, in its desperate effort to fight off Pennzoil and its ally, the notorious raider Carl Icahn. Most recently, Gleacher had earned enormous fees for himself and Morgan Stanley by masterminding Ronald Perelman's hostile takeover of Revlon Group, a battle that made headlines because of its unusual ugliness and because of Perelman's bulldog tactics. Gleacher's connection with Perelman briefly raised a concern at Gillette about the conflict of interest that would ensue if he took on the Gillette defense, and it turned out that the unknown raider was Revlon or some other former client of his. Gleacher brushed aside the concern. There was no conflict—it's the way business works on Wall Street, he assured Mockler and Zeien, adding years later that he had been "flattered to be asked by Gillette to take on the job."

The entire dealing with Morgan Stanley was also rather ticklish because the big investment banking house had represented Oral-B management during lengthy bargaining over the price and conditions of Gillette's 1984 purchase of the California toothbrush and dental products company. Gillette's negotiator in the difficult talks had been Zeien.

Mockler and Zeien were also concerned about Morgan Stanley's financial motivation to defend Gillette. Zeien refused to sign the standard Morgan Stanley contract for short-term takeover work when it was first proffered, arguing that its fees were too high and the arrangement lacked sufficient incentives for a successful defense against a raider. Zeien knew that investment bankers, even when they are hired to defend a target company, make a great deal more money when a takeover succeeds than when it fails. It was not until Gillette was fighting for its life a few weeks later that he and Gleacher finally signed off on a contract that Zeien would declare reasonable. Gleacher agreed to a fee of $1.4 million for defending Gillette, with a $3 million incentive to kick in if he was successful in repulsing a raider. Reflecting many years later about the tension over fees, Gleacher said that Zeien was correct to question the fee structure. "I don't blame him. The Firm stood to make a great deal of money if a takeover succeeded [$14.2 million, for example, if a $70 tender offer succeeded]. I convinced him our reputation for helping our clients was what counted most, not fees."

After all, there would be more deals, more work, more fees, in the future.

SORTING OUT LAWYER CONFLICTS

The Revlon rumors continued to circulate, though most analysts and press commentators concluded that Unilever NV, the Anglo-Dutch giant, was most likely to make a tender offer for the company. Inside Gillette, an indication that Revlon was behind the buy-up had surfaced the first week of November. Joe Flom told Joe Mullaney that he did not know for sure if Perelman was buying up Gillette stock, but if so, he probably would be unable to direct Gillette's litigation against a Revlon takeover because he would be caught in a conflict of interest. Mullaney knew, of course, that Flom was close to Revlon's Perelman. In fact, Flom and a young colleague, Donald G. Drapkin, had led the legal and strategic attack that had won Revlon for Perelman, and Drapkin had just announced he was quitting Skadden, Arps to work for Perelman full time. Mullaney realized at once that in all likelihood Flom knew Perelman's plans to go after Gillette and was obliquely signaling Mullaney, warning him that Skadden, Arps would not be able to act as Gillette's litigator against Perelman, if it came to that. A Perelman raid would require Flom, acting for Gillette, to haul into court an old friend and confidante, not to mention a man who had just paid his law firm several million dollars for legal help in the Revlon raid.

Flom and Mullaney both knew that certainly by Boston standards, and even by Wall Street's much looser rules of the game, this potential conflict would be impossible to overcome. Since Gillette had assumed all along that Skadden, Arps would defend the company in any takeover attempt, this was a serious predicament. Mullaney alerted Mockler at once, and both men agreed that Gillette could not chance getting caught without outside counsel in the event of a sudden raid. Mullaney first contacted New York's prestigious Sullivan and Cromwell and another Manhattan firm, but both law firms wanted to handle not just the litigation work that Gillette required but also the separate function of advising management and directors on takeover defense strategy and legal obligations to shareholders. That was exactly what Flom had been doing for Gillette, and neither Flom nor Gillette wanted to throw away the working relationship the famed lawyer had built up with Gillette's management and directors for a half-dozen years. The inherent conflict involved even in this more restricted legal role still bothered Mullaney, but Flom pleaded with him not to drop Skadden, Arps as corporate legal advisor. Although neither Mockler nor Mullaney liked the smell of it, they trusted Flom and valued his undoubted expertise, so they reluctantly agreed that Flom should stay on in that role.

"There was no conflict, this sort of thing happens all the time and Gillette people believed me when I explained this," said Flom in the summer of 1995, still active and still advising Gillette at the then age of 72. The small, slight lawyer, surprisingly soft-spoken for a man with a reputation for bombast and pushing the law to the edge, added, "I'm happy to say that in all the potential conflict situations in which I've been involved, I've remained on good terms with both sides afterwards."

Having heeded Flom's pleas that he be kept aboard as a legal adviser but not a litigator, and having rejected the all-or-nothing demands of the New York law firms, Mullaney had to find on short notice a willing litigator. He turned to an old friend, Patrick F. McCartan, who in 1986 was head of the litigation department at the big Cleveland law firm of Jones, Day, Reavis & Pogue. Mullaney and McCartan's careers paralleled in their early years. Mullaney had broken in as a lawyer at Jones, Day shortly after graduating from Harvard Law School in 1958. He and McCartan joined Jones, Day the same day. Mullaney stayed on for several years at the firm and was named a partner the same day as

McCartan. Shortly thereafter, the two men parted company. Mullaney left for Washington, D.C., where he worked as general counsel for about a year to the office of Special Trade Representative, headed by former Gillette chairman Carl Gilbert. With Gilbert's endorsement, Mullaney was recruited by Mockler to Gillette's legal staff in 1972. The Fall River, Massachusetts, native was named Gillette's chief legal counsel in 1975. McCartan stayed at Jones, Day and eventually became managing partner at the firm, which was among the nation's ten largest law firms in 1986 and, a decade later, number two in numbers of lawyers—about one thousand-two hundred.[1]

When he reached for his phone to call McCartan on Saturday, November 8, Mullaney had more than old friendship in mind. He knew that Jones, Day had lodged successful defenses in major takeover battles, including Exxon-Reliance and Marathon-Mobil. Unable to reach McCartan, Mullaney got through to managing partner Richard Pogue. After a flurry of calls to Mockler in the Boston area, Flom in New York, and Jones, Day lawyers in Cleveland, a deal was struck late Saturday afternoon. It was agreed that Jones, Day would be responsible for litigation in any takeover attempt made against Gillette. In addition, senior partner David Gunning was hired to provide an extra pair of eyes to assist Joe Flom in the separate function of advising management and directors.

John M. "Jack" Newman, Jr., a star litigator at Jones, Day, was assigned to the Gillette case and started learning all he could about Gillette that weekend. Newman had made a name for himself several years earlier as chief prosecutor for the U.S. attorney general in a major securities and insurance scandal in Los Angeles focused on Ray Dirks, a well-known corporate whistle blower.

"When I started looking at Gillette trading patterns, it was clear somebody was buying up Gillette and the word on the Street was that Ronald Perelman was a strong possibility," Newman recalled. "I quickly became convinced that the raider, whoever he was, was signaling the market and using arbitrageurs to secretly accumulate a big block of Gillette stock." Newman said he began to devise a theory of defense tying the raider to illegal stock parking, a scheme he had dealt with in which raiders tip off arbs about an impending raid in return for the arbs buying stock in the target company and "parking" it for resale to the raider. The advance planning based on Newman's hunch proved invaluable just a few days later.

The Jones, Day deal with Gillette for services in the event of a takeover attempt would stretch for several years and attach the Cleveland law firm to Gillette like a barnacle to a ship before the great takeover frenzy of the 1980s petered out, leaving in its wake a slew of shareholder law suits.

With a move against Gillette looking more likely all the time but the identity of the raider still guesswork, Gleacher flew to Boston November 12 to meet with senior Gillette executives and start full-scale planning in event of attack. The group reviewed a takeover attack contingency list that had been prepared by the company's in-house legal, public relations, and corporate secretary's departments—right down to such details as how to reactivate copy machines that automatically turn off each night at six, where to find someone at any hour who could operate fax machines, and how to secure scarce hotel rooms for directors. Gleacher began to prepare the executives for the need to think in terms of finding a friendly buyer. Other options were discussed. A full-scale meeting of the defense planning group, to include Pat McCartan of Jones, Day, had previously been called for Friday, November 14, at 10:00 A.M. in the Gillette boardroom.

The meeting could not have been better timed.

On November 13, 1986, at 3:58 P.M., two minutes before the Big Board closed, a block of 2.75 million Gillette shares was bought by Bear Stearns, an investment bank with close ties to the Street's most powerful arbitrageurs. A record total of 6,039,400 Gillette shares traded for the day, and the stock closed at 57 3/4.

At Gillette, senior officials knew the end of the waiting was imminent. The identity of the person or company buying up Gillette stock surely would be known within hours. The Chinese water torture was about to stop.

III

Fight for
Survival—
The Takeover
Threats

7

TEN DAYS
OF
TERROR

JOE MULLANEY WAS at his Back Bay home on Boston's Marlborough Street when the phone rang just before 7 P.M. Nov. 13. It was David Fausch, vice president of corporate public relations, who quickly passed on what he had just confirmed from several sources. The raider buying up Gillette stock indeed was Ronald Perelman, whose Revlon Group was launching a tender bid of $65 a share for all Gillette shares. Details of the $4.1 billion tender bid would be revealed in large tombstone advertisements in the *Wall Street Journal* and the *New York Times* the next morning, which would set the clock ticking for a ten-day period at the end of which Gillette directors would have to accept or reject a Revlon bid or come up with an alternative.

The first call to Fausch had come at 6:15 that Thursday evening from Larry Rand of Kekst & Company, Gillette's Wall Street public relations counsel. *Wall Street Journal* reporter Michael Miller, an M & A specialist in the New York newsroom, had called to say he was sticking around the office because he expected a Gillette story to break and he wanted Rand to be available for comment. Five minutes later, a reporter in the *Journal's* Boston bureau called Fausch asking for reaction to a reported bid of $65 a share by Revlon for Gillette, pinning it to a "reliable source." Fausch refused to comment on the unconfirmed report, which started a short, ritualistic journalistic dance. In a few moments the reporter called back with additional details but still no source. As before, Fausch declined comment. More minutes passed and at about 6:45 P.M., the phone rang and the same reporter was on the line, urgently demanding comment. When asked once again by Fausch for his source, the reporter exasperatedly replied that the details were in a tender offer advertisement that would appear in his newspaper the next morning. (The *Journal* supposedly had a "Chinese wall" between news and advertising departments that stayed down until about 7:15 or 7:30 P.M., when the *Journal's* early edition comes off the presses. After that, news production workers are free to steer reporters to the next morning's tombstone ads that formally identify buyers and targets in takeover bids, fulfilling SEC disclosure requirements. The wall seemingly was breached a bit before the deadline hour in the case of Revlon's hostile bid.) About the time Fausch was getting word on Revlon from the *Journal* reporter, Gillette's New York-based legal and financial advisers confirmed the news. After calling Mullaney, Fausch and Associate General Counsel Leonard Spalding began to work down an emergency call list of lawyers, bankers, and others who had to know right away. Mullaney called Mockler, as well as directors and some senior officers.

A hastily composed press release dubbed the "stop, look, and listen" statement was read at about 8:00 P.M. to the *Journal* and the *New York Times.* It stated, "The Gillette Company Board of Directors will carefully consider the unsolicited tender offer announced by Revlon Group Inc., in light of the best interests of the Company and its stockholders."

So it was Ronald Perelman, a brash figure on the Street who had used Drexel Burnham junk bonds to finance several highly leveraged takeovers in the preceding few years. The forty-three-year-old cigar-smoking financier, born and raised in Philadelphia but now ensconced in Manhattan's power district, the upper East Side, had acquired 9.2 million shares of Gillette, or 13.9 percent of the total outstanding, during a buying spree that started on October 31, according to documents he filed with the SEC. That made him Gillette's largest shareholder, by far. In contrast, the three largest institutional shareholders of Gillette were Rosenberg Capital Management, Lazard Freres & Company, and Miller, Anderson and Sherrard, which among them owned 4.4 million shares, or about 6.4 percent of Gillette's shares. Total institutional holdings of the company on November 13, 1986, amounted to 52.2 percent of the total, not counting the Revlon holdings.

Perelman's tender offer was straightforward and, to Gillette, harrowing. He offered to pay $65 a share for the remaining Gillette stock—a higher price than the stock had ever traded at—making the total bid worth $4.1 billion. His investment banker, Drexel Burnham Lambert, using language target companies had come to dread, said it was "highly confident" it could raise $3.9 billion junk bond funding. The remainder would come from Revlon and Perelman's privately held operating company, MacAndrews & Forbes. Gillette directors had ten working days to respond.

From Gillette's perspective, the news could hardly have been worse. Perelman had a reputation for buying companies and stripping them of their salable assets to finance his junk bond debt before moving quickly on to his next corporate raid. The specter arose of Perelman selling off Braun, Paper Mate, Oral-B, and any number of other Gillette nonshaving product lines to pay off the debt load he would incur with the high-yield junk bonds. It was assumed instantly inside Gillette and outside, too, that if successful, Perelman would keep the greatly profitable blade and razor operations, cut back on new product research and advertising to hoard even more cash, and retain a few toiletries lines that complemented Revlon's female-oriented lines. And then there was the matter of image. The prospect of abandoning King C. Gillette's creation to the New Yorker with a well-chronicled taste for glamorous night life and the lavish lifestyle of a free spender was unimaginable. Perelman's bravado could not have been further

from Colman Mockler's personal restraint and distaste for bragging and glitz, personal mannerisms that were reflected in the
management style of the conservatively run Boston business institution. Perelman versus Mockler, Revlon versus Gillette—this
truly was brash New York against Puritan Boston, and in the
bruising takeover battle that loomed, Puritanism seemed likely to
come out second best. Eric Gleacher, a hard-driving New Yorker,
would say from the perspective of ten years later: "It was good
for Gillette to have someone like me around, not hung up in the
Boston tradition. Gillette needed somebody like me."

Fresh in everyone's mind was Perelman's recent takeover of
Revlon, made in the name of Pantry Pride, a Florida food chain
that Perelman had acquired earlier in a hostile bid. The long, ugly
fight to take over Revlon and oust chairman Michel C. Bergerac
had shown off Perelman's relentless drive and financial skill.
Every time Bergerac upped the ante to fight off a Perelman bid,
Perelman raised the stakes. Sometimes he raised only a taunting
twenty-five cents a share, but each time the move forced Bergerac
to respond, and Perelman finally prevailed. Bergerac complained
to a *New York Times* reporter about the unfairness of a system that
encouraged him to greatly enhance the value of Revlon, as he had
done in a short period, but then allowed him to lose it all to a
pack of arbitrageurs backing a raider who forced a sale at an
inflated price that could only be financed with junk bonds.[1]

Perelman paid $2.7 billion for the cosmetics and health care
company plus about $50 million in fees to Drexel Burnham and
$25 million to Morgan Stanley for investment advice, among other
expenses. As for the huge debt burden he assumed, that was not
a problem: Perelman simply sold off the remaining assets of his
earlier acquisition—Pantry Pride—to get cash for Revlon. And
once he had Revlon, he began to sell off the billion-dollar collection of health care, specialty chemical, and prescription drug lines
that Bergerac had built up to complement the core cosmetics
business, in order to pay off junk-bond issues that financed most
of the deal. Then it was on to the next target—Gillette. If he had
his way, and there was little to suggest he would not on that
Thursday evening, in a matter of ten days or so he would become

the heir to King Camp Gillette's eighty-five-year-old company and the successor to John Joyce, Frank Fahey, Carl Gilbert, Vincent Ziegler, and Colman Mockler as the man who would decide Gillette's future and represent Gillette to the world.

"IT WAS COLMAN'S INSTINCT TO FIGHT"

Perelman's raid marked the start of "ten days of terror," Mullaney later said.

After the Thursday night phone call from Fausch confirming that Perelman was the mystery raider, Mullaney finished dinner with his wife and walked briskly through the cool autumn evening to the Prudential Tower. Fausch and Spalding were there calculating how to deal with the bombshell they knew would explode with the morning's first light. Mullaney got on the phone with Colman Mockler, who was at his Wayland home, in Boston's western suburbs. A little before midnight, Mullaney left the Pru and walked home for a few hours' sleep.

The next morning, executive secretaries and aides unaware of events arrived at Gillette headquarters and sensed a crisis atmosphere. Workers at Gillette installations as close as South Boston and as distant as Hong Kong soon received the news, too. At South Boston, reporters from the local papers quizzed early shift workers about their reaction to the takeover news as they entered the blade plant, often getting blank looks, for the news had not yet spread widely. Inside the factory, the talk was of little else as employees struggled to understand what was at stake. It boiled down to this: were well-paying jobs many workers considered theirs for life threatened by a takeover?

Mullaney was at his desk in his office next to Mockler's when a messenger appeared at 8:30 A.M. and presented a sealed envelope to Mockler's secretary, Mary Loftus. It was a letter from Perelman. At almost the same moment, Loftus took a phone call for Mockler; it, too, was from Perelman, and Mullaney remembers thinking that the timing was not a coincidence. Politely, as always, Mockler declined to take the call until he could assess the situation. The two men settled in Mullaney's office at a couch Mockler favored to review the cordially written letter, looking for signals. Mullaney recalls thinking the letter hinted that if $65 a share wasn't enough, there was more available. Perelman asked for an early meeting with Mockler to discuss the deal.

It was time to start the fortuitously timed takeover defense meeting that had been scheduled days earlier. Mockler decided to postpone calling back Perelman until at least after the meeting. He and Mullaney walked down a corridor with a few grim-faced colleagues, knowing they faced a tumultuous ten-day period that would decide the life or death of Gillette as an independent company.

As the meeting broke up nearly two hours later, Mullaney walked out a troubled man. Eric Gleacher and his crew of young analysts from Morgan Stanley and the lawyers from Jones, Day and Skadden, Arps had honestly assessed the bleak options open to Gillette. Gleacher said his top assistant, Andrew Liu, would immediately start evaluating Gillette's shareholder value by scrutinizing the worth of Gillette assets and future prospects, using computer models to estimate such factors as the value of new products and the company's own estimate of its future growth. In a few days, he said, he would be in a position to tell the directors if they reasonably could reject the Revlon bid as inadequate, or whether they were obliged to accept the $65 bid, or had to come up with an alternative offer to shareholders. Gleacher said he would immediately start a search for friendly buyers—"white knights" in the jargon of the Street—so that the directors would have an option to sell out to Perelman, if it came to that. He didn't say so, but everything from tone of voice to body language signaled that Gleacher thought the Perelman offer was very serious and posed a credible threat to Gillette's independence.

Pat McCartan, alerted to the raid by a call from Gillette, had caught a 7 A.M. flight from Cleveland to attend the meeting and had pored over the details in the *Wall Street Journal*. He outlined possible litigation strategies beyond obvious defensive moves that already were underway.

By the end of the meeting Friday morning, the reality of Gillette's plight was starkly clear. Perelman's tender offer of $65 a share might be high enough to win. At any rate, the bid could not be rejected out of hand in hopes that Perelman would disappear. Especially chilling was Gleacher's assessment of Perelman as a determined adversary. He knew the man's bulldog tactics well, having watched him and helped him in the prolonged fight to capture Revlon. He left the Gillette executives with the impression that the situation was not hopeless but that it would be prudent to start looking at once for white knights or some other alternative that might translate to loss of independence but would be better than selling out "to a guy who was easy to hate, running around with that cigar in his face all the time," as Joe Turley put it years later.

Mullaney remembers walking down the corridor from the boardroom about noon and thinking, "We're gone, Gillette's independence is finished. . . . My God, Gillette is gone."

The rest of that Friday is a blur to the many Gillette veterans who set about the grim work of defending their company's existence—the ultimate test a manager faces. One thing all agree on is that Colman Mockler assumed command quietly but decisively, setting a tone that would prevail throughout the ordeal. As he assessed events with his most trusted managers, Mockler worked to break the black mood. One participant remembers him saying with spirit, "We're not just going to roll over and die." He reminded them of how hard they had worked to position Gillette for major growth with new products and expansion to foreign markets and vowed he would do everything he legally could to keep the company from going down the drain.

"It was Colman's natural instinct to fight," Mullaney said, and his mood rubbed off on the others.

There were important decisions to be made. One of Mockler's first moves was to assign senior managers to an "A" team that would drop everything else and work exclusively on the company's response to the takeover. Assignments were made to the company's valuation, legal defense, and communications efforts.

The valuation group included CFO Thomas Skelly, as well as the corporate planning vice president, Paul N. Fruitt. Robert Ray and Kenneth Kames of Gillette's new business development department served as the M&A experts. They worked closely with Morgan Stanley and reported to Al Zeien.

The legal defense was headed by Joe Mullaney and his inside lawyers with outside counsel from Joe Flom and from Patrick McCartan, who directed litigation. The communications team included David Fausch and his outside advisers handling public relations, Milton Glass and his outside advisers handling investor relations, and Leonard Spalding to scrutinize news release copy and stand-by statements for legal concerns.

A second "B" team of operating managers, headed by Turley, was instructed to carry out the company's business as if there was no Perelman threat at all. "The last thing we wanted was to affect the worldwide business by reacting to shenanigans coming out of Wall Street," Skelly said.

The A and B teams would meet at the end of each day to brief each other and ensure that an accurate account of events was communicated around the Gillette empire. Top management recognized that workers at South Boston, Hong Kong, and points between would work more effectively if they were kept abreast of events. The structure of the A and B teams remained in place for the next year or so as raiders periodically threatened Gillette. When a crisis hit, the company had a battle-tested crisis management team that could be put to work at once. Operating managers understood that their job was to keep the company running smoothly, and they trusted the A team to keep them advised of events. "We all knew what buttons to push. It was quite effective," said Paul Fruitt.

As Gillette's liaison with Wall Street's investment bankers, Al Zeien had responsibility in two major areas. One was helping Morgan Stanley evaluate Gillette's worth, with special attention to explaining the company's upside potential beyond traditionally conservative projections and to make sure the bankers realized the importance of new products in the pipeline—in particular, the as-yet unnamed and unfinished Flag razor. To that end he worked closely with Andrew Liu, Morgan Stanley's chief analyst on the job, a young workhorse who impressed Gillette executives with his thoroughness and willingness to work prodigious hours. Zeien's other major chore was to help Gleacher develop alternatives to Revlon's offer, primarily to identify friendly suitors who might buy all or some of the company.

A critical decision was made before lunch on November 14 to reject Perelman's request for a return phone call or face-to-face meeting, a tactic that reportedly surprised and offended Perelman. "We decided it served no purpose and would be dangerous because you get into dialogue and people can reach different interpretations. So we decided it was best not to talk to Perelman," Mullaney said. In fact, Mockler and Perelman never met, then or at any later time. Gleacher, commissioned by Gillette to negotiate for the company, was the only Gillette envoy who talked or met with Perelman during the takeover attempt.

That Friday, directors were contacted and asked to stand by for a Monday meeting, by telephone conference call if necessary for out of towners, to be apprised of events and to consider the tone and contents of lawsuits that were being prepared. They were asked to be in Boston in person on Thursday, November 20, for a crucial meeting at which Gleacher would tell them if it was in shareholders' best interest to accept or reject Perelman's $65 a share bid.

THE BOESKY BOMBSHELL

The big break for Gillette—most people inside and outside the company came to believe it was the most critical factor in saving the company's independence—took place late that fateful Friday afternoon, November 14. The market had closed at 4 P.M. on an ominous note, with Gillette stock up exactly ten points to 67 3/4, almost three dollars above Perelman's bid and a sure sign that the Street thought a bidding war would soon force Gillette directors to capitulate and sell the company, if not to Revlon then to a more friendly suitor.

At 4:10 P.M., before Mockler and others had time to digest this news, a shocking story broke on news wires that would turn around Gillette's fortunes: Ivan Boesky—the biggest arb of them all, the feared, despised Ivan Boesky—had confessed to federal felony charges of profiting from insider trading. Boesky had become immensely wealthy through a seemingly uncanny ability to spot takeover stocks before others and profit as their share prices were driven up. It turned out that he was not uncanny after all, but just a greedy cheat who had grown rich by soliciting tips from some who attempted to manipulate the market. Acting on inside information is a criminal offense, and the feds had the evidence against Boesky. The news reports went on to say that Boesky had agreed to pay a fine of $100 million and, most important, had agreed to tell all to SEC lawyers in return for a reduced prison sentence. Since Boesky was the financier most linked to Drexel Burnham Lambert, and Drexel was the source of Perelman's money to buy Gillette, might there be an illegal Drexel-Boesky-Perelman link that would change Perelman's financing from solid

THE DOWNFALL OF MICHAEL MILKEN

The $100 million fine paid by Ivan Boesky was a record sum at the time but was more a slap on the wrist compared with the $1.1 billion fine later imposed on Drexel's billionaire deal-maker, Michael Milken. Milken pleaded guilty to SEC charges in April 1990 and served more than a year in jail. The man whose relentless hawking of high-yield junk bonds in large part made possible the 1980s takeover wave was barred for life from engaging in the securities business.

Milken was the most high-profile individual implicated by Boesky in his testimony to the SEC. No insider deal linking Milken with Perelman regarding the Gillette takeover surfaced during Milken's trial. According to Jesse Kornbluth, whose book *Highly Confident* covers the scandal, Milken called Perelman just before the raid on Revlon and Boesky's confession and argued against a Gillette takeover, but Kornbluth sheds no light on how Milken knew about the pending takeover bid or why he thought it unwise.

Drexel Burnham never recovered from the events that started with the Boesky confession and declared bankruptcy in February 1990.

to shaky? Boesky seemed certain to implicate Michael Milken in his criminal schemes. Were there Boesky-connected arbs, maybe Boesky himself, who bought up Gillette stock and "parked" it for the convenience of Perelman? (The *Wall Street Journal* reported a few days later that Boesky in mid-November had liquidated a fund worth $440 million that included takeover rumor stocks, including Gillette.)[2]

It did not take long for Mockler and the rest of the A team to sense the opportunities the scandal presented.

"That was a big break. It got the juices flowing," Mullaney recalls, and the Gillette forces moved toward a weekend of frantic activity in several cities in an improved frame of mind. Mullaney and McCartan realized at once that Boesky's confession provided an opening for them to frame lawsuits alleging his involvement with Perelman and the Revlon takeover bid. The confession also played into the defensive strategy of questioning Drexel's ability to come up with $3.9 billion to finance the deal. Boesky repeatedly realized enormous profits by investing in companies that later became takeover targets of raiders financed by Drexel. Had Boesky been signaled by Drexel or Perelman about the Gillette takeover?

Squads of lawyers from Jones, Day offices in Cleveland, Washington, New York, and as far away as Texas immediately began preparing lawsuits that would raise such straightforward questions. Phone lines and fax machines buzzed between Boston and the lawyers' outposts as the legal team raced to meet a Monday deadline for filing in Boston federal court.

McCartan, David Gunning, and Robert Profusek from Jones, Day set up camp in Boston to sort out legal strategy with Mullaney and the Gillette legal team. Jones, Day lawyers, directed by Jack Newman, worked through the weekend in Cleveland on drafting discovery procedures and poring over the SEC case against Boesky, keeping in constant contact with Boston. A so-called attack team of Jones, Day lawyers in New York methodically read newspaper reports and whatever documents they could find that might identify arbitrageurs, investment bankers, and others who could logically be served subpoenas demanding their sworn depositions. The weary lawyers and their aides completed the required documentation and drafts in Cleveland about 3 A.M. Monday. McCartan recalls that he flew back home to Cleveland for a few hours Sunday, scooped up the finished documents in the early hours Monday morning, and with Newman caught the 7 A.M. flight for Boston. "I kept on signing papers until we landed," McCartan said.

McCartan headed for Gillette's offices while Newman took the papers and went directly to the offices of Ropes & Gray, Gillette's Boston law firm. As soon as he got word of the board's approval that afternoon, he filed a lengthy lawsuit against Perelman or, more accurately, Orange Acquisition Corp., which was the formal name of the entity seeking to take over Gillette. The name Orange, according to Newman, was chosen by the New Yorkers to remind the Boston Irish at Gillette of the anti-Catholic Orange Order in British Northern Ireland, though given the mix of ethnicities and religions on both sides, the jab seemed feeble.

The forty-two-page lawsuit filed Monday afternoon asked the U.S. District Court in Boston to block Revlon from acquiring more stock, arguing that Perelman, through Orange, had violated both federal and state securities laws. The suit asked the court to rule that Gillette's 1985 poison pill provision or shareholder rights plan was valid in response to Perelman's earlier lawsuit that had sought to invalidate both the poison pill and the state's anti-takeover law, which the suit claimed was unconstitutional.

The heart of Gillette's lawsuit, the part that made headlines, charged that Perelman had secretly supplied insider information about his plans to acquire Gillette to "market players"—defined as professional traders, arbitrageurs, and other speculators—who would profit later by selling their stock to Perelman at a higher price. Perelman was accused of trying to place as much Gillette stock as possible in the hands of the market players. Subpoenas were issued to obtain records from Boesky's own firm, Boesky & Company; Bear, Stearns & Company; Ernst & Company; Gruss & Company; and Los Angeles-based Jefferies & Company. In all cases, the subpoenas demanded documents related to the Revlon refinancing, the purchase of Gillette shares, and any communications between the investment firms and Perelman. In addition, subpoenas were served to individuals, including Ronald Perelman, Michael Milken, and Ivan Boesky. Milken was served in a Hollywood sort of way, through the open window of his chauffeur-driven Mercedes as it turned into the driveway leading to his office at Drexel in Beverly Hills.

The aggressive strategy was risky as well as bold. Proving Boesky-Perelman-Drexel connections depended on finding support for the Gillette accusations through depositions and discovery proceedings that gave Gillette access to records and testimony under oath. Gillette believed the charges it made were true and reasonably could be proved in court. A few discovery moves urged by Jones, Day lawyers were rejected by Mullaney as off the mark, likely to open up the company to charges of a frivolous lawsuit. "It was my job to challenge the directors to accept an aggressive attack and I wanted to assure them these were reasonable moves," he recalled. The directors remained strongly supportive of Gillette's hard-nosed tactics throughout the week—a resoluteness that Gillette executives salute to this day.

"Colman had complete support of the board. We knew we were at risk as directors but we had confidence in Colman," said Lawrence E. Fouraker, former dean of the Harvard Business School and a Gillette director since 1973.

The timing of the Boesky scandal was like red meat to a hungry dog for the Gillette lawyers. It enabled the company to send a believable message to the world using tough legal language that could be paraphrased like this: "Don't expect Gillette to roll over and just take the best deal we can get. We're fighting for our survival, we're prepared to play rough, and the Boesky scandal plays right into our hands."

A SEARCH FOR WHITE KNIGHTS

While the lawyers were at work, Al Zeien and dozens of Gillette executives turned to the task of putting a value on Gillette to outsiders, which involved summarizing the company's assets, its plans, and its prospects for the foreseeable future. Fortunately, Paul Fruitt had just completed updating the company's five-year strategic plan, a sophisticated bottoms-up plan that started with Gillette's business units throughout the world. "The Book," as the document was called, lent credibility to the effort by Zeien and others to defend the bright outlook they painted for Gillette in sessions with Morgan Stanley's evaluators, Gillette directors, and prospective buyers.

CFO Tom Skelly took a room at the Sheraton Boston in the Prudential Center complex to put in more work hours over the weekend. He and others went through a role-playing exercise, positioning themselves as Ronald Perelman and saying in effect, "I'm Perelman and I want to buy Gillette for $4 billion plus. What are my obstacles?" From Perelman's perspective, Skelly concluded that a Revlon-Gillette combination would pay substantially higher taxes than Gillette as an independent, in part because of the IRS treatment of goodwill carried on the Gillette books. Skelly said the role-playing analysis helped Gillette defenders gain insights into Perelman's financial and tax-related options and also helped them to address tax concerns that potential white knights expressed in the days ahead.

Sunday night Skelly and Fruitt were driven to Logan for the forty-five-minute flight to New York's LaGuardia airport. As they settled into their seats, they glanced at a *Boston Globe* account of the Gillette plight and broke into laughter. The story speculated on how the Jewish New Yorker, Perelman, was going to coexist with all those WASPS at Gillette when he got his hands on the company. "The two of us got a kick out of that one, Paul being the son of Jewish immigrants and me the son of Irish immigrants," Skelly recalled.

The two men checked in at the Sheraton St. Regis and sat down to a late dinner. They were interrupted at 11:15 P.M. by a phone call summoning them to Morgan Stanley's nearby office at the Exxon building to work on the final draft of The Book, which would incorporate a few Morgan Stanley suggestions. Skelly remembers that those offices at midnight "were like South Station at rush hour," referring to Boston's busiest rail station. "The lights were on every place and the computers were going and all the young folks were running around in jeans. I asked one kid eating Chinese rice from a box about his social life and he said 'this is it.'"

Skelly said the young investment bankers seemed to work twenty-four hours a day and remembers in particular one young woman in sweatshirt and jeans who appeared never to sleep. He encountered her a few days later at a formal meeting of senior management to which she had been invited, this time dressed in a black suit and white bow tie. Sitting in the back of the room, she soon dozed off and slept peacefully as the meeting droned on.

A Downbeat Mood

In New York, the mood of the Gillette crew was downbeat Monday, November 17. The betting on the Street was strong that Gillette would be sold, if not to Revlon then to a higher-bidding friendly suitor. The Revlon tender bid had put Gillette "in play," that perilous situation in which a company loses control over its destiny, and potential buyers, friendly or hostile, engage in a bidding war that drives the price offered for the company to a level at which directors cannot reasonably reject it. There would be no shortage of friendly suitors, the *Wall Street Journal* assured readers.[3]

The *Journal's* headline that Monday reflected the mood of the Street, at least in the early hours of the day before the implications of the Boesky guilty plea began to sink in: "Gillette Appears to Have Little Chance of Staying Independent after Revlon Bid" said it all.[4] Analysts speculated that large consumer goods companies like the Anglo-Dutch giant Unilever, which would never consider a hostile bid, might welcome the opportunity to make a friendly bid. Other potential bidders prominently bandied about in the press were Colgate-Palmolive, Procter & Gamble, RJR Nabisco, and Philip Morris. Skelly and Fruitt settled down at Morgan Stanley offices along with Gillette's Robert Ray and Kenneth Kames, who also had come down from Boston to help explain the company's prospects to all comers who expressed serious interest. Their instructions were to share everything, literally to open The

Book and explain its numbers to any potential buyers who might be preferable to Revlon and willing to pay more.

"We were dead meat lying on Wall Street and the vultures were sitting on top of those buildings waiting to swoop down," said Skelly.

In effect, Skelly and his Gillette colleagues were there to "sell" the company, to provide information to potential buyers of the company in whole or part, or to persons who might have other alternatives in mind, such as joint ventures or leveraged buyouts. It was a tactic that had to be pursued because Gillette directors could not be expected to tell shareholders that the Perelman offer was inadequate, unless Gillette had been offered to others who had been given a chance to look at the company's books and make their own offers.

The rules of the game called for Gillette to weed out serious bidders from the frivolous by requiring that anyone allowed to look at The Book had to sign a confidentiality agreement. The agreement precluded the bidder from sharing what he learned with others and, very importantly, contained a standstill restriction that prevented the signer's company from acquiring stock and making a tender offer for Gillette without the assent of directors for a period of two years.

Forstmann Little; Kidder, Peabody; and Kohlberg, Kravis and Roberts—investment bankers all—signed the agreements and quizzed the Gillette executives at length after examining The Book. Merrill Lynch representatives showed up at the Exxon building but declined to sign the confidentiality agreement. There were "tire kickers" like Anheuser-Busch, which nibbled at the edges but never followed through with serious interest. "They'd wind us up and we'd repeat our story," is how Fruitt recalls the experience.

There was a lot of talk, but the flood of friendly suitors eager to acquire Gillette that the *Journal* predicted was proving more trickle than torrent.

In Boston, the directors met Monday for the first time since the Perelman-Orange attack. Five directors gathered at the Pru: inside members Mockler, Zeien, and Turley, as well as Raymond C. Foster and Lawrence Fouraker. The other six directors—Rita Ricardo

Campbell, Stephen J. Griffin, Herbert H. Jacobi, Charles A. Meyer, Richard R. Pivirotto, and Joseph J. Sisco—participated by telephone conference call. Mockler emphasized to them at the outset that their obligation was to shareholders, not management, and passed on the encouraging news that Morgan Stanley's preliminary analysis indicated that $65 was inadequate for shareholders. Mullaney and Flom, the latter on the line from New York, told the directors that they must seriously consider the tender offer, but if they decided it was a poor deal for Gillette's shareholders, they were protected by the business judgment rule that legally protects directors if they act in good faith, after appropriate investigation and a consideration of all relevant circumstances and with appropriate advice. McCartan told the directors that he thought the Perelman raid involved illegal tactics and outlined the basis for aggressive litigation that had been drafted; Mullaney got the board's unanimous approval to proceed with the lawsuit. Out-of-town directors were told to pack their clothes and head to Boston for a lengthy meeting on Thursday, November 20.

Skelly and Fruitt flew back to Boston on Tuesday night, November 18, and the center of action shifted to the Pru as the crucial Thursday morning directors' meeting loomed. By then, Gillette's efforts to turn the spreading Wall Street insider trading scandal to its advantage were bearing fruit as newspaper headlines focused on the sensational charge by Gillette that Perelman had violated securities laws by tipping off arbitrageurs.

The stock market reacted by dropping the price of Gillette almost ten points from the Monday high to the Wednesday close of 57 3/4, well below Perelman's $65 tender offer. The revelation on Monday that the SEC had issued a stack of subpoenas to Drexel officials at the time of Boesky's guilty plea gave traders pause about mighty Drexel's invincibility, however "highly confident" it claimed to be about financing Perelman. The subpoenas raised questions about Milken's involvement with Drexel clients, including raiders Carl Icahn and Victor Posner.

A story in Tuesday's *Wall Street Journal* put further heat on Drexel by disclosing that Milken's junk-bond financing operation had backed eight of twelve hostile takeovers the SEC was investigating with an eye to insider trading violations.[5] Gillette was not specifically cited, but the news played right into the hands of Gillette's lawyers and defense team. Drexel's managing director for corporate finance reminded reporters that issuing subpoenas does not imply wrongdoing, but few seemed to be listening.

On Wednesday evening, with the Gillette share prices plunging, Perelman released a defiant press release trying to reassure the Street that Revlon's financing was secure: "The Revlon Group Inc. said that Drexel Burnham Lambert today restated that it is highly confident that it can obtain financing for the acquisition of Gillette Company." Revlon, the statement went on, intended to vigorously pursue its tender offer of $65 a share. The statement included Perelman's branding of Gillette's charges "as a desperate and untruthful attempt to taint this offer in light of totally unrelated events of the past week. The charges are totally without merit and self-serving. Neither Revlon, MacAndrews & Forbes nor Ronald O. Perelman have ever had any business dealings with Ivan Boesky or any of his entities."

Howard Gittis, Revlon's vice chairman, told the *Wall Street Journal* that Gillette's decreased stock price might force Revlon to consider lowering its $65 bid. He said he was surprised that Gillette would "drag this into the gutter" by charging that Perelman had tipped off arbitrageurs in an effort to hype the stock's price.[6]

Drexel, mindful that failure to finance Gillette would be interpreted by friends and foes as a fatal weakness, issued a separate statement stating that the firm remained "highly confident" of its ability to finance Perelman.

Where Are the White Knights?

Although the combination of the Gillette legal offensive and the Boesky scandal had Perelman on the defensive, the situation midweek was still very much touch and go. Drexel's reaffirmation that it was highly confident about financing the deal calmed some investors, and Gillette's stock price steadied and gained slightly, in an encouraging development for Revlon. Perelman showed no

signs of retreat, and his $65 offer was still on the table for the
directors to consider. To the surprise of many, the search for
friendly suitors continued to come up empty, despite Gillette's
energetic efforts.

There was a surrealistic pause to the takeover drama when the
Gillette directors sat down around the boardroom table on the
morning of November 20. Colman Mockler opened the meeting
by reporting on his recent trip to the New Delhi blade plant. The
directors then considered and approved several expenditures: $3.2
million to increase production of Good News disposable razors,
$4.7 million to acquire a Chilean cosmetics company, and $12.5
million to fund the company's eyewear retailing venture (which
would be one of the first ventures jettisoned when the company
restructured). At about noon, the directors adjourned for lunch.

They resumed at 1:15 P.M. and this time got down to cases as
Joe Flom, Eric Gleacher and Andrew Liu joined the group. It was
Gleacher's duty as Gillette's investment banker to render the
"fairness" opinion—in plain English, to tell the directors whether
they could reasonably say no to the $65 offer. Gleacher told the
directors what they wanted to hear: that based on Morgan's still
incomplete analysis, he believed his preliminary advice that the
offer was inadequate would be confirmed. Everything Gleacher
said made it clear that he considered this a close call. And he
reminded the directors that based on past experience, there was
every likelihood that Perelman would keep on raising his bid.

Much of the meeting was given over to Andrew Liu's discussion of Gillette's five-year plan and how it related to shareholder
value. Liu and Gleacher referred frequently to their half-inch-thick
report coyly titled "Operation Smooth," which analyzed a company called "Company Smooth." The company was obviously
Gillette in every respect except for the code name. Company
Smooth was compared in whole and in its parts with nine leading
consumer products companies, including Procter & Gamble, Colgate-Palmolive and Bic. In another section of the report, Revlon's
assets, balance sheet, and management were analyzed and
profiled.

In one section of great interest to the directors, Operation

HOLD THAT CODE NAME

Investment bankers and corporate M & A managers cannot resist behaving like CIA spymasters when it comes to disguising corporate names, as the Operation Smooth report illustrates. In fact, a business spy might have been led astray by "Swiss Company," Morgan Stanley's name for Chesebrough-Ponds, by believing it referred to the country and not the national cheese, and thus guessing Nestlé.

Gillette code namers have come up with some other beauties. The code name for the secret negotiations leading to the purchase from Cooper Laboratories of Oral-B was High Noon, which had nothing to do with bright teeth. It referred to the movie *High Noon*, starring Gary Cooper.

Smooth analyzed the "unaffected price" of Gillette, that is, the price of $45 just before Perelman's buy-up began October 31. The report noted the $65 per share offered by Perelman was 44.4 percent above the unaffected price and indicated that sometimes an offer of this magnitude wins and sometimes does not.

The report's recapitalization analysis explored a ten-year estimate of the worth of Gillette as a whole, Gillette with all parts sold off except blades and razors, and several in-between configurations. Other sections of the report analyzed what Gillette would look like statistically after a leveraged buyout—no idle exercise, given KKR's interest at that time—and assumed Gillette's purchase of two other companies, measuring the "merger synergy" to be gained by acquiring companies thinly disguised as Stork Co. (Tambrands), and Swiss Company (Chesebrough-Ponds).

Gleacher spent a lot of time explaining his largely fruitless search for a white knight. He listed five American companies that had been contacted by him but had indicated no interest. They were the financial buyout company Forstmann Little & Company, Coca-Cola, American Brands, Philip Morris, and RJR Nabisco. In addition, four foreign companies had been contacted but expressed no interest: B.A.T. Industries of the United Kingdom, Fuji and Shiseido of Japan, and Switzerland's Nestlé. Black & Decker,

Johnson & Johnson, Procter-Silex, Healthco, and 3-M, plus Kao and Lion of Japan, had been contacted but were interested only in pieces; Black & Decker had an eye on Braun, for example. General Electric's Kidder, Peabody unit, American Home Products, Bristol Myers, Colgate-Palmolive, Procter & Gamble, Sara Lee, and Warner-Lambert, plus Beecham and Grand Metropolitan of the United Kingdom and Sandoz of Switzerland had also been contacted by Gleacher but said they were unlikely to proceed. Citicorp Industrial Credit, Metromedia Inc., Salomon Brothers, Shearson Lehman, and Merrill Lynch among financial companies, and Anheuser-Busch and Pepsi, had been contacted but had not yet responded.

Three companies were listed in the "interested" bracket: KKR, Ralston Purina, and Unilever. As it turned out, Unilever's interest was mild indeed. Joe Mullaney recalls the response of a British executive to the transatlantic phone inquiry Colman Mockler initiated as something like, "We're busy now, but why don't you pop over the pond sometime and let's see if there's something here to discuss." Ralston Purina remained in the mix until the final hours.

KKR showed serious interest in pursuing a leveraged buyout that would have included a heavy investment by top management at Gillette. KKR tax experts descended on Boston to take a closer look at tax ramifications, and talks went on until late in the week. According to Zeien, of the many options explored, KKR's LBO deal probably came closest to offering a realistic alternative to a Revlon takeover or Gillette's continued independence. But the KKR overture never really made it past first base because Mockler and Zeien were reluctant to talk about an LBO that would have enriched senior management but broken up the company as they knew it. That was not the Gillette style. KKR was told to go ahead and make an offer, but Gillette executives would not negotiate their own participation unless the directors agreed it made sense. "We got very much hung up with the fact they wanted major management participation," said Zeien. Mockler worried that LBOs crossed a line between management self-preservation at the expense of ordinary shareholders. All hands at Gillette agreed that the KKR contingent were both professional and respectful, not the so-called "vulture capitalists" that some had expected. When it became clear late in the week that Gillette would not opt for an LBO, the KKR team said thanks and goodbye, and that was it.

Joe Flom and Mullaney were there to guide the directors through their legal obligations to shareholders and to outline the legal protections afforded directors. Pat McCartan reviewed the litigation launched by Gillette and defensive moves underway to counter Revlon lawsuits.

The overtime meeting ended at 5:45 P.M. with directors still asking questions, especially about third-party possibilities. Three alternatives were discussed at length: play hardball, that is, take no action and rely on the market plus litigation to drive away Perelman; sell to Perelman or another party; or get rid of Perelman by buying back his shares.

SIGNALS FROM THE ENEMY CAMP

The first oblique signals that Perelman might be willing to deal for something short of a total takeover had come on Wednesday, November 19, the day before the meeting, with a call to Mullaney from Joe Flom. Flom reported that his Skadden, Arps partner Donald Drapkin had just talked to Perelman, who had suggested that if somebody from Gillette called him maybe they could work something out. Mullaney's first reaction was to blow up at Flom because he left the impression that Drapkin had raised the issue and Perelman had interpreted this as a signal that Gillette wanted to talk. That was contrary to Gillette's decision not to make the first move, and Mullaney was upset. Flom called back a short time later and explained to Mullaney that Drapkin had been talking to Perelman about other matters—Drapkin had announced he would soon leave Skadden to join Perelman full time—and that Perelman had raised the point, not Drapkin. That changed everything.

In the world of big-time takeovers, where lawyers and strategists search for verbal clues in coded conversations like this one, Flom's explanation made it seem that Perelman was sending a signal to Gillette via Drapkin that he wanted to talk.

About the same time that day, David Fausch recounted to Mullaney a similar elliptical message he had received the prior evening from Kekst & Company, a New York financial public relations firm hired some twelve months earlier to help with the New York media and investment community should Gillette be the target of a hostile takeover. The firm was the pre-eminent merger and acquisition public relations agency, with a long list of blue-chip clients, including Revlon during its raid on Pantry Pride.

When Perelman launched his hostile bid for Gillette, Gershon Kekst explained his firm's policy in cases where two clients were pitted against one another. Kekst would not work for the aggressor but would work to defend the client under attack. Fausch assumed this meant that Kekst account executive Larry Rand would not be dealing with Revlon or Perelman during the tender offer. When Rand told Fausch that Perelman had indicated some uneasiness about the Gillette takeover deal, Fausch assumed the exchange between Rand and Perelman was unrelated to the bid and did not challenge Rand as to why there was any contact with Perelman. But a few hours later, a *Wall Street Journal* reporter told Fausch that Rand had just given her Revlon's quarterly earnings release, and she understood him to say that he was also representing Gillette. She wanted to know how one PR firm could work for both sides.

So did Fausch. He called Gershon Kekst, who insisted that Rand was not working on the tender offer for Revlon but was servicing Revlon on the other public relations issues. Fausch refused to accept that this was just a nuance and not a conflict of interest and removed Kekst from the assignment. He kept the Kekst firm on retainer as a way to keep it true to its policy of working to defend a client in cases where two clients were in combat. Upon hanging up the phone with Kekst, Fausch called Jonathan Rinehart, who headed Adams & Rinehart, and retained that PR firm to work on Gillette's takeover defense.

The Kekst controversy highlighted the potential for conflicts of interest as the M & A game is played. The three major ad hoc takeover advisers to Gillette—Morgan Stanley, Skadden, Arps, and Kekst—all had worked for Ronald Perelman, though only Kekst

& Company's behavior smacked of having it both ways during the Revlon bid.

The A team met that night as usual to discuss the day's events and exchange news with the B team. The apparent signals from Perelman seemed strong enough to follow up, and it was decided to assign Gleacher, perhaps with Mullaney or Zeien, to contact Perelman after the Thursday board meeting finished. Gleacher wanted to meet Perelman alone, arguing that he knew Perelman well and was best equipped to sound him out and probe for openings, and he won his point. He contacted Perelman on Friday and found the Revlon chief in a talkative and amiable mood, obviously eager to explore options. Perelman sounded out the possibility of buying Oral-B. Almost casually, Gleacher inquired whether Perelman would consider selling his 9.2 million Gillette shares back to the company. After a few minutes more of sparring, the two men broke it off and Gleacher reported at once to Zeien.

The idea of anything resembling a greenmail payment, that is, getting rid of a raider by buying back his shares at a premium not available to other shareholders, was not the straight-arrow Mockler's notion of fair play, and he predictably was cool when the idea was broached. Greenmail was not uncommon in the mid-1980s, and Mullaney had already forewarned Mockler: "When I brought up the subject of working something out with Perelman such as buying back his shares, sometime in the middle of the week, he almost threw me out. He gave me a hard-eyed look, put both hands on his table and said 'not while I am here.' I almost ran out of his office. But I just wanted to get him thinking about it."

With no interest from any other buyer, friendly or otherwise, a late feeler from Ralston Purina was about the only alternative left for Gillette, and a lot of time and energy was spent on the matter before it evaporated at the last minute Sunday night. After some to-ing and fro-ing, mostly involving Ralston investment banker Bruce Wasserstein and Gleacher, Ralston CEO William P. Stiritz had become directly involved Friday when he phoned Mockler, an old acquaintance. Seeking details, Tom Skelly then contacted the CFO at Ralston and was told that Ralston was interested in acquiring a minority position in Gillette with a cross-investment by Gillette for a minority interest of Ralston.

Stiritz and a cadre of senior officers flew to Boston Friday afternoon. Mullaney and Mockler slipped out of the Pru for a few hours and huddled with the Ralston CEO and another executive in a room at the Ritz-Carlton Hotel overlooking Boston's Public Garden, expecting to hear a specific cross-investment proposal. It was Mullaney's impression that the Ralston executives instead wanted to talk about some form of leveraged buyout or Ralston investment that involved a special role for Gillette management. Mockler remained adamant about avoiding any appearance of management gain at the expense of other shareholders, so this line of discussion went nowhere, and the abbreviated meeting smacked more of executive small talk than fateful negotiations. During the short taxi trip back to the Pru, the puzzled Gillette executives decided that Ralston was interested in "taking a position," as Mullaney recalls it, but had as yet no specific plan in mind.

At noon on Saturday at the Sheraton Boston, Skelly and Fruitt, along with Gillette's top tax manager, Robert Sama, repeated to several Ralston executives their by-now familiar story of Gillette's current and future prospects. The outline of a preferred stock deal involving cross-investments began to emerge. The proposed deal would have Ralston Purina buying Perelman's block of Gillette stock. Ralston and Gillette would then make cross-investments of perhaps 15 percent in each other and would form a joint venture to develop Ralston's non-U.S. Eveready battery business. A possible change in Gillette's personal care operations outside the United States was thrown into the mix. In New York, Gleacher was directly working with Wasserstein to see what kind of a Ralston-Gillette deal could be struck, raising some concerns in Boston that the two M & A warriors might come up with something Gillette could not accept. There was a great deal of phoning back and forth between New York, Boston, and St. Louis, Ralston's home city.

Skelly, who was working from a room at the Sheraton Boston, called his wife, Patricia, and invited her to come to town for dinner and spend the night at the hotel. By Saturday evening, with the Ralston negotiations growing more tenuous, Gillette was giving serious consideration to buying back Perelman's stock. A team of

---

lawyers from Jones, Day and Skadden, Arps (corporate lawyers, not litigators) started work on drafting a buyback that would get both Perelman and Drexel off Gillette's back for a long time.

Skelly shifted his focus to accounting considerations of a stock buyback. Would authorities consider a buyback of Perelman stock greenmail for accounting purposes, thus opening up Gillette for hundreds of millions of dollars in added charges to earnings? Skelly and Sama, working with accountants from KPMG Peat Marwick, decided that if a Gillette buyback did not exceed a certain level of profit for Perelman, it would not constitute greenmail for accounting purposes, regardless of how the buyback would be reported in the media. The KPMG crew knew it was a sensitive point and retired to another room to have it reviewed by the accounting firm's SEC partners.

Skelly and his wife took the opportunity to go to dinner, which was interrupted before the main course arrived with an urgent phone call that took Skelly away from the table. After dinner, Skelly worked on the accounting consequences of a buyback for a while longer and then retired to bed at a late hour. At 6 A.M, he and his wife were awakened by the phone, and as Skelly engaged in a long, three-way conference call with KPMG officials in Boston and New York, his wife made up her mind to head back to their home and a bit of sanity.

Ultimately, KPMG's top brass agreed to render their opinion that a buyback under a certain profit level would not be considered greenmail for accounting purposes. The decision played an important part in the drama still to be played out late that night.

The action shifted to New York Sunday morning. Al Zeien flew to the city early in the morning in the company's Gulfstream aircraft, the much-used G-2 that was based at Bedford's Hanscom Field, about twenty miles from the Pru. Zeien knew that he had only a short time to get to midtown and confer with Gleacher before the climactic face-to-face meeting Gleacher had set up with Perelman, so he told the pilot to land at Teterboro, a small New Jersey airport closer to Manhattan than LaGuardia, where a limousine was waiting. As Zeien settled in the back seat, the limo driver stepped on the gas—and with a sound of scratching metal and squealing brakes, the big car rammed into an automatic gate and stopped.

The agitated driver jumped out and excitedly told Zeien that it was not his fault and that Zeien must wait there with him until his boss or the police arrived to record the accident. Zeien said to forget it and keep going. The driver would not budge, so Zeien jumped out and headed toward another car, hoping for a quick trip into the city. The limo driver grabbed Zeien's arm and told him he could not leave. "The whole company hanging in the balance and he's worried about scratches on his car . . ." Zeien recalled. "It's these little things you remember more than the big things."

Zeien managed to extricate himself from the Teterboro scene and was driven through nearly empty streets into Manhattan, where Gleacher greeted him with the news that he thought there was room for dealing. Gleacher asked what was going on with Ralston, was there a deal there? What did Mockler and the lawyers think about a buyback? Zeien recalls it as a chaotic scene: lawyers and Morgan Stanley people milling about, he on the phone with Boston talking about the worth of this or that part of Gillette, how to keep the Ralston prospect alive, and much more. Gleacher was told by Zeien that Oral-B definitely was off the table. Then it was time for Gleacher to drive to Perelman's townhouse on East 63rd Street.

"The only thing we had going for us was this idea of a blocking deal with Ralston. If you're defending a company against take-over, you've got to have alternatives, and we'd tried hard but really had nobody," was how Gleacher recalled his train of thought as he left for Perelman's apartment.

When he arrived, he found that Howard Gittis, Perelman's top assistant, was also on hand but no lawyers, as agreed upon. Gleacher started talking. He said that Perelman was in a difficult situation because of the Boesky-Drexel connections, and scandal figured in Gillette's thinking. "I told him if he stayed in the chase he might lose a lot of money because Gillette was trying to work out a deal with a white knight, and if Gillette succeeded in tying up the situation, that Gillette's stock would go down and then he'd lose a lot of money and that bad things would happen," Gleacher said.

And then Gleacher made his pitch. "I suggested to him that Gillette would buy him out, and that he'd make a little bit of profit, and that he would avoid a mess. And I knew right away from his reaction that he would go for it."

No specific buyback price was mentioned; no specific deal was discussed. Just talk—the sort of testing and give and take that later lead to deals. The numbers, and what Gillette would get in return for buying off Perelman, would be negotiated soon enough, in a few hours in fact.

Gleacher recalls it all as very informal, lasting perhaps twenty or twenty-five minutes. Gleacher had not had time to shave, of all things for a representative of the world's shaving leader. Perelman was wearing jeans. But everyone understood the high stakes. "In these situations you have to use your judgment without casting deals in stone. I'm there trying to persuade this guy to go away, and I couldn't stop and wait for instructions on exactly what to do." Gleacher told Perelman that he would be in touch later in the day and sped back to the Morgan Stanley office, where he filled in Zeien. Then Zeien, Gleacher, and various lawyers and bankers headed back to Teterboro, avoiding incidents at the parking lot gate, and took off at once for Boston to prepare for the critical board meeting scheduled a few hours later. Zeien broke the tension by instructing Gleacher that the best time to shave is during or right after a shower, not before—"Again, the sort of small stuff you tend to remember in these tense situations," Zeien said.

Back in Boston, Mockler apparently was still concerned about the degree of enthusiasm at Morgan Stanley for defending Gillette's independence and spent a few precious hours Sunday dealing with the famed investment banker James D. Wolfensohn, later to be chief of the World Bank, who had been recommended to him by director Larry Fouraker at the eleventh hour as a candidate to join the Gillette team as a second investment banker. In the haste of the moment, that did not pan out, though he was seriously considered. Wolfensohn was later hired in January 1987 by Mockler as a "second opinion" voice to back up Morgan Stanley on

M & A matters in a hushed-up move known to a few knowledge-able insiders as Project Revere, after the revolutionary leader.

Upon their return to Boston Sunday afternoon, Zeien and Gleacher briefed Mockler and the A team members on the Perel-man talks, reminding them that the prospect of buying back Perelman's stock at last gave Gillette a clear alternative to flat rejection or capitulation. Mockler, still concerned about the actual or perceived payment of greenmail, listened and then switched his attention to the Ralston deal.

Zeien turned to other matters, namely, making sure that Liu and Gleacher had all the numbers and rationale they needed to tell the directors again that Perelman's offer was inadequate in terms of shareholder value, leaving the door open for Gillette to retain its independence.

THE MIDNIGHT MEETING

The start of the director's meeting was delayed until 8:55 P.M. by a final effort on the part of Ralston to salvage a deal. The directors had convened in the thirty-ninth floor boardroom and a meal was brought in from the Top of the Hub restaurant, perched thirteen floors above them at the top level of the fifty-two-story Prudential Tower. The tension mounted as Ralston chief Stiritz and Wasser-stein talked on the phone with Mockler, with occasional brief time-outs for consultation with advisers. According to Mullaney, it became increasingly clear that Stiritz, presumably heeding Was-serstein, had moved well beyond earlier proposals calling for a relatively small preferred stock investment by Ralston and now insisted on a deal that called for an initial 22.5 percent equity investment plus options and rights to buy more Gillette shares. That smacked more of eventual takeover than minority invest-ment to Mockler. Finally, Mockler broke off the phone call by telling Stiritz the proposal would be considered and good-bye, we'll let you know. After a brief consultation, Mockler and his A team colleagues concluded that they would advise Gillette direc-tors that the Ralston proposal was not in the best interests of shareholders, and they headed down the corridor to the midnight meeting that actually did not end until after 1:30 the next morning.

Every director was on hand, as were the main players of the past ten days or so, excepting Joe Flom, who was in touch with the meeting via speakerphone.

"A tough meeting . . . a lot of angst and anguish," as Gleacher recalled it.

Tom Skelly remembered the serious attitude of the directors but above all that the board was resolute, with every director intent that personal feelings aside, it was not in the best interests of shareholders to let the company fall into Perelman's hands. Gleacher reviewed the matters discussed at the Thursday meeting and said that nothing new had developed to give hope that a white knight was waiting in the wings. He said Morgan's final opinion was that $65 was an inadequate price, given Liu's judgment that Gillette's value on an ongoing basis was between $62.30 and $72.94 a share.

Gleacher informed the directors that the Ralston deal had collapsed as far as Gillette management was concerned. He then described his talk that morning with Perelman. He told them he had advised Perelman of Gillette's interest in working out some form of cross-investment with an unnamed company. And then, in a dramatic moment, he described Perelman's reaction—his obvious interest—when told that Gillette would consider buying back the shares Perelman had accumulated. With Ralston dead, there were no more options; the way out for Gillette, Gleacher argued strongly, was to buy back Perelman's 9.2 million shares at a price well below the $65 that he would negotiate that evening and be rid of him. Gleacher told the directors that Perelman would go for it rather than face a messy fight in the context of the Boesky scandal.

The board did not act at once. Flom advised the directors that they could determine it would be a mistake to sell Gillette to anyone because of the bright future the company had as an independent. His remark sparked discussions in the vein of how bright is bright, with frequent resort to The Book. There were still questions about the Ralston deal to be asked and answered before that one was put away for good. But the big obstacle was the perception of greenmail, which was a sticking point for several directors, who besieged Gleacher and Zeien and others with questions. Gleacher insisted that this was the time to be realistic and go after a good deal—that night—rather than worry about perceptions. He told the directors that paying a small premium to buy out Perelman was an excellent investment, given Colman Mockler's earnest assurances that a mix of restructuring and excellent long-term prospects spelled much faster growth in sales and profits ahead.

As the directors pushed for more answers, it became evident that Colman Mockler was still bothered by the perception of paying greenmail. Zeien and others persuaded him that it was hardly classic greenmail, because the profit of perhaps $35 million that Perelman could expect would be relatively puny compared with most greenmail deals, including the $93 million payoff Sir James Goldsmith had extracted from Goodyear Tire and Rubber a few days earlier. Skelly reminded Mockler that the company's outside accountants, KPMG, had agreed that the amount Gillette was prepared to pay Perelman did not constitute greenmail in accounting terms. Pat McCartan, a keen observer of the night's action, believes the chairman finally was brought around to accepting a buyback by the conviction of the directors and management that whatever the public perception, Gillette would be a better investment for shareholders as an independent company. With the chairman's assent, Gleacher left the room to call Perelman and negotiate a buyback price.

During the evening, McCartan was called away for a phone

WAS IT GREENMAIL?

Gillette probably never will shed the popular perception that it paid greenmail to get rid of Ronald Perelman, and in a literal sense, the directors did vote in November 1986 to pay the raider a premium over the prevailing share price. But it was a matter of faith at the Pru then, as it was a decade later, that greenmail was more perception than reality in the Revlon raid.

It was not greenmail, Gillette argued, because the price paid to Perelman was within the stock's trading range, and at any rate, Perelman did not make an enormous profit on the deal.

The question was put to a vote at the 1988 annual meeting when Gillette shareholders supported, 56 percent to 44 percent, an anti-greenmail resolution. The nonbinding resolution precluded the company from buying back shares from any individual at a price greater than that available to other shareholders. The resolution was offered by California Public Employees' Retirement System (CALPERS), a major holder of Gillette stock, which claimed the resolution was needed to "terminate a practice we perceive to be 'greenmail,'" which, it went on, wasted company assets and damaged all other shareholders.

Gillette directors recommended a "no" vote on the CALPERS resolution, "not because the Directors approve of 'greenmail,'" but because, they said, the proposal could "seriously impair" their ability to act in shareholders' long-term interests. The directors further contended that the premium paid to Perelman, which CALPERS cited, was not greenmail at all but "well within the range of prices at which the stock had traded in the period immediately preceding the purchase." Furthermore, the directors noted, by early February 1987 the stock price had reached and even exceeded the price paid to Perelman.

The issue was resolved at board meetings in September and October 1988. In September, the board adopted a resolution required in the settlement agreement relating to the shareholder lawsuits against the company from the buyback of the Revlon stock. The settlement agreement restricted the company's ability to repurchase its stock from a shareholder who owns 3 percent or more of the company's stock at a price above "average market price" and stipulated that such repurchases must be approved by a majority of the stockholders.

In the October meeting, management reported to the board that in discussions with CALPERS, the latter had agreed to support an amendment to Gillette's bylaws, which incorporated the definition of "average market price," as well as supported the stipulation that repurchases above "average market price" must be approved by a majority of the stockholders, as opposed to the two-thirds majority expressed in the shareholder proposal.

call from the well-known New York lawyer Arthur Liman, who later defended Drexel's Mike Milken against insider charges, who was calling on behalf of Perelman. He said Perelman insisted on settling a matter involving his honor and integrity; Gillette, he went on, must retract charges made in lawsuits alleging Perelman had tipped arbitrageurs about his plans to make a tender offer. McCartan told Liman he did not think a retraction was called for but said he would discuss it with Mockler. After a brief discussion with Mockler, McCartan called back and agreed to draft a letter that, as it turned out, did not retract anything but was skillfully crafted to say that Mockler accepted Perelman's word that he did not tip off the arbitrageurs.

Gleacher shuttled between the boardroom and Mockler's office. There, his feet propped on the desk in a gesture unthinkable for the proper Mockler and which annoyed some Gillette executives who could see through the open door, he bargained with Perelman over price and other conditions. Finally, he returned to the boardroom and told directors that he had a deal, the best that could be had: $59.50 a share for all of Perelman's stock, plus $9 million to cover Revlon's legal and investment banking fees, for a total of $558 million. Based on the average price of $55.81 that Perelman paid for his Gillette shares, that meant a profit of about $34 million, plus the $9 million for fees. In return, Perelman pledged not to buy Gillette shares or attempt a takeover for ten years. In addition, in an unusual move that Gleacher suggested, the buyback deal included Drexel's agreement not to finance for at least three years any attempt to take over Gillette.

Flom and some Gillette directors made a half-hearted effort to go back and negotiate for a lower price, but Gleacher cut it short when he said he thought he had the best deal he was going to get and did not want to jeopardize the deal for what amounted to small change. Several directors grumbled about paying for Revlon's fees because they felt Gillette was being made to pay for another's mischief, but Gleacher said it was a standard practice in the M & A world that had to be swallowed.

Joe Turley went along reluctantly. He thought the Boesky plea had badly damaged Perelman. He felt that Gleacher had "patched up a little bit" with Perelman instead of pushing him to back off, and Gillette could have escaped without paying greenmail. "He [Perelman] was bagged. . . . He would have backed off," he said years later.

"The board hated this deal, but I liked it," said Gleacher.

The meeting broke up at 1:30 A.M., with the directors told to reconvene in a few hours right after an early breakfast, to sign off on the formal deal. The weary Bob Profusek of Jones, Day had worked through the night Saturday and all day Sunday preparing legal papers that would be needed at once for any of several moves the directors might make. Sometime Sunday afternoon, he recalled, the tide turned from Ralston and toward a buyback. By late in the evening, after the New York–Boston shuttles had stopped running, the buyback seemed all but certain. Profusek rushed to Logan Airport, where he boarded the waiting company Gulfstream and took off for New York. On landing, he headed directly to the Revlon offices, where he spent a second-straight sleepless night, this time working with Revlon lawyers to arrange the stock purchase papers and finalize the sensitive standstill language.

The lawyers were racing to complete paperwork so that the deal would close before the market opened. They almost made it, though not without a lot of shouting, cursing, and banging of desks. Ronald Perelman was there for most of the time and was among the loudest of the shouters and noisiest of the desk bangers, Profusek recalled. "You've got to understand, Revlon has a different sort of management style, very abrasive and angry compared with the calmer and more dignified Gillette approach," he said. The mood was not particularly hostile, he said, just ill-tempered, with fatigue breeding distrust and unseemly outbursts. One hitch that infuriated Perelman and set off a torrent of abuse developed at the last minute, when Revlon lawyers were unable to locate all the Gillette shares held by Perelman, most of them at Drexel. It turned out to be a mechanical matter, but for a while it raised the question of whether Revlon actually had in its possession all the shares that it had claimed.

For its part, Gillette was prepared. Treasurer Lloyd Swaim,

anticipating the potential need for a huge sum of money first thing Monday morning, had made sure hours earlier that J. P. Morgan would make available to Gillette the funds needed to support the one-time stock purchase. Finally, the money and stock were exchanged and the trade "crossed" just moments after the market opened. Once the block trade had crossed, the tension deflated like air from a pricked balloon. Profusek staggered to a nearby hotel and at 11 A.M. finally went to bed for a few hours sleep—to be awakened thirty minutes later by a call from Joe Mullaney, who had questions about the grudging but not inaccurate language used in the Revlon press release.

Years after the "midnight meeting," Eric Gleacher remains convinced that the Boesky scandal was pivotal to Gillette's victory and that Boesky's confession to the SEC and all comers "scared the hell out of Perelman." Gleacher said that he told Gillette directors that Perelman would not be implicated by Boesky—indeed, unlike Drexel's Milken and so many other Wall Streeters, Perelman never was tied to any of Boesky's numerous insider scams. But Gleacher said he also told Gillette directors that Perelman was running scared and did not want to be tied to Drexel, if Drexel was tied to Boesky. Of course, the Boesky scandal was the beginning of the end for Drexel, which declared bankruptcy in February 1990, fatally hurt by its links to Boesky.

Gleacher now says, "I can absolutely assure you that the Boesky scandal changed Ron Perelman's mindset. I know what he was thinking because we talked about it later." Minus the Boesky scandal, Perelman could have had Gillette for $70 a share, he concluded, because there were simply no other bidders that were interested, and the $65 share price was so close to what he and Liu thought was a "can't reject" offer. "The Boesky stink scared him off from raising his bid," Gleacher said.

Perelman, interviewed in 1995 in *Cigar Aficionado* magazine, said that he was "suckered" into thinking Gillette was about to do a deal with Ralston that would have made a clean Revlon takeover impossible to complete.[7] Gleacher rejects that version: "I did not mislead him."

Al Zeien speaks for many at Gillette who agree, a decade after the event, that the timing of the Boesky scandal was fortuitous. "We were lucky," he said, adding that shareholders who stayed with the company have nothing to complain about—a financial understatement the salesman side of King C. Gillette would have enjoyed. A share of Gillette at the end of tumultuous 1986 was worth $49.25, but with several stock splits and reinvested dividends escalated in worth to $759.56 at the end of 1996.

8

AN END
TO
GRADUALISM

THE HASTILY SCRAWLED morning-after sign that secretary Nancy Gosson put up by her desk on the Prudential's thirty-ninth floor read "Gillette 1, Perelman 0." It was a deft metaphor in a baseball town whose citizens recently had suffered a World Series loss to the New York Mets in a setting of defeat snatched from victory, when Red Sox first baseman Bill Buckner misplayed a potential game-ending ground ball that extended the Series to a final game that the Sox lost. There were hugs and handshakes and lots of happy chatter as word of Revlon's withdrawal spread around the Gillette floors at the Pru and soon throughout the company, as an employee bulletin from Colman Mockler was flashed to Gillette's many outposts around the world. But there was none of the champagne-on-ice ritual that had become common in victorious executive suits during the takeover era. Champagne at the office was Perelman's style, not Gillette's; New York, not Boston.

A major shared emotion was a sense of relief as the tension of the preceding ten days evaporated. Al Zeien's secretary, Janice Daley, remembered thinking that at last she could get the laundry out of the back of her car. She had been carrying it there for days, working such long hours that she passed her dry cleaner on the way in to work before the business opened and returned home after it closed. "We were all wondering whether this would be over in time for a normal Thanksgiving," she recalled. "We didn't know what would happen. I had a knot in my stomach much of the time."

At least one valued employee, in the information technology department, had quit because he said he could not work under the strain of not knowing who his boss would be. A twenty-four-year veteran worker at the South Boston plant told an interviewer she was confident that the company would come through, but some coworkers literally were worried sick at times during the takeover threat. These were exceptions. Most Gillette employees, especially the veterans at the South Boston blade plant, told reporters from Boston papers that they did not lose any sleep because they were confident all along that Gillette would figure out how to shake off Revlon and save their jobs.

Tom Skelly said that the people who were dealing directly with the takeover probably stayed more composed than those who were to one side of the battle. Lawyer Pat McCartan remarked that the stress level at Gillette during the relentless pressure was measurably lower than at other companies he had served as counsel during takeover struggles. He credited Mockler's calm demeanor for setting the tone. Mockler no doubt smoked even more than usual as he dealt with one crisis after another, but he had always been a heavy smoker. It was one bad habit this very disciplined man was never able to beat.

There was weariness along with the relief. Despite arriving home at about 2 A.M, Skelly was up by 7 A.M. conferring with colleagues. Treasurer Lloyd Swaim checked the reaction of financial markets, talking to bankers and rating agencies. Both men knew that although Perelman was out of the way, the company had been forced to add a load of debt to its balance sheet and faced interest payments the scale of which Gillette had never dreamed of owing. But the company was intact; that was the main thing.

There was one emotional moment at midday Monday, when Colman Mockler strode into a room crowded with fifteen or twenty of his closest associates, who had been summoned to hear a detailed postmortem. "Everyone there stood up and clapped. Colman blushed," recalls lawyer Len Spalding.

And that was it. Mockler recovered quickly, thanked his colleagues for their hard work, and moved at once to the urgent business at hand, which was how to restructure the company to increase short-term profits and build up the price of the stock without sacrificing the company's long-term future. Everyone in the room knew they had to make good on the promise that Gillette could better serve shareholders as an independent company, and they knew they had to make it happen in a hurry or face more takeover threats.

Within minutes of the announcement of Perelman's failure to take over Gillette, the company's stock had started to drop, adding to its vulnerability. It lost as much as 10 3/4, falling to 45 7/8 before steadying there. Arbitrageurs and short-term investors who were now stuck with shares they had bought in the 50s and 60s, in hopes of a quick killing, railed to the press about being victimized by greenmail. Gillette officials expected shareholder lawsuits to follow.

Perelman had said he would pay $65 a share. Gillette had rejected him and told shareholders the company had a bright future. How long would it take the company to get the stock back to $65, and in order to do that, what had to be done? It was a reality check that could not be put off. The predators had forced the issue.

RESTRUCTURING BEGINS

"You know, one of the best things that happened to Gillette was Ronald Perelman. He made us think about ourselves and where we were going," Skelly said, voicing a sentiment widely held by Gillette veterans a decade after the great scare.

Paul Fruitt put it another way: "The Perelman attack marked an end to gradualism." Fruitt was right. The company had been making some moves to tighten up and reorganize priorities, but it had to move boldly now. The luxury of gradualism was over: Gillette had been bloodied, and sharks were out there waiting to strike if the company failed to make good on its promise to maximize shareholder value. Maximize shareholder value— MSV—became a mantra among executives and directors.

Before the Thanksgiving turkey was carved on Thursday that week, the restructuring process was underway.

Skelly remembers a meeting early in the week when Mockler started off by asking a room filled with senior managers, most of them frequent business travelers, "Number one, who here thinks we should continue to fly a corporate jet?" Nobody voted yes. Mockler thanked them for the vote because he said there was no way he was going to fly to some distant place in a private jet and announce a factory had to be closed. Approval to sell the Gulfstream G-2 and cancel an option to buy a G-4 was just the start, but an important symbolic move, to the shrinking of businesses, factory closings, sell-offs of marginal units, and most difficult of all, the first-ever major layoff of Gillette employees that everybody knew had to come.

Not that any corporate break-up of the sort that Revlon presumably had in mind was in the works. Gillette's stance was that it could restructure and tighten its belt without resorting to extreme measures, such as selling off a major division like Braun. The company had taken on new debt to finance the buyback, but its balance sheet was strong, and there was no need to sell whole divisions to pay for the debt, as Goodyear Tire had been forced to do in order to finance its greenmailing of Sir James Goldsmith. No draconian measures would be needed to substantially increase Gillette shareholder value, cash flow, and stock price, said Milton Glass, the long-time investor relations chief who had earned Wall Street's trust as a straightshooter. Investors appeared to be listening, with First Boston and Paine Webber both increasing their earnings estimates. The stock slowly drifted upward to $47 at midweek.

All this was reassuring, but until Gillette managers took action to make it happen, restructuring was just a big word that meant nothing.

The meetings that started before Thanksgiving and picked up again in earnest the following week put everything on the table. "I thought it was an amazing coming together of what's right for Gillette. There were not a lot of arguments, instead, there was amazing cooperation," said veteran administration chief William J. McMorrow. He saw Gillette's ability to make painful cuts without a lot of internal backbiting as a good test of the Gillette culture under stress.

"There was very little naysaying. We tried to be humane but everyone was asked to do their share," Fruitt recalled.

Fruitt kicked off the first post-Thanksgiving Day meeting with a two-hour presentation that included a review of the company's revised long-range plan up to 1990. It was similar to the valuation presentation provided to Morgan Stanley and prospective white knights two weeks earlier, when the company was seeking to justify its prospects for a bright future. That plan and the 1987 budget, which Fruitt then knew by heart, served as the starting point for the restructuring of Gillette.

Next, the company moved into an emergency phase that required tough decisions by senior operating managers all over the world. The company was tearing up its 1987 budget plan and demanding immediate cost cuts and the lopping off of underperforming business units, plus an 8 percent reduction in personnel. This was the real thing, not just hopeful numbers-crunching in a planner's computer. The managers had two weeks to consider which factories to close and which product lines and business units to sell. Across the board, personnel reductions had to be made. Advertising had to be curtailed. Specific solutions and figures were demanded. Any Gillette group that was not part of the company's core businesses and did not show significant potential for near-term payoff was considered expendable.

Managers were told an urgent emphasis must be directed toward short-term cash generation. At the same time, they were told that as they looked for big savings they must not do anything that would damage the company's long-term growth prospects. Deadline for the restructuring plan was December 15, three days prior to the next directors' meeting.

Under Mockler's direction, Skelly and Swaim arranged for a $750 million line of credit with a number of banks headed by Morgan Guaranty; $215 million was drawn down by year-end. It was a new world for Gillette's financial managers. By year-end 1986, the company's net debt had swelled from $378 million a year earlier to $997 million. Standard & Poor's downgraded Gillette debt to A2, hardly a junk-bond rating and, in fact, a gentle downgrading that recognized Gillette's strong balance sheet, but it was still a new experience for a company used to A1 and nothing less.

McMorrow, working with Mockler and others, put together severance packages that were considered unusually generous by most other corporate managers. All employees laid off because of the restructuring, including the members of the G-2 flight crew who, strictly speaking, were not Gillette employees, were awarded early retirement benefits if they were within five years of becoming eligible. Employee savings plan accounts were fully vested and various other benefits sweetened. Looking ahead, a plan was crafted to give forty-six key executives—excluding CEO Mockler and President Joe Turley—two years' pay in the event of a hostile takeover, the rationale being that these players almost certainly would be fired by new owners.

A Boeing Company executive later told Tom Skelly he was surprised that Gillette's severance benefits were extended to so many. He said that Boeing managers, their hands tied by regulations related to government contracting procedures, had carried out major layoffs with far less attractive severance packages. Gillette was free to set its own standards, and the company proved that its reputation for paternalism was not misplaced. Employees who were laid off rated Gillette with a "G" for generous, by most accounts, and there was not much badmouthing of the sort so destructive to employee morale. In the difficult months that followed, many Gillette executives credited the goodwill created by the company's severance policies with playing a big part in Gillette's fast recovery from the Perelman attack.

Selling off the Losers

Derwyn Phillips had been instrumental in acquiring for Gillette many of the entrepreneurial business units that were being targeted for severe cutbacks or elimination, like Misco. He had been an advocate of buying entrepreneurial start-ups that needed a lot of nurturing but had big payoff potential down the road. It had to be painful for him to choose which of his "babies" to sell off, but he recalled the period as interesting, as well as difficult.

"We sat around a table and held up our hands and said 'that can go, that can't go,' and we negotiated goals for layoffs and plants that had to be closed down. It was crisis management effectively at work," he remembered.

Phillips noted that he came to Gillette as a top salesman from Canada who had been schooled in a period when the gospel was "build, build, build. . . . I was taught to double the business or be considered a failure." He had had to oversee a lesser restructuring process once before—in 1977, when the separate Toiletries and Personal Care divisions of Gillette North America were merged into the Personal Care Division. That move had involved some blood-letting, but nothing like this.

Fruitt credited Mockler's strong moral compass and understanding of finance with making him well suited to the unpleasant task. Terminating faithful employees was uncharted territory for Gillette, but there was no turning back. And so the meetings continued on an almost daily basis until the broad outlines of a restructured Gillette emerged. In effect, the managers had to draft an overall plan that produced the cost savings and cash flow numbers needed to design a detailed plan of action to submit to the board.

Fruitt and Bill McMorrow were chosen to make the presentation to the directors. The plan they proposed showed a new Gillette, slimmed down by the sale of the French luxury products company S. T. Dupont, the Misco computer catalog business, the Elizabeth Grady skin care salons, the Digital Learning software venture, Optimum View eye care, and the Noelle day spa retailing ventures, among others. It was proposed to delay introduction or eliminate some new products from the Paper Mate Division and Oral-B. Plans to introduce nonshaving products to Third World countries were temporarily shelved. Product lines that were doing well in one market but failing to produce in another were to be discontinued in the unprofitable markets; Braun products would be pulled back from Latin America, for example. Two or three Gillette European factories would be closed, along with various warehouses and facilities, and several Oral-B and writing instrument plants around the world. The Rockville lab building near Washington, D.C., was to be sold. Directors were told at the December 18 board meeting that the estimated savings from divestitures and layoffs would be enough to boost earnings in 1987 and beyond.

The directors signed on, putting it to management to make the proposed changes or come up with equally beneficial alternatives. Their work had to include hard numbers and had to be completed by mid-February, so that a revised 1987 budget could be approved by the directors at their February meeting and the company's books closed for 1986.

A press release issued after the December meeting did not disclose which business units would likely be sold off or factories closed, but the release did not hold back on the real shock for Gillette employees around the world. The directors announced a reduction of 2,400, or 8 percent of the Gillette workforce. That was the item that made the next day's headlines. The stock closed at an even $50.

Directors also ended conjecture by approving a one-time pretax charge of $190 million against 1986 earnings (soon revised upward to $205 million) to cover restructuring costs, mostly severance pay for laid-off workers, plus the costs of fighting the takeover. This put Gillette in the red for the fourth quarter, but as Milton Glass noted, it was good use of "the accounting profession's greatest gift to corporate America"—a one-time special write-off that clears the books and often is considered by Wall Street as beneficial. When the smoke cleared weeks later, the company's net income for all of 1986 after special charges was still in the black at $15.8 million, or $0.25 per share, though off 90 percent from 1985. It was duly noted that profit from operations before special charges was up 8 percent, to $411 million in 1986.

In a press release the company announced that it had begun to purchase some of its own shares on the open market, which was the start of a previously announced plan to buy back up to 7 million shares, or about 12 percent of outstanding company stock. The reduction of shares outstanding had the effect of improving per-share earnings.

In addition, the board announced the phasing out of oil and gas ventures in Ohio and Texas and said the company would sell off unnamed pieces of real estate. Mockler and Zeien had been the prime movers in Gillette's financial backing of several American oil and gas exploration companies during the 1970s oil crisis, when Arab suppliers cut production. The idea had been to protect Gillette against an unexpected cutoff from the raw material feedstocks needed for the company's plastic razors, cartridges, and pens. The ventures did not amount to much as the price of oil and gas slipped far below those of OPEC crisis days and curtailed incentives for American producers to add to reserves. The prospect of a shortage of supply had become remote by late 1986. So the decision to wind down Gillette's participation in oil and gas ventures was an easy one.

The budget cutters hardly paused to take a bite of Christmas candy. The next two months were a constant round of meetings and decision making, all with MSV in mind. By February 19, 1987, the fruits of their labors were spelled out as the directors sat down to an all-day meeting.

In the morning session, they approved some routine matters and some not so routine. A 2-for-1 stock split was approved. Directors were thoroughly briefed on a shareholder resolution for the upcoming annual meeting that demanded that Gillette leave South Africa, an issue that had been dogging the company for years. They advised a "no" vote to shareholders. In the afternoon, the restructuring plan, largely intact from the December 18 presentation, was discussed in detail and approved.

The rest of the winter and spring of 1987 went by in a blur. The company's managers had to implement the restructuring plan by laying off workers and selling off businesses. By year's end, the company had sold S. T. Dupont to a Hong Kong group for $53.4 million, its 40 percent interest in the Eyeworld retail spectacles business to a Japanese company for $7.5 million, and the Misco computer supplies operation to a British firm for $20 million, all of which were better deals for Gillette than estimated in the restructuring plan. Braun withdrew from Argentina, Jafra pulled out of Canada and closed eleven small overseas operations, and the Liquid Paper factory in Greenville, Texas, was sold. The Rockville Research facility was sold and personnel moved to leased quarters in nearby Gaithersburg, Maryland. Fulfilling Mockler's first sell-off decision after the Perelman buyback, the G-2 aircraft was sold for $4.4 million, and the company hangar in Bedford, Massachusetts was closed.

"We all loved that plane. I can remember Walter Hunnewell calling me up on a moment's notice and saying it's time to check on some matter in South America and could I go along? So I'd drop everything and hop into G-2 and we'd be off," recalls Milton Glass. As Gillette's travel needs grew significantly in the 1990s, the company kept to its policy of flying commercial airlines and chartering private jets only when urgently needed. With its global operations and corporate policy demanding executive travel, Gillette became one of the best corporate customers any travel agency or airline could hope for.

The rest of the 1986 restructuring plan was completed by the end of 1988. It had been a significant restructuring but far from the drastic bust-up that Perelman was thought to have had in mind.

The downsizing was made more palatable in the first months of 1987 by the upturn in both sales and profits by the company's core groups as the global economy improved and foreign exchange rates turned more favorable for Gillette. Together with savings from the restructuring that began kicking in, the company posted record earnings for the 1987 first quarter on the way to the record profits and sales for the full year in which Gillette would crack the $3 billion sales mark for the first time.

Al Zeien, who spent many hours with Eric Gleacher in a

continuing effort to place a long-term value on Gillette, told the directors as early as their March meeting that Morgan Stanley analysts thought the company's value was "considerably higher" than in November 1986. Zeien explained that it was important to focus on increasing the company's long-term prospects because the threat of takeover raids was still out there. He noted that Gleacher had had a call from "a person who could be characterized as a corporate raider" holding about 2 million Gillette shares who wanted to sell them back to the company. It was almost surely veteran raider Irwin Jacobs, who, press accounts later noted, was a leader with other arbitrageurs behind heavy post-Revlon trading that started new takeover speculation.

Zeien added that the company had received an "expression of interest from another large consumer goods company" inquiring about prospects for a friendly transaction. "Pro-active defensive measures" amounted to time well spent, he said.

The April 17, 1987, annual stockholders' meeting held at Gillette's Andover Manufacturing Center turned out to be largely sweetness and light keyed to the good news of higher earnings and share prices that had moved into the low 60s, near the $65 per share tender offer made by Perelman. Analysts who had grumbled that Gillette would never be the same again praised the company's quick turnaround. The stock split adopted that day was seen as positive. The news drowned out the lingering cries of greenmail from a few shareholders who refused to forgive Gillette for the buyback that netted Perelman about $34 million in profits.

It was too good to last.

THE UNWELCOME RETURN OF
RONALD PERELMAN

Only seven months into the ten-year standstill agreement that forbade him from making an unsolicited purchase of Gillette stock until late 1996, Perelman sent a two-page letter dated June 16, 1987, to Gillette directors, in care of Colman Mockler. It was accurately described by *Boston Globe* reporter Alex Beam as "about as welcome as a four alarm fire at the Pru."[1]

Perelman requested the consent of directors to allow Revlon to make a cash offer of $40.50 a share (equivalent to $81 before the two-for-one split that had just taken place) for all Gillette shares. It was an underhanded or ingenious move depending on one's point of view, and it confounded lawyers who thought that the language in the standstill agreement was bullet proof. By requesting permission of the directors to make another bid—and then stating publicly the price he was prepared to offer—Perelman was trying to put the company in play once again and make it impossible for Gillette to snub him. Lawyers noted that even if the Revlon bid was ignored, the move could start a bidding war from others. If Gillette was forced into the arms of even a friendly buyer by November 1987—the one-year anniversary of the Revlon buyback—the price protection clause of the buyback deal would kick in, and Perelman would receive at least an estimated $200 million. It was a clever move that, regardless of legality or morality, paved the way for further turmoil as what became known as Revlon 2 kicked off five dangerous months.

"He certainly violated the spirit, if not the law of the standstill deal," Glass said. Lawyers fretted about possible violations of law, pointing out that this was the first known challenge to the standard standstill deals common to many takeover resolutions.

Perelman asked for an answer in ten days, but he did not have to wait that long.

On June 18, Gillette released a terse statement acknowledging receipt of the Perelman letter "delivered late yesterday [June 17] without prior notice and on an unsolicited basis." The statement noted that a regularly scheduled meeting of the board of directors would take place that same day, and another statement would be forthcoming. When the second statement was released a few hours later, it said that the board had considered the unsolicited bid and refused to consent to it. For the first but certainly not the last time, the directors stated publicly, "The board is firmly of the belief that Gillette has a bright future as an independent company," a pithy slogan traceable to a remark by Joe Flom to the directors near the climactic moment of the first Perelman attack. Speaking for the directors, Mockler cited the price protection clause and suggested that Revlon was trying to put Gillette in play. Gillette lawyers had been authorized to consider and start litigation against Revlon, the statement concluded. Although Gillette did not follow through with a suit against Perelman, lawyers researched the standstill law, and the possibility of a suit remained in the Gillette defense arsenal.

Perelman fired back at once and, in a second letter to Mockler, wrote that he was "disturbed to read of your hasty rejection." He said he would waive any gain triggered by the price protection clause and said the sole reason for the bid was to combine Revlon and Gillette. He urged reconsideration.

A week later, Gillette's directors reconvened for a special session and were assured once again by Eric Gleacher and Joe Flom that they could reasonably ignore Perelman. Mockler sent a letter to Perelman, and a concurrent press release restated that Gillette had a bright future as an independent company and that this was not an appropriate time to sell. Mockler pointed out that the company had posted a 33 percent first-quarter earnings gain and expected comparable progress in the second quarter. Mockler accused Perelman of violating the intent of the November 1986 agreement and tried to make clear that Gillette would not bend: "In the circumstances, Gillette does not intend to consider or respond to any further communications from Revlon which are in violation of the agreement" and would not deal with "arbitrarily imposed deadlines."

The stage was set for a nasty and tense summer during which Gillette frequently was the most actively traded stock on the New York exchange, a worrying sign that speculators thought Gillette was back in play.

Lawyer Len Spalding, referring to many weekends lost to emergency legal work, said only half jokingly, "The summer was ruined." If not entirely in play, Gillette was being stalked.

The nastiness had already started, in fact, when Perelman publicly challenged Gillette to see for itself how solid his financing package was by contacting Revlon's lead lender, Citibank. Lloyd

Swaim did just that, and acted immediately on what he discovered. "We told Citibank that we were very unhappy with their role in Revlon's offer and that we would sever whatever relationships we had with them," Swaim told the *Wall Street Journal*.[2] That abruptly ended a twenty-two-year banking relationship. Citibank had been the number two lender in a group of nine banks put together by Morgan Guaranty to loan Gillette $750 million in revolving credit to buy back Gillette shares. At Gillette's insistence, Citibank was dropped from the group.

Citibank officials said they were sorry to lose a valued customer. But money talks, and unlike several other big banks, the powerful New York institution refused to take a pledge not to finance hostile bids against important customers. Swaim replied that Gillette was "even more disturbed that Citibank didn't have the courtesy to advise us of their role even after Revlon's letter was sent."[3] Gillette discontinued its relationship with Citibank worldwide, except in one or two instances where another international bank was not available or when Citibank provided a special local need. It was not until several years later that Gillette reestablished banking relations on a controlled basis with Citibank.

In the wake of Gillette's refusal to consider Perelman's offer, the first of several shareholder lawsuits was filed against Gillette, charging the company with stifling free and open bidding for the company in order to entrench the "lucrative, powerful and prestigious" position of Gillette officers and directors.

Irwin Jacobs, chairman of Minstar Inc. in Minneapolis, surfaced publicly and attempted a legal shakedown by disclosing that he owned a substantial but less than 5 percent stake in Gillette, having started to accumulate shares right after the Revlon buyback. He said he expected the board to act responsibly and if it did not, he would have to look at what was necessary to protect his investment.[4] Flom and Gleacher advised the directors to ignore Jacobs, whom they did not consider capable of mounting a takeover bid.

Gillette executives and directors could not ignore the speculation that Revlon 2 set off. At least this time, no ten-day gun was aimed at the company's head. As the company's stock climbed toward the 40s (it had been in the 80s, pre-split), rumors flew that Procter & Gamble, Hanson Trust, Nestlé, and Unilever, among others, might yet wind up with Gillette. The company took the position that it was not for sale, and Morgan Stanley did not make any attempt to find a friendly buyer for Gillette or any of its parts.

Morgan did keep updating its valuation of Gillette based on the company's most current strategic business plans. At the July board meeting, Gleacher reassured the directors that the goals set out in the restructuring plans for maximizing shareholder value appeared to be realistic, based on results. The directors noted the encouraging trend of improved profits and sales and decided it was time to spend some money; $9.7 million was authorized to acquire the Levi Strauss building in Mexico City and relocate Gillette's fast-growing Mexican manufacturing operations there.

Quietly, Morgan's analysts, working with Al Zeien, explored alternatives, such as a major recapitalization that could be considered in event of an all-out move by Perelman or another raider.

Not so quietly, Massachusetts governor Michael S. Dukakis, getting ready for his successful bid to win the Democratic presidential nomination for 1988, sensed political hay to be made from defending home-state companies from out-of-state raiders. He pushed through the legislature a tough anti-takeover law that he signed with maximum hoopla at Gillette's softball field adjacent to the South Boston plant. Workers cheered Dukakis when he said that he hoped the new law's delaying tactics would give Gillette more time to compete in the razor wars, rather than having to "ward off these characters who keep coming here trying to take over your company." Gillette is incorporated in Delaware but is classified as Massachusetts-based for purposes of the anti-take-over law because it is headquartered in the state, where the majority of its U.S.-based employees work at the South Boston plant, the Pru, and the toiletries plant at Andover. The legislation, drafted with the help of Leonard Spalding, became known to many as the "Gillette Law."

The most innovative defensive measure discussed that summer evolved from a serious dialogue between Zeien and Colgate-Palmolive CEO Reuben Mark. Which side started the dialogue is unclear, but for a time it looked like some form of joint venture uniting the two great rivals might happen. From Gillette's perspective, the idea was to construct a joint venture that would in effect have made Gillette so complicated in structure that it could not have been acquired without a raider acquiring parts of Colgate, too. One proposal was to form a third company that combined the international businesses of Gillette and Colgate. Other versions were discussed. Although the move was seen primarily as defensive, Zeien said there was an element of "Hey, isn't this a great business idea," including visions of synergy-related cost savings.

Zeien cooled on the idea when the talk turned to how the joint venture would be organized, with the central question of who would be in control. What if the Italian manager of the international venture said he wanted to sell more Colgate toothpaste but claimed he could not sell more Gillette blades? Who would decide on the joint venture's share of blade and razor research back at South Boston? Zeien concluded that there must be clear-cut management control from one party—the reason Gillette holds out for management control if not always majority ownership in its joint-venture blade plants in emerging nations. Gillette had to deal with the real world, not business school case studies, Zeien reasoned, and management control was the real issue, not cost savings. The talks with Reuben Mark were cut off, ending any prospect of an action that would have had a profound impact on the world consumer products business if it had become reality.

As the half-year earnings report showed, Gillette's relatively modest restructuring plan had improved profit performance without slowing growth, and the company's major businesses were doing well, including the chronically underperforming Paper Mate group. Mockler had supported retention of Paper Mate when proposals to sell it off were on the table during the post-Perelman restructuring, just as he had a few years earlier. "It seemed like everyone else wanted to sell, but Colman wouldn't do it," Joel Davis, who then was head of Paper Mate, said when he had later become senior vice president for corporate planning at Gillette. There was a price: Paper Mate had to swallow the biggest single personnel cut of any surviving group.

By midsummer 1987, Davis and Mockler were in a strong position. Profitability of the Stationery Group (successor to the Paper Mate division) had taken off and was on the way to an almost five-fold gain on much-increased sales from 1986 to 1988. The operating profit margin had been only 4 percent at the end of 1986, but it grew to 10 percent in 1987 and 15.1 percent in 1988. Davis credited the two-year surge to an exciting new product, the Flexgrip stick pen; high-margin new products that came with the completed acquisition of Waterman SA of France; and what some came to call the "predator's bonus," the sharply reduced operating costs forced by the restructuring cuts.

Revlon 3: Perelman's Last Gasp

He just would not go away. On August 17, Ronald Perelman made a third try, and Revlon 3 was both arrogant and scary. This time he asked for the consent of the directors to bid $45 in cash and $2 in securities for all Gillette shares, or $5.4 billion, getting uncomfortably close to the point where the directors could not reject the Revlon bid out of hand, standstill or no standstill.

Perelman chose to lecture the Gillette directors. He claimed that $47 represented a 45 percent premium over recent prices. "No option available to you as a stand-alone company—a recapitalization, a leveraged buyout, a share repurchase program—can compare with a combination with [Revlon]," he wrote in a letter to Gillette, in which he also scorned "general statements about a 'bright future as an independent company'" and challenged Gillette to allow shareholders to decide for themselves. He declared the time had come for "dialogue rather than threats of frivolous lawsuits" and charged the directors with treating Gillette as their "private fiefdom." He said Revlon would not accept a peremptory rejection and would leave its request outstanding until at least September 15.

The company responded to Revlon 3 with a curt suggestion that the bid "may well be another violation" of the standstill agreement but did not reply to the actual offer at once. Gillette closed the day up 3 1/4 to 43 3/8, then dropped back slightly the next. Perelman responded with a letter to Mockler declaring that he was "shocked" to read the *New York Times* headline "Proposed offer of \$47 is turned down," although that was not Gillette's precise position.[5] He demanded to know if the *Times* headline was true or false. "The time for equivocation has passed," Perelman concluded.

Gillette ignored him for the moment.

In comparison to the excitement and stock churning generated by Revlon 2, Wall Street shrugged off the \$47 offer.

"I think this indicates desperation more than sincerity; Revlon needs money," said Shearson Lehman analyst Andrew Shore. He said he thought that Gillette would emerge relatively unscathed, adding, "It isn't afraid of Perelman anymore." E. F. Hutton analyst Lynn Hyman said that Gillette stock should have moved up more sharply on the basis of Revlon's offer. She expressed skepticism that Revlon 3 would get any farther than Revlon 1 and 2.

With timing that to some observers roused suspicions of an arrangement with Revlon, Irwin Jacobs waded in with unsolicited advice to the directors: If \$47 is the best deal you can get, so be it. Take it and stop this prattling about a bright future as an independent, he advised.[6] Gillette strategists noted that the "bright future" phase was getting deep under the skin of raiders and arbs, and Ronald Perelman in particular, according to reliable reports, and decided to use it until the enemy screamed. Wall Street took only cursory notice of Jacobs' challenge.

After letting Perelman cool his heels for a week, Gillette directors met in special session August 24 and authorized a terse statement rejecting Perelman's request for an immediate response. With what struck some as inspired mischievous intent, the statement solemnly reaffirmed that the company had a bright future as an independent company, by now a Gillette refrain almost as familiar as the old "Look Sharp, Feel Sharp" ditty and, as an attention-grabber, almost as effective.

At the next Gillette board meeting, the directors heard an upbeat review of the progress of restructuring by Al Zeien and Bill McMorrow, and then turned to the Perelman request to reopen bidding. Mockler told them that a Gillette-Revlon combination made very little business sense, since only a small part of Revlon's products were sold through trade channels common to Gillette.

Eric Gleacher then candidly addressed the question of valuation in light of Revlon's $47 offer. Gillette's stock price could
exceed $47 sometime the next year, he said, and 1991 projections
of $80 to $85 per share remained reasonable. If the board decided
to sell the company, he went on, it was reasonable to ask for a
premium above $47 ranging from 20 percent in a strong market
and 50 percent in a low market. He said it was understood in the
market that Gillette is not for sale and that Morgan had not sought
out other offers.

On the downside, he said that Revlon might be willing to pay
a surprisingly high price to buy Gillette because Revlon badly
needed cash flow and was not concerned about earnings per share,
it being a private company. Gleacher and Flom advised the directors that Perelman and his aide, the former Skadden lawyer Donald Drapkin, had approached them about possible alternative
Revlon investments in Gillette. Both said they understood that the
board wanted no negotiations whatsoever at the time, and nothing
came of the contacts.

The many advisers and non-directors present then left the
room—but in a bit of comic sideplay, Gleacher reappeared to say
he had received a call from Irwin Jacobs, who threatened to start
a proxy war unless the directors went along with Revlon's request.
The Minneapolis raider had apparently called the *USA Today* col-
umnist Dan Dorfman a day or so earlier, which resulted in a
Dorfman column that ran the same day the Gillette directors met.
Dorfman's column speculated that Jacobs and another business-
man, Carl Pohlad, might start a proxy fight or make a bid for
Gillette; now Jacobs was making a belated follow-up call to
Gleacher. Don't worry about Jacobs, Gleacher said, and left the
room again. The directors talked some more and then authorized
the statement declaring that they would not consent to Perelman's
request.

When Perelman's deadline of September 15 came and went
without response, the irritated Revlon leader extended it again to
October 15. The day came, and Gillette ignored him once more.
The next day, Gillette announced sharply higher third-quarter
earnings and sales, well above the Street's expectations. Analysts
hailed the company's restructuring as a success and said that the

company's performance would make it more difficult for any raider to complete a takeover. Revlon's vice chairman, Howard Gittis, declined to say whether Revlon would make another bid.

IMPACT OF BLACK MONDAY

On October 19, 1987, Black Monday, the Dow Jones average tumbled 508 points or almost 23 percent, the worst single-day drop in more than seven decades. Gillette fell 8 3/4 points and closed that Monday at an even $24. The next day, the stock fluctuated, dropping to a low of 17 5/8, recovering later in the day to close at 24 3/4 as unknown bargain hunters bought heavily.

Al Zeien, in Germany on business, could not believe it when he called home Monday night at about 5:30 P.M. Boston time and his wife told him the market was down 500 points. "'Joyce, you mean 50.' She said 'No, 500.' I got sore at her and she said if I didn't believe her to turn on my television. I did and she was right, of course."

In Boston, Paul Fruitt took a long view, noting that the crash pretty well ended the takeover threat as raiders licked their wounds and bankers cut off their takeover funding. "We all thought it marked the end of the takeover era for the time being. It hurt to see our own stock get hit, but as the unkind jokester said, it was a little bit like watching your mother-in-law go over the cliff in your new Lincoln," Fruitt said.

A few weeks after the crash, Mockler announced a major management reorganization that had been in the works for nearly a year. The repeated Revlon takeover threats had diverted management attention to the more urgent matter of defending the company and delayed the move. The reorganization created a two-group structure that Gillette strategists considered best suited to produce the promised bright future in an increasingly globalized economy. Gillette North Atlantic, organized on a product line basis, included the company's traditional shaving, personal care, and writing instrument businesses in the slower growing, more mature markets of Europe, the United States, and Canada. Derwyn Phillips was named vice chairman and put in charge. International/Diversified, under Vice Chairman Al Zeien, included the traditional businesses in the faster-growth rest of the world, plus Braun, Oral-B, and Jafra products everywhere. The new organization anticipated the approaching early retirements of Joe Turley, then sixty-two, president and COO, and Rodney S. Mills, executive vice president of Gillette International. The post-crash period that winter provided a welcome chance to focus on something other than sharks and raiders. At last, Gillette managers were free of distractions and could concentrate on the future.

But it was not to be. The worst threat of all to Gillette's existence loomed just ahead. Unknown to Gillette officers, a trio of bottom-feeding New York speculators scooped up a million shares on October 20, the day after Black Monday, when Gillette shares sold as low as 17 5/8. Soon after the new year started, with about 6 percent of the company's equity in their pockets, the Coniston Partners would launch a proxy war that put the company's future squarely in the hand of shareholders. The stockholders would prove almost equal parts loyal and fickle, making 1988 a year of suspense.

9

The Ivy League
Predators

THE NEW YEAR had started on an optimistic note as the reorganized Gillette team began work around the world. The euphoria at the Pru about getting back to business as usual lasted exactly one week.

On January 7, 1988, the takeover wars resumed with two surprise announcements that ended a hiatus following the Black Monday market crash. Hoffman-LaRoche launched a hostile $4.2-billion bid for Sterling Drug, and E-2 Holdings, a publicly traded unit of the Beatrice Company, announced it had acquired about 5 percent of American Brands. The E-2 chief let it be known that he would launch a hostile bid if management did not agree to break up the company.

To the takeover community and especially the arbitrageurs, who had taken such a beating in the crash, it was like announcing two Texas oil gushers after a year of drilling dry holes. "The 'arbs' were back in business," author Milton Moskowitz commented in a prediction that turned out to be right on the mark.[1]

Gillette was back in the business of fending off rumors. In *USA Today* Dan Dorfman kicked in early with speculation that American Brands would seek a merger with Gillette as a defensive move to shut out E-2. Gillette stock, which had been at $30, moved up to about $33. Shearson Lehman analyst, Andrew Shore, thought he knew why. It has nothing to do with E-2, he told reporters. The gain in Gillette shares was in response to reports spreading on Wall Street that three young New Yorkers known as the Coniston Partners were loading up on Gillette shares and would try to put the company in play or gain control of the board. Old reliables Unilever PLC and Hanson Trust also surfaced in the press as rumored suitors for Gillette, but the more persistent reports were about Coniston, a partnership that invested large pools of investment money for wealthy individuals.

Paul E. Tierney, Jr., one of the three managing partners at Coniston Partners, declined comment when queried, which of course did nothing to stop the speculation. By the end of January, the Coniston rumors were more rampant than ever, and Gillette's stock was among the most heavily traded on the New York Stock Exchange. It was reported—and denied by Chairman Alan "Ace" Greenberg—that Bear Stearns, one of the arbs' favorite investment houses, had received an "open ticket" to purchase up to 3 million Gillette shares.

Finally, on February 11, Coniston filed a 13-D form with the SEC and made it official: Coniston had acquired 6,791,900 shares, or about 5.9 percent of Gillette stock at an average price of $31.50 a share. Tierney told reporters he had tried to reach Colman Mockler to ask for a meeting to discuss ways that Gillette might improve the company's performance. Yes, he said, a proxy fight for control of the board was a possibility if Mockler did not satisfy the group.

That brought out the doomsayers in full force. Andrew Shore said Gillette's days as an independent might be drawing to a close. Adding insult to injury, Ronald Perelman's name surfaced when reports speculated that Coniston was acting as a stalking horse for him and would sell the company to Perelman if it gained control.

Mockler returned Tierney's call the next day, but the two men hardly moved beyond introductions. Mockler declined to provide confidential information that Tierney wanted and put off Tierney's request for a further meeting when it became clear that Tierney had no specific agenda to discuss.

Separately, Gillette announced settlement of all sixteen shareholder lawsuits against the company stemming from the buyback of Perelman's stock in 1986, with Gillette agreeing only to pay certain legal fees "to avoid the expense and distraction" of the suits. Shareholders who sued got nothing. Joe Mullaney declared it a total vindication. It was an "end chapter one, start chapter two" sort of day.

Coniston Partners continued to lob grenades at Gillette for several days, complaining with increasing pique that the company had botched a chance to make money for shareholders when it rejected Perelman's request to make a $47 bid in September 1987. Face facts, give up the fight for independence, and sell off the company while the time is ripe, Tierney and his partners urged. The unsolicited advice grew increasingly testy as Coniston waited for the requested meeting with Mockler that they must have known the determined Gillette chief would not suffer. For its part, Gillette realized a new crisis was about to break. Paul Fruitt and his planners used the time to update the one-year and five-year strategic plans they had last reworked in detail when the company restructured following the Perelman buyback. Their new projections showed the company moving smartly toward and beyond the high shareholder values already promised, bolstering the company's consistent position that selling out to another company would be counterproductive for stockholders.

On February 19, Coniston formally announced it would launch a proxy contest to solicit shareholder votes to elect four Coniston nominees to the Gillette board at the April 21, 1988, annual meeting of stockholders. Their goal, the Coniston partners candidly explained, was to persuade other Gillette directors to put the company up for sale to the highest bidder. Gillette management realized that the election of four directors hostile to management and the removal of Mockler, one of the four directors up for re-election, would signal a fatal lack of support by shareholders and would have made it extraordinarily difficult for Gillette to carry out its strategic plan and retain its independence. The four Coniston nominees were the three partners and David H. Strassler, a former chairman of UA-Columbia Cablevision, who headed Weston Associates in Great Barrington, Massachusetts.

Gillette said it would resist "vigorously" efforts to unseat its directors and accused the Coniston Group of plotting to sell the company or rip it apart and sell the pieces. Mockler urged shareholders to sit tight, vote against Coniston, and watch the company's earnings grow.

THE CONISTON RECORD

The Ivy League predators, as the well-educated Coniston Partners were often called, were riding high that winter. The name "Coniston" came from the street in Short Hills, New Jersey, where one of the partners lived, but the partners marched to financial battle under many names. The proxy contest against Gillette was waged by a couple of limited partnerships named RB Partners and RB Associates of New Jersey (RB for razor blades), apparently controlled by another partnership named GTO, the initials of Keith R. Gollust, Paul Tierney, and Augustus K. "Gus" Oliver, the Coniston Partners. The three men invested on behalf of a maze of single-purpose U.S. and foreign investment groups linked together, often in limited partnerships, to form the Coniston Group—hence, the Coniston Partners or just plain Coniston as the takeover group was called in the press. As Gillette complained loudly and often, it was next to impossible to identify the major backers of the partners because their identities were masked in limited partnerships that preserved anonymity.

The Coniston Partners were known in the takeover trade as strategic block investors, and according to *New York Times* reporter Randall Smith, "in investment style, Coniston often acted like corporate raiders such as Carl Icahn or Irwin Jacobs."[2] Coniston typically bought 6 to 10 percent of the stock of a target company, sometimes more, and then used that holding as a strategic block—

a club to bully managements into drastic action like divesting assets or selling their company to a white knight.

The partners were the opposites in personal style from most of the rough, tough raider fraternity, and indeed, they considered the word "takeover" offensive. "We are not in the takeover business, we are in the investment business," Gollust told the *Boston Herald*.[3] Gollust, a Princeton graduate with a B.A. in mathematics, left a Wall Street investment bank to strike out on his own in 1976. He was joined two years later by Tierney, who had earned a philosophy degree at Notre Dame and gone off to Chile for two years with the Peace Corps before returning to earn an MBA from Harvard as a prelude to several short-term financial jobs. Gollust, who was forty-two at the time and clean-cut, showed up in scores of newspaper and magazine photos, in contrast with the long-haired Gus Oliver, the youngest partner, who had graduated from Yale. After earning a law degree, Oliver joined Skadden, Arps, where he learned the takeover trade from Joe Flom.

At the time of their attack on Gillette, the partners had scored major successes. Employing a code-named attack company named LA Partners—for Air Lines spelled backwards—Coniston netted a profit of $175 million at Allegis, the travel conglomerate whose core was United Air Lines. At Allegis, they parlayed a 13 percent strategic block into a power block that forced the board to fire Chairman Richard Ferris, put nonairline assets up for sale, and undertake a $2.8-billion stock buyback. Earlier, Coniston had bought up a block of Storer Broadcasting and forced the Miami company into a $2.1 billion leveraged buyout by threatening a proxy contest. That move had yielded Coniston $39 million.

THE FIGHT FOR SHAREHOLDER SUPPORT

Gillette realized that once again it faced a fight for survival. Managers put anything that could wait on hold and organized an all-out campaign to identify even relatively small shareholders and reach them in person, by phone or by letter. Gillette sent out a half-dozen mass mailings containing its 5 1/2 by 7 inch blue proxy cards (Coniston's were white) that listed Gillette nominees. Accompanying letters talked up Gillette prospects, deplored Coniston's intentions and abilities, asked why Coniston's investors were not fully identified, and urged recipients to fill out the blue proxies and return them at once.

Colman Mockler and a few other senior executives fanned out from New York to California to meet with the biggest institutional managers. They tried, often with very little success, to convince them to forego short-term gains from a forced sale of the company and support management as it enhanced shareholder value by moving Gillette to much greater long-term gains. It was an uphill battle to persuade institutional managers, given the typical institution's priority on locking in the short-term gains that usually are generated by forced sales. Still, since institutions now held 65 percent of Gillette's 115 million shares, it was imperative for Gillette to convince at least a few institutional holders to vote for management. The effort had to be made, however discouraging. Tom Skelly recalled that Mockler and Milton Glass visited six or more of the biggest shareholders (institutions voting a million or more shares) and came away without winning a single vote.

As it turned out, Gillette's margin of victory would come from the near-total loyalty of its small shareholders, many of them employees and retirees. Management recognized this loyalty and went all out to make sure the small shareholder vote was delivered. At first a team of forty executives was drafted to work with their proxy solicitor Georgeson Co. and people both inside and outside Gillette, with the goal of contacting every holder of fifteen hundred shares or more. That proved unworkable when Georgeson staffers failed to follow through in many cases. Three weeks into the battle, Gillette regrouped. Bill McMorrow organized the campaign and kept score while dozens of Gillette managers and employees started tracing shareholders and contacting them, an often convoluted process given changes of names, deaths, address changes, shares registered in street names, and the like.

Tom Skelly recalled how employees eagerly plunged into the proxy campaign. "A lot of employees had felt helpless during the

Perelman raids but now there was something they could do. They'd show up and stay all night to call stockholders if asked to do it and it paid off." Skelly noted wryly that the efforts of the rank and file paid off a lot better than a trip he and Zeien made to Chicago, where the two men made what they thought was a convincing presentation to more than a dozen Allstate Insurance investment managers, who grilled them about their optimistic projections—and after changing sides at least once, ultimately voted their 614,500 shares for Coniston. "I guess they didn't believe us," Skelly mused.

Mike Hawley, at the time vice president for operations services, had his share of calls to make, though he was one of those operating executives who was expected to keep his eye on the real world and make sure the products kept pouring out. He recalled the difficulty of getting his message through to institutional managers eager for short-term gains. They did not want to listen to appeals he and other Gillette managers made that were based on their respect for a company of flesh and blood humans who actually made and brought to market high-quality products. "Let's face it," he said. "Institutional managers could not have cared less whether we were making beans or snowshoes. They were only interested in return on investment."

A special Euro team was formed in London to contact shareholders abroad. In Boston the "700 Club" was formed to deal with stockholder inquiries, so named because the phone bank crew displayed evangelical salesmanship along with their informational duties. Understandably, shareholders were confused as the mailings and proxy cards kept coming at them in waves. How often could they vote? Was Gillette the blue card or the white one? Does this have anything to do with dividends? Canvassers repeatedly found small shareholders antagonistic to raiders, reflecting the Main Street versus Wall Street ethos that accurately reflected this proxy battle. On a more pragmatic scale, many long-time shareholders said that it did not make sense to face the capital gains taxes they would owe if the company was sold.

One Gillette caller reached a New Hampshire shareholder and was mortified to learn that the man's wife had died a few hours earlier. He started to apologize, but the man cut him short with kind words and said, "Don't apologize, we have great respect for Gillette and you have our vote."

A senior executive reached a shareholder, a widow, in Virginia one afternoon and gave her his best spiel. There was a pause. She thanked him, pledged her vote, and thinking he was calling locally rather than from Boston, changed the subject. "Was he doing anything tonight and would he like to get together with her for a drink. . . ."

Coaxing Mockler to Boast a Little

Jones Day litigators and advisers worked long hours in Washington and New York as well as Boston. Bob Profusek, the Jones, Day lawyer who drafted the overnight buyback agreement with Perelman, lived in Dallas but commuted to a room at Boston's Ritz Carlton each Monday. "At the Pru, Bob and I worked like dogs on proxy materials, the advertisements, and defensive strategies," Leonard Spalding recalled. "We'd send out to the Au Bon Pain for ham and Swiss croissants about 3 or 4 P.M. and keep on working until midnight. Then he'd go back to the Ritz and get a good meal from room service while I went home and usually settled for a peanut butter sandwich and a beer."

One of the running gags during the tense days of the proxy war was that Gillette had overlooked a perfect defense: it should have adopted a bylaw forbidding takeover by any person whose hair is more than three inches long on the day the takeover contest is started, referring, of course, to Coniston Partner Gus Oliver's shoulder-length hair. This was attributed to Skadden, Arps's Boston-based Gillette liaison, Lou Goodman.

Spalding recalls a hectic afternoon when he was working two phones simultaneously from Gillette's offices as a printer's deadline for a newspaper advertisement to shareholders loomed. One call was to a Jones, Day lawyer in Washington, who in turn was on the line with an SEC lawyer seeking final clearance on some controversial point in the ad copy. Spalding's other line was open to the public relations counsel David Duffy of Adams & Rinehart in New York, who also was working on the ad. Duffy in turn was on the line with both Spalding and the impatient printer.

Coniston's big-name proxy solicitor, Donald F. Carter of The Carter Organization, Inc., was masterminding an aggressive campaign that tried to counter every Gillette move. Boiled down, the Carter message was, "Don't believe those greenmailers at Gillette who turned down $47 a share just a few months ago in order to keep management entrenched. Don't believe their talk about a bright future as an independent company. Vote for Coniston and we'll make sure you make a good profit right away by forcing them to sell their company to the highest bidder."

Coniston concentrated on the decision makers at the major institutional holders, where the partners could count on receptive listeners. Indeed, some institutional managers, including Michael Price of the Mutual Shares Funds, were later singled out in a Gillette lawsuit against Coniston as undisclosed investors in Gillette and in other earlier targets of Coniston. The suit eventually was withdrawn. Price denied anything illegal but later ended his direct investment in Coniston.

Gillette strategists convinced Colman Mockler that he must shed his usual reserve and tell shareholders what management deeply believed: that an extraordinarily promising new razor product in the pipeline would greatly enhance shareholder value before long. Mockler, by nature averse to boasting, was reluctant to make claims for a product that, after all, did not yet exist in commercial form. He had never done that, and it did not seem quite right to him.

One executive recalls a chorus of highly paid and exasperated advisers pleading with Mockler, in effect saying, "Damn it Colman, your company is fighting for its existence, we're sitting on a great piece of news, and it's no time for holding back." Mockler agreed reluctantly. A proxy mailing to 27,000 shareholders that went out in early April under Mockler's name cited Gillette's exceptionally strong first-quarter earnings and then disclosed that the company had developed a new blade and razor that "provides a significant improvement in shaving" and would be introduced in late 1989 or early 1990. In case anyone missed the point, the

---

next day Milton Glass told analysts that the new product Mockler had mentioned would be "the biggest advance in shaving since the Trac II." Knowledgeable Gillette-watchers on Wall Street and in the media picked up on the disclosure. But Mockler's disclosure apparently did not persuade institutional managers who did not think in terms of 1989 or 1990—that was a year or two out, too far in the distance, too long-term.

The Tito Factor

The proxy fight grew increasingly bitter. When the Boston-based supermarket chain Stop & Shop ended a takeover attempt by accepting a $1.2 billion leveraged buyout deal that gave all share-holders a smart gain, Gillette was advised arrogantly by investor Michael Price to do the same. Gillette fired back with proxy mailings and newspaper ads that raised questions about Conis-ton's "intricate web of relationships . . . undisclosed investors including substantial foreign ownership," and demanded that Coniston reveal its backers and explain its relationship with the Swiss financier Tito Tettamanti, a major financial backer. Coniston refused and charged Gillette with trying to scare shareholders with veiled references to foreigners with Italian surnames.

Gillette played heavily on the purely financial background of the Coniston trio. When accused by Gillette of having no business experience, Paul Tierney replied testily that he "wasn't in this contest to become a vice president of manufacturing in the razor blade business," a remark that a decade later still angered Gillette veterans with long memories. They resented financial hotshots sneering at production managers who actually make products and get their hands dirty now and then, as one of them put it.

In a move that Milton Glass called critical to Gillette's eventual victory, a group of Gillette operations executives trooped to New York on April 14 to outline Gillette's prospects. John Symons, who had moved from London to Boston as head of the North Atlantic Shaving Group, made the most dramatic presentation, which in-cluded more on the tantalizing shaving breakthrough product that Mockler had mentioned. The optimistic reports were aimed at persuading on-the-fence proxy holders to think long term and vote for management. Glass was convinced that this was accomplished, though others at Gillette played down the meeting's impact in light of the institutional disloyalty as measured by the actual proxy results.

A week before the election, the gloves came off, and Gillette dropped a bombshell that heated up the proxy fight by several degrees—and which three months later would explode in the company's face. In response to an amended SEC filing by Coniston that disclosed the identities of certain of its investors, Gillette sued in federal district court in Boston charging that Coniston had failed to disclose information required by the SEC and had used false and misleading information in its proxy fight against Gillette. The suit further claimed that Coniston had hidden partners and supporters who operated within a complicated web of foreign and domestic companies, and that Tito Tettamanti and Michael Price, among others, were involved in various other Coniston schemes. It charged that Price, as president of Heine Securities, had accumulated 2,229,300 shares of Gillette that should have been disclosed by Coniston in its proxy filings. Gillette asked for a temporary injunction to prevent Coniston from soliciting votes but withdrew the request a few days later.

Gus Oliver called the suit a "ludicrous, last-ditch effort . . . to turn the election around." Coniston filed a counterclaim four days later alleging that Gillette had violated SEC rules by bringing the lawsuit as a means to make false, misleading, derogatory, and unsupported charges in an effort to "pollute the market in the crucial last week before the election." Responding to the counterclaim, Jones, Day's Pat McCartan told the court that Coniston had no desire to operate a business and that the three partners were only the arbitrage arm of Tito Tettamanti.

As the lawyers wrangled, Gillette placed a full-page advertisement in the *New York Times* and the *Wall Street Journal* on April 19 and in the Boston papers, the *Chicago Tribune,* and the *Los Angeles Times* the next day. Under a heading that read "The Coniston Group: Who Are They?" a complex chart prepared by Jones, Day lawyers identified more than two dozen investment groups in the

Bahamas, Grand Cayman Island, Monaco, Luxembourg, Panama, the Channel Islands, and Switzerland linked with some U.S. entities as the Coniston Group, with Tito Tettamanti listed at the top of the chart. It became known as the Tito chart and, frequently, the "infamous" Tito chart. Jones, Day lawyers had prepared it for internal use and reviewed it with the SEC in an effort to understand how Coniston was organized, but it seemed to Mullaney and others that it was too good not to share with the public. There was no real debate about publishing it. Mockler was reluctant at first but, true to his consensus style, signed on when Gillette's A team and outside consultants unanimously approved, and the chart ran in several U.S. newspapers.

Oliver expressed outrage. He claimed that the Tito chart unfairly insinuated Mafia-like connections by emphasizing Coniston's foreign holdings and served to mislead shareholders at the last second without giving Coniston time to respond.

That set the tone as shareholders filed in to the fateful annual meeting at the cavernous warehouse of Gillette's Andover, Massachusetts, plant, where a large tent had been put up. A touch of last-second puzzlement had been added that morning by the *Boston Globe*'s headline "Gillette Reportedly Has Six Suitors in Wings." The story, by Robert Lenzner, reported a "revelation" that Gillette had secretly obtained agreements from six potential suitors in an effort to fend off the Coniston takeover bid. The story appeared to contradict Gillette's consistent position that no prospective buyer had surfaced. It was attributed to a shareholder owning 1.3 million Gillette shares.

A Gillette spokesman responded that the incident sounded like "ancient history." It turned out that Lenzner had been contacted by Guy Wyser-Pratte, an arbitrageur at Prudential Bache, who had been told accurately by Al Zeien during a last attempt to win his vote that several companies had signed confidentiality agreements with Gillette. They had—but that was in 1986 and, in one case, 1987. The agreements were the standard standstill agreements that permit a prospective buyer to look at a company's confidential numbers and strategic plans but stipulate that if they do not act at the time, they must not make an unsolicited bid during the

———

ensuing two years. There was no new development, no scheme to deceive shareholders. The fact remained that no prospective buyers had showed interest in buying Gillette.

Boston's rival paper, the *Herald*, played it straight in its election-day coverage. "D-Day for Gillette" blared the page one headline on April 21. Indeed, nobody knew who was going to win this one.

The Votes Are Cast and the Suspense Builds

Len Spalding had convinced himself that all was lost and was in a glum mood as he walked through the warehouse to the tent. Treasurer Lloyd Swaim was in a more hopeful frame of mind, having just seen the final tally by Bill McMorrow, the company's unofficial scorekeeper. McMorrow's tally reflected significant last-gasp changes and indicated a 6 percent Gillette win. But the tally by Coniston's vote counter, Donald Carter, indicated that Coniston would win. When Carter encountered a Gillette adviser he knew, his greeting was, "I'll be here next year and you won't." Some of the Gillette insiders headed for a command post that Georgeson had established in a trailer at the back of the tent to wait out the tense proceedings.

As might be expected with Colman Mockler in charge, the meeting was uncommonly civil. Mockler spoke his piece and then politely introduced Paul Tierney, who gave Coniston's pitch. Both men knew their words were more for posterity than for undecided voters, because by then all but one hundred or so last-minute proxy cards had been collected. When the floor was opened for questions and comments, there was a moment of anticlimax. The first person to speak inquired about the use of animals in product testing, an old perennial at Gillette shareholder meetings, before another questioner delved into the subject on the minds of most of the large crowd—Gillette's continued existence as an independent company.

Finally, Mockler announced the election closed and added what everyone knew, that it would be at least a week before the results were known. The meeting ended shortly before noon. An

ANIMAL RIGHTS RESOLVED

An end to a costly animal rights campaign waged against Gillette for many years finally came in 1996, when Gillette reported that no laboratory animals were used to test any consumer products in the previous twelve months.

Gillette had paid a price for demanding stringent product quality and safety standards since 1986, when a group of animal rights activists infiltrated a Gillette laboratory and photographed a rabbit being tested for an anti-dandruff formulation that, ironically, was never brought to market. Although the testing was in full compliance with government regulations, various groups, most notably People for the Ethical Treatment of Animals (PETA) demanded a boycott of Gillette products. PETA activists disrupted company functions for the next ten years, demonstrating in rat and rabbit costumes and occasionally picketing the homes of Gillette executives.

Gillette spent millions in funding outside research for the development and validation of alternative test methods and in countering PETA's extravagant claims of animal torture. By 1995, the company had reduced the number of animals required to meet government-mandated product safety tests from almost 4,000 in 1986 to 388 (379 rodents and nine rabbits) and, finally, no animals at all in 1996. PETA thereupon ended its campaign.

unmarked van backed up to the Andover plant, loaded boxes containing 100,000 ballots, and headed off for the Delaware offices of the official vote tallier, Corporation Trust Co. There, in a room traditionally called the "snake pit," the official count would be made, with observers from both sides monitoring the process.

As the truck moved out to Interstate 93 to start the long drive south, news reporters swarmed after Coniston and Gillette officials.

Gillette spokesmen were noncommittal, though privately most were fairly confident of victory based on what they were hearing from the Georgeson command post. The company line was, "We're confident but we will wait for the official results."

The Coniston side didn't wait. Paul Tierney told reporters it appeared from their unofficial count of votes that Coniston had won. He warned Gillette directors not to do anything drastic pending certification of the newly elected Coniston nominees. Gillette executives were taken aback by Tierney's confidence. Mockler told reporters that Gillette disputed Coniston's claim to victory and again said that Gillette would await official word of who won. Tierney's "victory" statement made headlines the next day and discouraged some of the Gillette faithful in the hinterland, though Wall Street played down the victory claim and, with Gillette management, settled in to wait for the official results.

Mockler wanted more reassurance and got on the speakerphone with Georgeson's vote monitor, Maria Weisensee— a woman who had struck Gillette officials as streetwise and savvy. "Honey," she told Mockler in her heavy Bronx accent, "this election is over and you won." Still, there were anxious days to pass before the official results were known.

Vote counting was slow going in the Delaware snake pit as Corporation Trust counters had to cope with a ton or so of blue and white cardboard proxies, many of them outdated and invalid. In a proxy contest, only the latest vote counts. Shareholders are free to change their mind until the last minute, and many do just that. Thus, pro-vote Gillette proxies received in early April may be canceled out by a card received a week later and then canceled out again. The final date on the proxy card is the determining factor. After invalid cards were discarded, it turned out that 84 million of 115 million eligible shares were cast—less than both sides had expected.

Gillette's vote monitor at the snake pit told Mockler that even though the final vote was not yet in, prospects for a narrow victory looked good. Finally, on May 2, both sides were alerted to hook into a three-way conference call at 10 A.M. the next morning to hear the final tally reported from Corporation Trust in Delaware. McMorrow with several others crowded into Joe Mullaney's office to hear the verdict. As he tells it, "A man's rather phlegmatic voice came on, and the first thing he said was that 84 million votes were cast. Then he said Gillette won 44 million—and we knew we had won." As the tension broke, McMorrow ducked next door to call

Colman Mockler. The boss had escaped to Bermuda with his wife for a few days' rest.

Remembering that Mockler was one of the nominees up for re-election, McMorrow said, "Good morning, Mr. Chairman. . . ." McMorrow noted that Mockler was subdued in response, but obviously relieved.

A postmortem revealed that the margin of victory came from small shareholders, whose 20 million votes split 19 million for Gillette and only 1 million for Coniston. By contrast, about 40 million of the 64 million votes cast by institutions backed the Coniston nominees.

McMorrow had expected at least 95 million votes to be cast. Pondering the smaller vote, he and others at Gillette realized that most of the arbitrageurs who were still holding Gillette stock—stuck with it, from their point of view—had leaped at the chance to sell during late March and early April, when Gillette shares peaked as high as 49 one day. The share prices had temporarily soared because of unfounded rumors that a Japanese cosmetics giant and then Philip Morris had expressed interest in acquiring Gillette. With their stock sold and no stake in Gillette any longer, the arbs had not returned their proxies, even though they were eligible to vote as holders of record on March 7, the deadline for voting rights. This was one time that Gillette was grateful to the generally hostile arb community. "To their eternal credit, the arbs didn't meddle in the affairs of a company they no longer were involved with," said Skelly.

Coniston's Gus Oliver vowed the battle was not over. At the very least, he said, Coniston would press ahead with its lawsuit charging Gillette with misleading shareholders. He hinted at demanding a recount, obviously surprised with the final tally, because Donald Carter had been telling the partners all along that Coniston had won. Carter apparently had miscounted, perhaps stopping his tally too soon and missing last-minute switches or perhaps double-counting major institutional blocks.

Postmortems were consistent. Neither side believed that the Tito ad was a deciding factor, though Gus Oliver thought it showed desperation on the part of Gillette and made Coniston

Right: Succeeding the famous diamond-and-arrow trademark as the company's symbol was the Gillette omnimark introduced in 1970.

The Gillette Company

Nothing will ever be attempted if all possible objections must be first overcome

Above: Vincent C. Ziegler, a salesman from the Midwest, was chairman of Gillette from 1966 until his retirement at the end of 1975. During his tenure, sales of the company more than tripled. He died in 1979.

In 1921, Max Braun founded a machine shop in Frankfurt, Germany, that grew into the modern Braun AG. In 1948, he invented an electric shaver that soon became the European leader and was the major reason Gillette acquired Braun AG in 1967.

Dieter Rams, a well-known adherent to the German Bauhaus Movement of functional design, served as Braun's chief designer for almost 40 years.

Stephen J. Griffin was elected president of Gillette in 1976. His long career included a stint as chief of Gillette's international group when overseas sales began to gain great momentum.

William G. Salatich, then head of Gillette North America, hams it up in the early 1970s with one of the world's most famous personalities—heavyweight boxing champion Muhammad Ali.

If the shave bites, he'll bite right back.

Hear Telly exclusively on MCA Records.

No guy loves a blade that nicks and scrapes. Especially if he's used to injector blades. Well, now meet Gillette Twinjector® twin injector blades. As safe as any single injector blade. But they shave close, smooth and comfortably. Because, for one thing, *They fit your injector razor.* Twinjector blades have rinse slots. To reduce clogging. And they fit your present injector razor. Would we give you a rough time?

The Gillette Twinjector® Shave. Beautiful, baby.

Tough-guy television actor Telly Savalas extols Gillette Twinjector blades in an ad from the late 1970s featuring his signa-ture growl, "Beautiful, baby."

Above: Through its Toni division, Gillette was for many years a major sponsor of the Miss America Pageant. Miss America 1971, Phyllis George, is pictured in an ad for the company's Adorn and White Rain hair care products.

Left: In 1979, Gillette introduced the Paper Mate EraserMate pen, the first ball-point pen with truly erasable ink.

Right: Colman M. Mockler, Jr., was the "quiet man from finance" who headed Gillette for 15 of the company's most tumultuous years.

Below left: Outdoor advertising for Gillette blades in China.

Below right: Gillette capitalized on the Japanese passion for baseball in this promotional display for the Atra shaving system, which is called Actas in Japan.

Above: A Japanese ad for Liquid Paper correction fluid.

Left: Bette Nesmith Graham, founder of Liquid Paper Corporation, created an industry when she concocted typewriter correction fluid at her kitchen table. Gillette purchased the company from her in 1979.

Left: Matching a global brand with a global sport, Gillette has been a principal sponsor of World Cup soccer since 1970.

Far left: In 1983, Gillette Chairman Colman Mockler, Jr., cut the ribbon at the official opening of Gillette's first joint-venture blade manufacturing plant in China.

Left: Outspoken former London policeman John W. Symons, who headed first European and then North Atlantic operations at Gillette during the stormy 1980s, championed the introduction of the Sensor shaving system.

The tombstone ad that appeared in *The New York Times* and *The Wall Street Journal* on November 14, 1986, officially started the takeover raid by Ronald O. Perelman's Revlon Group.

Financier Ivan Boesky pleaded guilty to insider trading on the same day that Perelman launched his first bid for Gillette. Boesky's woes played right into the hands of Gillette strategists fighting off Perelman.

Ronald Perelman, the rough and tough New York raider who was public enemy number one at Gillette during the takeover wars of 1986 and 1987.

Investment banker Eric Gleacher was just as tough a street fighter as Perelman, and he was on Gillette's side of the battle.

Above: Famed takeover lawyer Joseph Flom of Skadden, Arps, Slate, Meagher and Flom, New York, was in Gillette's corner during the takeover wars, pitted against old friend Ronald Perelman.

Right: Massachusetts Governor Michael S. Dukakis, with Gillette President Joseph F. Turley peering over his shoulder, tells a crowd of workers outside Gillette's South Boston factory that he will introduce tougher anti-takeover legislation.

Above: Gillette Senior Vice President Joseph E. Mullaney, left, testified in June 1988 at a hearing before the Anti-Takeover Commission at the Massachusetts State House. Mullaney forcefully criticized hostile raiders and their tactics.

Below: The infamous "Tito" chart that Gillette published in several national newspapers just before the climax of the proxy fight with the Coniston Group. The chart later imperiled Gillette when a federal judge said that the ad may have misled stockholders.

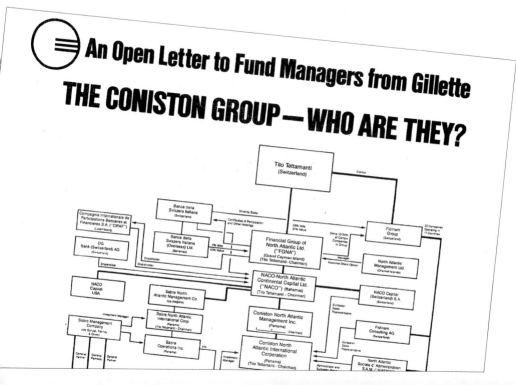

Above: The Coniston Partners: Augustus "Gus" Oliver, Keith Gollust, and Paul Tierney.

David L. Ryan/The Boston Globe

Below: The *Boston Herald* found the Gillette versus Coniston fight irresistible fodder for its cartoonists and layout staff.

TUESDAY SPECIAL

BUSINESS

GILLETTE REGULARS vs CONISTON RAIDERS

COLMAN MOCKLER **JOSEPH TURLEY** **LAWRENCE FOURAKER** **HERBERT JACOBI**

In Gillette's corner...

Gillette Co. is an 87-year-old Boston personal care company that dominates the worldwide razor blade business with outlets in more than 200 countries. The management directors' slate says that increased profit from operations, new products and spending reductions can boost Gillette's annual growth by more than 12 percent for each of the next five years.

KEITH GOLLUST **PAUL TIERNEY** **AUGUSTUS OLIVER**

Not pictured: Director candidate David Strassler

...the Coniston team

Coniston Partners, a New York investment group with a 6 percent stake in Gillette, say they seek to "maximize shareholder value" for Gillette's 27,000 shareholders by promoting a slate of directors who will entertain all offers for the company.

Gillette buffeted in proxy battle

By DAVID CALLAWAY

THE Gillette Co. took a blow yesterday from its fifth-largest shareholder. The California Public Employees Retirement Fund, which holds sh.......

been the wild card in the fight since it began in mid-February.

Almost none are talking and many have decided to withhold a decision until Thursday's 10 a.m. deadline.

'We think

Street arbitragers and other professional investors who hold roughly 20 percent of the shares.......

lette's management failed when it elected to pay.......

Right: Under the steady leadership of its chairman, Colman Mockler, Jr., Gillette fought off several hostile takeover attempts to remain a vigorous, independent company.

Below: The front page of the *Boston Herald* on April 21, 1988, said it all. On this day stockholders decided the outcome of the proxy fight for control of Gillette waged by the Coniston Group against Gillette's management, led by Colman Mockler, Jr.

WORLD NEWS

HIJACKERS OF KUWAITI JET GO FREE

Shiite Hijackers of a Kuwaiti jetliner, yesterday walked away scot-free: Page 3

WEATHER

TODAY: Possible rain
High: 50s.
TOMORROW: Sunny with high of 50 to 55.
Details on Page 34

TODAY'S TV: Page 59

WITH MONTREAL

prospect of falling behind
the Canadiens, stormed
night, 4-3: Back Page

Thursday April 21, 1988

Boston Herald

Telephone (617) 426-3000 · · · 25 Cents 35¢ BEYOND 30 MILE ZONE

D-Day for Gillette

Shareholders to decide proxy fight

By DAVID CALLAWAY

THE FATE of Boston's largest manufacturing company and its thousands of workers will be decided today in an Andover warehouse where Gillette Co. shareholders will vote whether to back a corporate raiders' bid to oust four company directors.

Long careers of many top Gillette executives could fly out the window if Coniston Partners wins its hard-fought 2-month-old proxy battle, one that experts rate as too close to call.

"Like any election, we won't know the results until the ballots are counted." said Gus Oliver, one of the three Coniston partners. "The indication is that we have a lot of

support. My own impression is that there is not a lot of people sitting on the fence."

About 1,000 shareholders are expected to attend today's meeting and Gillette proxy solicitor John

Wilcox said many large shareholders will wait until the last moment to make a decision.

"Gillette has been the underdog all along," said Wilcox, a solicitor at Georgeson & Co. Inc. in New York. "It's been an uphill fight, but we're certainly

Turn to Page 45

Raisin'
the roof

Warren Buffett, the Sage of Omaha
and possibly America's most successful and famous investor, knew a
good thing when he poured $600
million into Gillette and became the
company's largest stockholder in
1988. This was just before the company's stock began a long, strong
increase in value.

look sinister. Both sides agreed the loyalty of small shareholders was critical. The Coniston Partners had given up trying to solicit small shareholders a few weeks into the campaign, when the trio encountered nothing but rock-solid support for Gillette and often found themselves being harangued by employees or company pensioners as opportunistic outsiders before they could get a word in. Predictably, neither side was happy with their press coverage. Gillette officials were particularly upset with what they considered kid-glove treatment of Coniston by the New York financial press. Coniston felt that the press was sloppy and sometimes offensive, singling out specific long feature articles in the *New York Times* and *Barron's* magazine. The articles led Gus Oliver to comment many years later that he "almost sympathizes now with [former Vice President] Dan Quayle and that's saying a lot."

Oliver pointed out that Coniston would have preferred a process less confrontational and costly than a proxy fight as a means of changing Gillette management but from the start knew that there was no chance of Gillette cooperation. Years later, Oliver said that the group saw great value in the company, with blades and razors as a platform supporting personal care products and other business, but that he had no idea just how very great that value would become.

Oliver also said that despite Gillette's claims, Coniston never intended to sell off pieces of the company, except perhaps for Paper Mate; the partners insisted throughout the battle that their strategy was to put the company up for sale and install new management that would exploit the existing franchise more aggressively. The strategy would have worked, according to Oliver, if some viable party had expressed interest in buying Gillette. Despite many rumors to the contrary, Oliver said Coniston never talked to Ronald Perelman about buying Gillette. Perelman encouraged such speculation with comments like one he made at Drexel Burnham's annual "Predators Ball" in 1988, where the Revlon chief reportedly said he hoped Coniston would win, and if so, he would think about making a bid.[4]

Gillette insiders agreed that the lack of any buyer interest in the company was a great boost for management because it put

Coniston's strategy in doubt. To Eric Gleacher, "They simply did not recognize that there were no other buyers, that this company had been shopped around with no takers." Joe Mullaney may have put it best. "We were sort of in play, but without other players."

There were some nuisance offers to deal with, of course. For example, Gillette received a form letter from an international broker named Jaa Je Ess, who declared he knew of someone who might be interested in buying Gillette. Gleacher testified that it was not regarded as a serious offer when it was cited in court proceedings much later.

When it finally became clear that Gillette had won the proxy fight, Colman Mockler sent a message addressed to every Gillette employee, noting that their support as shareholders was a key factor in the victory. He thanked them for their "even more important performance in carrying out the work of the company in the face of uncertainty and distraction." And then, just so nobody would miss the point that he was pleased, Mockler declared a special holiday of one day off with pay for all employees throughout the world.

Gillette's joy at winning was tempered by the realization that nine of their ten biggest institutional holders voted with Coniston, including the California Public Employees Retirement Fund, the College Retirement Equities Fund, and the New York State Common Retirement System. Gillette executives were bitter about their lack of loyalty and did not readily forgive. A former Gillette manager later called the institutional defectors "shortsighted. These guys were not investors, they were holders of stock who would sell Gillette or anybody else down the river for a $3 short-term gain." Only Sun Banks of Florida among the top ten went with Gillette, persuaded by Milton Glass in the end that prospects for a quick, sure gain were overcome by Gillette management's argument that they should be given a chance to produce superior long-term value. Citicorp, parent of Citibank, which Gillette had angrily cut off from further business less than a year earlier, voted its 754,000 shares for Coniston.

To be sure, enough shares were voted for Gillette by small- and medium-sized institutions to make the difference when combined with the solidly loyalist individual shareholder block. It took a lot of last-minute work. A critical late reversal was engineered by Glass just a few hours before the vote, when he convinced an executive he knew at a major Midwestern consumer products company to countermand a pro-Coniston vote by a professional money manager who ran the company's pension fund. That one switch swung nearly a half-million votes out of the Coniston column to Gillette, and there were similar countermands in the final twenty-four hours as Gillette executives leaned on personal contacts at other corporations holding Gillette shares in their pension funds. These late reversals may have made the difference between winning and losing, according to Lloyd Swaim.

TITO TETTAMANTI, REVISITED

The Tito ad came back to haunt Gillette in a big way. It turned out to be the key factor in a no-jury trial heard by federal judge Mark L. Wolf, during which Coniston lawyers tried to prove their April 19 counterclaim against Gillette, claiming that Gillette had misled shareholders.

Judge Rya Zobel had been scheduled to hear the trial, but in a possibly fateful move, she recused herself at the last instant when she read the Coniston brief and realized Colman Mockler's key role as the last man to approve the April 19 advertisement. Mockler was a Fellow of the Harvard Corporation; she was a Harvard Overseer.

Gillette lawyers considered Coniston's case fairly weak. During the trial that started in late June, Coniston lawyers seized upon Gillette's alleged desperation that supposedly led to untrue claims of Tettamanti controlling Coniston and innuendo that the Swiss financier might be involved in arms deals or drugs. When Tettamanti was deposed by Gillette's lawyers, he had proved nimble. Putting his name at the top of the infamous chart, he said, was a "perfidious way to scare" stockholders into believing that "a very bad Swiss guy" is trying to put his hands on an important company like Gillette. He indignantly brushed off innuendo about drugs and arms shipments. "Frankly, I'm more than willing to accept that if you go into the ring you can be hit, if you are in boxing, but there are certain things that are not allowed." He claimed that he was a passive investor and did not interfere with Coniston investment decisions, no matter what the chart showed or papers unearthed by Gillette suggested.

Private detectives hired by Gillette to find out what they could about Tettamanti and the Coniston Group had turned out to be singularly unsuccessful, perhaps counterproductive. Coniston lawyers, who called the Miami-based investigators "Private Eye" in court documents, obtained copies of their reports to Boston and at the trial threw the reports back in Gillette's face. Their reports had concluded that "Dr. Tettamanti is well-known and respected in financial circles and is not associated with any known unethical or illegal practices." The same reports noted that detectives sent to Chile and the Caribbean had looked into the practices of Gollust, Tierney, and Oliver and, "with the exception of minor traffic violations," had found no damning evidence. Gillette was desperate and had overreached, the Coniston lawyers told Judge Wolf.

The case, argued on behalf of Gillette by Jack Newman of Jones, Day, effectively countered many of Coniston's allegations, such as the last-minute charge from the Prudential Bache arbitrageur Guy Wyser-Pratte in the *Boston Globe* about supposedly secret confidentiality agreements that stopped would-be bidders from going after Gillette. But unfortunately for Gillette, Judge Wolf focused on the April 19 ad with the Tito chart. The advertisement had been a pet project of the Gillette litigation team, especially Joe Mullaney, and Gillette's proxy strategists in general. Jones, Day had assured Mullaney that the chart in final form was safe to run; Pat McCartan noted years later that Judge Wolf notwithstanding, he believed that the chart was an effective piece of work that was 100 percent accurate. "I loved that chart," Eric Gleacher said. Though in hindsight a few Gillette people claimed that running the Tito ad was risky, there is no evidence that at the time anyone said to stop or even slow down.

At any rate, Judge Wolf had the only opinion that counted.

Once again, Gillette's world was turned on its head July 6, when Judge Wolf rapped his gavel and, after a few opening remarks, declared that he wished to avoid further suspense regarding his opinion, which he said would take several hours to express. "I will tell you that I am persuaded that the Coniston Group has proved that the April 19 advertisement [the Tito chart] violates SEC Rule 14a-9 [securities law prohibiting false and misleading statements]."

Gillette's in-house lawyer, Bill Mostyn, was in the courtroom using a bulky cellular phone to deliver a real-time account of the opinion back to Gillette colleagues. As he remembers the scene, there was a disruption as several reporters and interested observers dashed out of the chambers to phone their offices, causing Judge Wolf to comment that their exit was premature because they would miss the rest of his opinion. Indeed, the judge went on to say, it appeared that Coniston also had violated federal securities law. Evidence suggested to him that Tito Tettamanti might be one of several controlling persons of the RB partnerships, he said, and failure to disclose this may have violated securities laws. Moreover, Judge Wolf declared that the rest of Coniston's claims against Gillette were unconvincing—but the April 19 ad could not be overlooked, and Gillette could not be excused for running it. The rest of the morning was given over to how Judge Wolf arrived at his decision. Finally he ended by saying he would next consider Gillette's charges against Coniston and set a pre-trial hearing for the coming week. He caught everyone's attention when he suggested, almost casually, that he might void the proxy results and order another proxy battle, or perhaps even order a special meeting of shareholders, with Archibald Cox or someone of that stature as a monitor. Judge Wolf was thinking big thoughts.

Despite the qualifiers, it was a stunning blow to Gillette.

Although most of the Gillette crew were astounded by Judge Wolf's decision, there were straws in the wind at the time that should have been a warning of danger. The day before the trial was to begin, for example, Judge Wolf suddenly called Colman Mockler and Joe Mullaney to his chambers for several face-to-face meetings with the three Coniston partners. The Partners told Judge Wolf that they would be happy to settle then and there if Gillette management would agree to hire another investment banker and try to sell the company. Mullaney recalled the judge's annoyance when Mockler dismissed the idea, the judge apparently not understanding that Coniston was seeking to win in a settlement what they had lost in the proxy contest. Pat McCartan was not surprised. ". . . I had bad vibes about this judge after sitting in on part of the trial," he said.

Gillette had no time to sulk. Judge Wolf scheduled phase two of the trial to start in about a month, after his vacation.

A COSTLY GOOD RIDDANCE

After Judge Wolf's decision, the old speculation hit Wall Street about Gillette looking for a friendly buyer to end its nightmare and avoid another proxy contest. As usual, many names were mentioned, but no bidders surfaced.

In a sort of political sideshow, both Joe Mullaney and Coniston's Paul Tierney appeared before a Massachusetts anti-takeover legislative committee in late June to defend their positions on corporate takeovers. Mullaney had always mixed easily in the Irish-American-dominated politics of Boston and Massachusetts and often was the company's spokesman on political matters, but the Boston press found it intriguing when that least likely of political backslappers, Colman Mockler, showed up at an unrelated reception hosted by the state senate president, William "Billy" Bulger, at Anthony's Pier 4 restaurant. Bulger represented South Boston, home of Gillette's largest factory.

Gillette was unconcerned about takeover law at this point. The company's focus was entirely upon the upcoming trial and the likelihood of a new proxy fight. The Jones, Day lawyers thought the judge most likely would order a new election of directors, whatever he decided on the merits of the case. The Coniston partners also thought the judge was likely to order a new election but not for several months and not until he had heard the Gillette arguments, which, he had already hinted, showed some merit. They realized that any finding against Coniston by the judge would have to be noted in future Coniston proxy materials. Legal costs were mounting. Another proxy contest would be costly, and there was no assurance of a Coniston win.

Coniston blinked first. On July 11, Gus Oliver told Joe Flom, his old boss at Skadden Arps, that he wanted to discuss a settlement involving a buyback; nothing came of the first proposals because Gillette would not consider any buyback idea that did not include all shareholders. After the court rejected Coniston's request for an immediate new election, Oliver approached Flom again, and this time Flom was ready: he suggested the outlines of a complex "put rights" buyback that eventually formed the settlement.

Four days later Flom, Gleacher, and Andrew Liu met with the three partners, and there followed on the weekend twenty-four hours of back-and-forth phoning among Mullaney, Oliver, and Mockler. Finally, on the evening of July 20, a deal was struck. Flom and Mullaney spelled it out for the directors on July 21: Gillette would buy one of every seven shares held by all shareholders of the company at $45 a share, on condition that Coniston drop its lawsuit and buy no more shares nor seek control or influence the company for three years. Gillette agreed to lift standstill agreements for nine signees, which at any rate were to expire in November of that year. Technically, it was a put rights dividend deal in which each shareholder could either sell one of each of seven shares held back to the company or sell the put rights for cash. Total cost to the company was $720 million, or the cost of buying back 14.3 percent of its outstanding shares. For the Coniston Partners, it meant a profit of about $35 million. Al Zeien told the directors to think in terms of a large cash dividend: Is it financially viable? He said that for Gillette it meant an increase in debt from $1.1 billion to about $1.8 billion, which put the company into a negative debt-to-equity position at the end of the year. Zeien and Gleacher said the deal was doable, financing could be arranged, and there would be no material effect on the company's ability to pursue its strategic business plan. Colman Mockler emphasized that the put rights proposal was consistent with the company's intention to accelerate the stock repurchase program.

Nobody at Gillette was happy at the prospect of walking away from a legal fight its lawyers were convinced it could win. But Gillette's leaders did not need to be reminded that there are no sure things in dealing with the courts. Do it, authorize us to complete this deal, Gleacher and Flom advised directors. Put a two-year nightmare behind you and move aggressively toward that bright future, without any more outside disruption.

The directors were receptive and authorized further talks but expressed strong objection to paying the $6 or $7 million in legal costs that Coniston had incurred and demanded Gillette pay for. Paying off Perelman's legal debts in 1986 still bothered some of them. After a week of negotiations that proceeded along these lines, an oral agreement on the buyback was reached late Saturday, July 30, subject to board approval. In the end, Coniston gave up its demand that Gillette pay its legal expenses.

On July 31—"Sunday, naturally," said Len Spalding, who had seen another summer disappear into seven-day work weeks—the Gillette board of directors approved the deal. There was one more detail. The wary Gillette team did not trust Judge Wolf to go along with the settlement and dismiss the case, because he had expressed doubts when advised of this possibility when contacted by phone at his Martha's Vineyard vacation house. So Newman dispatched a Jones, Day legal aide, Sally von der Hoya, to the Vineyard to deliver a thick sheaf of documents providing legal precedent for such dismissals. After a long, hot day that included getting stuck in the fog and barely escaping back to the mainland on the last flight from Edgartown, von der Hoya returned, mission accomplished.

When the $720 million buyback was announced the next day, it was generally interpreted as Gillette getting off a sharp hook with minimal damage. Wall Street was surprised and, as always, skeptical: "The stock is still basically in play" an analyst at Josephthal & Company said, speaking for many so-called experts. This time they were wrong. Gillette was as safe as it could ever be from predators.

There were human casualties. For Colman Mockler, the trial and Judge Wolf's determination that Gillette had misled its shareholders was as difficult to take as anything that the Revlon crowd had thrown at him. He was a proud man and internally incapable of shrugging off assaults on his integrity. Just how great a toll the two years of fighting for Gillette's corporate life took on Colman Mockler's own life will always be a matter of conjecture.

IV

FAST TRACK
TO
GLOBAL
LEADERSHIP

10

WARREN BUFFETT
COMES
ABOARD

THE OUT-OF-COURT settlement that rid Gillette of Coniston put the company in an unaccustomed position. To finance the repurchase of 15.6 million shares, the company was forced to borrow heavily and wound up 1988 with stockholder equity at a negative $85 million, compared with plus $599 million a year earlier. In short, the company was highly leveraged and owed a lot of money. Colman Mockler assured shareholders the debt load was manageable given Gillette's ability to generate cash and its continued access to unused lines of credit, and he noted that the financial rating agencies, Moody's and Standard & Poor's, had retained the company's investment grade ratings.

Moreover, Gillette's business fortunes clearly had been on the upswing throughout the tumultuous years of Revlon 1, 2, and 3 and the Coniston attack, making prophets of those who had promised skeptical shareholders that Gillette had a bright future as an independent company. While the lawyers and proxy fight managers held center stage in 1988, the company's operating managers produced an overall sales gain of 13 percent to $3.6 billion, with earnings up more sharply on the strength of fast-rising foreign profits.

Mockler reported to shareholders that strong performance came from broadly based geographic and product line gains, and also reflected cost savings from the company's 1986–87 restructuring. Several product lines outside wet shaving reported strong sales, with notable gains registered by Braun dry shaving and small appliance products outside Europe, especially in Japan. International growth, particularly in Latin America, was producing big numbers. There were good results both at home from Atra Plus and abroad from its international twin, Contour Plus, and other "Plus" shaving products. Worldwide sales of Gillette double-edge blades continued their gradual decline, but that was welcome news, the result of Gillette's relentless campaign to upgrade double-edge blade users to twin-blade systems. Even with the decline, the company retained its traditional world leadership in the double-edge blade form invented by King C. Gillette.

And yet that debt-heavy balance sheet rankled. For the first time in memory, Gillette suddenly had to cope with negative equity, which forced a strict discipline in the use and control of funds. It was awkward timing, because by the spring of 1989, Gillette was committed to introduction "within the next year, of an innovative shaving system whose superior performance represents a significant advance in consumer satisfaction." That comment in the 1988 annual report referred, of course, to the promising new product that Mockler had cited in less definitive terms a year earlier in a letter to shareholders urging them to stick with Gillette in the proxy battle with Coniston. Gillette had to deliver as it entered the costly final stretch prior to launching an important new product, when capital spending requirements increase. It was financially manageable but distressing for Mockler, given his caution regarding debt, a perception sensed by one of America's smartest investors as he scrutinized Gillette's annual report at his home in Omaha.

"I'LL PROPOSE MYSELF"

Gillette Director Joseph J. Sisco remembered clearly his third-man role between Colman Mockler and the famed investor Warren E. Buffett. A Middle East and South Asia specialist who was the highest-ranking career diplomat in the State Department when he served as undersecretary for political affairs in President Gerald Ford's administration, Sisco had negotiated the Egypt-Israel ceasefire of 1970. He later served as chancellor and as president of American University in Washington, D.C., and after retirement started his own management consulting company, Sisco Associates. He knew both Buffett and Mockler well, having served as a director of Gillette since 1979 and as a director of GEICO Corp., a casualty insurance company controlled by Buffett.

When the phone rang at Sisco's home one evening in spring 1989, Warren Buffett was on the line, calling from Omaha. Buffett had been sitting in his favorite reading chair perusing annual reports the way some men read the sports section of newspapers, poring over details indicating strengths and weaknesses in company balance sheets like others look for runs and errors in baseball box scores. Gillette's 1988 annual report caught his attention. "It was my thought that they might be interested in a big investment in their shares because they had used up all their capital in repurchasing shares," Buffett later recalled as he explained how he came to add Gillette to the string of blue-chip investments owned by Berkshire Hathaway Inc., his publicly owned holding company. Buffett said he did not know anyone at Gillette well, but it struck him at once that Gillette seemed like a conservatively managed company and its managers probably were not comfortable being so stretched financially. And then he saw Joe Sisco's name as a director. He remembers that he thought, "Well, I'll just call Joe and as my friend Katharine Graham [former *Washington Post* chairperson] used to say about guests sometimes, I'll propose myself." A moment later he was on the line with Sisco asking him to approach Colman Mockler and find out whether Gillette would welcome an investment proposal from him. "I told Joe, look, if they have an interest, fine. If they don't, that's fine too." Sisco readily agreed to Buffett's proposal, assuring him that Mockler would get along well with him.

As Sisco tells it, "I contacted Colman right away and it was clear to me that Warren's proposal struck him positively." He called Omaha back and told Buffett about Mockler's reaction, adding, "I think you two fellows ought to get together." After that, Sisco stepped back to watch events unfold.

Buffett said he did not recall any "Bingo, let's do the deal now" sort of response when he first contacted Mockler the next day, but he "felt there was an interest." Mockler informed Zeien, Mullaney, Skelly, and a few others about Buffett's interest. The men agreed that it would be desirable to have a big infusion of capital from a friendly investor like Buffett but only on terms that could be defended as fair and reasonable to all shareholders. They agreed there was no need for a white knight deal because the company was in no need of rescue. Mockler started the ball rolling but cautiously, as was his wont.

The first face-to-face meeting between Mockler and Buffett took place a few days later in Omaha as Mockler, Skelly, and Mullaney were returning to Boston from a business trip to Mexico. Buffett remembers shaking hands with Skelly and Mullaney as they alighted from a chartered plane parked away from the main terminal and then driving Mockler in his aging car to the Omaha Press Club, a favorite haunt, for lunch and talk. This was a "size each other up" sort of meeting, Buffett said. He recalled that the Press Club was mostly empty as they sat down to the sort of no-frills meal both men enjoyed—hamburgers and Coca-Colas. "We did have some sort of exotic dessert, I remember, a combination of ice cream with candy bars on top and a lot of chocolate sauce," Buffett said. "We hit it off, a couple of Midwestern boys. I liked him, the chemistry was good. It was like meeting a girl, it didn't take five minutes. And I could tell he was very able." Buffett said that he told Mockler that if Gillette was interested, he would really like to invest in the company. He suggested a preferred stock purchase, Buffett said, probably because he was in a mode of making preferred deals at the time, having recently concluded such deals with USAir and Champion International. "I do know that I told him 'any amount between $300 million and $750 million, and he could pick the number, whatever he felt was appropriate.'" Then Buffett drove Mockler back to the terminal to rejoin Mullaney and Skelly, where he found the two men somewhat annoyed because they had tried in vain to find a good steakhouse but had been forced to settle for hamburgers, which they held in less esteem than their boss and his host.

Back in Boston, Mullaney called Gillette lawyer Len Spalding and told him to start work on a preferred stock deal.

The minutes of the June 15 directors' meeting a few days later note that "Mr. Mockler introduced the subject of a possible investment in the company by a premier long-term investor, whom he identified." Mockler told the directors that a convertible preferred deal was likely but stressed that he had not discussed any terms with the investor. He reviewed the positive aspects of the investment, such as cleaning up the balance sheet and freeing capital for investment. He obliquely referred to the takeover raids of the past. The investment, he said, "would support the belief that Gillette can carry out its strategic plans without undue concern for the disruptions and distractions of the past few years." The directors authorized Mockler to move ahead and negotiate a convertible preferred deal, subject to their final approval.

Mockler asked Gillette CFO Tom Skelly and Treasurer Lloyd Swaim to alert J. P. Morgan/Morgan Guaranty Bank, which had replaced Morgan Stanley as the company's lead investment banker, but said not to reveal the identity of the potential investor. That raised concern among the investment bankers, who were leery of Gillette doing a deal on possibly onerous terms just to clean up the balance sheet. A deal without too many strings attached would be okay, the Morgan bankers advised, but Gillette did not need to act out of weakness. It was only after the name of the mystery investor was revealed a few days later that J. P. Morgan gave wholehearted approval to go ahead with negotiations.

There was a lot of work to be done. Charles T. "Charlie"

Munger, Buffett's confidant and California-based partner in Berkshire Hathaway, became actively involved along with lawyers and bankers from both sides, including the ubiquitous Joe Flom for Gillette. The deal hit a snag from the point of view of Gillette negotiators because Buffett's lawyers demanded terms they considered unreasonable, given Gillette's strengths. The two sides kept coming up with dividend rates and convertible terms that were far apart. Buffett's first proposal was for a 9 percent dividend with shares convertible into common at $45 a share, or a 9.5 percent dividend with shares convertible at $50 a share, with Gillette not permitted to "call" the deal—convert the preferred to common—for eight years. Gillette rejected that and came back with a proposal of an 8.5 percent dividend with shares convertible at $52, with Gillette able to call the deal in two years under certain conditions. The two sides jousted for a couple of weeks, and by the first of July, it appeared the deal was in deep trouble, though as Buffett recalled, "I always thought the deal was likely to work out because Colman and I wanted it to work out. I worried that the lawyers or the bankers would screw it up, but in the end, I would say I always felt it likely we were going to make a deal."

At the Gillette end there was hope, too, but also concern from negotiators who could not understand why the Buffett forces were so far from them on the formula for valuating the company, which seemed to be the stumbling block preventing an agreement. Something seemed to be wrong. Mockler decided a face-to-face meeting was needed to avoid a breakdown caused by misunderstanding on how each side arrived at their divergent valuations. On the Fourth of July, Mullaney drove from his vacation home in Westport, Massachusetts, to the small airport at Hyannis, on Cape Cod. He met Mockler, who had driven from his weekend place at Chatham on Cape Cod, and the two men took off in a chartered plane for Omaha to explain to Buffett personally what they thought was fair and reasonable to Gillette shareholders and how they got to that point. It was a friendly meeting. The issue was not resolved at the time, but it was agreed that both sides would reassess their positions and keep on trying. Mockler and Mullaney returned to their homes that evening in time for holiday fireworks.

It took a week or so, but on July 12, negotiators tentatively agreed on terms, and Mockler phoned Buffett after the stock market closed that day with Gillette's proposal. Within the hour, Buffett called back with his approval. Terms called for Berkshire Hathaway's insurance subsidiaries to purchase $600 million of 8 3/4 percent convertible preferred stock from Gillette at $1,000 a share. Each preferred share was convertible after two years into 20 shares of Gillette common stock at $50 a share, representing about a 20 percent premium over the then-prevailing Gillette share value. The 12 million common shares represented about 11 percent of Gillette's total voting shares, making Buffett far and away the company's largest shareholder. Gillette was required to redeem the shares at the end of ten years. The deal included a provision insisted upon by Gillette that allowed Gillette to redeem the shares at $50 within the first two years if the common stock price increased to at least 125 percent of the conversion price, or $62.50, for at least twenty consecutive trading days. In that event, Gillette could call the preferred stock, saving $60 million plus accrued dividends.

At Gillette's board meeting on July 20, Morgan's managing director, Roberto Mendoza, gave his blessing on the deal as "fair and reasonable" to shareholders, and the directors unanimously approved it. The deal was announced the next day after the market closed, with Gillette stock at just over $42. The national press played it up as an anti-takeover measure by Gillette, but Gillette spokesmen stressed that the deal was "strictly financial and strategic" and noted that it had been initiated by Buffett. They said any anti-takeover effect was purely incidental.

"I've dealt with a lot of people, and no one was easier to deal with than Colman Mockler," Buffett later said. "And a great numbers man, a great analytical mind."

As part of the deal, Buffett was elected a director of Gillette.

Some institutional investors grumbled that Gillette was giving Buffett a deal nobody else could get, but as the stock's value soared above the conversion price, the complaints stopped. It turned out to be a sweet deal for both sides. "The deal with Buffett helped everyone," Peter Lynch, the renowned manager of Fidelity's Magellan Fund and a long-time bull on Gillette, told Roger Lowenstein, author of *Buffett*. Gillette used up most of its proceeds to pay off short-term debt, which cleaned up its balance sheet. Technically, the transaction was listed to one side of the balance sheet as "mezzanine preferred," meaning neither debt nor equity, but the rating agencies considered it equity and, coupled with the company's fundamental strength, upgraded Gillette's credit rating to A- by Standard & Poor's and Baa1 by Moody's. By the time the transaction was completed, the normal cash flow from Gillette's blade and razor business had, at any rate, wiped out the negative equity and pushed the ratio slightly into positive territory.

Gillette's stock reacted so well that the company was able to shrug off the negative impact on the stock market of Iraq's invasion of Kuwait in late 1990 and met the two-year deadline for early redemption, avoiding a $60 million payout. The deal signaled to investors everywhere that if a long-term investor as smart as Buffett wanted to buy Gillette shares, then the company's prospects must be excellent.

Buffett said later that he made a mistake. He said he should have used his $600 million to buy common shares rather than insist on a preferred stock deal that cut his risk. If he had bought common, he said, he would have wound up with 15 million shares for $40 a share, instead of 12 million shares at $50 a share under his preferred deal, which gave him a higher dividend yield plus an option to convert at a fixed price. But not a bad deal either way, he laughed, as he paced about his Omaha office on a hot August day in 1995. He was in a good mood because he had laid out $2.3 billion that morning to acquire the shares Berkshire Hathaway did not already own in GEICO. Running through the numbers in his head, he noted to a visitor that his $600 million Gillette investment in 1989 had more than tripled in under six years to about $2.2 billion, which neatly covered his GEICO purchase earlier in the day. He said he could not think of any better place than Gillette for his money.

Buffett, by any calculation one of the richest men in America and often regarded as the nation's most astute investor, is famous for putting huge sums of money into a handful of companies he understands and which he believes are unmistakable leaders in their companies. In 1996, Berkshire Hathaway's biggest holdings were American Express Company, Coca-Cola Company, Walt Disney Company, The Gillette Company and The Washington Post Company. It also had large but lesser holdings in Sears, Roebuck; Dean Witter, Discover & Co.; PNC Bank Corp.; Viacom; and Merrill Lynch. As he readily concedes, he has made his shares of mistakes along the way—USAir and Champion International preferred stock deals made the same year as the purchase of Gillette preferred failed to work out, for example, and his bet that he could resurrect Salomon Bros. at a profit to Berkshire Hathaway did not pay off.

Of his many success stories, Buffett singled out Coca-Cola and Gillette as "fabulous global companies." He noted that the two companies have market shares in a great many countries that exceed their American market-leading shares. "Both companies have products that travel well, low-priced items that people everywhere consider necessities. . . . I'm telling you, for many people everywhere Coke is a necessity, and of course, blades are necessities," said the billionaire who quaffs Cherry Cokes like a child drinks milk and who considers shaving with his Gillette razor a gratifying daily experience.

Buffett said he made his early fortune in "my cigar butt phase," buying very low-priced stocks forgotten or overlooked by almost every investor but with enough value to promise some appreciation. But that was thirty years ago, he said, and by the time of his Gillette purchase his investment aim was to find a business with a great franchise, pay a fair price, and hold on for the long term. Buffett said he bought Gillette for its management, too, "because of Colman. But I could not feel better about Al [Zeien]. He really knows products, as well as marketing and finance. It's unusual to find a guy that combines that."

One thing changed quickly when Buffett joined the Gillette board. Cokes replaced Pepsi at Gillette cafeterias and vending machines around the world. And knowing Buffett's personal fondness for having several Cherry Cokes daily, the company took heroic measures to make sure that his favorite refreshment was available even in places where cherry-flavored colas are not locally in demand. When Gillette directors were scheduled to meet in

Kronberg, Germany, at Braun AG's headquarters outside of Frankfurt, an urgent call was made to Boston for a couple of cases of
Cherry Cokes.

STEEL MAN VS. PLASTIC, ROUND TWO

During the year and a half that Mockler and his senior staff were
preoccupied first with fighting back the Coniston proxy challenge
and then concluding the negotiations with Warren Buffett, John
Symons fought to complete the "steel man" crusade he had begun
in Europe. His chance came when Gillette reorganized at the start
of 1988 to emphasize a product line approach over geographic
structure—a key step in its transition to a global enterprise. Mockler gave Symons the powerful job of Blade and Razor Group
president under the new Gillette North Atlantic structure, with
responsibility for technological direction, manufacturing, and
marketing the company's shaving products in Western Europe
and North America. It was, in effect, recognition of his success in
Europe and a challenge to Symons to repeat that success in North
America and the broad pan-Atlantic market.

Whereas Symons had been pretty much free to run his own
show in Europe he had to fight the battle of "steel man" versus
"plastic man" all over again when he moved to Boston. Despite
support from Mockler and Zeien, there was no certainty he could
win out over the views of many men and women from the Safety
Razor Division (SRD) in South Boston who had been largely
responsible for so many shaving product successes through the
decades. With good reason, SRD believed its technologists and
marketers were at the heart of Gillette's success, not just in North
America but worldwide. Their view, by and large, was that Gillette
should dedicate its best technology and marketing efforts to disposable razors and worry about a next-generation system to replace the aging Atra Plus in due time. The top strategists from
SRD were convinced that the entire shaving market was moving
relentlessly toward domination by disposables and that Gillette's
best hope was to adopt its technological advances in a superior
line of disposables to hold off Bic and Schick.

The launching of the code-named Flag blade and razor system in 1990 (see Chapter 11) marked the ultimate victory of Symons' steel man philosophy, which espoused the preeminence of systems over disposables. But first the stage had to be set for Flag, North American priorities and mindset had to be changed, and even the company's attitude toward the manly act of shaving had to be readdressed. Symons had a three-part strategy planned: reposition Gillette as the premier wet shaving brand in the eyes of men everywhere, follow this by launching a new blade and razor system that would set a world standard for quality, and lastly extend the Gillette brand name beyond blades and razors into male grooming aids and toiletries. The idea was to make shaving something more than scraping hair off the face and part of an overall Gillette grooming process instead.

Joel Davis started work as president of the Stationery Products Group in the new Gillette North Atlantic structure the same day that Symons took over as president of the Blade and Razor Group. He knew from working with Symons in Europe that his colleague would bluster and demand and do anything to get his way, no matter what others thought.

"John was not a consensus manager," Davis observed with understatement. "He had such a clear idea of what he wanted to accomplish and he couldn't care less whether others agreed." Davis said that Mockler must have made up his mind to change the prevailing blade and razor strategy when he appointed the messianic Symons because he had to have known that Symons would surely shake up entrenched management to get what he wanted. "Colman was a different sort of leader. He never could have done this himself, but I believe he used John as his foil, his agent for change."

From the beginning, Symons was determined to re-establish the strong male heritage of Gillette by focusing advertisements on the masculine feel-good experience of shaving with a handsome razor made of steel. He thought of it as recapturing the old magic of the Gillette shaving experience.

Never subtle, Symons caught everyone's attention shortly after he arrived in Boston in 1988. At a meeting about advertising strategy for the "Essence of Shaving" campaign then underway,

Symons listened impatiently to plans for advertising and promoting disposables, with only a secondary focus on systems. Abruptly, he broke in and issued an order that changed the course of events. From that moment, he said, advertising would end for the Good News disposable and the lower-priced, heavily promoted Micro-Trac disposable. No money would be spent to advertise *any* disposable product. Advertising dollars would support only Atra Plus, Contour Plus, and other systems. A later tally of advertising outlays showed the impact of that order. From $9.9 million in 1987, advertising in the United States for male disposables fell to $4.4 million in 1988 and to zero in 1989 and 1990. It had already been cut to zero in Europe.

As technologists ended work on disposables and started an all-out effort to finalize the design and manufacturing processes for Flag, Symons turned to the immediate challenge of enhancing Gillette's male imagery. He selected old colleagues from the European razor campaigns, Peter Hoffman in marketing and Sharon E. Keith in market research, as key players on the Blade and Razor Group marketing team. A new advertising message began to take shape, though not until Symons traveled to New York with Hoffman to chastise BBDO for what he did not like in the current campaign and demand the time and attention of the agency's top talent for a bold new message he had in mind. BBDO's London office had orchestrated the Gillette pan-European blade advertising strategy, so Symons was hardly an unknown to the New Yorkers. He made it clear that he was in charge in both Europe and North America, that a great deal of business was at stake, and that BBDO would have to earn it. He told BBDO precisely what he wanted: a simultaneous American-European ad campaign that emphasized the universal manliness of shaving and established Gillette as the male grooming company that understood what men wanted. The Gillette name was to be emphasized as the premier brand name in shaving. Sharon Keith's market research had shown the great value of Gillette as a world-recognized brand name that resonated with male shavers, and Symons felt sure that he could take advantage of this brand awareness to sell razor systems and, later, Gillette-branded male toiletries.

Peter Hoffman became the point man with BBDO. He told the agency that the new Gillette North Atlantic structure required a global approach, and he requested that BBDO star Phil Dusenberry work on the Gillette account. Dusenberry was widely known in ad circles as the creative force behind memorable ads embracing large, simple themes laced with heavy emotional content and pulsating music. He was deeply involved in the pioneering "Pepsi Generation" ad campaign, which was among the first consumer ads to stress the emotional promise of good feelings for the consumer over the story of product content. Dusenberry later came up with the phrase "GE, we bring good things to life," one of the most successful emotion-over-function ads of all time. He was hired by the Ronald Reagan campaign team to handle the ads in Reagan's second presidential campaign. A sports lover who would fly anywhere in the world to attend a heavyweight boxing match, he had worked on various Gillette accounts through the years. By 1988 he had become vice chairman of BBDO Worldwide and chairman of the flagship New York office. Hoffman put Gillette's vision to him: Recapture the spirit of Gillette's dominant male image, of a company that knows and understands men throughout the world. What Gillette wanted was a powerful, emotional campaign theme that captured the Gillette male imagery and would connect with men anywhere in the world.

Dusenberry signed on with his colleague Ted Sann as the day-to-day account manager and client contact. Throughout the winter and spring of 1988 they worked on the project, with Gillette putting heavy pressure on BBDO to produce in a hurry. Money was spent with an abandon that must have astonished Mockler, but the chairman kept hands off. Hoffman wanted a strategic emotional ad that would last twenty years, something like the enduring "Look Sharp, Feel Sharp" campaign. Sometime in the spring the BBDO team toted up to Boston about twenty-five sample print ads with various messages like "you can see it written on his face" and "the look, the feel, the pride" and spread them around a conference table. One theme caught the attention of the several Gillette executives anxiously hoping to spot a winner. It was "Gillette, the Best a Man Can Get." Hoffman recalled there was a unanimous "that's it" reaction for the seven words that had been scrawled on a scrap of paper along with several other possibilities by BBDO staffer Michael Scheback. From that moment on, it was a matter of execution, making the "Best a Man Can Get" theme come alive and work well in one commanding TV ad that met Symons' goal of establishing an emotional relationship between men and Gillette. BBDO commissioned composer Jake Holmes to come up with music and lyrics.

Hoffman and his colleagues knew instinctively that the "Best a Man Can Get" theme worked because it caught their vision of the company: Gillette equals men; Gillette products are the best you can buy; Gillette products will make a man the best he can be. Hoffman worried how well the English words would translate into other languages. The BBDO team showed the line to its sister agencies around the world and discovered to their relief that with relatively minor adjustments, it worked well as an expression of male bonding with Gillette. Sometimes the translation was better than hoped for. For example, the Italian translation became "The Best of a Man" and, according to Gillette's local management, seemed to capture the Italian spirit, as well as the way local marketers were positioning the business. Dusenberry was relieved that the Gillette line did not run into the problem that Pepsi had encountered in Thailand, where the Pepsi jingle translated as "Pepsi brings your ancestors back from the grave."

By July 1988, BBDO had created five television ads built around the "Best a Man Can Get" theme, and the Gillette crew was off to Manhattan to choose the winner. One video proclaimed a "mankind" theme, featuring a choral group much like the Mormon Tabernacle Choir celebrating the greatness of man and mankind. Another took more of a hard hitting, MTV-youth approach, with fast cuts. Finally came the fifth presentation, BBDO's favorite, which had been saved for the last. It showed many visual vignettes that celebrated various aspects of manhood: masculinity (sports shots, working man); sensitivity (man with baby); sexiness (man gets woman); family (father and adult son). It was accompanied by pulsating music with words vital to the ad's message: "You're looking sharp, you're feeling good, you've come so far. We know how to make the most of who you are. From father to son, that's what we've always done. Gillette, the Best a Man Can Get."

It was a hit with the Boston contingent. The emotional bonding with Gillette they had hoped for was there. Dusenberry immediately walked the Gillette team across the hallway and showed them variations of the "Best" theme in nonvideo forms that BBDO had prepared with the idea that these could be used in packaging and promotional materials.

Keith's market research had proved the Gillette name enjoyed practically icon status in terms of brand recall. With that in mind, and with the "Best a Man Can Get" theme accepted as the all-encompassing Gillette theme, the North Atlantic marketers decided it was time to dress up the old Gillette brand logo. It had already been decreed that the Gillette name would share equal billing in terms of size on shaving products, reversing the old system whereby the word "Atra," for example, was two or three times the size of the word "Gillette" on packaging and promotional materials. The famed New York identity consulting firm Anspach Grossman Portugal—boasting a client roster of recognized American brands, such as Quaker Oats, Sara Lee, and Texaco—was given the assignment. The newly designed Gillette brand logotype on razor packaging, and later on all North Atlantic operations' stationery and facilities, was a fatter, bolder version of the old Futura typeface but tilted to the right and depicting a more forward, more masculine image.

To show off the new advertising and marketing approach, a briefing was held a few weeks later at the Harvard Club in Boston's Back Bay, where Symons' team and BBDO heavyweights led by Dusenberry presented their recommendations to Mockler and other top executives. Sharon Keith described the extensive research that had been conducted to measure consumer reaction to the proposed ad campaign. Then Gillette executives were treated to a sixty-second version of the "Best a Man Can Get" ad—a splicing together of footage taken from several commercials and edited to create a live-action preview of what would become the final ad. Accompanied by the just-composed score, the imagery created by Dusenberry and his crew was powerful. The excitement in the room was obvious.

The grand strategy to reposition the Gillette image for male shavers was coming together even as the countdown to the launch of Flag continued. A legal question remained: Would the phrase "the Best a Man Can Get" be construed as a performance claim or puffery by the big three television networks? Gillette's assistant general counsel, James P. Connolly, worked with Hoffman and Keith to substantiate the performance of Atra Plus as the best shaving product available through a hierarchical technology-based assessment process. A research protocol was based on the following assumptions: Twin blades perform better than single edge; shaving systems perform better than disposables; pivoting-head razors are better than stationary ones; and products with a lubricating strip are superior to those without. With this approach, Gillette's consumer-use tests had only to include products with those features, namely, Schick Ultrex Plus and Wilkinson's Profile Extra. In a major paired-comparison study, Atra Plus won decisively. Armed with this ammunition, Connolly trooped to ABC, CBS, and NBC with the ad during the winter of 1988 and won their approval.

The "Best a Man Can Get" ad made a rousing Super Bowl debut in January 1989. It marked the start of an unprecedented $80 million simultaneous European-American ad campaign supporting Atra and Contour Plus. The television ad showed the same music and visuals for all markets but ran in fourteen languages in nineteen countries. It seemed to work. Unit sales of blade cartridges for Atra Plus and other systems moved up to 33 percent in the United States in the first six months of 1989 from the prior year's all-time low of 31.7 percent, the first gain in share for cartridges since the mid-1970s, when disposables were introduced.

Symons was gleeful. Engineers had by then solved many of the manufacturing problems that had held back the launch of the new product that would replace Atra. The target for pan-Atlantic introduction of the new razor was moved up slightly, to early 1990. Things were looking up for Flag, a product that had been in the development process for more than ten years. It would be introduced to the trade in the fall of 1989 with not a few persons inside and outside the company convinced that Gillette's future as a fast growth company was at stake.

11

COUNTDOWN

TO

SENSOR

TECHNOLOGY HAS BEEN at the heart of the corporate culture at Gillette since King C. Gillette's invention of the safety razor. It had taken a half-dozen years to find William Nickerson, the technologist who made a patentable prototype of the founder's vision of a blade and razor system. Then it took another year or two for Nickerson to design and build machines that could harden and sharpen thin sheet steel and stamp out blades in sufficient numbers and quality to make Gillette Safety Razor Company a viable manufacturer. With a few bumps in the road along the way, The Gillette Company has been making and marketing the industry's most technologically advanced shaving products ever since.

As Al Zeien put it in a lecture at Yale School of Organization and Management in 1991, Gillette funds technology on two beliefs—there is a better way to shave and Gillette will find it; there are better ways to manufacture Gillette products, and Gillette will find these, too. The ten-year countdown to the Sensor shaving system makes these points well, with the ultimate success of the Flag project dependent on technologists designing a product that shaves better than any before it and then figuring out how to manufacture the product efficiently in a high-speed process.

The concept of shaving facial hair with independently moving twin blades—the heart of the Sensor system—took a first move toward reality in 1979 at Gillette's Reading U.K. laboratory. Researcher John Francis devised a means of mounting tiny springs to twin blades within a cartridge, the idea being that two blades moving separately up, down, and sideways would follow the contour of a man's face and would produce a closer and more comfortable shave. For that breakthrough mechanical design achievement, he received the first of an eventual twenty-two patents incorporated in Sensor. His invention came about fifteen years after other researchers under Dr. Norman Welsh at the Reading lab had developed the first twin-blade cartridges, which led to the 1971 launch of the Trac II razor system. In the spirit of the Gillette credo that the company is always at work on the next-generation blade and razor, the Trac II was barely on the market before Welsh's researchers had begun looking for a better way to shave.

Nobody at the English laboratory or at Boston knew quite what to do with the complex spring-mounted blades. It was difficult to place the moving blades in cartridges even in small test quantities. Engineers at once foresaw obstacles to anything resembling cost-efficient mass production. The temptation was to move on to product ideas with a more obvious payoff, like better disposables. But there was just one thing about the experimental spring-mounted blades. Even the first rather crude hand-built models made for human testing at the lab produced closer shaves than the latest twin-blade models on the market, which featured fixed blades in a pivoting cartridge.

Al Zeien, among others, took note and became convinced of the long-term worthiness of the moving blade concept, which had been dubbed "Flag" not for patriotic reasons but as an acronym for "floated angle geometry." Flag actually was not one Flag, but

Flags 1–7. The concept of spring-mounted blades mounted in a cartridge was Zeien's favorite among the seven moving-blade designs that were competing to determine which would be developed. Zeien's sponsorship counted for a lot, because in late 1980 he had been elected a director and vice chairman of the board in charge of technical operations and new business development. That gave him great clout as a technology advocate and decision maker. Trained as a marine architect and engineer, Zeien brought strong ideas to the place of technology.

Zeien was determined to strengthen Gillette's mastery of technologies that were needed to develop next-generation products. To that end, he hired Dr. John Bush in 1979 from General Electric as corporate R & D vice president, with orders to build up the company's existing strength in high-speed photography techniques so that researchers could mount cameras between the blades in a twin-blade cartridge, enabling them to photograph the act of shaving.

One of Zeien's first moves was to install a program management system that consolidated all technical activity—R & D, engineering, and manufacturing—by product category across the entire company. This enabled him to direct resource allocation from a corporate perspective and to significantly increase the amount of technical effort directed toward new product activity. The people in the laboratories grumbled for a while, but Zeien made it clear that program managers would report directly to him on a frequent basis.

To fill the crucial program management job at the Safety Razor Division, Zeien pulled a young technical manager from the ranks and assigned him the job of developing a new shaving system based on moving blades. Edward F. DeGraan, then thirty-seven, had hired on at Gillette as a manufacturing trainee after graduating from Boston's Suffolk University. He eventually wound up as manager of the Puerto Rico factory dedicated to making Cricket lighters and, with the sale of Cricket, was back in Boston in a short-term marketing job when Zeien recruited him to head the Flag project.

"WE'LL FIGURE OUT HOW TO MAKE IT LATER"

DeGraan remembered one of his first meetings with Zeien. The latter laid out a slew of drawings and specifications on a table and said, "Your job, Ed, is to get the product I've defined into shape for testing and to conduct a broad-scale consumer use test as soon as possible." Zeien told him he had gone through all the aspects of Flag and reviewed very small-scale test results, and he was convinced that spring-mounted blades were the best option among moving-blade concepts. DeGraan recalls with great clarity his saying, "We'll figure out a way to manufacture it later." The moving blades were to be developed at this early stage for both a disposable razor and as a cartridge for a system razor.

DeGraan was impressed that Zeien had cut through the technological clutter and made a firm decision among the seven Flags and had gone a step further to define the product he wanted in great detail. The razor had to have a pivoting head that held twin blades with individually mounted springs and a blade guard that moved on a plane, like the blades that followed it. It was up to DeGraan to coordinate the work of R & D and product engineering departments and to advance that concept into a product that could be tested by thousands of consumers against Gillette's current top system, the Atra.

Every four to six weeks DeGraan met with Zeien and others to review the program. Zeien's commitment and his encouragement to the many technical people working on Flag was critical. In the early 1980s low-cost disposables had become the hot shaving product worldwide, grabbing market share from systems. Some at Gillette who knew about Flag despaired of spring-mounted blades or any new technology changing what they saw as the inevitable commoditization of the shaving market, where price would gain priority over quality. Flag technology might make a disposable perform better, they argued, but it would be so costly to develop and produce that a Flag-based disposable would not be able to compete on price. DeGraan said he interpreted Zeien's emergence as Flag's sponsor as a signal from Colman Mockler that Gillette believed that the wet shaving business should and could be driven by the best technology available, not price. He and his colleagues certainly needed the boost from senior management. Flag lost its divisional sponsorship from the Safety Razor Group in 1983 and was kept alive only by the intervention of Zeien and Mockler, who funded the project with money controlled by the chairman's office.

By mid-1983, DeGraan's team had solved enough technical problems to produce a limited number of twin-blade, spring-mounted cartridges that were deemed fit to be included in large-scale consumer tests. These critical tests involved many hundreds of shavers who compared Flag with Atra and other products. The results of the consumer use test, or CUT in Gillette jargon, surprised even the most ardent advocates of Flag. In every measurement of comfort and closeness, Flag scored decisively higher against Atra and the other products, providing test results the likes of which had not been seen since the first twin-blade Trac II model was tested against double-edge blades. These were astonishing results.

The findings kept the corporate dollars flowing for the Flag product, but not everyone was pleased. Major players at Gillette were still concerned about the ultimate cost of a Flag-based product in a market they assumed would be dominated by low-priced disposables. Meanwhile, Flag's complexity increased as Zeien insisted that the newly developed lubricating strip for Atra and Good News be incorporated into Flag's design.

The technological challenge for DeGraan now shifted in large part from product R & D at the U.K. laboratory to process engineering and manufacturing concerns at the South Boston manufacturing plant. The challenge became "R & D has delivered the product, now what's the process?" DeGraan recalled the extreme pressure on process engineers to develop workable ways to design the equipment that would mass produce Flag within reasonable cost parameters. By the first quarter of 1986, he said, "The fog began to lift a bit." Encouraged by Mockler and Zeien, DeGraan went before the board of directors in June 1986 for what he remembered as an extraordinary experience. I told them, "We've got great news, we've got a wonderful new product. I wish I could tell you I knew how we are going to manufacture it, but I can't. If we introduce this as a system, here's the product cost estimate. If we make this as a disposable, here's another product cost. We need $10 million right now." He showed them schematic drawings and a very rudimentary form of a system razor with the handle made of plastic. He described some of the plastic materials that Gillette was trying to mold, he described the challenge of linking assembly machines, and he talked about the problems of laser welding that had to be overcome. It was the first time the directors had heard a technical description of Flag. Legal chief Joe Mullaney stressed that the company was seeking as much patent protection as possible.

In a sweeping move of support, the directors voted the money without challenge to the technology. "The main thing they wanted to know was how fast can we get the product," DeGraan said. It was less than six months before Perelman's first raid on the company.

In April 1987, DeGraan was back again. He told the directors that a lot of progress had been made on Flag as a product, but he needed another $10 million to build a pilot manufacturing line to determine how to assemble the product at high speeds and low cost. He estimated a Flag product could be launched in late 1989. This time he showed some beauty shots of the product in prototype form and showed off a systems razor made mostly from plastic. Again, it was a technological review with little or no mention of marketing strategies, and again the directors voted to fund the project. It was proof to DeGraan that senior management and the board retained Gillette's historic commitment to technology-driven new products, despite the pressure to reduce costs forced by the Revlon attack and the restructuring that followed.

Production Challenges

Process engineers and manufacturing experts struggled with unprecedented production challenges. About ten thousand feet of the main assembly area at the South Boston plant was partitioned off and made secure from prying eyes as DeGraan's pilot line took shape. By early spring 1988, work on Flag had progressed to the point at which engineers were confident a cost-efficient product could be launched by late 1989 or 1990. It was great timing, because the technological green light came just before the fateful vote by shareholders that would determine whether Gillette would remain independent or be swallowed up and sold off by the Coniston Partners. Whether Mockler's letter telling shareholders they could expect the introduction of a major new product tilted the close vote to Gillette is arguable, but it certainly caught the eye of experts who had followed Gillette through the years and knew the company's reputation for introducing successful new shaving products.

The appointment of John Symons as president of the Shaving Group of Gillette North Atlantic at the start of 1988 had added both focus and pressure for DeGraan and his Flag engineers. DeGraan had flown to London to brief Symons on the moving blades project a year or so before the Englishman was promoted to his North Atlantic job, and Symons had been enthusiastic. But he had been upset to learn that Flag technology was being developed for use in disposables as well as systems, and he also thought it heresy that plastic was the material of choice for the permanent handle of the proposed razor. Immediately after Mockler asked him to move to Boston, Symons had telephoned DeGraan and instructed him to stop work on Flag disposables and on the plastic handle.

Within days of arriving in Boston in January 1988, Symons called a meeting in the South Boston factory cafeteria to restate his orders, because there was still some ambivalence about stopping R & D work on Flag disposables. Symons made it clear that he wanted priority on the Flag system razor, period. He also restated his opposition to plastic in the system handle, his English accent growing more pronounced as his voice rose, and he exhorted the technology team to think of quality and the glories of Gillette, past and future. Think steel, not plastic. He received a standing ovation.

The handle on the razor that finally was launched in 1990 was stainless steel with bits of plastic added for a better grip. In prototypes, plastic had worked as well as metal for the handle in a manufacturing sense, and Gillette had greatly upgraded its in-house abilities to produce and mold plastic materials and to use the material in production lines in a cost-efficient way. But Symons was adamant that the handle of the razor that soon would be christened Sensor must be made of metal to give it a manly, high-performance feel. To save money by building the system with plastic was penny wise and pound foolish, he maintained, dooming to failure his grand strategy to convince shavers that Gillette understood what real men wanted. "We can't allow an image of blue, hollow, and plastic," he preached incessantly, referring to the Good News disposable.

Perhaps the most difficult of all production problems that had to be solved was how to attach the tiny springs to the blades at the extreme speeds required for efficient production of blade cartridges. By that time, it had been determined that laser welding was the only way to go, but learning how to apply that esoteric technology to Gillette's world of high-speed blade production raised a host of questions.

Al Zeien said that mastering the laser challenge and devising automated quality control techniques were keys to breaking the stumbling block of how to make hundreds of millions of Sensor blade cartridges at a reasonable cost. One of the big process engineering challenges was how to weld the blades without upsetting the hardness or the sharpness of edges and, at the same time, weld them at the required high speeds. Some arithmetic told the engineers that each blade cartridge needed thirteen spot welds plus two false welds at each end, meaning a total of fifteen welds that had to be precisely made, with one-ninetieth of a second allowed between welds. With this in mind, machinery had to be designed, built, tested, and installed on the factory floor. It had to run twenty-four hours a day, with minimal human supervision.

To assure quality control, Gillette engineers had to learn to work with electronic scanners able to measure deviations meas-

HONERS—THE FACTORY ELITE

Through the decades, the honer's work has changed as better ways to harden, sharpen, and convert strips of steel into blades have changed the nature of their work, but their basic job of monitoring quality and correcting mistakes remains strikingly similar. By the mid-1950s, the honer's best friend had become a microscope. At a time when the daily output of double-edge blades at South Boston was about 10 million, a crew of nearly forty honers worked each shift in the strip-edging department. Their work revolved around a narrow, 24-foot-long sharpening machine that processed a blade-width strip of lacquered steel moving continuously past twelve grinding and honing wheels and four leather stropping wheels. At one end of the machine the sharpened strip was cut into individual blades that were stacked on a metal holder.

The old-time honer squinted frequently into a microscope looking for imperfections, which he corrected by adjusting grinding wheels to ten-thousandths of an inch. The honer also had to keep a sharp eye on lights, gauges, and indicators, which, among other things, counted blade output per minute. The honer had to know what to do when a wheel wore down, when the steel strip broke, and how to correct variations from the norm. He had to be alert to when the coil of steel feeding into the machine wore out and had to be spot-welded to a new one. Although computers soon enough took on most of the work of the 1950s honers, the human touch in blade making survives.

ured in microns. A micron is twenty-five thousandths of an inch, a measurement invisible to the human eye, like "measuring" vitamins. Scanners built into the assembly lines had to keep up with production speeds that enabled Gillette to turn out hundreds of millions of cartridges a year right from the start. Only the most sophisticated machines would do. The legendary honers at South Boston, acknowledged since William Nickerson's days as the factory's elite and the highest-paid skilled workers on the site, had to learn a new set of skills enabling them to monitor computer-controlled instruments and take appropriate actions. Today, honers are among the highest-paid workers at the plant, but instead of hands-on mastery, the Sensor-generation honers essentially monitor blinking, largely noiseless machines that produce "the sharpest edges ever honed" from spools of Japanese, British, or Swedish steel wound in spools up to thirty-six miles in length.

With the technology under control and a broad marketing strategy in place, the board gave final approval in mid-1988 to spend what was needed to launch Sensor. It turned out to be more than $150 million in the eighteen-month run-up to launch. Manufacturing the Sensor tested all the manufacturing expertise Gillette could muster. Problems remained to the very end and very slightly delayed the planned launch. Nobody in the shaving industry knew more about cutting steel into blades and making plastic parts with injection molding than Gillette, but Sensor was on such a different scale of complexity than Trac II—ten separate parts in each cartridge versus six in Trac II, for example.

To complicate matters, the marketing strategy for Sensor required simultaneous introduction in nineteen countries on two continents—a nearly global launch for the nearly global company Gillette had become. It is one thing to design a universal product and adopt a universal ad campaign. It is quite another to produce tens of millions of that product from the first day. The Sensor launch was dependent on Gillette factories in South Boston and Berlin gearing up simultaneously for the most high-tech manufacturing effort in the company's history. South Boston, as always, served as the mother plant and technology transfer center and was the key training site for many German engineers, who learned what did and did not work right along with their American compatriots. According to DeGraan, the two plants functioned seamlessly, each tied to the same cost accounting scheme that averaged the German and American costs into a common cost applied to the entire North Atlantic market. One result was that it became in the best interest of management at the German plant for South Boston to perform well, and vice versa. This cooperative effort added a new twist to the traditional intra-company competitions between widely separated factories to produce at the most efficient rates.

SELLING THE SENSOR

Once the Flag technology was mastered and the unalterable decision was made to go ahead with a made-from-metal systems razor, attention shifted to marketing strategy. What would the new razor be called? What features would be stressed?

The first step had been the crucial build-up to reposition Gillette as a quality maker of high-performance razor systems. As was noted in Chapter 10, John Symons worked with his marketing chief, Peter Hoffman, throughout 1988 and 1989 to set the stage for Sensor's launch. He decreed that the Gillette name must be restored as a brand name for shaving products made by a company that understood men and what made men feel good about themselves. BBDO was assigned to bring that image alive. The resulting "Best a Man Can Get" theme was first used to support Atra in the United States and Contour in Europe, a year before Sensor was launched.

Symons influenced the design of the Sensor from an aesthetic viewpoint. He ordered the use of stainless steel for the handles because he wanted the look and feel of a classic metal razor. He rejected hundreds of handle designs as too light, too short, or too dark until finally approving the final look, right down to the black plastic used for the trim and hand grips. Hoffman said it was all part of Gillette's effort to bring the concept of value back to the shaving process, to make the statement that shaving is an important part of the male grooming ritual and that choosing Gillette products makes a difference.

Symons was so concerned about detail that he vetoed many versions of the Sensor packaging before being satisfied that there was a proper masculine sound and feel as the package was ripped open. He demanded the easiest possible way for the user to clamp the replacement blade cartridge onto the razor.

In fall 1989, after a year of hints and promises about its new shaving system and a year devoted to repositioning Gillette products as "The Best a Man Can Get," the company pulled the trigger on phase two of its image makeover when it introduced Sensor to the press and the trade. The name itself remained a well-kept secret until the media introduction. The choices had been narrowed to Sensor or Zebra, the former representing space age, high-tech, male panache. Zebra was the favorite of those who thought that the image of the swift and striped African beast was mirrored in the black-on-silver stripes of the sleek razor handle.

The media launch in October 1989 was a celebration designed to raise expectations further, and it worked. The public relations firm Porter-Novelli had been retained months before, working with Hoffman's staff and corporate public relations staff to pique media awareness and create press kits that translated all that technology into readable copy. The message "Gillette Is about to Change the Way Men Shave Forever," which would appear as teaser TV and newspaper ads, was etched onto the glossy invitations sent to the media and security analysts who were to attend the product unveiling on October 3. That day, about eighty reporters (a separate briefing was scheduled later for analysts) crowded into the elegant Pierre Hotel in New York City. At precisely 9 A.M., a synthesizer played the "Best a Man Can Get" song as computer-generated graphics flashed wall-sized images of manly men, beautiful women, loving fathers, achieving executives, high-flying athletes, and of course, Sensor razors greatly magnified to show every hair-slicing detail. The press was bombarded with information. Most of it was about Sensor, but for those with a deep appreciation for minutiae, there were such facts as the average man has thirty-thousand face whiskers and generates 27 1/2 feet of facial hair in his lifetime, having spent 139 days of that lifetime removing that hair before it reached such unfashionable length.

To skeptics who wondered if men would pay the $4 yearly premium for Sensor over what it cost to shave with an Atra Plus, or almost twice as much as it cost to shave daily with Bic throwaways, Symons confidently predicted that consumers would gladly spend a few dollars more to enjoy the best shave a man could get. For about six cents a daily shave or $20 a year, including an initial outlay of $3.75 for the razor, men the world over would enjoy their remaining days spent shaving, exuberant Gillette spokesmen promised.

In expansive terms, Symons told the assembled reporters that Gillette would spend $110 million in 1990 to advertise the product and another $65 million to promote it (through incentive sales programs, special store promotions, and the like) in Europe and North America. He forecast first-year sales at $206 million and a 15 percent market share in three years. Big numbers, a big show—and it produced big headlines. The *New York Times* headline must have pleased Symons.[1] "Gillette Challenge to the Disposables," it proclaimed, noting that disposables held 43 percent of the U.S. blade market in dollar terms and 56 percent in unit sales but that Gillette was confident Sensor would cut into the throwaway market.

Perhaps more important than the headlines was the general approval by securities analysts. Brenda Lee Landry of Morgan Stanley issued an immediate bulletin to her clients. "It's a winner," she said, issuing a "buy" recommendation. Other analysts generally liked what they saw. Few accepted the life or death scenario that had been conjured by some media and investment analysts, who wrote that Gillette was taking a huge risk by putting all its eggs in the Sensor basket at a time when most customers were satisfied with low-cost disposables. Andrew Shore of Shearson Lehman Hutton decided that the Sensor story was not about market share versus competitors but "a vision of how to make more profit from a sluggish market." He concluded that Gillette would do well with Sensor.

A Bic spokeswoman said she did not think Sensor was such a hot item.

All this followed an ambitious show put on for Gillette's entire European and North American sales force, who had assembled a few weeks earlier at a sports arena outside Washington, D.C., for their first look at the new product. The simultaneous North Atlantic launch marked by far the biggest test of the evolving global strategy at Gillette: one product, one ad campaign for nineteen countries, with the same visuals and music, and only the language altered for local understanding.

Symons was at his evangelical best as he stood under a single spotlight in a darkened hall, fists clenched and arms upraised, and exhorted his Gillette sales troops to move out as he had once done and sell Sensor to accounts in every hamlet and city in their territory. More music. Moving lights. It was show biz. Symons loved it.

The epilogue to the Sensor story was a happy one for Gillette. In 1990, the year of the launch, 24 million Sensor razors were sold, far above the company estimate of 18 million. Instead of producing and shipping an estimated 200 million Sensor blade cartridges, Gillette shipped 350 million. For a short time, demand was so strong that advertising had to be pulled in an effort to let the South Boston and Berlin factories—both operating twenty-four hours a day, seven days a week—crank out more product. Sensor captured 9 percent of the total North Atlantic blade market by year-end. The new razor provided momentum that pushed company sales up 14 percent and decisively over the $4 billion level.

Not surprisingly, investors were impressed with this development. From a low of $33 in early 1990, the price of one Gillette share moved up to just under $50 at year-end, representing a yearly gain three times better than the Dow Jones industrials. It was, concluded Al Zeien, the most successful product launch in the company's history. Of course, Sensor did not produce instant profits. Zeien said Sensor did not break into the black for two and a half years, until the second half of 1992. But the psychological boost was immediate, and the stage was set for many years of profits from replacement Sensor blade sales.

The boost to employee morale from Sensor's successful launch is difficult to overstate. The company was only a year and a half removed from the takeover threats and the Coniston proxy fight. Although sales and profits had moved up smartly, employees had read much in press accounts about a mystery razor often portrayed as a "bet your company" gamble. Company officials scoffed at the notion, but the perception was widespread. The undiluted good news that came with Sensor's instant success proved a tonic beyond dollar value.

GILLETTE REORGANIZES

Colman Mockler surprised nearly everyone outside Gillette's inner circle when he announced on November 15, 1990, that he intended to retire at the end of 1991, when he would be nearing sixty-two years of age. He said he wanted to set in motion a process of orderly management succession. With the directors' approval, he chose Al Zeien as president and chief operating officer effective the first day of 1991, a move that singled out Zeien as Mockler's indicated choice to succeed him. Joe Mullaney was named a director and vice chairman-legal. Robert J. Murray was named to be one of three executive vice presidents, assuming direct control of the North Atlantic Group, Gillette's largest operation. If there was any challenge to Zeien, presumably it would come from these men.

In the shuffle, the post of vice chairman-North Atlantic held by Derwyn Phillips was eliminated. Removed from any chance to succeed Mockler, Phillips decided to retire. He was ready to leave the daily grind at any rate, Phillips later said from his summer residence on the rocky shores of Marblehead, Massachusetts.

In a strange turn of events, John Symons was gone by Christmas of 1990, victim of the reorganization that had eliminated his base of power as president of the shaving and personal care group. There was no place for the combative Englishman to go but home. On November 19, 1990, he tendered his letter of resignation as an officer of the company in a one-sentence pro-forma document, though he made clear to friends that he was not happy about being pushed aside. The old London cop, who did not claim to be a diplomat, had never learned to take no for an answer to his pet ideas. "Watch out when Old Snowy gets red in the face right up to his white hair. He's about to explode," an English colleague had warned one Boston executive who inquired about Symons' disposition. He had often been proved correct. Despite the unqualified success of Sensor, Symons' insistent demands that he run the show his way and his contempt for the company's nonshaving businesses alienated him from many at headquarters. He was a hero to many at Gillette, and an unusual and irreplaceable manager when Gillette badly needed his leadership. But his personality was not suited to Gillette's corporate style for day-to-day management at a senior level. He was sixty-one when he retired.

At their December meeting a few weeks later, the board hailed Symons' twenty-three years at the company with language more colorful than the usual boilerplate of farewell resolutions. The directors thanked him for his "astute and vigorous leadership in the development of the company's commitment to the strategy that Gillette Is the Best a Man Can Get."

THE SHOCKING DEATH OF COLMAN MOCKLER

The euphoria built up by Sensor's year-long success burst in a heartbeat late in the morning of January 25, 1991, just two months after Mockler had announced his impending retirement. Mockler had concluded the regular Friday morning meeting of the chairman's office, a group consisting of himself and his three most senior corporate colleagues. There had been some joking about the big incident of the week—a *Forbes* magazine cover story lauding Mockler in almost fulsome tones and portraying the dignified leader as a sort of modish Superman in a double-breasted suit, wielding an ax-sized Sensor as he stood atop a mountain with vanquished foes below. That had been good for some laughs, not the least by Mockler himself. A week earlier, public relations chief Dave Fausch, just prior to leaving for a vacation in Hawaii, had given Mockler a prepublication copy of the magazine and asked for his reaction to the piece. When Mockler called Fausch back to his office about thirty minutes later, the boss peered at Fausch, grim-faced. After a lengthy pause, Mockler remarked, "I don't wear double-breasted suits," and then broke into an explosive laugh.

Tom Skelly, the company's senior financial officer, remembered how the chairman's office members kidded him at their January

25 meeting about the *Forbes* story, advising him that now was the time to rent a jet and with his wife make a farewell tour of the Gillette empire, with Mockler predictably demurring from such a grandiose gesture. The meeting broke up about 11:30 A.M. Shortly thereafter, Mockler followed his usual routine and headed down the hallway past other executive offices to check stock market conditions on a computer at the end of the corridor. About halfway there, he suddenly collapsed on the carpeted floor and died almost instantly from a massive heart attack.

Dr. William Greer, the long-time company doctor, was summoned from his office one floor above by an employee who mistakenly told him that Mockler had fallen and injured his leg. In his long career at Gillette, Dr. Greer had answered many emergency calls. Eight times he had been called to resuscitate heart attack victims, and six times he had succeeded. When he arrived on the thirty-ninth floor moments later, he headed down the empty hallway toward a group of men and women huddled around the fallen Mockler. Several people with CPR training had tried to revive Mockler but without success.

"He was dead—no question, but we tried anyway to resuscitate him," Dr. Greer recalled. "There was nothing we could do. Sometimes it just happens, a rupture or something and there's nothing you can do. It was a sad day."

An ambulance crew soon arrived, but the paramedics could do nothing to revive him. Mockler was removed to University Hospital, where he was officially pronounced dead. Efforts to reach his wife and other family members had already begun. Senior officials were adamant about saying nothing to the media or to NYSE officials until Mockler's family had been notified. In a great irony, his wife, unknown to those trying to locate her, was literally next door in another part of the Prudential Center, attending an evangelical conference at the Sheraton Hotel. She was finally located by a Gillette manager who was a fellow church member, and accompanied back to her husband's office.

The hours before Joanna Mockler was informed were tense. Three times, reporter Ron Suskind from the *Wall Street Journal* called the company's public relations office to inquire about rumors that had begun to circulate about Mockler's death, growing increasingly insistent and demanding. Each time he was held at bay with a response that told him nothing: "Someone will get back to you." Complicating matters, Dave Fausch was in Hawaii. He headed back to Boston at once when he was informed, but it fell to Corporate P.R. Director Joan Gallagher to announce the tragic and, in business terms, sensitive news. At about 3:15 P.M., the company issued a short press release: "The Gillette Company regrets to announce the death today of its Chairman and Chief Executive Officer, Colman M. Mockler, Jr. Mr. Mockler died unexpectedly of a heart attack at Gillette headquarters."

At 3:17 P.M. the Dow Jones newswire flashed a bulletin: "Gillette says chairman, CEO Mockler dies of heart attack." In a singular response that only Wall Street could give, the price of the company's stock hardly fluttered after word of his death crossed the broad tape, closing at $65, or up a fraction from the previous day's close. It was the Street's way of saying that Mockler had left Gillette in great shape as a business and with a plan of succession apparently in place.

Obituaries the next day commented on Mockler's many achievements as a human being who cared about others, on his strong code of ethics, and on his successes at Gillette. Many writers singled out his singular contribution to his alma mater, Harvard University, where he had served as a member of the university's major governing board, the Harvard Corporation. A front-page story in the *Boston Globe* described him as "the quiet chairman . . . who fought off corporate raiders and kept the company both independent and prosperous."[2]

Funeral services were held at Mockler's home church, the Grace Chapel in Lexington, Massachusetts. Hundreds of friends and colleagues from Gillette assembled for a service where matters of the Holy Spirit and salvation were treated seriously by the presiding ministers, just as they were by Colman Mockler during his lifetime, both on and off the job. The next week, a memorial service honoring Mockler was held at Old South Church in Boston's Back Bay, a few blocks down Boylston Street from Gillette headquarters. It, too, was a distinctly religious service and allowed employees the opportunity to mourn this loss openly and reflect on the larger message of Mockler's life. Later, hundreds more of his friends attended a service at Harvard's Memorial Chapel. Physicist Charles P. Slichter, a fellow Harvard Corporation member, caught the essence of Mockler's personality when he noted that it was Mockler's style at meetings to let others have the first say, speaking infrequently but then always to the point, sensible, adding a new dimension. Slichter noted that Mockler's heart attack occurred a few weeks before the search committee, on which both had served, had made a final choice of Neil Rudenstine to be Harvard's twenty-sixth president. He said that he knew that Mockler was voting yes when the final vote was made.

After a few days, news reports began to speculate on Mockler's successor, always noting that Zeien was the front-runner for the dual role of chairman and CEO but also analyzing the prospects of Mullaney and Murray. Mullaney had support within the company, including some board members. Murray, at forty-nine much younger than either Zeien, sixty, or Mullaney, fifty-seven, and well known to outsiders, was considered by some Gillette-watchers a long-shot possibility for the CEO role. Alice Longley of Donaldson, Lufkin & Jenrette and Andrew Shore of Prudential-Bache were among the few investment analysts to go out on a limb, speculating that Mullaney would most likely get the nod as chairman. At Gillette there was suspense but hardly great surprise when the directors met February 21 and, at the end of a busy day that included their declaring a two-for-one stock split and a 15 percent dividend increase, announced their unanimous choice of Al Zeien as chairman and chief executive officer.

Activities at Gillette moved ahead, "steady as she goes," as Zeien said that afternoon. In the company's annual report, published just a few weeks later, Zeien paid tribute to Colman Mockler in business language any executive would savor. The Gillette Company, he noted, continued its strong momentum of recent years, achieving record sales, income, and earnings per share in

1990. This performance, Zeien concluded, reflected the vigorous and growing company to which Colman Mockler's leadership had contributed so much. In more personal terms, Mockler was eulogized elsewhere in the report as a man who would "be remembered by his friends and colleagues as much for his exemplary personal qualities as for his outstanding professional achievements."

12

AL ZEIEN
TAKES
CHARGE

AL ZEIEN HAD just turned sixty-one when he took over, an "old man" at Gillette, where senior executives tend to join the company early and retire early after thirty-five years on the job. A few foolish outsiders thought that Zeien would be a caretaker CEO who would keep the Sensor-generated momentum going but not start major new initiatives or shake things up . . . would hand the company over to a younger man and retire after a few years to a life of leisure. Anyone who knew Zeien at all had a good laugh at this fantasy.

Alfred M. Zeien is a first-generation American. His father moved to the United States as a young man from Luxembourg, and his mother emigrated from France. They came through Ellis Island, courted, married, and settled down to raise a family in the multiethnic New York City neighborhood of Jackson Heights. Zeien's father, who spoke four languages, was an able cabinet-maker who thought his children should learn practical skills. At home, Al Zeien learned French, the language his parents often spoke around the house. He learned to build furniture and install wiring and plumbing fixtures before he was out of high school. He excelled academically, graduating first in his class in both elementary and secondary school, and as a result he had exceptional college opportunities to sort out when he turned seventeen. Harvard and MIT both offered full scholarships, but Zeien was intrigued by another school, the little known but greatly respected Webb Institute of Naval Architecture in New York. Climbing the corporate ladder at Gillette was child's play compared with getting into Webb, as Zeien tells it. Of eight hundred applicants, two hundred young men were invited to a series of tests at the school gymnasium. After the first day of tests, a few dozen names were called, and those boys who failed to survive the cut filed out. The process was repeated for days until finally, the two hundred were winnowed to sixteen survivors who were admitted to Webb. Zeien was one of nine who graduated, a bona fide naval architect eager to put his skills to work. Shunning big corporations, Zeien started a design firm in Connecticut, where he and five employees designed yachts, did the lofting, and ordered materials for specialty yards up and down the East Coast while his wife Joyce sold real estate in coastal Connecticut. Demands of the Korean War changed the nature of boat building, and Zeien decided to move on and attend Harvard Business School. There he became intrigued and fascinated by the nuclear submarine program led by the legendary Admiral Hyman Rickover. At twenty-six, Zeien became chief estimator at the General Dynamics shipyard at Groton, Connecticut, and at twenty-eight he was sales manager. Five years later, he was working out of General Dynamics headquarters in Manhattan, in charge of mergers and acquisitions, and learning some Wall Street lessons that would prove critical twenty years later at Gillette.

His biggest M & A coup at General Dynamics was the acquisition of a big shipyard at Quincy, Massachusetts, just south of Boston. Before long the erstwhile M & A manager was posted to Quincy as operational head of the shipyard—and he was only thirty-four years old, with eight thousand employees working for him. No romanticist about the marine industry as a business,

Zeien had accurately read the handwriting on the wall and concluded that U.S. shipbuilding was in for hard times. He started to
look around, and in 1968, just after Gillette concluded its purchase
of Braun AG in Germany, he was hired by Gillette and sent
immediately to Frankfurt to start up an international division for
Braun as its general manager.

"I came home to my wife the night I signed on and told her I
had decided to leave the marine industry and go into consumer
products, that I had joined Gillette, and that we were going to
move to Germany right away. I remember she looked at me and
said, 'But I just bought a puppy today.'" The dog went along with
the Zeiens when they moved.

Zeien's first job at Braun was to strip the company's five
operating divisions of their non-German businesses and consolidate them in an international operation. This was his first taste of
at least incipient globalization. The job successfully completed, the
Zeiens returned to Boston in 1973, where he was appointed a
group vice president in the Diversified Companies operation for
a short time, before being hastily recalled to Braun the next year
as head of the domestic or German half of the company, which
had gone into a sudden tailspin when government-recommended
retail price supports were withdrawn. He stopped a flow of red
ink at the division and convinced Colman Mockler to resist those
who wanted to sell Braun and be rid of its problems. Zeien was
elected chairman of the board of management—Braun's top job,
and reorganized the company to fit the increasingly multinational
world of Gillette. He is regarded by most Gillette-watchers as the
man whose faith in Braun's future saved the company from being
sold. This accomplishment loomed large a dozen years later when
Braun had become a global force in electric shaving and small
household appliances and Gillette's second most profitable division after blades and razors.

When Zeien returned to Boston to stay in 1978, he assumed
the role of Gillette's most senior technical manager, and as related
in Chapter 11, he played a pivotal role in developing the Sensor
razor. He reorganized the company's technical operations and its
approach to developing new products. In a different role, he was

a key player as Mockler's contact man with the investment and banking communities during the takeover wars.

A COMPANY'S MISSION AND ITS VALUES

One of Zeien's first moves after his election as Gillette chairman in 1991 was to introduce a mission and values statement that Gillette employees worldwide came to recognize as the outline of Gillette's long-term strategy—nothing less than Gillette's blueprint of how it would transform itself to a truly global company. The statement's key phrase is this: "Our mission is to achieve or enhance clear leadership, worldwide, in the existing or new core consumer product categories in which we choose to compete." Zeien emphasized the importance of the statement. "It says we will not become involved in any way whatsoever in a core business in which we are neither the worldwide leader or have a plan in place to become the worldwide leader." Put another way, the days of buying or developing new product lines that could not show a reasonable promise of global leadership were over. During his first few months as CEO, Zeien devoted much of his time to personally promoting the mission and values statement. Traveling about the world, he made it clear that the corporate credo was not to be made into a plaque and hung on the office wall next to a sailboat picture but was instead a living document designed to emphasize the company's strategic mission. Zeien told many interviewers to focus on the words "clear leadership, worldwide," which was his test of globalism. He emphasized that the standard is tougher than, for example, the standard at General Electric, where Chairman Jack Welch demands that GE be number one or number two in a given geographic market like North America or the United Kingdom but not worldwide.

The document also laid out the company's values, focusing on Gillette's relationship with its employees, customers, and the nations and communities where it does business. The idea of a written guideline had first been raised by Mockler, and more than one executive, past or present, claimed to have produced a comparable mission statement during the Mockler years, only to see the idea of codifying the company's mission gather dust once it hit the boss's desk. It was never "sold," as Zeien put it.

At about the same time that Zeien was promoting the mission and values statement, the company came up with a new corporate logo to replace the Omnimark logo that had lasted remarkably long as these things go—since 1970. The Omnimark was a circle with three horizontal bars that represented quality, integrity, and activity. The new logo bore a resemblance to the old but used a bolder, italicized typeface and repositioned the circular shape to suggest a stylish letter G. The three bars remained, representing the much-used tag line that proclaimed Gillette's commitment to globalism—world-class brands, world-class products, world-class people.

Whether the mission and values statement really meant something beyond noble words got an early test when Joel P. Davis, then running the Stationery Products Group, came to Zeien one day in 1992 with the statement in hand and, in effect, dared the CEO to support a controversial acquisition. Buy Parker Pen Company, he urged, and Gillette will be the undisputed world leader in the nearly $8 billion writing instruments business. It was a big step, buying the world's second largest pen company, but Davis was persistent. After nearly forty years in the stationery business, much of it spent scratching and playing catch-up, he argued that this was Gillette's chance to achieve once and for all "clear leadership, worldwide" in one of the company's "existing core consumer product categories"—language from the mission statement not lost on Zeien.

Gillette had been a force in the pen and mechanical pencil business since 1955, when Paper Mate was acquired. In world markets, and especially in North America, Gillette had fought the good fight for decades against low-cost competitors like Bic, Scripto, and Pilot, selling refillable products and inexpensive stick pens, specialty pens, and an array of related stationery products.

Joel Davis, had returned from Europe in 1983 to take over as marketing chief at Paper Mate when worldwide sales for the stationery products business were about $250 million and profits were negligible. His strategy had been to add more high-value products and lessen dependence on U.S. sales. Product innovations such as the Flexgrip pens with rubberized barrels helped, but the breakthrough that moved stationery products from a mostly domestic underperformer to a profitable global unit was the 1987 acquisition of Waterman Pen Company, a leader in luxury pens.

When he heard in 1985 that French-controlled Waterman might be up for sale, Davis asked Jacques Lagarde, who at the time was in charge of Gillette's operation in France, to sound out Francine Gomez, Waterman's mercurial director-general. Mme. Gomez was a Parisian legend, moving easily in and out of the capital's political, cultural, social, and business circles with a high degree of visibility. A long period of negotiations began with the strong support of Gillette International's executive vice president, Rodney S. Mills, and indispensable help from André Doucet, a French citizen who had moved to a post in the New Business Development division at Gillette following divestment of the luxury goods maker S. T. Dupont.

Gillette's European legal chief from the London office, Robert G. S. Forrester, soon became a key player in the politically charged negotiations with Mme. Gomez. She finally accepted a Gillette offer after winning promises that the company would keep Waterman's design and production facilities in France.

Initially, she was happy with Gillette's handling of Waterman. She visited Boston, where she was fêted by Gillette leaders and Boston's tiny French community. However, the honeymoon was short-lived. Just before Christmas 1988, she resigned as Waterman president and director-general in "complete disagreement" with Gillette's plans to sell the stylish, expensive line of Waterman pens in such office discount stores as Staples. Sell a $400 Waterman for $200 at a discount store that sells paper clips in an adjacent aisle? To her that was sacrilege, like peddling Rolls Royces fender to fender with Fords. To Davis it was a smart move, making the fine pens available at an attractive price in stores frequented by businesspeople, who were the pens' target customers. Davis was correct. Within a year or so, Waterman had made deep inroads into the luxury pen market in the United States, where many consumers bought pens selling for $1,000 or more in luxury goods stores, and others sought out $100 pens marked down significantly at office discount stores.

The Waterman franchise gave Gillette a stronghold on the high-end market to go with its strong position in lower-priced Paper Mate pens. The earnings of Gillette's worldwide stationery business more than quadrupled from 1986 to 1988, attaining respectable if hardly bladelike profitability.

The Addition of Parker Pen

If an acquisition worked once, why not twice? Parker Pen was the biggest maker of high-quality pens, and the addition of this British company to Gillette's Stationery Products Group would give the company unbeatable strength in mid-priced pens and a second major source of high-end writing products. Gillette earlier had tried to buy Parker but gave up late in 1985, when an investor group that included members of the Parker family got the inside track, and it became obvious that outside bidders would be shut out. Now it was 1992, and suddenly the company was up for sale again. Joel Davis got the word on Monday in February after a cross-country flight to Santa Monica on Paper Mate business. When he checked his Boston office after arriving about noon, there was a "good news/bad news" message from the New Business Development vice president, Ken Kames. "Ken told me the good news is that Parker is for sale and the bad news is that Zeien, Mullaney, and Skelly had already talked about it and concluded they did not even want to look at Parker's numbers," said Davis. Mullaney, the legal vice chairman, was concerned about antitrust obstacles. Skelly, as chief financial officer, worried about a very large investment in a Gillette product line that had never been very profitable.

Davis knew he had a lot of selling to do inside Gillette, and he took aim right at the top in a meeting with Al Zeien. Mullaney and Kames were also there. On the speakerphone from his home in London was the English barrister, Bob Forrester, described by

GLOBAL SCARS FROM ANTITRUST

Gillette's legal chief, Joe Mullaney, had every reason to be wary when he raised the spectre of antitrust problems from both Washington and Europe if the company went after British-owned Parker Pen Company.

Late in 1989 Gillette, together with a group of investors and a management group from Swedish Match Company, announced their intent to buy the disposable lighter, match, and Wilkinson Sword blade and razor business from Stora AB of Sweden. Gillette was interested only in the Wilkinson blade and razor business. The deal was structured to give Gillette 100 percent control of Wilkinson operations, except for the European Community (EC) nations of Western Europe, where Gillette knew antitrust considerations clearly prohibited the company's participation. The company planned from the start to liquidate its minority interest in the other businesses.

In the United States, Wilkinson had only 2 percent of the blade market, but despite this low figure the Justice Department argued that the deal broke U.S. antitrust laws. In 1990 Gillette agreed to sell off its U.S. interests in Wilkinson to avoid lengthy and expensive litigation. European court rulings in 1992 forced Gillette to dispose of its Wilkinson interests in all of Western Europe—not just the EC—plus Eastern Europe and Turkey. As a result, Gillette wound up in March 1993 selling both its North American and European interests in Wilkinson to Warner-Lambert, parent company of Schick razor. Gillette retained full control of the Wilkinson business throughout Latin America and Asia, and restricted control in Australia. But for the North Atlantic Group, the Wilkinson deal had proved unrealizable after long and costly months of legal wrangling. Mullaney knew the proposed Parker deal would revisit many of the same issues.

Davis as "my ace in the hole" because, after all, this was another European affair with Waterman-like overtones. Davis made his pitch directly to Zeien, making his case on the mission and values statement's stated goals. He contended that adding Parker would strengthen the Stationery Products Group at every price point in every distribution channel in every writing system in every world market, making Gillette the clear worldwide leader—exactly the criteria of the mission and values statement. It would enhance profit margins and add global reach, Davis argued.

It was a persuasive business argument, but there remained the antitrust doubts. What did Forrester think? "A 50-50 bet, but I'm not telling you we can't do this," Forrester said from London. The glass was half full, he was saying. The skeptical threesome of Zeien, Mullaney, and Skelly were persuaded, at least to the point that Zeien told Davis to check it out and see if a deal was possible.

After a few weeks' study, Davis was convinced that the deal made business sense and could be done. He was given a green light by the board to approach Parker. Davis arrived at the Parker headquarters in Newhaven, England, on April 9, 1992—he recalls the date because it was his daughter's birthday and because John Major scored an upset win that day to retain his seat as England's prime minister. Gillette and Parker officials sparred for a while— they were rivals in the marketplace so there was some strain—but in the end, Gillette was invited to submit a bid along with a few other suitors. A short time later, Davis returned to Newhaven with an attractive bid. He and Kames had convinced Zeien that Gillette had to bid high because if competing bids were close, the antitrust uncertainties would make it easy for Parker to choose another to forgo legal skirmishes. Parker accepted Gillette's bid of £285 million (U.S. $458 million) in September 1992.

That was the easy part. The French, English, and American regulatory authorities had to be convinced that the deal would not harm their respective national interests. First came the French. At a Paris meeting of regulatory authorities, seated between Parker chairman Jacques Margry, a Frenchman who had lived in England for years, and Waterman's chief, Jean Veillon, Davis struggled to understand the dialogue. Finally, he asked Veillon to interpret what was being said. "They hate it," he replied. Davis spent most of December 1992 in France reassuring French authorities that Waterman's French production would be unaffected by Parker. He signed off on several commitments to retain Waterman jobs, and just before the new year, the French authorities agreed to the deal.

Attention turned to England, where the Monopolies and Mergers Commission, or MMC, grilled Gillette and Parker separately for days on end. Davis grew concerned that the English would attach impossible conditions. But on February 10, 1993, he got a jubilant call from Forrester—"The MMC approved the merger without conditions."

Now it was up to the United States, where Justice Department lawyers since mid-autumn had been asking for more and more and yet more detail. Most of the requests were for arcane manufacturing information showing how much it cost to make Parker products and how and where components were secured.

Davis noted a critical difference between the English MMC and the American lawyer-dominated process. The MMC members were businesspeople, and they understood that the acquisition had not much to do with manufacturing but everything to do with marketing. The American lawyers were mired in information not always relevant to the case. Time was growing short. Gillette needed a decision or the deal was dead. Finally, in March, just a few weeks after the change in administration from President George Bush to President Bill Clinton, the still-leaderless Justice Department moved, and it was bad news. Justice sought a temporary restraining order, which in effect would have killed the deal because Parker's owners were growing impatient for closure and had set a deadline for early May.

Gillette sought at once to block the order by arguing to Federal District Court judge Stanley Sporkin, who had come to prominence as a tough enforcer at the Securities and Exchange Commission. To the huge relief of Gillette, Sporkin turned down the government's request for a temporary injunction, issuing a strong and dramatic argument supporting Gillette's position. According to a *Boston Globe* account of his decision, Sporkin said in court that "Only rich people buying expensive fountain pens would get hurt. . . . It's a status thing for them. I buy an 87-cent pen and it does the same thing," Then he reached under his robe into his shirt pocket and brandished a throwaway pen, adding, "Trust-busters have better things to worry about than a monopoly of fountain pens."[1]

Judge Royce Lamberth echoed Sporkin's sentiment on May 6, when Lamberth declined in federal district court the Justice Department's request to issue a preliminary injunction against Gillette. On May 7, 1993, the deal was closed, and Parker Pen became a Gillette business, the largest component of the Stationery Products Group. The Justice Department, which still had legal room to challenge the deal, eventually dropped the case, influenced by these decisions and Gillette's own legal position.

A lot of tough business decisions still had to be made about brand strategy and how to sort out the overlap in low-, mid-, and high-price markets. Davis knew that it was critical to keep the product personalities of Waterman and Parker distinct. Waterman pens, like those in its lacquered maroon-and-gold Expert 2 line, were admired for their French flair and sense of style; these were products that gave the user great pleasure. Parker pens, like the black-and-white-marbled Duofold fountain pen, had a reputation for Anglo-American functional integrity and impeccable technology. It was decided to run Parker, Waterman, and Paper Mate as distinct businesses under the Gillette umbrella, with global marketing plans directed from respective headquarters in England, France, and the United States but coordinated at Boston—a different structure than the more centralized blade and razor operation.

SENSOR FOR WOMEN, TOO

Not long after Sensor's smashing debut, Gillette began at last to come to grips with women's shaving needs. The company had tinkered halfheartedly with slightly feminized knock-offs of male razors, beginning in 1915 with MiLady Décolleté and, in more modern times, with Daisy, Lady Sure Touch, and Just Whistle, a 1980 product whose name struck many as patronizing. Just Whistle produced nominal sales for ten years until it was straightforwardly renamed Atra for Women, an accurate description because the product was a slightly curved and slightly longer-handled blue-green version of the standard Atra razor. Atra for Women produced respectable sales despite no advertising, and that opened some eyes.

Research dating to 1959 had revealed significant differences in the way men and women shave and how they viewed the experience. Men shaved about six times a week, which was twice as often as women. Men changed blades after ten to twelve shaves, women less frequently. Predictably, men spent more money on shaving than women, who often borrowed their mate's razor.

Gillette marketers learned from a study in the late 1980s that men and women perceived shaving quite differently. Men viewed shaving as a skill, but women viewed it as a chore. Men valued weight and balance in a razor as a sign of quality. Women feared a heavy razor, afraid it would slip from their soapy hands in the shower and cut them. When men cut themselves, they blamed the razor. When women got a nick or cut, they blamed themselves. Additionally, women believed that twin-bladed products were more likely to produce nicks or cuts, whereas the opposite is true. Thus women tended to settle for cheap single-blade disposable products, a finding that distressed Gillette executives.

Sharon Keith, the North Atlantic Group's vice president for marketing research, recognized the untapped potential, as did some of her male colleagues. But there was internal naysaying and indecisiveness about diverting manufacturing space and marketing attention from the male shaving enterprise, especially when the company was spending hundreds of millions of dollars to reassert its masculine image. The relentless "Best a Man Can Get" theme hardly seemed a promising message for women—though confounding many assumptions, Keith's research showed that "The Best" ads were not a turn-off to women but instead appealed to many of them because the ads portrayed men as sensitive fathers and husbands.

The solution was perhaps two parts technology and one part clever marketing.

In 1991, technologists at the company's South Boston industrial design center came up with several variants of a female Sensor. One prototype was basically a pink Sensor, representing Gillette's traditional approach. But the prototype that excited all who saw it was a strikingly different product than the standard Sensor. Jill Shurtleff, a graduate of the Rhode Island School of Design, was the chief industrial designer of the winning prototype. She literally shed blood in her work, personally testing every wet shaver on the market, and became convinced that existing T-shaped razors, like the Atra for Women and Daisy disposables, were ill conceived for shaving female underarms and legs.

When the standard Sensor was introduced, market research showed that women preferred the performance of the spring-mounted blades but did not like the way the razor felt in their hands. The metal handle was too heavy and was too likely to slip in the wet confines of shower or bath, where most women shave. Shurtleff came up with a lighter plastic razor with a much broader and more deeply ribbed handle to replace the slim handle of the T-shaped razor. She designed it for maximum maneuverability, literally to fit in the palm of a woman's hand and to function as an extension of her fingers. The tactile waves on the handle made the razor easier to hang onto under wet and slippery conditions. The Sensor for Women was made of translucent light bluish-green plastic. In every way, except for the interchangeable Sensor blade cartridge, it was a product distinct from the silver and black T-shaped, metal, and masculine Sensor razor.

North Atlantic chief Bob Murray asked directors for funds to produce 6 million Sensor for Women razors. Then he took a closer look at Keith's research and upped that to enough money to produce 12 million. Several more times he went back to the board with Zeien's strong support to request funds for increased manufacturing capacity before Sensor for Women was introduced in the summer of 1992.

A $14 million advertising campaign for the first year included prime-time television as opposed to the customary placement during the daytime soap operas and immediately the product took off. Demand far outstripped supply for many months as pleasantly surprised Gillette executives scrambled to increase output. Elegant television and print ads positioned shaving as a meaningful part of a woman's beauty regimen, with watery images of a woman demonstrating how the razor would seamlessly glide over her legs. In the Gillette North Atlantic region, using Gillette's formula that women account for $1 of every $7 spent for blade and razor products, women's shaving by the mid-1990s made up the group's second-largest business, outselling male toiletries as well as the company's traditional line of deodorants and antiperspirants.

"Finally, a razor worth holding on to," was the advertising tagline that eventually was translated into French, Italian, Spanish, German, Russian, Polish, and other languages. The global demand for Sensor for Women was an eye-opener for Gillette. It had been assumed from market surveys and anecdotal evidence that North American and British women were far more likely to shave, and more often, than women elsewhere. Strong worldwide demand for Sensor for Women called that assumption into question, with sales apparently more related to income than geography. Women everywhere, it seemed, wanted their own razor, and millions were willing to pay a premium for it. The old imaginary line through the map of Europe, with women shavers concentrated to the west, fell as quickly as the Berlin Wall had done a few years before. Women in Eastern Europe and much of Asia responded to the advertising. The St. Petersburg, Russia, periodical *Smena* told its readers that consumer tests showed that men think women like pink but women "hate this color and prefer any other color to it." With the green and white Sensor for Women, *Smena* rhapsodized "Gillette has realized every woman's dream for smooth legs with no nicks or cuts." Another magazine, *Vecherniy St. Petersburg*, predicted in 1995 great days ahead for Sensor for Women, priced at 27,000 rubles (approximately U.S. $5), because research showed that 80 percent of Russian women shaved legs and underarms with "inconvenient men's razors." Clearly, Gillette had another fast-selling universal product for its global marketing machine.

Product designer Jill Shurtleff joined the marketing effort, which was keyed to the theme "a product designed by a woman, for women." As chief technology spokesperson, she traveled extensively during product launches. Her goal, she said, had been to "create a product that customers have an emotional reaction to, an Italian approach as opposed to the German or functional approach." She earned professional honors from the prestigious Industrial Designers Society of America, and her visible success was good for the image of Gillette, too. It showed that a company positioned as a manly enterprise, where women were conspicuously missing from corporate officer ranks and scarce among senior managers, had recognized the value of women shavers and had rewarded and empowered a key female employee for her good work.

The subsequent success of Sensor for Women and later Sensor-Excel for Women convinced senior management of the merits of manufacturing and marketing separate razors for men and women. In 1996, one of the North Atlantic Group's most powerful posts, vice president for business management, Blades and Razors, which was held by long-time Gillette marketer John Darman, was split to create the new position of vice president for business management, female shaving, to be assumed by Mary Ann Pesce, a Wharton graduate with fifteen years' experience in Gillette's personal care and shaving operations.

Sometimes no end of technology will overcome cultural objections to a product. A significant number of European women remove unwanted hair with epilators, which literally pluck hairs from the body. When Braun, the world leader in this category, introduced the Silk-épil epilator it was touted as less painful and more efficient than other models on the market and a sensible alternative to depilating hair with wax. But American women have simply refused to tolerate the pain involved with ripping out hairs, even though the grooming lasts longer than shaving. Although Braun has had good success in Spain and Italy with Silk-épil, and to a lesser extent in the rest of Europe, the figures tell the story: Epilator usage among European women was 14 percent in 1996 versus one half of 1 percent for women in the United States and Canada.

THE GILLETTE SERIES IS BORN

One day in 1990 John Symons strode into the office of Peter Hoffman, his North Atlantic marketing chief for blades and razors. You are now in charge of extending the Gillette brand approach into men's toiletries, he was told. It was not unexpected. Expanding the Gillette brand name beyond blades and razors into male toiletries and shaving preparations—male grooming products in general—had always been part of the Symons strategy for Gillette, and this was the time to do it, by capitalizing on the momentum of Sensor and the "Best a Man Can Get" theme.

The idea would succeed or fail on innovative technology, and Hoffman's instructions to the R & D department were demanding: Gillette wants new toiletries and shaving products that are the best a man can get—new and better product forms like clear gels, superior chemistry, innovative ways of dispensing the product, and new emphasis on fragrance. We'll call these products the Gillette Series, he said, and they must compete for market leadership in every part of the world.

After an investment of $75 million and day and night work, the company had come up with fourteen products by the end of 1991, and marketers were eager to launch them right away. For once, Al Zeien put on the brakes. He decided that a few of the fourteen products were "punk," as indicated by poor results in consumer use tests (CUTS) against leading competitive products. Once, twice, and then three times the launch of the Gillette Series was put off until all fourteen of the products scored better than rivals in Gillette's all-important CUTS.

"I thought we had just one shot at getting this right, and we must have the best products to win. Timing wasn't so important. Quality was," Zeien said. The Gillette Series finally was launched in September 1992, followed with a major advertising push at the 1993 Super Bowl game. There were six gel, foam, and nonaerosol shaving preparations for both normal and sensitive skin; six deodorants and antiperspirants in stick, aerosol, and clear-gel forms, and two aftershave skin conditioners in gel and lotion forms.

The company's clear gel form of antiperspirants was the first major new product form in the category in a decade and was accompanied by a patented dispensing system. The stick deodorant entry was developed with an active ingredient synthesized from moss that grows at the base of French oak trees. Not just any old moss but a type that, in the hands of chemists, made it possible for Gillette to get rid of the white-flake phenomenon plaguing other types of stick dispensers.

Gillette had never paid much attention to fragrance in its male grooming products, but that changed, too. Gillette's chief perfumer, Carl A. Klumpp, was widely respected in the consumer products industry as a professional who understood the importance of smell to female products like Toni home permanents, for which he had devised a minty flower aroma to mask an otherwise sulfurous odor. He was directed to turn his skills to male products.

The further challenge was to come up with so-called global odors, to create scents that would appeal "to the tire hauler in Arkansas, the doctor in Chicago, the waiter in Paris," as reporter Barbara Carton described his task in the *Wall Street Journal*.[2] Klumpp knew that Europeans were more comfortable with fragrances, whereas American men professed indifference. European men liked stronger odors like Smoky Tabac, but Americans often did not. He concentrated on creating "macho scents" like citrus, pine, and woodsy herbs that would be globally acceptable.

After much collaboration with fragrance-supply companies, he began a series of elaborate tests to identify a middle-of-the-road yet distinctive fragrance that would appeal to men everywhere. The result was Cool Wave, the first in the Gillette Series line of deodorants, antiperspirants, and shaving preparations introduced first in the United States, in Europe shortly thereafter, and eventually around the world. Cool Wave was from the French chypre family with a few citrus notes added; a year later came Wild Rain, from another French family, with a floral, woodsy scent like pine; and next was Pacific Light, for sensitive skins. More are sure to come. Hoffman believed that global fragrances, that is, those pleasing to consumers throughout the world, were a major reason Gillette Series products enjoyed quick success in the market for male grooming aids.

Series products received heavy advertising support and were selling in eighty-one countries by the end of 1996. Worldwide sales of the new male grooming line led an increase in sales for the entire toiletries and cosmetics product segment to nearly $1.4 billion that year. Profits were sharply increased, a hopeful sign. In the many years since Right Guard and Foamy for men and the Toni products for women were added to the Gillette portfolio, personal care products often produced strong sales for Gillette but seldom exciting profits. Products that failed or lagged wiped out the profits from winners, and historically the group as a whole had suffered when compared with blade and razor profits. For decades, Gillette ran its personal care business as a brand management operation in the manner of powerhouse competitors such as Procter & Gamble, with great amounts of time and money spent building up separate brands. Moreover, personal care products were weighted to domestic sales.

Zeien has been confident that the Gillette Series strategy of showcasing the globally familiar Gillette brand name with deodorants and antiperspirants and shaving preparation products will make it easier to sell these products profitably in world markets. As Zeien sees it, the more nonshaving products that Gillette can introduce into international markets, the more profitable the blade businesses there will become because both product groups win by sharing warehouse, distribution, and other overhead costs. An increasing flow of new Gillette-branded personal care products will prove a "real global weapon" as Gillette continues to grow its total business away from the more established markets of North America and Europe. He asserts, "The best is yet to come."

Zeien likes to disarm critics who say the company should focus more on blades with such information as this: In the Asia Pacific region in the mid-1990s, the toothbrush business was two to three times bigger—he does not say more profitable—than blades.

A SENSE OF URGENCY

To a remarkable degree, the modern Gillette builds on the company's past. While Zeien has changed many of the old ways of doing business, that does not mean he has forsaken the company's history of growth through new products and geographic expansion. He just has wanted to do it faster by creating a sense of

Right: Gillette introduced a new omnimark in 1993 that reflects its world-class brands, products, and people.

Above: A playful Forbes magazine cover in early 1991 showed a triumphant Colman Mockler, Jr., brandishing an outsized Sensor razor. Mockler was shown a prepublication copy of the cover a few days before he collapsed and died of a heart attack January 25, 1991.

Following the death of Colman Mockler, Jr., Alfred M. Zeien was elected chairman. During the 1990s, Zeien led Gillette to its most successful years as he made the company a truly global force in consumer products.

Above: On October 29, 1993, President Bill Clinton came to South Boston, where he campaigned for passage of the North American Free Trade Act, using Gillette's blade and razor plant as the backdrop.

Left: With Chairman Alfred Zeien, President Clinton inspects blademaking equipment at the company's South Boston plant. Historically, Gillette has supported free trade as good for its global business.

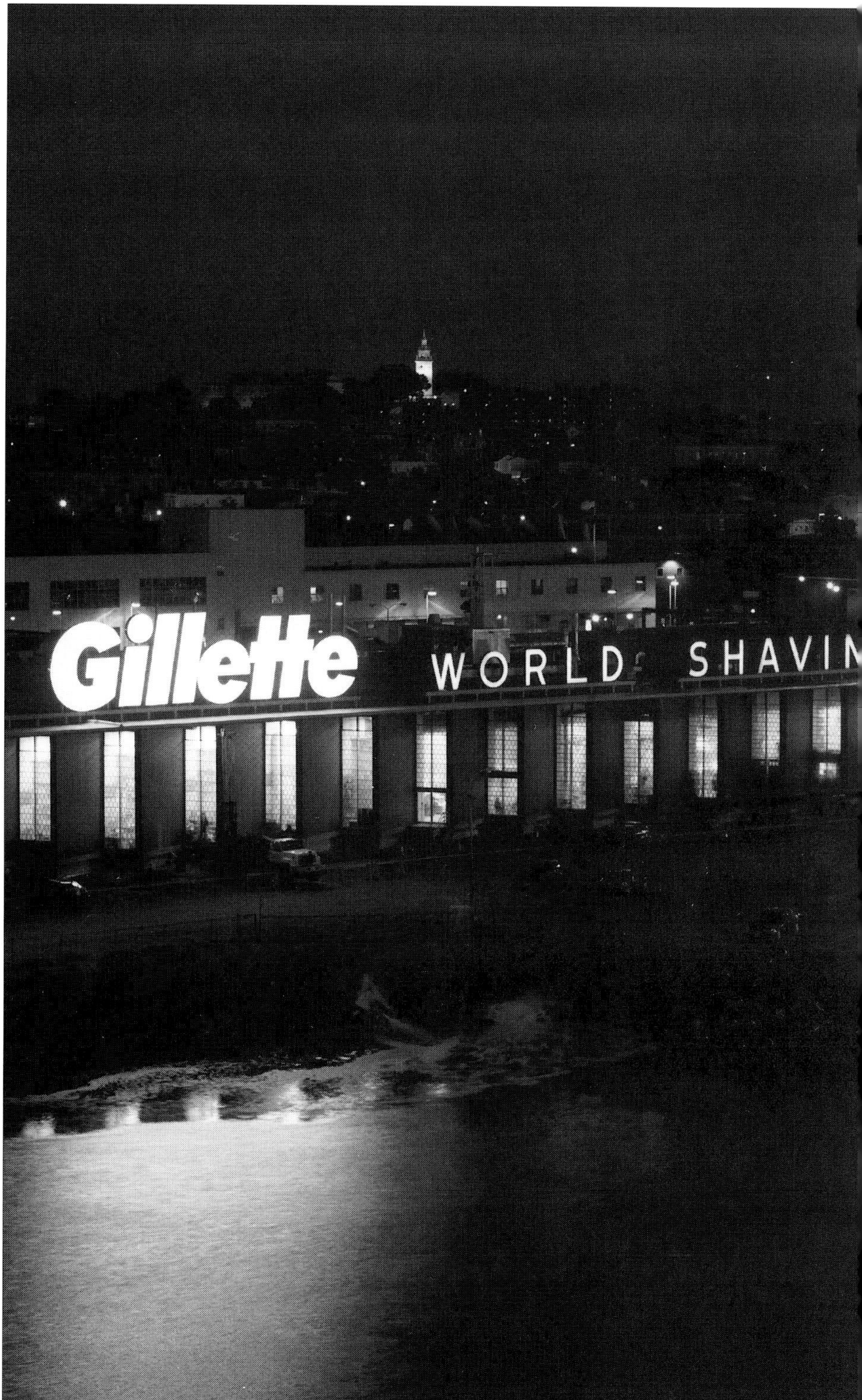
Gillette
WORLD SHAVIN

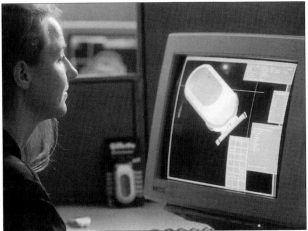

Above: Industrial designer Jill Shurtleff played a major role in creating the top-selling Gillette Sensor for Women shaving system.

Left: The 1.2 million-square-foot South Boston razor and blade factory has been Gillette's most important single plant since the company began making blades on the site in 1905. It literally is "World Shaving Headquarters."

Left: World Cup soccer was the focus of this 1994 advertisement for the Gillette Slalom razor in St. Petersburg, Russia.

Below: The worldwide leader in double edge blades, Gillette sells these products under a variety of brand names overseas.

Beneath the Rule of men entirely great, The pen is mightier than the sword.

Edward Bulwer-Lytton
(Richelieu 1839)

THE SIGNING OF HISTORY

In 1987, Presidents Ronald Reagan and Mikhail Gorbachev exchange Parker pens after signing the INF Treaty, signaling an end to the Cold War and initiating a series of pacts sealed with Parkers.

On June 17, 1992, President George Bush and Russian President Boris Yeltsin emphasize the power of the pen after signing the historic arms reduction accord with Orange Duofold Roller Ball Pens.

The end of World War II in 1945 brought hope for world peace. Today each treaty brings to light the tragedies of conflict. But, most importantly, each treaty demonstrates an undying quest for peace. Details of these powerful moments are etched in history forever bearing witness to the ideal that, truly, the pen is mightier than the sword.

LIFETIME GUARANTEED

✦ PARKER

THE PEN THAT BROUGHT PEACE TO THE WORLD

The world had been at war for six years before peace came. It had taken months to orchestrate:

Limited in production to 1,945 pieces worldwide, each writing instrument is individually numbered, and engraved with the signature of General Douglas MacArthur.

Shortly after midnight on May 7, 1945, General Dwight D. Eisenhower, resting at allied headquarters in Reims, France, receives word that it is time to sign the surrender agreement. Although General Eisenhower is not destined to pen his name to the Armistice (an honor reserved for President Truman), he brings two Parker 51 Fountain Pens to the table for the signing. Afterwards, a smiling Eisenhower makes the "victory sign" using the surrender pens. On September 2, 1945, the U.S.S. Missouri sits in Tokyo Bay. On her deck, amid a sea of military uniforms, is a long table with surrender documents ending the war in the Pacific. General Douglas MacArthur, representing the United Nations, uses his wife's 20-year-old Parker Duofold to sign these historic documents. Then, Admiral Chester Nimitz acting on behalf of the United States comes to the table. For this momentous occasion he also chooses a very special writing instrument — a Parker 51 Fountain Pen presented to him by a friend shortly after Pearl Harbor in anticipation of that moment. The very act of signing is a powerful message of peace delivered with confidence and pride. And in each instance, the message is delivered with a Parker pen.

The solid 18K gold emblem embedded in the pen crown features the "Ruptured Duck" symbol, created for honorable service recognition of World War II veterans.

Since 1899 when the Lucky Curve was used to end the Spanish American War, Parker pens have helped declare that "The pen is mightier than the sword." To recognize the 50th anniversary of the war's end, Parker is proud to present this World War II Commemorative Pen fashioned after the original Duofold given to General MacArthur by his wife, Jean, for the surrender signing. Each limited edition pen features the General's signature and a solid 18K gold die-struck emblem of the "Ruptured Duck." While the origin of the term "Ruptured Duck" is unknown, the logo is based on the Honorable Service Lapel Pin issued to every World War II service member honorably discharged September 1939 and December 1946. In Department of Defense and Commemoration

"TODAY THE GUNS ARE SILENT. A GREAT TRAGEDY HAS ENDED."

GEN. DOUGLAS MACARTHUR • SEPTEMBER 2, 1945

In 1993, Gillette acquired the illustrious Parker Pen Company, whose writing instruments have figured in many significant moments in history. The addition of Parker to the company's Paper Mate and Waterman brands enabled Gillette to become the world leader in writing instruments.

The Gillette Series line of men's toiletries—shave preparations, deodorants/antiperspirants, and after shaves—has strengthened the company's position as the premier male grooming authority worldwide.

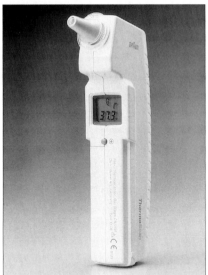

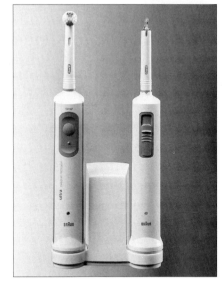

World leaders in their respective market categories are,
clockwise from top, Oral-B
toothbrushes, Braun Oral-B
oral care appliances, and
Thermoscan infrared ear
thermometers.

Launch ads for the SensorExcel shaving system were identical across continents, with only the language changed to meet the needs of the different markets. Shown are German, Greek, Italian, and French versions.

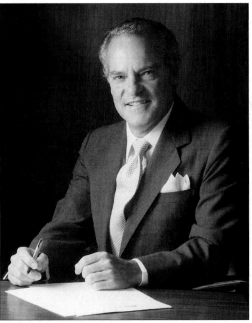

Above: Henry R. Kravis negotiated for KKR, the investment group that controlled Duracell, in talks that ended with Gillette's acquisition of the worldwide battery leader. Kravis became a major stockholder of Gillette and joined its board of directors.

Left: Duracell PowerCheck Mobiles, which supported the introduction of Duracell PowerCheck AA batteries, operated in cities across the United States during the summer of 1996.

Gillette Chairman Alfred M. Zeien, left, and President Michael C. Hawley.

urgency, by getting things done in one year instead of two, in three weeks instead of a month. The SensorExcel, for example, followed Sensor by only three years, which was a much shorter period between major razor innovations than in the past.

When Zeien assumed command in 1991 he was determined to accelerate global expansion; by 1996, prior to the Duracell acquisition, a total of 70 percent of sales and 72 percent of operating profits were generated outside the United States, up from two-thirds of sales and profits in 1990. The company was well positioned in large world markets that were just opening up, like China. The proportion of total sales from Gillette products that are worldwide leaders in their markets climbed from 55 percent in 1990 to 81 percent in 1996.

Zeien insisted on an increased rate of new product introductions. He asked his senior managers to get out of Boston and move around the world on a more frequent basis and set an example by scheduling himself at least one international trip each month. He demanded more speed in decision making and more speed in accomplishing goals—virtues learned, he said, from his father. He aimed for more consistency of performance from quarter to quarter and through 1996 he got it, with each quarter's sales and profit topping the previous one.

Growth Drivers

One of Zeien's consistent messages from the time he took over was preaching the gospel of "growth drivers," namely, heavy investment in research and development, capital spending, and advertising. The idea was to stimulate top-line sales volume in both the short and long term. According to Zeien's formula, total spending on growth drivers should rise at least as fast as sales. In 1996, for example, spending on growth drivers rose 18 percent to $1.74 billion, while sales rose 10 percent to $9.7 billion.

New products came far more rapidly in both shaving and nonshaving fields. More than twenty new Gillette products were launched in 1996, matching the pace of 1995, which was an all-time high for the company. During the 1980s Gillette averaged seven or eight and sometimes ten or twelve new products yearly, launching not just any new product but products that claimed or aspired to worldwide market leadership. The company's total oral care sales, for example, keyed to world leadership in markets for both manual and mechanical toothbrushes, more than doubled from 1990 to $900 million in 1996. One measure of the new product success was the number of me-too brushes and oral care products from Colgate, Procter & Gamble, and other competitors that began to show up on pharmacy shelves. Over all, the speed-up strategy seemed to be paying off. In 1996, a total of 41 percent of Gillette sales came from products introduced in the last five years, up from 30 percent in 1990.

Zeien attempted to change the style of Gillette's management, to make it less cautious and more alert to opportunities, more open to communicating company goals and outlook to outsiders. A gregarious executive as compared with the more introverted Mockler—his colleagues could hardly ever persuade Mockler to boast about company prospects before a group of strangers—Zeien enjoys jousting with analysts. He also understands perception and symbolism. When Greyhound was merged into Dial Corporation in 1991, he quickly accepted when NYSE officials offered Gillette the symbol G, to replace GS. Only twenty-three NYSE companies are assigned single letters.

The senior vice president for personnel and administration, Robert DiCenso, noted that Zeien was much more the top-down manager in contrast to consensus-minded Colman Mockler, who always listened and said thank you. "If Al saw flaws in your presentation he'd challenge you on the spot . . . and you always knew where you stood right away."

DiCenso rated Zeien as more aggressive, especially in moving Gillette ahead in new products and top line growth. His is a fast growth philosophy, quite distinct from the more typical American company in the 1990s era of downsizing, when cost cutting rather than capital expansion is viewed as the safe way to increase profits.

Jacques Lagarde put it this way: "Colman Mockler saved the company, that's clear. And he re-focused Gillette. Al Zeien changed the way Gillette operates."

Zeien's summation is that Gillette's "history gave me one great advantage and that was Colman Mockler's legacy. He gave the people of this company a tremendous sense of trust. Colman built a culture where people at the top trusted people in the field to work in the best interests of the company, and vice versa. We could never have moved so fast without this sense of trust."

Zeien surprised just about everyone in February 1995 by recommending to the board that Michael C. Hawley be elevated from executive vice president, international, to president and chief operating officer. Many inside and outside Gillette had expected the promotion would go to Robert J. Murray, executive vice president for the North Atlantic Group, or perhaps to Jacques Lagarde, executive vice president for the Diversified Group, as prelude to the top job when Zeien retired. Several months after the Hawley announcement, a disappointed Murray said he would retire after thirty-four years at Gillette. Murray later took a job as chairman and president of New England Business Service Inc., a company he had served as a board member.

NOW, ABOUT THAT BRIGHT FUTURE

After nearly five years as chief executive, Zeien stopped to take stock just before the books closed on 1995. As he reviewed events with the board, it was natural that he recalled the difficult days of the hostile raids by Ronald Perelman and the Coniston proxy fight. He remembered how Gillette had got under the skin of the New York raiders by repeating over and over that the directors advised shareholders to reject interlopers because Gillette had a bright future as an independent company. He reminded the directors that in fall 1986, just before the Revlon takeover attack, Gillette stock had a market value of less than $3 billion, and Perelman valued the company at about $4 billion. By the end of 1990, the market value had climbed to $6 billion and, by December 1995, to $24 billion—eight times the 1986 figure.

"The judgment of the Board of Directors that Gillette had a 'bright future as an independent company' has been emphatically confirmed," he concluded. At the end of 1996, one year later, shareholder value was $43.2 billion.

Zeien has not had to spell out the gain in shareholder value to long-time employees of Gillette, especially those who kept on buying company stock through the Gillette savings plan, in good times and bad. A few examples: a female South Boston factory employee retired at fifty-eight after twenty-six years of service with a final annual salary of $45,449. In addition to her pension, she walked out with $971,800 in her savings plan, which largely reflected the increased value of Gillette stock over her years of employment. A male employee who retired after just twenty years of service had $1.1 million in his account, and a thirty-five-year veteran at the factory retired at sixty-two years of age with $2.3 million in his savings plan. They are among dozens of Gillette's South Boston employees who retired as millionaires and can attest to that promised bright future.

13

THE
SIXTH
LEG

NOT LONG AFTER Al Zeien became CEO, he began telling anyone who asked that Gillette was looking for "a new leg" business to make the company not just bigger but better. He first spelled out the criteria for a new leg acquisition at the 1992 shareholder's meeting. Later, as he refined his concept, he said a "sixth leg" would add to an "already sturdy stool" held up by Gillette's five existing businesses—blades and razors, toiletries and cosmetics, stationery products, Braun electric shavers and appliances, and Oral-B dental products. Zeien took the long view: The greatly profitable blade business earned about two-thirds of the company's earnings, as it had for years, but shaving is an essentially static unit market. "Its basic limitation is that we really can't get very many people to shave more than once a day." Go back to about 1975, he would say, and the world market has stayed at roughly 20 billion blades, with longer blade life offsetting increased world population gains.

The way out of the box, he would tell listeners, is for Gillette to grow its nonblade business at a faster rate than the blade business. With blades accounting for two-thirds of earnings, an added new business would make no sense unless it not only increased the one-third contribution of nonblade earnings but also increased the *rate* of earnings growth fast enough to generate the 15 percent or greater annual increase that Gillette shareholders had come to expect in the 1990s.

To achieve that kind of growth, the sixth leg would have to share synergy with the current Gillette businesses, in particular, benefit from the company's global distribution system set up to sell blades. As Zeien saw it, Gillette was like a factory at 75 percent capacity but with global management and distribution strengths in place to expand closer to 100 percent.

In the spring of 1995, Zeien decided to speed up the search and appointed Joel Davis senior vice president for corporate planning, with instructions to focus on the sixth leg. Using the exacting strategic and financial standards laid out by Zeien in his 1992 "new leg" speech, Davis and veteran acquisitions scout Ken Kames laid out those requirements in a pithy one-page document entitled "'New Leg' Acquisition Criteria." Any new business acquired by Gillette must bring with it world leadership or a realizable plan to achieve it. It must be a technologically based consumer products company or business. It had to be a global business with potential for geographic expansion. It must fit with the Gillette culture and have important synergies, such as compatible distribution channels.

Those were just the strategic "musts" specified in the document. It would also be "desirable," according to this newly established criteria, to acquire a business selling a nondurable product through existing channels with few competitive challenges and a strong domestic position. It would be desirable to have transferability of management skills in a recession-resistant business consistent with Gillette quality and image.

Financial criteria for the sixth leg candidate were equally exacting. The new business had to add to long-term earnings growth and must immediately contribute at least 10 percent sales and operating profit and accelerate the rate of Gillette's earnings and revenue growth. It would be desirable to acquire a company for no more than $5 billion in Gillette stock, the criteria sheet stated. It could not be a hostile takeover.

Zeien realized that the new business would have to be paid for with Gillette stock to avoid the crushing costs of amortizing goodwill that accompanies a cash transaction. He thought that good candidates were out there and always had been, but he knew it would be difficult to acquire a strong business that fit the criteria until Gillette got its P/E (price to earnings ratio) into the 30s. That would make it easier because it would lessen the total number of shares Gillette would have to pay out.

In August 1995, J. P. Morgan and Merrill Lynch were hired as investment bankers to help in the search. An elaborate and secretive process was put together, code-named Project Alaska. A list of seventy-five hundred consumer product companies in several nations was quickly winnowed to forty-four, with a few judgment factors thrown in to further narrow the list. The ATF (for alcohol, firearms, and tobacco) factor kicked in to exclude businesses or situations that Gillette wanted no part of. The list was pared to twenty, then to eight, and with one Zeien veto, to a final seven. On November 15, it was concluded that the world's leading producer of alkaline batteries, Duracell International Inc., was the top choice. Duracell was given the code name Mt. McKinley, for Alaska's highest peak.

"It would be nice to say that we went through all that exercise to discover Duracell," Zeien said. "But the fact is that Duracell was on just about every list we had around here for five years."

In early winter 1995, Zeien was directed by the Gillette board to initiate negotiations with Henry R. Kravis, general partner of Kohlberg, Kravis, Roberts & Co. Inc. (KKR). KKR was a small group of wealthy investors that owned 34 percent of Duracell's stock and controlled the destiny of the seventy-year-old battery company.

DURACELL'S EARLY DAYS

The corporate origins of Duracell go back to the business partnership struck in the 1920s between a wealthy young New Yorker, Philip Rogers Mallory, and Samuel Ruben, a largely self-taught scientist and inventor, also a New Yorker.

Philip Mallory was the fourth-generation scion of a New England Yankee family that had made a maritime fortune in sailmaking and then building and operating ships during the nineteenth century. According to James P. Baughman, author of *The Mallorys of Mystic,* Charles Mallory was on his way from Waterford, Connecticut, to Boston to find a job in 1816 when he stopped at the small port of Mystic, Connecticut, and decided to settle there. He established a sail loft and eventually became a prominent shipbuilder and owner. Succeeding Mallorys took the family enterprise into the era of steam- and diesel-powered ships, with major focus on building the nation's largest coastal and intercoastal shipping enterprise. The 125-year maritime dynasty of the Mallorys of Mystic is memorialized at Mystic Seaport, a major museum and showplace of American maritime history that was financed in part by the Mallory family estate.

Philip Rogers Mallory—known even then as P. R.—was studying at Yale College in 1906 when his father sold the prospering family business at a handsome profit to Charles W. Morse, one of Wall Street's richest and best-known financial manipulators of the time. Morse's goal was to build a coastal shipping cartel that would dominate shipping at the vital port-to-railroad juncture. His ambitions proved too great, and with powerful rail interests engineering his demise, the Morse bubble burst quickly, precipitating Wall Street's Panic of 1907.

P. R.'s father, and later his older brother Clifford Day, regained control of the business and led the recovery from the Morse debacle. Until Clifford Day's death in 1941, the Mallory shipping enterprise, with nonfamily investors deeply involved, flourished again. But P. R. had been disillusioned in 1906 by the sellout to

Morse and the prospect of working for someone else. With his brother Clifford back in the shipping business, P. R. moved on.

He entered Columbia Law School, dropped out in 1910, and started a Wall Street investment banking career. In 1916, with the help of his father, he raised $40,725 and formed a company to make tungsten filament wires. He named it The Mallory Company.

Mighty General Electric was not amused about an interloper chipping at its filament business and began a long court battle charging patent infringement. In 1924, GE prevailed. That might have been the end of P. R. Mallory Company, as it was now called, except for the intervention of Ralph Terry, a senior GE executive who was said to have been embarrassed by the heavy hand of his employer in crushing its small competitor. In 1925, Terry helped arrange for Mallory to buy an outfit that supplied GE with welding tips and electrical contacts, and the company expanded into other electrical components, such as automobile fans.

In 1925 Mallory met Samuel Ruben who, like him, had left Columbia without a degree, eager to make his mark on the world. Ruben, a precocious young scientist, had found financial backing with the help of a Columbia professor who recognized his brilliance and helped him set up a laboratory in New Rochelle, New York, where he could conduct electrochemical and electrophysics research and pursue a career as an inventor. Ruben met Mallory one day when looking for a piece of equipment, and the entrepreneur and the scientist-inventor recognized that each had what the other needed: Mallory needed Ruben's inventive genius, while Ruben needed Mallory's financial and manufacturing savvy to bring his inventions to market.

At first, the two men just talked. P. R. Mallory Company formed a joint venture with GE to make tungsten carbide cutting tools, started other electric components businesses in New York and New Jersey, and consolidated manufacturing operations at Indianapolis, where the components supplier waited out the Great Depression.

Mallory himself never moved to Indiana. As founder-president, he conducted his company's business from Tarrytown, New

York—a fortuitous location given its proximity to Samuel Ruben's laboratory at New Rochelle. He and Ruben soon made the first of many important business deals. Ruben had invented a rectifier, a device that converted household AC current to DC current. He licensed Mallory to manufacture the product, which was used to recharge radio batteries. Ruben upgraded his device to eliminate a persistent humming, so that radios could operate when plugged into wall outlets. Under another license, Mallory's firm manufactured an electrolytic capacitor invented by Ruben. Though he never worked directly for the company, Ruben remained the inventive heart and soul of P. R. Mallory Company for several decades.

MALLORY ENTERS THE BATTERY BUSINESS

As World War II neared, the company increasingly became a supplier of metallurgical products and radio components to the U.S. military, with government support backing Ruben's research and Mallory's manufacturing. Turning from rectifiers and capacitors, Ruben concentrated on storage battery devices. By the time the United States entered the war, he had developed a mercuric oxide cell for the U.S. Army. The mercury cell packed far more capacity into less space than conventional zinc carbon batteries and was better suited for military needs, like powering walkie-talkies and other gear whose use was critical in the extreme climate of the South Pacific. The company turned out millions of mercury cells at Indianapolis for the war effort, earning numerous wartime "E" for excellence awards for production of what became known as Mallory Tropical Batteries.

Ruben's wartime mercury cell was expensive to make, and there were few carryovers from the military work to consumer applications, with one exception. Ruben developed for Mallory a mercury battery that could power miniaturized hearing aids. Until the late 1940s, hearing aids were two-part devices, with the earpiece connected by wire to a battery that typically was clipped inside clothing. The button-sized P. R. Mallory mercury cell battery for hearing aids was small enough to rest in the earpiece and do away with the need for wires. Enough hearing-impaired men and women were willing and able to pay the relatively steep price for the first nonwired hearing aids to make the battery business a modest success.

Much larger consumer markets for miniaturized radios and other devices began to grow rapidly after 1952 with development of the transistor. This low-power semiconductor device replaced bulky vacuum tubes, which had high-power demands, and set off a revolution in the design of business, entertainment, and communications devices, making it practicable to build portable battery-powered consumer products. The first transistor radios reached the market in 1953 and were instantly successful. They were powered by conventional zinc carbon AA-sized batteries, and Union Carbide Co.'s Eveready division and Inco Inc.'s Ray-O-Vac churned out millions of batteries for device makers and for a growing consumer replacement market. The batteries did not last very long, but they were priced right and performed well enough to satisfy customers in love with their battery-run gadgets. The era of portable power for the masses was underway, with radios everywhere, from backyards to beaches.

But P. R. Mallory Company was shut out. Basically a military supplier of high-performance batteries, the company had no inexpensive batteries for the new mass market and, what's more, had no experience selling directly to consumers. It acquired a Cleveland maker of zinc carbon products in the mid-1950s, but the venture soon failed.

Samuel Ruben began in earnest to develop an alkaline battery that would leapfrog the less powerful zinc carbon battery and give equipment makers and consumers a choice of a better-performing product. Eveready and Ray-O-Vac also had researchers working on alkaline batteries, but Mallory's needs were more desperate, and Ruben's talents were up to the challenge. In 1955, he developed an alkaline manganese battery that was more compact, durable, and longer-lasting than anything seen before. Mallory supplied the manufacturing know-how for the new battery.

Mallory sold its alkaline battery to manufacturers in the original equipment market (OEM). By far, the most important early customer was Eastman Kodak, which needed a very small and powerful battery for its electricity-draining flash units; Mallory started producing Ruben's AAA-sized alkaline batteries exclusively for Kodak's flash units, but there was a catch. At Kodak's insistence, Mallory licensed Eveready and other competitors to make AAA batteries for the large replacement market created by the repeated use of flash cameras. Mallory had no choice: Lacking a consumer distribution system, the company had to give up the lucrative replacement market to licensees, domestic and foreign.

Despite being shut out from consumer sales, Mallory's alkaline battery business began to grow steadily, with its competitors focused on meeting the much larger demand for zinc carbon batteries. In need of funds, the company sold stock to the public in 1957, about the time that founder P. R. Mallory was handing over the reigns of the company to his son G. Barron Mallory, who was chairman from 1960 to 1968 and remained a director for many more years. The company started up alkaline battery plants in Kentucky and Tennessee in 1960 and 1961.

In 1964 the name Duracell was registered as a trademark in the United States, and the company began to make the changeover from selling branded Mallory batteries to branded Duracell batteries. The battery design was dressed up with consumers in mind, copper and black colors replacing the old Mallory black and white. Moves were made to lessen dependence on OEM and military sales and before the decade was out, the company was making batteries in Mexico, Germany, and Canada and attempting to penetrate foreign markets, a neglected area until then. But it was slow going. Despite the company's technological achievements and superior alkaline batteries, neither Mallory nor Duracell was a household word, and the company was losing ground to competitors who understood what consumers wanted and how to sell to them.

MALLORY LEARNS THE CONSUMER BUSINESS

The arrival of Peter G. Viele in 1973 marked the beginning of the modern Duracell company. Viele was a rising young marketing manager who had earned high marks at Philip Morris and at General Foods. He was named president of Duracell Products, a business unit of the parent P. R. Mallory Company that was dedicated to the marketing, sales, and distribution of Duracell batteries to consumers. A headquarters building was built on the lower slopes of the Berkshire Industrial Park in Bethel, Connecticut, not far from Viele's Wilton home. With a heavy dose of advertising, the Duracell brand name began to enter the public consciousness, and not a moment too soon.

With competitors showing double-digit year-to-year growth in battery sales, Duracell had to play catch-up in a hurry. Total Duracell battery sales climbed from $62 million in 1971 to $116 million in 1975, for the first time accounting for nearly one-half of total P. R. Mallory Company sales. Nearly all the increase came from alkaline batteries sold through newly established consumer marketing channels, with digital watches, hand-held calculators, and smoke detectors generating particularly strong battery replacement sales that year. (Ironically, this was when Gillette was divesting itself of several consumer electronic businesses acquired during its helter-skelter diversification period. Gillette had learned the hard way that it was not well equipped to compete with Japanese makers of price-sensitive devices like calculators.)

Duracell began television advertising under Viele, the idea being to educate consumers about the virtues of long-lived alkaline batteries as opposed to zinc carbon batteries. "No regular battery looks like it or lasts like it," was the message pounded home by countless ads extolling the copper and black Duracell alkalines. On television and in print, the famous Duracell pink bunnies began to strike their snare drums, and they drummed . . . and drummed . . . and drummed . . . to pound the message home. Some fifteen years after Duracell's pink bunnies retired from U.S. television (they continued drumming away on television screens in Europe, Latin America, and Asia), Eveready launched a campaign to sell its competing Energizer line of alkaline batteries. Eveready's parody of the Duracell bunny employs a laid-back nineties bunny wearing Hollywood-style shades and banging a big bass drum to make the same point of longevity. Duracell executives are convinced that many television viewers see the Energizer bunnies and immediately think "Duracell," which creates a confusion bonus for their own copper and black batteries.

Eveready's Energizer campaign came late, well after Duracell had seized the lead in the premium-priced alkaline battery market. The failure of Eveready to react to Viele's aggressive consumer marketing in the 1970s and 1980s gave Duracell the opening it needed to survive and prosper and position itself for the superior long-term growth that alkalines offer over zinc carbons.

In one sense, Duracell was too successful with its charge into the alkaline consumer market. Its pink bunny campaign started in the 1970s marked the end of P. R. Mallory's existence as an independent company. In 1978, Los Angeles conglomerateur Justin Dart pounced. "I'll never forget sitting in the Indianapolis office on a November morning when the phone rang and we learned that Dart Industries Inc. was about to tender $46 [increased to $51] a share for the company," recalls Gregg A. Dwyer, who later became senior vice president and general counsel of Duracell. Dwyer knew at once that Mallory's corporate life was about to change forever. Dart acquired Mallory for $252 million cash and immediately began selling off the company's nonbattery businesses, many of them to Connecticut-based Emhart Corporation. The company's name was officially changed to Duracell International Inc. in 1980.

Soon Dart merged his company with Kraft Inc., to form Dart & Kraft Inc. Duracell prospered in the unlikely mix of companies under the Dart & Kraft umbrella and under Kraft alone, after Justin Dart sold his half of the business to the big food company to work as an adviser to his long-time friend, President Ronald Reagan.

Tragically, Viele, who had been made Duracell's chief executive, suffered a fatal heart attack while on a business trip in 1982, just at the point when his company was poised for accelerated growth. He was forty-nine, a young man, especially when compared with P. R. Mallory and Samuel Ruben, Duracell's indispensable pioneers. Mallory died at his Fishers' Island, New York, home in 1975 at the age of ninety, and Samuel Ruben also lived to an advanced old age. Like fellow college dropout and inventive genius, Edwin Land of Polaroid, Ruben was always addressed as "Dr. Ruben," a title that he formally acquired in 1981, when Columbia awarded him an honorary Doctor of Science degree at commencement exercises, citing him as a "scientist, electrochemist, and inventor."

By 1988, Duracell sales were approaching $1 billion, and the company was challenging Eveready for leadership in the worldwide battery market, with a clear lead in the fastest-growing alkaline battery segment. When Kraft decided to concentrate solely on its food businesses and put Duracell up for sale, KKR moved quickly. In what was heralded as one of the most successful LBOs of all time, KKR paid $350 million in cash and $1.45 billion in borrowed money to Kraft and walked off with Duracell, which it took private. KKR later reduced its holding to 34 percent after a few successful stock offerings, and Duracell once again became a public company in 1992. Sales that year totaled $1.6 billion. By the time Al Zeien started discussions with Henry Kravis early in 1996, sales had grown to $2.3 billion.

GILLETTE TAKES AIM AT DURACELL

Zeien was dubious that he would get a quick deal, but it was time to test the waters; KKR made no secret that it intended to cash in on its Duracell investment. But Gillette's investment bankers, he reckoned, were willing to spend a lot more of Gillette's money to get a deal than he was. He told Gillette's board that he would offer a little less than $6 billion in Gillette stock, or about $1 billion less than the price Project Alaska's investment bankers recommended.

To avoid attention, Zeien met with KKR principals Henry

Kravis and Scott M. Stuart at a corporate apartment in New York owned by J. P. Morgan Co., the Gillette bankers. It was not the first time Zeien had dealt with KKR. In 1986, during the Revlon takeover push, he had been Gillette's point man in negotiating with KKR principals, who proposed taking Gillette private in a leveraged buyout, but the talks went nowhere.

Not long before the men met in New York, there had been a negative incident for Duracell. Chief Executive Charles R. Perrin had warned Wall Street analysts that Duracell earnings would fall short of 1996 projections, and as was usual in such cases, the company had been punished by the market. Duracell stock had dropped almost 20 percent in a month to 45 1/8, while Gillette's shares stood at 54 1/8 on January 19, edging Gillette toward the higher P/E ratio that Zeien thought was needed to make the financial numbers work for a deal. At this meeting and a follow-up in Boston two weeks later, however, the two sides were far apart in what Gillette would pay for Duracell. Zeien advised Gillette directors in February that he planned to break off talks, at least for the time being. Project Alaska was frozen in ice.

Davis' sixth leg team went back to the boards and tried to come up with another suitable candidate. They knew, of course, that other companies or businesses would fit the Gillette criteria. Zeien could name several—General Electric's lightbulb business for one and Johnson's Band Aid business for another, but obviously these were not for sale at any price.

The more work the planners did, the clearer it became that Duracell still was the best fit. And as the winter and spring months sped by, the stock market was helping as Gillette's P/E ratio rose steadily while Duracell shares slumped. Zeien was content to wait for the market to help him out and was in no hurry to go back to Kravis. By the time of the June 19 regular board meeting in Boston, Gillette stock stood at 58 7/8, and Duracell's had fallen to 43 3/8; the directors agreed that Zeien should resume discussions with Kravis. Gillette's P/E had moved into the low thirties. Zeien tracked down Kravis and negotiations resumed, this time with the numbers working strongly in Gillette's favor.

On July 10, Kravis and Stuart flew to Boston to meet with Zeien at the Ritz-Carlton hotel, near Gillette headquarters. Kravis still asked for a price Zeien considered unreasonable, but the Gillette chief sensed that the KKR figure was far from final and that Kravis was taking the Gillette overture more seriously.

His intuition was confirmed two days later, when a group of KKR executives flew by helicopter to Duracell's hilltop headquarters at Bethel and disclosed to a shocked group of senior managers that KKR was talking with Gillette about an acquisition. CEO Charles Perrin, who subsequently declined a Gillette offer to stay on, and his fellow Duracell executives were dismayed to learn they had been left out of the loop on the most important corporate news imaginable for them, personally and professionally. Morgan Stanley was at once retained as financial adviser to Duracell's full board of directors in order to render a fairness opinion on takeover terms and to make sure senior management was taken care of when Duracell was sold. Management owned about 10 percent of Duracell's stock.

Starting July 29, Zeien and Kravis began a series of telephone negotiations. Zeien worked hard to persuade Kravis that KKR and other Duracell shareholders would gain great value by exchanging Duracell shares for Gillette stock, what he called the "change to a better horse" concept.

Kravis' starting point was one share of Gillette for one share of Duracell, with Zeien countering at 0.875 shares of Gillette for each Duracell share. On the advice of Morgan Stanley, Duracell's directors rejected the 0.875 offer on August 22, but negotiations continued. Zeien was in New York August 27 on the floor of the New York Stock Exchange, watching Gillette shares rise yet again, when he was called to the phone for a penultimate discussion with Kravis. The two men agreed to make every effort to conclude a deal. Two days later, Zeien and Kravis talked once more and agreed to recommend to their directors that the deal be done on an exchange of 0.904 shares of Gillette for each share of Duracell, a deal worth roughly $7.3 billion for Duracell shareholders at that day's price of Gillette shares.

"I didn't doubt that KKR would sell Duracell. The question was whether they would sell at a price that made sense to

Gillette," Zeien said later. At the time agreement was reached, Gillette's P/E multiple was trading at a rich thirty-three times trailing twelve-month earnings. Zeien's patience had paid off.

The Deal Is Completed

The big issues that still faced negotiators before the deal could be put to a vote of both boards on September 12 related to the "what ifs." What happens if a third bidder comes in? What happens if the deal is called off? What is called the due diligence phase was underway, with both companies exchanging reams of confidential information about each other. Consultants were engaged to check against nasty surprises like environmental hazards or the sudden emergence of new technologies that might render alkaline batteries obsolete. Ken Kames was front man for the Gillette due diligence team.

There were less than two weeks to hammer out the details. Kames and his crew worked through the long Labor Day weekend without pause. On September 4, Gillette representatives and their bankers met in New York with Duracell management and their investment banker. The next day, Duracell representatives flew to Boston to meet secretly with Gillette management at the Sheraton Hotel. Complicating matters, the Gillette directors had long been scheduled to hold their September meeting in London. That meant that Zeien and several other senior executives had to be in England during the final days, keeping to a prearranged mix of ceremonial meetings, dinners, and theater-going in order to avoid the appearance of anything unusual.

Back in Boston, Davis broke off for a few hours for a family wedding in Connecticut on Saturday, September 7, but that night he got from Gillette lawyers a preliminary copy of the final draft of the acquisition agreement, which would be presented to directors in London for their approval. He reviewed the draft Sunday and flew to London on Monday. Kames flew over the next day. There were still key issues unresolved, including severance arrangements and management fees for the bankers. Trans-Atlantic phone lines were busy day and night as the two sides haggled over details.

On Wednesday, the Gillette directors assembled at the historic Cliveden House, an estate overlooking the River Thames near Windsor Castle that once was owned by Viscount Astor. Cliveden was more historic than convenient, given the lack of the very latest telecommunications equipment.

Adding to the pressure, Gillette executives in Boston had learned that the *Wall Street Journal* would run a story in its Thursday, September 12, editions disclosing the pending deal several hours before it was scheduled to be voted on. The story was sure to set off an avalanche of questions from Wall Street and the world business media. As a result of the news leak, the starting times for both board meetings were moved up several hours in an effort to have the deal officially approved by the time the NYSE began trading at 9:30 A.M. Thursday—an especially awkward turn of events for the Duracell directors, who had to start their meeting at 6:30 A.M. in New York in order to listen to the full presentation, deal with last-minute questions, and vote to sell their company before trading began. Originally, Gillette had planned to announce the acquisition after the market closed Thursday.

Gillette and Duracell negotiators and lawyers talked through the night Wednesday to finish up the last details. But shortly after the Gillette meeting began about 10 A.M., London time (5 A.M. New York time), a simmering problem erupted that threatened to muddy or possibly derail the deal, despite the elaborate planning.

Warren Buffett, Gillette's largest shareholder, objected to paying KKR the $20 million fee that Kravis demanded for advisory services, even though KKR also was the seller. Zeien had reluctantly agreed just the night before to pay the fee, along with $10 million to Duracell banker Morgan Stanley for two months' work, for a total of $30 million to KKR and Morgan Stanley. Buffett contended $18 million was more than enough. Gillette had agreed to pay a total of just $16 million to its two Project Alaska banks, which had been working with the company for more than a year.

Buffett was being consistent. For years, he had fought a war with Wall Street bankers over what he considered outlandish fees for minimal services. In 1991, when he temporarily took over as chairman of Salomon Inc. to salvage his major investment in that firm, he sharply cut the pay of Salomon bankers. In 1995, as the largest shareholder of Capital Cities/ABC Inc., Buffett had complained openly about what he considered excessive fees charged by investment bankers for their role in the Walt Disney Company's takeover of Cap Cities, for the deal was a friendly one, hammered out almost entirely by executives of the two companies.

Buffett told Zeien and other directors that he thought that the Duracell acquisition was good for Gillette and he would vote for it, but that he objected as a matter of principle to paying the $30 million in advisory and banking fees. Zeien was concerned. He thought that reneging on the $30 million might open up for reconsideration certain concessions that he had demanded during negotiations, such as cutting back on costly golden parachutes for Duracell executives. He explained to the directors that he had already raised a fuss and had refused to agree to the first KKR-Morgan Stanley demand for $40 million in fees, having knocked that fee down to $30 million. Buffett held his ground.

Zeien was incredulous that a nearly $8-billion deal (the fast-rising Gillette stock price had increased the acquisition's value more than half a billion dollars since it was announced) was floundering over $12 million in fees, but he remained calm. He realized he must once again phone Henry Kravis, who at least was in Europe, at the Ritz Hotel in Paris, coordinating arrangements for a birthday celebration for his wife. But first he wanted a plan. After conferring with his Gillette colleagues, Zeien decided to pursue a multiple vote scheme that would show the world that Gillette directors approved unanimously of the Duracell acquisition as a strategic action.

The directors first voted unanimously, 12–0, to approve the acquisition subject to lowering the KKR fees from $30 million to $18 million. Then they took a second vote to approve the acquisition with the $30 million in fees intact—the same motion that Duracell directors were voting on in New York. On this vote, Buffett abstained along with fellow director Michael B. Gifford, the managing director of Britain's Rank Organization PLC. Gifford told Zeien that he thought his vote, added to Buffett's, would give Zeien more leverage in dealing with Kravis.

With that, Zeien reached Kravis in Paris and put the matter to him. He told Kravis that he had two votes, one unanimous for the acquisition with KKR fees reduced, the other with two abstentions but with the full fees included, and asked Kravis whether he wouldn't rather have the unanimous vote. Kravis asked Zeien to call back in a few minutes. When he did, Kravis told him that he would not back down on the fees and that Duracell's board, in fact, had moments earlier voted to approve the merger agreement as agreed on, with the $30 million in fees intact.

To avoid misunderstanding, Zeien told Kravis that he would ask for a third vote by Gillette directors with the fees intact. He hurried back to the Cliveden meeting room, where it was early afternoon and the directors had been meeting for about four hours. On the third vote, Gillette directors approved the Duracell acquisition 11-0, with only Buffett abstaining. The Omaha maverick had made his point of principle. And Zeien had gotten on the record the board's unanimous approval of the most important acquisition Gillette had made in its long history.

The sixth leg had been added, subject to the formal shareholder approval at the end of the year. The Gillette Company now represented nearly $10 billion in sales and employed close to 43,000 people.

A Global Payoff Looms

In London, Zeien had little time to savor the deal. News of the acquisition was released immediately but still came too late to catch the opening of trading in New York. At the bell, investors proved wary about the high price Gillette was willing to pay—it was reported accurately in the *Wall Street Journal*'s exclusive story that morning—and drove the stock down at the opening. It was up to Zeien to reassure analysts and the news media that Gillette had a big winner well worth the high price it had paid.

Zeien moved into another room at Cliveden for a news conference by conference call that gave reporters and securities analysts in America a chance to question him. The deal was perfect for Gillette, he said, not just another diversification but the sixth leg the company had been seeking, the ticket to a higher rate of earnings for years to come as Gillette sold its compatible mix of batteries and blades through a single global distribution network.

The prospects of converting huge markets outside the United States and Europe from lower-value zinc carbon batteries to longer-lasting alkaline batteries were excellent, Zeien said—"and if that upgrade concept sounds familiar to you, it should—carbon zinc is to batteries just as double edge is to blades. Let me state the obvious: We have a new core global business with high-growth potential and many characteristics similar to Gillette's core blade business."

Wall Street and the media bought Zeien's story.[1] By day's end, Gillette shares had gained almost a point, rising to $66. It was the start of a steady climb that moved shares up another 20 points by December 30, 1996, the day the Duracell acquisition was officially approved by shareholders, thus adding more than $4 billion to Gillette shareholder value and about $1 billion to Duracell shareholder value.

Gillette wasted no time integrating Duracell into its global operations. Duracell was divided into two parts. A North Atlantic division was created at Bethel to be headed by Gillette veteran Ed DeGraan, who was the manufacturing technology stalwart of the Sensor razor system. Almost three-quarters of Duracell sales were in the United States, Canada, and Europe. Outside Europe and North America, Duracell operations were phased into Gillette's existing international operations, batteries with blades, so to speak, to take maximum advantage of the synergy counted on to sharply increase Duracell's presence.

The $9 billion world market for batteries in 1995 was split into $4 billion for alkalines, $3 billion for zinc carbons and $2 billion for rechargeables. Gillette projected a $15 billion battery market by the year 2000, with alkalines growing at 20 percent annually to $7 billion, zinc carbons remaining at $3 billion, and rechargeables more than doubling to $5 billion, as power-hungry laptops and cell phones fed demand. In the United States, where 87 percent of sales were alkaline at the time of acquisition, Duracell had about 48 percent of the total battery market in revenues, compared with 36 percent for Ralston-Purina's Eveready. World-wide, the two companies were neck-and-neck in total market share.

At Bethel, DeGraan is surrounded by a cadre of youthful Duracell managers and technologists working in a showplace headquarters that was opened in 1995. The handsome Berkshire Park headquarters environment proved something of a culture shock for Gillette executives in terms of place and work style when compared with the relatively mundane high-rise offices (but with great views) and the more formal management style at the Pru-dential Tower. Gillette executives were more used to pigeons in the Pru Plaza than to the wild turkeys freely roaming the Duracell grounds. What was more important, however, was that Duracell and Gillette managers seemed to share the mindset that comes with organizations that demand fast growth, quality products, and world leadership in mass-produced consumer products.

V

GILLETTE'S
GLOBAL CULTURE
IN
PRACTICE

14

THE
DEVELOPMENT OF
GLOBAL SKILLS

THOMAS W. PELHAM, the intrepid first Gillette sales chief, had just returned to Boston in the summer of 1915 after a perilous, some would say foolhardy, trip around the world via Vancouver, Vladivostok, Manchuria, Russia, and finally home, dodging German submarines on the last leg. He reported to his boss that Gillette had established eight sales subsidiaries covering North America and parts of Europe. Gillette blades made in Boston and Montreal—the war had forced closure of Gillette-owned or contract blade plants in Germany, France, and England—were available from jobbers located throughout the rest of Europe, Asia, the Far East, and Latin America. Pelham was particularly excited about Russia. During two weeks in Petrograd, he had watched his agent, A. G. Micheles, sell $50,000 of Gillette blades and razors almost overnight with little more than a small advertisement announcing the shipment's expected arrival and declaring "no honing, no stropping, beware of substitutes!" No matter that

Imperial Russia was in turmoil, that the Bolshevik revolution was on the near horizon—what a market!

He witnessed a tumultuous May Day parade of 1 million militants who temporarily took over the imperial city. Where a statesman might have seen 1 million revolutionaries, Pelham noted in his diary the awesome sight of "black men from Turkestan, Mohammedans, Tartars from the Caucasus, Kurds from the Trans-Caucasus, Mongolians, Manchurians, Laplanders and people from every part of Russia"—all potential Gillette shavers. "Russia is one of our great markets for the future," he concluded, though there would be a seventy-year pause in sales forced by the Bolshevik Revolution of 1917.

Revolution, world war . . . these were mere interruptions to the inevitable Gillette global invasion, as far as Pelham was concerned. When he addressed the annual meeting of Gillette salesmen in 1918, the final bloody year of World War I, Pelham conceded "increased difficulties" in shipping blades to Europe and the Orient but defiantly told his sales troops that the company would continue shipments, "[except to] governments with which we are at war." Pelham further declared that "we do not propose to let any difficulty . . . interfere." Gillette's policy was that once a foothold had been gained in a country, it was to be retained even at the expense of a "temporary monetary loss due to such setbacks as floods, revolutions, elections, crop failures, and unexpected fluctuations in currency."

This cocksure declaration of permanence has remained a cornerstone of Gillette's global culture to the present times. Listen to Michael Hawley, speaking as Gillette president almost eighty years later: "The hallmark of Gillette is permanence. When Gillette goes into a market we're going to be there a long time." Gillette's history of gaining a head start on competitors by moving rapidly into emerging markets and then staying there, regardless of difficulties, often gave the company an insurmountable lead over late-arriving competitors, as in Latin America. Gillette's "toe in the water" strategy—the earthier "foot on the ground" metaphor is preferred by post-Mockler Gillette executives—is as old as Pelham's determination in 1915 to ship blades to Russia before the revolution broke out and as fresh as Gillette's re-entry into Russia in 1990, less than a year after the end of the Cold War. Gillette's historic mindset made quick entry a natural reflex.

But the mechanics must accompany the mindset. As the company moved into new world markets, it developed a range of skills to complement its global reach and the means to make geographic expansion work.

BLADE MAKING AROUND THE WORLD

Development of a blade manufacturing process that allowed Gillette to build profitable but very small factories around the world helped to propel global expansion from the late 1960s through the mid-1980s. George O. Cutter was largely responsible for the so-called mini-plant. A manufacturing executive who was later to become vice chairman for technical operations, Cutter served for a while in the 1960s as head of international operations. While in that position, he ran up against the increasing problem of protectionist nations levying tariffs so high that Gillette could not price its imported blades to compete effectively against the much cheaper blades made by local competitors. Sometimes there were barriers to manufacturing, too, though Gillette's decision to cooperate with host nations like Malaysia and prerevolutionary Iran in joint venture factories (see chapter 3) eased the political obstacles to manufacturing abroad. But economic obstacles remained in nations with home markets too small to support the output of a normal-sized Gillette blade plant. Cutter used his technological skills to address that concern.

Then as now, Gillette's blade plants housed high-output machines designed to run at very high speeds with a minimum of manpower. These mainstream plants filled the needs of a major host country like Brazil and also turned out tens of millions of blades that were exported to neighboring nations. The system worked well when trade barriers were low. But it broke down when smaller nations in Asia, Latin America, and the Middle East levied sky-high duties on imported blades but were too small in population to justify a large plant.

Cutter's solution was the mini-plant, a rogue approach to blade making that depended on the use of hardening and sharpening machinery much less costly than normal Gillette-designed machinery. For one-third the price of Gillette equipment, he bought off-the-shelf German blade-making equipment that was scorned by Gillette engineers for its lack of sophistication. Cutter's solution was to "doctor" the machines, fitting the front and back ends with proprietary Gillette sharpening components and certain other parts. The hybrid machines yielded high-quality blades but at a very low rate, sometimes only 20 million blades a year—just enough to satisfy the home markets of small nations. The mini-plants were inexpensive to build and maintain, and the slow speeds of blade making made possible such economies as using water rather than oil during the sharpening process. The small factories were labor intensive compared with more automated mainstream plants, but this mattered little in the lower-wage countries where they were installed.

Mini-plants began to spring up around the world and operate at such low costs that Gillette could price their quality blades at levels competitive with generally inferior local products. The joint venture at Kuala Lumpur, Malaysia, first proved it could be done, and then mini-plants were built in the Philippines, Indonesia, Morocco, Egypt, Thailand, and in several other nations whose protectionist policies made importing impractical. Though the era of the mini-plant lasted only twenty years, until freer trade policies opened up the global economy, it was a phenomenon that went beyond manufacturing in importance for Gillette. With each small factory came a mini-Gillette organization, with a general manager, financial manager, factory manager, transport and materials managers, and so on. These were excellent training grounds for the breed of global managers that Gillette would later need in large and small operations scattered around the world.

Executive Vice President Robert King said that the mini-plants' success signaled to the international business community and to doubters within the company that Gillette had acquired the practical means to back up its global focus. It was more proof that the company would not be deterred from moving into markets it wanted to serve, whatever the political and economic roadblocks.

The mini-plant era wound down in the late 1980s as the Uruguay round of GATT tariff reductions took effect and as agreements creating regional trading blocs were signed, such as the U.S.-Canada Free Trade Act and later, the North American Free Trade Act, or NAFTA. As tariff walls fell, exporting again became a viable way of doing business. Several of the mini-plants were closed and production was consolidated in larger plants.

Long before mini-plants, Gillette employed in-house manufacturing skills to recycle and retrofit aging blade-making machines no longer needed in the United States or Europe for new factories established in world outposts. Veteran Gillette international executive Rod Mills recalled spotting a fifty-four-year-old made-in-Boston Gillette machine churning out blades at an Asian plant where it had been installed for many years. That is admittedly an extreme case, but it makes the point. Refurbished and well maintained, and long since depreciated so that the cost of factory start-ups was sharply reduced, such outdated machines in their old age were still productive, helping Gillette make low-cost entry into all corners of the earth. Recycling continues to this day. In the 1980s and 1990s, Gillette entered India, China, and Russia with a combination of exported products and locally made double-edge blades manufactured wholly or in part from recycled equipment from Gillette plants elsewhere.

When there is no longer any way to recycle a machine one more time, disposal is not a casual matter. Gillette remains secretive about its technology, as any photographer who has ever tried to take a photo inside a Gillette plant without prior clearance knows. Outmoded machines are disassembled, and the proprietary parts are pulled out or broken up before the machines are junked. Gillette record-keepers note the serial numbers of destroyed equipment and products, such as the 15,223,314 blades packed in wooden boxes that were dumped in the ocean at the outer limits of Boston harbor "in not less than 12 fathoms at mean low water" on June 1, 1938.

In modern times, the venerable South Boston plant serves as the training ground for technologists from other Gillette sites, a sort of "world university" of shaving technology. For a while in 1990, German engineers and a cadre of highly skilled workers transformed the South Boston plant into a little Germany as Gillette prepared to start Sensor lines simultaneously in South Boston and Berlin. A few years later, Brazilian technicians and managers replaced the Germans as Gillette made preparations to extend Sensor and SensorExcel production to Manaus, Brazil. The block-long sign over the 1.2 million-square-foot factory proclaiming "World Shaving Headquarters" is no exaggeration.

GLOBAL UPGRADING

CEO Zeien is adamant that Gillette's time-tested "Stone Age" marketing strategy for developing nations is a thing of the past, gone with the realities of the global economy and its wide disparities in income. The evolutionary or Stone Age strategy, as it came to be known, was to move into a new market and offer primarily double-edge blades, on the theory that consumers would recognize the Gillette quality compared with local products and would not aspire to anything better for a number of years, giving Gillette a profitable run as it built up its distribution system. Then Gillette would employ its famed upgrading strategy, which was to move its double-edge customers to higher-priced products like Trac II or Sensor, and to nonshaving products.

The upgrading strategy remains in place, but the emphasis has changed. Premium-priced Gillette products like SensorExcel, Braun Oral-B plaque removers, and Parker pens are made available at once and advertised widely in most new markets. The change came about when Gillette realized that sizable pockets of urban affluence existed in virtually all the large countries it entered, and millions of middle and upper income consumers were ready to buy the company's higher margin products. Gillette moved into India, Russia, Turkey, Poland, and other almost wholly double-edge-blade markets with advertising aimed at upscale customers. Demand for the Sensor for Women razor in Russia was too strong to meet from almost the first day television ads ran, supplemented by advertising posters displayed at kiosks along St. Petersburg's Nevsky Prospekt and in a few other Russian cities.

Gillette does not expect to upgrade overnight the majority of its double-edge-blade customers in Russia or in other mass markets where huge numbers of people subsist at poverty level. Despite worldwide advertising blitzes that never mention double-edge blades, and despite worldwide availability of the latest Gillette system products, double-edge blades still accounted for slightly more than 50 percent of all blades sold in the world in unit terms in the mid-1990s, a quarter century after the introduction of twin-blade systems. The Stone Age strategy, in its deliberately gradualist form, is a relic of the past, but upgrading from double-edge shavers will continue well into the twenty-first century.

NURTURING A GLOBAL CULTURE

When Colman Mockler took over as chairman and CEO in 1976 he was, by Gillette standards, an international neophyte, having spent only a year or so in London early in his career. Yet during his fifteen years at the top he kept Gillette ahead of most American multinationals that were moving toward the ill-defined concept of the global economy. One of Mockler's first moves was to elevate an international specialist, Steve Griffin, to the post of president. Griffin had no doubt about Mockler's commitment to global expansion. He said that Mockler, renowned for his ability to grasp the significance of numbers, understood that one day the fast-growing second and third world populations would provide the engine for Gillette's long-term growth.

Mockler was not a happy foreign traveler and he did not like exotic foods, but he could easily digest the financial reports coming in from Mexico and Brazil and other points south. There was no need to endure spicy food and tropical heat to recognize that Gillette's Latin American business was taking off and deserved strong support. Griffin persuaded Mockler to travel to Asia in the late 1970s, particularly to Japan and to such destinations as the Europeanized city of Sydney, Australia, which was Gillette's Asia-Pacific headquarters until business logic later dictated a move to the more typically Asian Singapore. Joe Turley, who succeeded Griffin as president, often served as Gillette's ambassador to foreign governments as well as to employees around the world. Turley's trips to the Middle East and Asia and behind the Iron Curtain sent a strong message about how Gillette valued its overseas presence and the potential for expansion to regions for the moment out of reach.

Rod Mills, executive vice president for Gillette International, was another of Mockler's key agents for cultivating the global outlook that Mockler wanted throughout the company. A talkative, tireless activist, ready to jump on a plane at a moment's notice, at ease in foreign settings, not afraid to play the provocateur internally, Mills was the perfect complement to the reserved Mockler on trips abroad. According to Mills, Mockler would frequently say, "Look at our business—most of it is with 6 percent of the world's population." And then he would do some quick multiplication and declare that if the company could do this well with 6 percent, think what it could do if it reached the rest of the world.

Mills said some London-based Gillette old-timers did not know what to make of Mockler's calls for more internationalism when he first became chairman and guessed incorrectly that he just wanted a short-term sales push. He recalled a group responsible for Gillette operations in the Middle East and the Indian subcontinent that responded to Mockler's request for new ideas by rehashing an old sales campaign. Mills had to intercede for his polite chief to make it understood that Mockler had asked for long-term planning to prepare Gillette for the more or less borderless world that he sensed was coming.

Mockler set up a discretionary Third World fund of about $1 million under the office of the chairman, assuring managers far from Boston a sponsor, or at least a hearing, for their projects at budget time. He regularly flew in key foreign managers to educate the board about Gillette's global aspirations. It was also a chance to solicit the directors' support for unlikely projects, like the blade factory at Manaus in the Amazon jungle, which was favored by the Latin America chief, Gaston "Tony" Levy. Levy got the money for it. "I think Gillette's international managers made remarkably detailed and persuasive presentations to us. I know of several companies where directors never got the kind of detail and chance to ask questions that I experienced at Gillette," said Director Joe Sisco, recognized for his knowledge of international economic development.

GAINING BETTER CONTROL
OF FOREIGN EXCHANGE

Through necessity, Gillette became more financially sophisticated as it grew more global, particularly in matters related to foreign currencies and exchange rates, which were areas critical to the health of any American company that generated three-quarters of its operating profits outside the United States. Country managers were expected to protect profits from local currency fluctuations and get as many dollars back to Boston as possible. In pre-computer days, however, there was no effective way to control the process from Boston or London. In the pre-jet, pre-fax era, local treasurers had little contact with Boston.

In his many years as corporate treasurer at Boston, Milton Glass worked to bring the worldwide financial operations of the company under better control, always with the aim of getting money earned elsewhere back to Boston in U.S. currency. Along with his successor, Lloyd Swaim, Glass was a master of the arcane world of forward exchange and currency swaps to hedge foreign currency transactions. It required a lot of know-how, including the ability to interpret economic and political trends in nations ranging from stable Switzerland to volatile Argentina. Glass was an early innovator in arranging complex financings in Eurodollars or other currencies that were advantageous to Gillette in terms of interest rates and tax implications.

The global Gillette of the 1990s could scarcely exist without the world-shrinking impact of the jet airplane and the computer. Jacques Lagarde contends that Zeien's familiarity with international Gillette businesses, because of his frequent travel, has been a key to his ability to keep the company's geographically scattered managers marching in the same direction. He notes, only half jokingly, that Gillette's centralized computer controls are so melded with the company's global operations that two computer-literate people theoretically could manage 50 percent of Gillette's business from Boston.

Nowhere is computer power more evident than in the company's worldwide cash management system that went into full operation in 1993. It frequently is cited at meetings of corporate international managers as one of the most sophisticated cash management systems in use by any global enterprise. Gillette's treasury department started moving in earnest toward a more centralized and automated way to control the movement of cash around the world in the aftermath of the 1980s takeover scares, one aim being to increase efficiencies and reduce costs. The effort bore full fruit soon after the arrival in Boston in 1988 of Gianulderico "Gian" Camuzzi, an Italian national who had worked several years for Braun's finance department in Germany. Camuzzi's streamlining of Braun's treasury procedures had caught the attention of Lloyd Swaim, who brought him to Boston as his chief assistant.

In short order, Camuzzi designed a new cash management strategy and devised a computerized system to make it work. His former colleague at Braun, Walter Ochynski, wrote the software that enabled the system to go online. The object was to hedge the company's exposure to inflation and redeploy cash generated by the hundreds of non-American Gillette businesses overnight, every night. It took a few years of work with national authorities to exploit the full tax implications of the cash flow system, and once that was accomplished, the system began full operation in 1993, keyed to a company "treasury center" in Zurich.

Each night, cash that has accumulated in Gillette bank accounts around the world is "swept" or transferred to Zurich in what is known as the "midnight sweep." The subsidiary receives credit from Zurich in its own interest-bearing account, or if it is short of cash, the manager writes a check that Zurich will cover. One goal is to avoid fees that banks charge for holding and moving cash. Another is to minimize taxes levied on bank accounts by ending the day with a zero balance. The Swiss treasury center operates as Gillette's in-house international bank, dispensing cash to Gillette offices each morning in dozens of currencies, as needed. Only a few developing regions of the world, accounting for about 15 percent of Gillette sales, are outside the system, and that percentage is decreasing as bankers in developing nations gain computer skills.

The Zurich treasury center, like the subsidiaries, ends the day with a zero balance, no cash position. Any cash that is left over by mid-afternoon in Zurich is sent to Boston, following a daily 8:45 A.M. call from Boston to Zurich (2:45 P.M. Swiss time) during which transactions are confirmed, interest rates and political trends discussed, and other matters resolved. Swiss tax laws made Zurich the ideal venue for the Gillette treasury center, which otherwise would be located in Boston. As it is, Camuzzi and his small crew of about a half dozen assistants aided by computer and communications technology control the global operation from the forty-eighth floor of the Prudential Tower as if the company's treasury center was in the next room, instead of across the Atlantic. The daily call is made to Zurich from a "war room" that looks like a commodities trading pit, with a large-screen monitor flashing real-time financial information from Reuters under four clocks set to the time in Singapore, London, Boston, and Zurich.

Camuzzi says the system saved approximately $5 million in 1996, mostly in reduced foreign exchange payments, interest payments, and bank fees. Excess funds are immediately invested in interest-bearing vehicles or used to pay down debt. When a Gillette unit anywhere needs to borrow money, it is done centrally through the purchase of commercial paper, allowing Gillette to benefit from low rates because of its strong credit rating. Gillette has dispensed with banks for most cash management services, and its balance sheet shows the impact. At the end of 1995, the company reported sales of $6.9 billion and carried only $48 million in cash and short-term securities—about the same as in 1968, when sales were $553 million. And there has been a big savings in manpower over the old days, with about fifteen treasury specialists split between Boston, Zurich, and Braun's German headquarters, or about half the number it took to do the same work in the 1970s. "The system works like a bloody Swiss clock," Camuzzi said, with an inventor's pride.

Intuition continues to count in the computer age. The suggestion to Camuzzi by a Swiss banker that the Italian central bank was on the verge of dropping support for the lira prompted Camuzzi that very day to exchange lira for marks. When a few days later the lira was devalued by 5 percent, Camuzzi had saved Gillette millions of dollars, the currency that really counts at Gillette. Then there was the day in 1992 when Camuzzi sold most of the company's sizable holdings in English pounds at the equivalent of $1.85, just after the Bank of England raised interest rates, which pushed the pound temporarily higher. Gillette's treasury heads were certain the pound would soon falter and drop back below $1.85. A few months later, when Gillette needed millions of pounds to buy British-owned Parker Pen, the pound had sunk to $1.70, and Gillette came out on the right side of the fifteen-cent spread between sale and purchase.

OLÉ! GILLETTE DISCOVERS WORLD SPORTS MARKETING

With global operations comes global marketing. For the company that built a bond with American men through its Cavalcade of Sports broadcasts, the challenge shifted over the years to building a bond with men throughout the world. Gillette sponsored bullfighting in Mexico and bicycle racing in France, but it soon focused on soccer as the best way to reach sports fans worldwide. Soccer, or football as it is called everywhere except in the United States, is the world's most popular sport, played and watched by more men and increasingly women than any other sport. The World Cup soccer tournament, staged each four years, is by far the single largest sports event in the world apart from the Olympic Games. For Gillette, the World Cup has become what baseball's World Series once was—the signature event tying Gillette to male customers via sports.

Gillette's first involvement with the World Cup dates to 1970, when the company spent about $100,000 to become an official sponsor of the games, held that year in Mexico. With sponsorship came the right to display the Gillette logo on the perimeter boards surrounding the field, in view of tens of millions of television viewers whenever cameras following the action picked up the logo in the background. Brazil got into the finals (losing to Italy), its presence a big break for Gillette, because a prescient Gillette manager had signed up a young Brazilian star named Pelé to promote the company's products. Pelé soon became probably the most recognized sports figure in the world.

Gillette executives in Boston, where soccer in 1970 was about as popular as snooker, were impressed with the immediate payoff of the Mexican games sponsorship, especially in Latin America, where Gillette sales perceptibly increased during the month-long series of games, and the company signed on as an official sponsor of the World Cup for the foreseeable future. The Gillette logo on the perimeter boards ringing the interior of the world's most famous soccer stadiums became a familiar sight to television viewers from Chile to Sweden.

By the time of the 1994 World Cup, Gillette was the oldest continuous sponsor of the Cup series, and it decided to pull out all the stops. The company spent almost $22 million over the four years leading up to the event, including about $12 million to become one of eleven official sponsors. The sponsors at the 1970 Mexican games, except for Gillette and Italy's Martini, had been

Mexican companies trying to reach the local market; globalism had not yet caught on with corporate marketers. But by 1994 the roster of sponsors included exclusively global or multinational companies: Gillette, Coca-Cola, Energizer (Eveready), Fujifilm, General Motors, JVC, Mastercard, McDonald's, Snickers (Mars), and Philips. Using formulas far more complex than the x's and o's of soccer strategy, Gillette's international advertising director, Tim Schramm, calculated that the prime stadium sign positions negotiated by Gillette (behind left goal and along the right midline) were on camera for an average of eight minutes and eight seconds per game during the fifty-two-game playoffs. During the championship match before 100,000 fans at Pasadena's Rose Bowl, where Brazil avenged its 1970 loss to Italy with an overtime victory, the Gillette signs were exposed on television for ten minutes and fifty-six seconds. Altogether, the television audience for the World Cup's fifty-two games totaled 32.1 billion, with games carried in practically every nation where Gillette blades are sold.

Schramm figured the exposure of Gillette's stadium signage on television had the equivalent value of one minute and twenty-one seconds of TV commercials (2.7 thirty-second commercials), or put another way, thirty seconds of board exposure was equivalent to five seconds of a commercial. In dollar terms, he estimated it would have cost Gillette at least $46 million to buy the equivalent amount of advertising time in major world markets.

Schramm called the World Cup the perfect match for Gillette's global marketing and promotion efforts. The company flew 1,024 men and women to Los Angeles for a week of wining, dining, and entertainment prior to the finals at the Rose Bowl. Most were international distributors and retailers, along with various VIPs and winners of Gillette incentive contests. Gillette had become so convinced of the ability of World Cup sponsorship to reinforce the Gillette brand name internationally that Schramm said the company probably would sign up for four of the possible 32–36 stadium signboards available for the 1998 World Cup, to take place in France, assigning spots to Braun as well as the Gillette brand name.

FINDING, TRAINING, AND KEEPING
GLOBAL MANAGERS

When Vincent Ziegler started Gillette's expatriate program in 1967, it marked the beginning of Gillette's systematic buildup of its corps of global managers. The program was designed to ensure that Gillette managers would be compensated on equal terms wherever they served, to encourage the sort of managerial mobility vital to any company bidding to become a serious presence in international business. Mobility is especially important to Gillette because the company's history is one of generally looking within its ranks when hiring senior managers.

About a dozen years later Gillette finally adopted a formal company-wide program of management incentives keyed to performance-based pay, a step considered somewhat tardy by the standards of most large American companies. By the time the performance incentives were in place by late 1979, Gillette's program had a distinct global cast. Mockler demanded that all executives at the eligible grade levels receive the same treatment, wherever they happened to work. William McMorrow, the company's top personnel manager, questioned him on this point. He told Mockler that many American companies doing business overseas reserved management incentive schemes for domestic managers. He told him that Gillette did not need to extend its plan to other nations as a recruiting tool because Gillette jobs generally were considered a plum without any special incentives. Mockler insisted that it was the fair way, and he thought it would prove wise in the long run.

Gillette generally gets high marks for its treatment of employees worldwide, at all levels. In a *Boston Globe* exposé by Mitchell Zuckoff of American exploitation of workers in Indonesia, Gillette served as the point-counterpoint "good guy" for its more benevolent personnel practices.[1] In Mexico, in response to the negative impact on paychecks caused by the devalued peso, Gillette employees in 1995 received a 17 percent cost of living adjustment in addition to merit increases averaging 8 percent. The starting pay of employees at the company's *maquiladora* (border) factory in Mexicali, while far below California wages, was 29 percent above the minimum Mexican wage, rising to 47 percent after thirty days, with fringe benefits worth 43 percent of salary in 1995. The attractiveness of the company cafeteria and recreational facilities at Gillette plants in Brazil and Argentina appeared to an observer superior to such amenities at older Gillette plants in the United States and England.

The more rapidly the company expanded internationally, the more acute became the need for identifying and training managers who could succeed as expatriates. Montreal, Canada, played a special role as a training ground, stretching back to the company's early days. A blade factory and national headquarters flourished in Montreal from 1906 until 1988, when the economic logic of large-scale manufacturing for a single North American market finally prevailed and the plant was closed.

In all those years at Gillette Canada, managers faced the same problems of distribution, pricing, factory management, labor management, and dealing with strong political leaders that challenged Gillette managers in markets with much larger populations. There was a different currency, exchange rate difficulties, and two cultures to sort out, yet Montreal was only a few hours north of Boston by train, and it became even less removed with the advent of airplane travel. Senior operating heads at Gillette in the 1980s and 1990s were top heavy with men who had started or spent a few years at Montreal, including Canadians Rod Mills, Derwyn Phillips, North Atlantic executive Ronald J. Rossi, and Braun Chairman Archie Livis, plus many Americans and others who spent time as expatriates in Montreal.

It was a rare Gillette senior executive in the 1990s who had not logged time as an expatriate. President Michael Hawley (Hong Kong, Canada, United Kingdom, Colombia, Australia) is just one example. When the expatriate program was formalized in 1967, about one hundred managers qualified, and these were mostly North Americans and British. By the mid-1990s, the company had nearly four hundred expatriate managers from forty-three nations.

Nearly half of them were in at least their fourth country. A British citizen who had replaced a Mexican was in charge of Turkey; a Swedish-born British citizen was at the helm in Russia, with a staff made up of British, Argentine, and American managers. All reported to José Ribera, a Spaniard based in England, where he oversees the AMEE operation covering Africa, the Middle East, and Eastern Europe.

Al Zeien told a group at St. John's University, where he was awarded the Colman Mockler Distinguished Leadership Award, that the major factor affecting Gillette's growth through the year 2000 will be the company's ability to grow its international expatriate program. According to Zeien, it takes about twenty-five years to build a solid expatriate workforce to the point that the company routinely has a good choice of candidates within its ranks for middle and senior management posts. The typical expatriate candidate has had a good business education, has spent a few early years at Boston, goes back to Japan or Pakistan or wherever home is for a few years, and then moves to three or four other Gillette posts in other nations—about a twenty-five-year process in all. Zeien considers the transferability of management to be the glue that holds the various parts of the company together.

As the company evolved from strictly blades to a multiproduct company, many fast-track senior executives worked for years at financial jobs away from their home countries. Executive Vice President Bob King began advancing through the ranks as a controller in Peru, a nation he had paid scant attention to before being asked if he would work there. It seemed like a good adventure and a path to better jobs at Gillette; moreover, his wife was willing, so it was off to Peru but not just as a numbers man. King noted that the Gillette concept of a controller has never been that of the classic "sharp pencil" or "bean counter." A Gillette controller is more of a financially trained generalist who is expected to perform his functional disciplines in finance, accounting, and treasury within the general context of the overall business, and to develop analytical and strategic planning skills along the way. King said the typical young controller in a foreign subsidiary does all the normal accounting chores in addition to collecting money from customers, negotiating promotional terms with salespeople, and keeping track of interest rates and cash flow. He has the responsibilities of a chief financial officer rolled into a full-service job performed in a sovereign country. That means the controller had to learn how to deal with often-volatile fluctuations in exchange rates—a make-or-break challenge when it came to returning profits in dollars to the parent company, especially before the computerized Boston-Zurich treasury system was instituted. It was part of the Gillette international experience that set the company and its managers apart from some American competitors that moved into high-inflation nations like Argentina before they knew how to cope with dollar exchange problems.

A management trainee program was established in the early 1980s at Boston headquarters for up to a dozen or more promising foreign students recruited from leading American business schools. Latin American chief Tony Levy had a special interest in promoting the plan. He wanted to attract bright young Latin American students who could eventually return to their homelands as Gillette managers, though not before experiencing, as expatriates, a few years at Boston and perhaps another one or two tours in other parts of the Gillette world. Gillette's trainee program was expanded, and it became a key part of the company's global culture because it helped the company train its own corps of global managers from the ground up.

Executive reviews begun by Ziegler and Mockler to identify promising managers who would be both able and willing to tackle management jobs outside their home countries became increasingly important to Gillette under Zeien's leadership. He told a Dow Jones interviewer that he spends about 50 percent of his time dealing with "people matters" or, to put it another way, management development. Much of that time is spent on personal reviews of eight hundred executives a year. "I told my personnel people that was impossible, that I didn't know eight hundred people, but when I reviewed my calendar I saw they were right," Zeien said. From his first year as chairman and CEO, Zeien made it a point to travel outside the United States every month of the year because "that's where the people are." In a global business like Gillette's

Zeien said, with seventy-five profit centers scattered around the world, the home office must delegate a great deal of decision making, and he wanted to make sure his managers everywhere shared with him the same goals and objectives. "Managing a global company is a lot different than managing people who have an office down the hall."

The ability to speak English is a unifying factor wherever in the world Gillette people work. Managers whose first language is not English are expected to have enough fluency to conduct business in the language—a common-sense policy inasmuch as English is the global business language.

STRUCTURING FOR A ONE-WORLD BUSINESS

Rosabeth Moss Kanter observed in her 1995 book *World Class: Thriving Locally in the Global Economy* that global structure follows global strategies (and global procedures and systems follow global structures). Gillette's modern history makes her point. Late in 1987, with the takeover threat from Ronald Perelman apparently over, Mockler announced a profound reorganization to take effect in 1988 that indeed reflected Gillette's gradual adoption of global strategies begun about twenty years earlier. As Kanter put it, the company moved beyond a structure suited to multinational operations to a transnational structure keyed to worldwide management of several different core product lines, with blades and razors at the top, of course.

In many ways, the 1988 reorganization implemented by Colman Mockler reflected the successful reorganization of Braun implemented by Al Zeien in the 1970s. As in the Braun reorganization, Mockler employed a matrix approach that centralized strategic decision making on a product basis but reserved for local managers the powers and resources to run their own shows and, in particular, to sell Gillette's worldwide products based on local retailing conditions. Gillette was split into two operating units. Gillette North Atlantic was charged with responsibility for the blade and razor, personal care, and stationery products businesses in both Western Europe and North America—the most advanced world economies and, significantly, the more mature and slower growth regions for Gillette. Gillette International/Diversified was given responsibility for these traditional product lines in the rest of the world, which encompasses the heavily populated, fast-growing markets where Gillette foresees some of its fastest growth. This two-world, mature growth/fast growth structure was later adopted by such global consumer products rivals as Colgate Palmolive. In addition, Gillette International/Diversified was given worldwide responsibility for Braun, Oral-B, and Jafra product lines; later Diversified was expanded to include North Atlantic Stationery Products.

As if attuned to Gillette's planning, the much-discussed but elusive global economy began to open up in the late 1980s. Tariff boundaries around the world were lowered, and regional trading blocs helpful to Gillette's globally structured business were formed in North and South America and Asia. China's free market reforms continued. Eastern European nations looked west for new business. The collapse of communism in Russia and other former Soviet Union nations made it possible for capitalists to move in, and Gillette responded. Western Europe, on cue in 1992, became the world's largest trading bloc. Despite separate currencies and certain nontariff barriers, the European Union proved compatible with Gillette's earlier pan-European restructuring.

Zeien contends that even the company's core product line of blades and razors was operating only on a multinational basis as opposed to global prior to 1991: "The company made certain products in Malaysia, others in France, and tailored the products to those national markets. Gillette no longer does this." A *New York Times* headline in a January 3, 1994, story captured the point: "Gillette's World View: One Blade Fits All."[2]

Few consumer goods companies met Zeien's test for global in the late 1990s. He cites Coca-Cola and parts of Johnson & Johnson, like Band-Aids. Many companies, he contends, are still multinationals, like the canned soup company that sells its soup everywhere but varies the soup taste for different markets—it is not a global company because the soup it sells in New York is different from the soup it sells in Paris or Moscow. Zeien said that Gillette recognizes that people in Egypt are not exactly the same as those in Malaysia but that Gillette offers them the same spectrum of products made to the same world standards under the same factory principles. Gillette may sell more of one product to the Malaysian and more of another to the Egyptian, but the product is the same. That is the meaning of Gillette's global mindset. With global skills to complement it—and continued good luck in the geopolitical forces shaping the global economy—a bright future seemed to be Gillette's to win or lose.

15

LATIN AMERICA
SHOWS
THE WAY

GILLETTE PINS MUCH of its optimism for strong growth well into the twenty-first century on its assuming market leadership in populous China, India, and Russia, nations largely closed to Gillette and other Western companies until recently. In many ways, the history of Gillette in Latin America suggests what can be expected. There the company encountered the same challenges it contends with in its new emerging markets: autocratic and sometimes unstable governments, arbitrary price controls, economic nationalism, high rates of inflation, and a market split between great masses of poor people and relatively smaller numbers of upper- and middle-class consumers.

In Latin America, Gillette's managers learned to cope and compete. Over many decades the region has emerged—from having been a Gillette backwater into what is now the most profitable segment of the Gillette world, based on percentage of sales. The response to a visitor's question by Carlos Enrique Daireaux, general manager of Gillette do Brasil in Rio de Janeiro, says it all: "What does Gillette make in Brazil? We make money!"

In 1996, Gillette do Brasil posted pretax profits of $72 million on sales of $286 million, making Daireaux's point. Brazilians bought more Gillette blades and razors in dollar terms—$218 million—than any nation except the United States, moving ahead of the perennial runner-up, France, in the mid-1990s.

And that's just Brazil. Mexico led other Latin nations in overall sales and profits in most postwar years until the 1995 recession and peso devaluation hit hard and sales plunged 37 percent to $199 million. Mexico recovered in 1996 to post $224 million in sales, which ranked it seventh among all nations, whereas Brazil finished fifth overall. Argentina has been a consistent profit center for more than fifty years, despite political turmoil and savage periods of hyperinflation, and in 1996 Gillette products accounted for an astonishing 95 percent share of the nation's razor and blade market, a few points higher than other Latin countries in this most Gillette-friendly of all regions in the world in terms of market share.

GETTING STARTED

Gillette started selling blades and razors in Mexico in 1906. "I will say that anybody who has carried on in Mexico for twenty-two years, as we have done, had to take a darned good beating," wrote long-time president Frank Fahey in a 1928 *Blade* article. Well worth the struggle, he might have added. The early years in Mexico set the stage for a sustained era of growth in Mexico, especially after 1949, when a small factory in Mexico City was expanded and Gillette Mexico began a major push to sell more goods both domestically and for export to Central America and elsewhere.

Shortly after the end of World War I, Gillette had established an office in Buenos Aires to coordinate an import and distribution network throughout Argentina, that most European of Latin nations. Other distribution networks were put in place gradually throughout Latin America and the Caribbean as the company followed its classic "toe in the water" strategy, moving aggressively into less-developed nations ahead of most U.S. consumer goods companies. Once there, Gillette fought to stay the course despite military, political, and social upheaval.

As sales and distribution networks took hold, blade manufacturing followed, starting with Brazil in 1931, when the merger with AutoStrop yielded a blade plant in Rio de Janeiro. AutoStrop had been turning out blades and razors since 1926 in rented factory space in the city's Vila Isabel section. São Paulo later took over as Brazil's manufacturing center, but Gillette stayed put in the carefree city of the Cariocas. Headquarters staff eventually settled in the downtown Botafogo business district, where executives enjoyed splendid views of Sugarloaf Mountain across the bay.

The early postwar years in Brazil were all about patience and digging in. The company focused on building a distributor network that functioned in the remote villages and cities scattered around the interior of the world's fifth largest country, as well as in the crowded coastal regions where most of Brazil's 160 million residents live. Brazil, the most populous Latin nation, is one of the world's fastest-growing countries. Its demographics are attractive for a consumer products company like Gillette: 48 percent of Brazilians in 1994 were under the age of twenty-one as compared with 33 percent in the United States. Brazil's 1994 per capita income was just over $3,100—less than one-half Argentina's average—but high nonetheless by Latin American standards.

Gillette was established as a modest exporter of blades and razors to its Argentine operation when World War II broke out, giving the company a sudden opportunity to reap the spoils of war. A German blade company hastily abandoned operations in Buenos Aires in 1942, and Gillette's Argentine subsidiary seized the chance to fill the void by building a new blade plant. Thus it was that Gillette, famed supplier of blades and razors to American soldiers fighting the Germans, became the major blade supplier to a nation whose government only got around to declaring war on the Axis powers three weeks before the Germans surrendered in April 1945. Because it was already established in Argentina, Gillette was able to keep making and selling blades throughout the long, dark postwar years when General Juan Perón's government and other military juntas pursued economic self-sufficiency and shut off Argentina to outside investment. The plant provided jobs, and Gillette's blade packages were stamped "made in Argentina," so that the economic xenophobia of the Perónistas was deflected.

The new manufacturing plant completed by Gillette in Mexico City in 1949 concluded the first stage of Gillette's strategy of establishing a manufacturing presence in each of Latin America's "Big Three" nations, which together account for 70 percent of the region's nearly half billion people. More and larger plants eventually were established by Gillette to serve not only Mexican and Latin American markets but also to produce certain razor products and Braun home appliances for export to the United States and Europe.

In the rest of Latin America, Gillette sometimes established operating companies that served logical groupings of small nations—the Andean region and the Caribbean, for example— working with local jobbers when that made more sense than immediately incorporating Gillette-owned companies. But whether in Colombia, Chile, Peru, or wherever Gillette incorporated and put up the company flag, it usually got there before American or foreign competitors, and its managers made clear that the company was committed to staying for the long term rather than just signing up a few agents and skimming off fast profits. The fast-growing populations of Latin American nations provided sufficient incentive for Gillette to adapt to difficult conditions and sell blades while bullets flew and currencies collapsed.

LEARNING TO COPE WITH EXTREMES

The extreme differences between rich and poor in Latin American economies affect the way business is done. About 8 percent of Brazilians account for almost two-thirds of total consumption. The bottom 67 percent of the population accounts for only 11.5 percent of consumption. Nei Eduardo P. da Silva, director of manufacturing for Gillette do Brasil, pointed to a sprawling hillside *favela* (shantytown slum) looming directly above one of Rio's most fashionable districts and conceded that he, a native-born Carioca, could not safely venture into the essentially lawless area. But he said that Gillette agents can and do service the slums' merchants with products, just as Gillette agents in the hinterlands make sure that blades are available to the rural poor.

Argentina's per capita income of about $8,000 in 1995 was about double that of Mexico and more than twice that of its huge neighbor, Brazil. Especially in the capital district around Buenos Aires, where a third of the nation's roughly 35 million residents live, there are relatively fewer people living in hopeless poverty than in the great cities and rural outbacks of Brazil and Mexico.

A few cities in Latin America, including Rio, have long had crime problems that required extraordinary security measures to protect employees from kidnapping and extortion. In Rio, drivers and armed guards were assigned to about a dozen Gillette executives and their families. Often, the same drivers and bodyguards are assigned to watch over families and transport wives to grocery stores and children to school. The shiny new company car with the black-suited driver and his muscular sidekick, sadly is not unique to Rio. It has become a recognizable part of the business scene in other parts of the world where Gillette is located, and is one of the costs of doing business globally. The same measures taken by Gillette in Rio are in place in St. Petersburg, where Gillette's Russian operation is headquartered, for example. Managers in these postings are made to understand that such precautions must be accepted as part of the global business routine, like vaccination shots and visa difficulties.

Just as Gillette learned to sell in markets with great disparities between rich and poor and found ways to protect its employees from crime, the company's managers learned to cope with unstable government and hyperinflation in major Latin markets. Carlos Daireaux listed some of the factors contributing to a cumulative 87.7 billion percent inflation from 1981 through 1993: a chaotic parade of eleven finance ministers, twelve central bank presidents, twelve economic stabilization programs, five price freeze periods, eleven official indexes to measure inflation, twenty-four foreign debt negotiation proposals, sixteen salary policies, eighteen changes in foreign exchange rules, twenty-four proposed budget cuts, and five different currencies, with nine zeroes cut out. Various governments tried to curb demand, control prices, confiscate money from companies, and at one point, even tried to seize cattle—about the only measure that did not complicate life for Gillette, Daireaux noted wryly.

How Gillette's Latin American managers dealt with hyperinflation and still sent profits home to Boston is examined later in this chapter.

WALTER HUNNEWELL'S LATIN AMERICA

One way to track Gillette's deep penetration of Latin America is to start in Boston in 1945, when a young Harvard College graduate named Walter Hunnewell returned from war service looking for work with a taste of adventure. Hunnewell had not particularly enjoyed Harvard, where he earned his undergraduate degree in 1939, though later studies at Harvard Business School opened up intriguing job possibilities. He joined the U.S. Navy and as a young lieutenant served aboard a ship in the Mediterranean war theater. It proved in many ways a satisfying interlude in Hunnewell's life. The war over, young Hunnewell, a member of a long-established New England family, was determined to escape the family investment business and find work outside. He landed at Gillette, which sent him in 1948 to Mexico, where his long romance with Latin America began.

A few months after moving to Mexico City, Hunnewell replaced the general manager, who had quit unexpectedly. More important, he met and married his wife, Luisa. The lifelong New Englander settled down for what turned out to be a long career linked primarily to Latin America. Upon his return to Boston from Mexico, Hunnewell advanced rapidly through the ranks, helping to establish company-owned sales and distribution companies in Chile and Colombia to replace local jobbers and working on projects in the Big Three Latin nations.

In 1958, Hunnewell became manager of the Latin American

Division and was named group general manager of the successor Latin American Group in 1961. He was to spend seventeen years in these posts. "I don't think anyone at Gillette before or since held one job for so long," Hunnewell mused many years after his retirement. Former colleagues told stories of Hunnewell's legendary frugality, like the time he returned home from a long trip with a ropelike fabric about his waist. He explained that he had a perfectly good belt at home and saw no need to buy a new one in Rio. He could be almost as tightfisted about Gillette budgets, but at the same time he was probably the company's leading advocate for Latin involvement during an era when that was not always popular.

Hunnewell ended his exclusive preoccupation with the Latin American Group in 1974, when he was elected senior vice president and deputy general manager of international operations. In 1976, he was appointed executive vice president of Gillette International. But Latin America remained his first love, with Europe lacking, he felt, the exciting growth prospects of Brazil and Mexico. He noted that his feelings were not always shared by the man who was his boss for much of his career, CEO Vincent Ziegler, who enjoyed traveling in Europe and expended much of his business energy there.

According to Hunnewell, Colman Mockler was another Europhile in terms of personal interest, but he had a lively appreciation for Latin America's contribution to Gillette. When military and political turmoil scared many American companies away, Mockler continued to commit money to increased manufacturing ventures and supported any measure he thought was needed to maintain Gillette's edge. Al Zeien continued aggressive expansion in Latin America as a cornerstone of his global strategies. As the twentieth century nears its end, Gillette is so entrenched that many Latin customers don't ask for blades, they ask for "Gillettes," just as Americans once asked for "IBM machines" rather than computers, and English asked for "Hoovers," not vacuum cleaners.

After Hunnewell, a succession of Latin American managers fought to keep Gillette a household word under difficult circumstances. Chief among them was Tony Levy.

WORKING UP THE RANKS

The unlikely saga of Tony Levy underscores Gillette's ability to identify and pay heed to promising managers toiling far from Boston headquarters. Levy is an Italian-born Jew who, in the early 1950s, was working as a pharmaceuticals salesman in Egypt. He was living there with his family when Arab nationalist revolutionaries headed by Gamal Abdel Nasser seized power. After Nasser abolished the monarchy and expelled the British from the Suez Canal, life became difficult for many foreigners. By 1956, conditions had become intolerable, and Levy packed up with his wife and child and boarded a ship for Brazil, landing in São Paulo with $380 in his pocket, no job, and able to say just a few words in Portuguese.

Levy had scarcely heard of Gillette. He set out to search for a job with a company where he could eventually use his language capabilities in English, French, or Italian. Each morning, he rode to the top of one or more of São Paulo's new skyscrapers and walked down floor by floor, looking for signs on doors that would indicate whether the company's working language matched his abilities. On his downward treks he got a few offers to work in sales but he was looking for something better, with managerial responsibility. Finally, on the eighteenth day of his search, he decided to follow a lead on a French company located on the tenth floor of a building, but he inadvertently got off an especially balky elevator at the seventh floor. Hot and in a foul mood, he decided against walking up three more floors and punched the elevator "up" button. As he waited, he turned and saw the name "The Sydney Ross Co." on a door. At that moment a receptionist happened to poke her head out the door, and Levy asked her if the company was English. No, she replied American—a division of Sterling Drug. Levy gave the receptionist his card, and her boss asked him in for a talk. After a short interview, Levy was advised to go to Rio and discuss job opportunities with the Sydney Ross Brazilian manager.

Off to Rio went Levy, and after a long discussion about Egyptology and architecture and other nonbusiness matters, he was offered a trial as sales supervisor, with the job to be his if he learned Portuguese in ninety days. That proved no obstacle for linguist Levy, who worked with Sydney Ross salespeople by day and studied Portuguese at night, gaining enough language skill after forty-five days to impress his boss and win the job.

After three years with Sydney Ross, Levy was ready for a better job. He went to a headhunter who sized him up and, in short order, singled out three prospects, including Gillette. He chose Gillette when the headhunter assured him of its reputation as a family company that cared about its employees. Levy had several interviews with Gillette do Brasil's general manager, Franklin Ford Doten, whom Levy recalls fondly as a heavy, cigar-smoking New Hampshireman. Doten did some creative tinkering to find a job that met Levy's demand for managerial responsibility, and the next day Levy began a thirty-five-year Gillette career, very soon taking over as general sales manager in Brazil, as Doten had promised. From there Levy moved up rapidly, with assignments in England, Canada, and Boston.

By 1973, he was back in Brazil, this time in charge, and like all Latin American managers, committed to a policy of defending the company's profitable domination of double-edge blade and razor sales. Very soon he would be trying to upgrade faithful double-edge customers to the revolutionary twin-blade razors that had just been introduced in the United States as the Trac II. The Bic disposable's challenge to the comfortable status quo was on the horizon.

LEVY TACKLES HYPERINFLATION

But first, there was that seemingly intractable Brazilian headache, inflation, which was getting worse, not better, as Levy moved into the top job in Rio. Brazil's wild ride in the postwar years had been fed by the needs of a fast-growing population concentrated in the coastal strip between Rio and São Paulo, one of the world's largest cities. Brazilian governments, faced with governing a land mass larger than the United States minus Alaska, spent heavily trying to persuade coastal inhabitants to move inland to the new capital of Brasília and other hinterlands. Unbroken years of deficit spending financed by heavy foreign borrowing fueled impressive rates of growth but infected the nation's currency. The inflation that was accepted as a natural part of the Brazilian scene, like coffee and corruption, lurched from tolerable to intolerable to truly outlandish hyperinflation that peaked in 1993 at 2,567 percent, then suddenly fell to acceptable levels.

Levy knew the headache of inflation from a householder's pragmatic point of view, having handled his family's finances in Rio when inflation often was at a rate of 40 percent to 50 percent a month. In his earlier days, he and his fellow workers sometimes were paid by Gillette twice a month instead of monthly, and then for a time every Friday afternoon, two hours early, so that the money could be deposited in banks or spent before the weekend. Back in Rio as general manager, Levy was sure that he could deal with inflation's impact on business as a whole.

He set up the Gillette Erosion Protection Plan. It dealt with how to sell, how to collect (receivables should be cash when possible), and how to pay (delay as much as possible). Levy's plan required that Gillette reevaluate assets weekly, rather than monthly, as required by law. Inventories had to be kept at low levels, the aim being to push products into the hands of distributors so they could generate cash sales. High discounts were approved for cash sales on the theory that it was wiser to pay discounts for cash deals in a hyperinflationary situation than to be paid in full but forced to wait for the normal thirty- or sixty-day billing cycle. Levy and his financial staff spent a lot of time developing a refined discount schedule, taking various rates of likely devaluation into consideration. Managers throughout Brazil were required to attend "Erosion Protection" seminars.

The program worked, Levy claimed. Profits returned to Boston in dollars more than doubled in his four years on the job. Levy recalls Walter Hunnewell saying, "Tony, please come up here to Boston and explain to the directors how you do it." The directors could not understand how dollar profits were increasing at a time of hyperinflation and frequent devaluation. What was going on? Was Gillette involved by any chance in payoffs to the country's traditionally corrupt bureaucracy?

Levy told them that the key to Gillette's success was the simplest of maxims: "Think dollars." Many of Gillette's American competitors had failed to follow this maxim, he noted, despite posting good sales in local currencies. When Levy took charge of all Latin countries he refused to accept profit and loss statements in any currency except dollars.

Argentina suffered through even worse bouts of inflation and government instability than did Brazil. The peak years of Argentine hyperinflation occurred briefly in 1976 and then for a number of years consecutively, starting in the mid-1980s through the early 1990s. Accountants were forced to abandon computers and cover reams of papers with handwritten zeroes to keep up with figures that moved into the trillions for a while. Yet Argentina almost always managed to post strong profits.

"We thought we knew something about inflation after years of 100 plus annual increases, but then came 1989 and hyperinflation like we had never seen," recalled Carlos Ruiz Echazu, general sales manager in Buenos Aires. Argentina's consumer price index shot up 4,923 percent that year from a "mere" 388 percent in 1988. "If we didn't hustle, the grocery clerk would mark up goods in the next aisle before we could get there," Echazu said.

In an unusual turn of events, Argentina's extreme inflation actually protected Gillette's market dominance because some competitors simply did not want to cope with it and left the country. Nobody wants to invest in times of hyperinflation, explained Jorge E. Micozzi, an urbane Argentine financial manager who served in various Gillette posts in North and South America, including Gillette headquarters in Boston before being named general manager of Gillette Argentina in 1991.

Micozzi said speed and flexibility were the keys to weathering the inflationary period. As in Brazil, Micozzi said Argentina's managers were instructed to think in dollar terms, though, of course, they had to make pricing decisions in pesos. During the toughest periods of inflation, the company had to increase product prices twice weekly, a difficult procedure that had to balance what the market would pay for Gillette goods against what the dollar impact would be when the pesos were converted. In effect, the company was financially driven in the worst inflationary years.

There were a lot of allied financial complications. In the worst days, the company could not get normal credit from banks, nor loans—not even from old friend BankBoston, which is a major American banking presence in Latin America, particularly Argentina and Brazil. Mockler and later Zeien served on BankBoston's board, in part because of Gillette's extensive presence in Latin America. Unable to borrow during hyperinflationary periods, Gillette sometimes had to negotiate U.S. dollar-denominated bonds to raise cash. In general, managing inflation involved a sophisticated and perilous hedging of dollars, buying and selling at appropriate times. It meant keeping up with laws and regulations that changed overnight. It meant communicating almost daily with key suppliers. Frequently, it meant demanding payment in advance.

It all added up to many fifteen-hour days, just to keep up with the paperwork associated with pricing changes and ever-changing government regulations. Micozzi said Gillette's Argentine company never failed to return dollars to Boston in modern times, with the single exception of 1989, the year the Consumer Price Index shot up almost 5,000 percent.

THE PRESTOBARBA STRATEGY

Latin American Gillette managers took a different tack in dealing with the challenge of disposable razors in the mid-1970s. From Caracas to Santiago, they had the benefit of forewarning as they watched French-owned Bic upset Gillette plans in Europe and North America. They noted that for once, a competitor blade maker enjoyed the heady role of getting there first and starting a price war that cut into Gillette's market share. It did not escape their notice that blade profit margins dropped sharply when the price of Gillette disposables was slashed close to Bic levels.

But Bic was not yet in Latin America, and Levy and his colleagues had time to plan. They recognized that the Latin American market was still overwhelmingly double edge, and that the low-priced twin-blade disposable sold as Good News in the United States was a value-added product for Latins that could be sold as a premium-priced step up from double-edge blades.

Levy named the Latin version of the Good News the Presto-barba, and the ubiquitous blue-handled razor became an instant success in the 1970s. It has remained a major source of sales late in the twentieth century, twenty years after its debut. The Presto-barba is especially popular with younger men and women, who make up a disproportionately large segment of Latin shavers.

To make sure that the Prestobarba would retain a long life as a premium-priced disposable, Gillette adopted a defensive pricing strategy for its Latin American Group. The company offered consumers two versions of the same basic disposable razor. The strongly advertised market leader Prestobarba was made from blue plastic. Lower-priced versions were made from yellow plastic, sporting such names as Permasharp in Mexico and Probak in Brazil. They housed the same blade cartridge as the Prestobarba but the word "Gillette" is not on the packaging, and very importantly, the yellow off-brand models are not advertised. They sell at retail for at least 10 percent to 15 percent less than the Presto-barba. Throughout the region, the well-known and very profitable Prestobarba disposable became Gillette's best-selling high-margin razor.

The cannibalizing strategy, which was a variation of Gillette's 1921 strategy to fend off competitors after King Gillette's original blade patent expired, came from a computer study by planner Carl Hoefel showing that if a product was the first to be sold in a market, its potential was very great; if second to market, it would do fairly well; if third, its potential was limited, and so on. Basically alone in the disposable field with the Prestobarba, Levy and colleagues decided to outflank Bic by putting unadvertised yellow-handled twins to the Prestobarba on the market before Bic could get there, reserving the second-to-market slot for Gillette. The strategy worked, with latecomers fighting for tiny shares of market.

Gillette managers in Russia, Poland, and several Asian and

Middle Eastern markets with similar market dynamics took note and copied the Latin model of creating off-brand disposables.

ENSURING BETTER JOBS FOR LATIN MANAGERS

In his early years, Tony Levy was determined to end the practice of automatically dispatching North Americans and occasional Englishmen to the senior operating jobs in Latin America. "I made a solemn promise to myself that I would train and replace the first-line expatriate managers with locals, and also second and third level managers in finance, marketing, production, and administration," Levy recalled. He himself had been the first Latin American—adopted, if not by birth—to hold the top job in Rio.

Armando Silva, who started work at Gillette's Rio outpost in 1934 and was still on the payroll sixty-two years later—almost certainly Gillette's all-time leader in longevity on the job—remembered that "I broke Tony in." He said Levy did not require as much care and handling as a succession of straight-from-Boston executives who preceded him.

Levy felt that the North Americans who dipped in and out of Latin America for a few years in executive jobs seldom trained replacements. He believed that Gillette's growth in Latin America depended on the cross-training of young managers, exposing a marketing manager to finance, and a production manager to finance or marketing, for example, within each country or organization. He also lobbied for funds to move Latin managers with special strengths to temporary postings where they could learn more, and then make sure they were moved back to the Latin American Group. In a few years Latin America was "converted," that is, most general manager posts were filled with local Latins, and with some exceptions, second- and third-level positions were filled either with locals or other Latins.

When Levy succeeded Rod Mills as chief of Gillette's international operations in 1987, he took the regional cross-training idea to the next logical step. He converted Latin America from an importer of talent to an exporter, dispatching dozens of able Latin managers to Gillette outposts in Eastern Europe, Asia, and the Middle East—the very nations likely to be in need of people who knew how to confront inflation and distribute products to markets split between rich and poor.

By the mid-1990s it was unsurprising to find an Argentine personnel specialist, Juan Gallo, working in Russia after a stint in Boston or manufacturing specialists like the Brazilian engineer and master storyteller Aluízio Sturzenecker popping up for a few years in India, then a few years in Russia, with occasional short-term assignments in Turkey or China or wherever Gillette needed him.

In a restaurant in his latest home city of Manaus, Brazil, Sturzenecker talked engagingly about the exhilaration and the downside of unexpected late-night calls from Boston asking him to move to one or another foreign outpost that suddenly had need of his talents. He recalled the hot night in India, where he and his family had finally settled down to something approaching routine, when the phone rang and the voice from Boston asked him if he would like to be a candidate for a new job in St. Petersburg, Russia. He figured that he might as well be a candidate because he could always withdraw later. So he said yes, and the Boston voice responded with enthusiasm, "Great, you're the only candidate, and we'd like your decision in forty-eight hours." Weeks later, the Sturzeneckers were en route to Russia, where they stayed long enough to accumulate a wardrobe of fur coats and Cossack-style hats before being sent to Manaus, an equatorial city where the temperature seldom dips below a very sticky 85 degrees Fahrenheit in any month of the year. Sturzenecker has not yet got rid of his furs because, as his wife reminded him with faultless logic, he'll never know where in the Gillette world he'll end up next.

Ricardo Maddalena, in his early thirties, had been assigned to jobs in Brazil, Argentina, and Mexico and been posted for temporary duty to Braun in Germany before he landed the marketing manager's job in Rio, where he paused briefly before being promoted to a post in the Latin American Group in Boston. "And I have thirty years to go!" he exclaimed. His Brazilian boss, Carlos Daireaux, well traveled himself, said that Gillette seldom loses people despite the travel demands. "Gillette people are very loyal and they won't leave because they want to work for the leader. Our wives are jealous of Gillette." He's right, on the latter point. Most Gillette wives and families appear to take the travel in stride and most thrive on the adventurous lifestyle, which is leavened with good perks and a lot of home leave, although there are occasional broken marriages that are blamed on the pressures of global business. Gillette personnel managers make it clear that the company does not demand that its employees move, and managers can reject assignments, though it is obvious to any ambitious person at Gillette, or anyone considering an offer from Gillette, that almost all executives in the top ranks have worked abroad.

Argentina's Micozzi believes that Boston, considered by many Americans as one of the nation's most parochial cities, is a felicitous headquarters site for a global company. "Boston, the Boston culture, travels well, better than, say, New York or Cincinnati," he commented. "Most of us have traveled around the world and worked in other nations, but we are comfortable with the Gillette culture everywhere. This culture comes from Boston and by and large it is conservative, and slow to make drastic changes, with the result that people are comfortable."

———

SUCCESS IN THE AMAZON JUNGLE

The remarkable history of Gillette da Amazonia SA at Manaus reveals much about how Gillette's global culture encourages good ideas to unfold in unlikely places, such as the heart of the Amazon rain forest.

The Portuguese established Manaus in 1669 at the point where the Rio Negro joins the Amazon river, about twelve hundred miles from the coast. The tiny jungle outpost suddenly boomed in the late nineteenth century, when the Amazon region became the world's major supplier of natural rubber. British rubber barons moved in for a few decades and Manaus became a British colonial capital, with the bosses and managers living in relative comfort, even building an ornate opera house in 1890. Countless native

Amazon rubber tappers loaded their canoes with rubber drained from *seringuera* trees and paddled to Manaus, where the rubber was sold to agents and then loaded on barges for the long trip to Belém at the Amazon's mouth, and beyond.

According to the local story, British seamen sneaked *seringuera* seedlings to Malaysia and other relatively accessible places and put an end to the Amazon monopoly. The development of synthetics to replace natural rubber sealed the city's doom. The British abandoned their "London on the Amazon," leaving behind the Opera House, and such infrastructure as the world's largest floating dock. It is a lengthy platform perched atop barrels that rise and fall as the river seasonally swells and ebbs based on the amount of rainfall.

As it became evident that rubber had no future and timber operations could not expand forever, Brazil became desperate to attract industry to Manaus to provide jobs for the area's indigenous Brazilians, called Indians to distinguish them from Brazilians of European and African descent.

The Manaus Free Trade Zone and Industrial Park was established in the 1970s to encourage foreign companies to set up factories by promising tax breaks and incentives—the drawback being Manaus' location thousands of miles from anywhere. It is a five-day barge trip upriver from the Atlantic port of Belém and four days going back. There are no reliable roads to the south, east, and west; the sole road north is not for the timid. It is more than three hours by air to Manaus from either Rio or São Paulo. Still, the incentives offered by Brazil's government were so tempting that several Japanese consumer electronics companies overcame the improbable logistics and had started production by the time Tony Levy caught the bug in 1975. The Brazilian government made him an offer that Gillette could not reject—at least that is what Levy preached when he persuaded Boston executives that Gillette's future lay in the Amazon jungle.

Companies that located in the Manaus Fiscal Incentive Area were promised an 88 percent reduction on import duties and an impressive range of reductions and outright exemptions from sales and income taxes. Gillette was promised a site in a handsome industrial park with plenty of space, modern infrastructure, maintenance of green space, and environmental controls. Government programs to aid schooling and post-school technical training were promised to companies wary of installing expensive production machinery without sufficient skilled labor to keep the plants running.

It was a real-life industrial version of Hollywood's *Field of Dreams* fantasy about the baseball park built in an Iowa cornfield on the premise "Build it and they will come." Brazil's plan to tempt modern industry to a remote jungle site worked, if success is defined as sudden industrialization of a forgotten and decaying river city bypassed by the twentieth century. From a population of 350,000 in 1960, the population of Manaus climbed to 1.6 million in thirty-five years as Indian families migrated to the city, and a sizable middle class of managers, bankers, and the like moved from the south to support the industry. Manaus now accounts for nearly 80 percent of the total population of Amazonas, Brazil's largest province, with an area about two times the size of France.

By 1995, nearly three hundred U.S., Japanese, and European companies, including Honda, Sony, and Philips, had invested more than $5 billion in the government's industrial parks, creating about 44,000 jobs in factories landscaped with the exotic plants and flowers of the jungle. The Manaus park where Gillette is located is more attractive to the eye and has more employee amenities than the typical asphalt and brick industrial parks that scar the outskirts of many cities in North America.

Are You Crazy?

Manaus turned out to be a success story, but it was considered a risky move at the time Levy flew to Boston to make his pitch to the directors. He had a selling job to do.

"Walter [Hunnewell] and the others in Boston thought I was totally crazy and Walter told me 'don't even appear here,'" Levy recalled. But of course, Levy knew something about selling and ignored the good-natured warning from his boss. After his pitch, the directors paused and then told him to go ahead. Levy had already begun a tiny Manaus operation to assemble pens, hiring six Indian workers and a supervisor in what he remembered as a "rented shack" near the decaying downtown area. The workers proved adept, and the Paper Mates rolled off the makeshift line. Eventually, as many as one hundred native Amazonians were employed to assemble millions of Paper Mate products, but Gillette's real goal was to establish Manaus as a center for blade and razor production.

Manufacturing cartridges for twin-blade razors presented a much more complex manufacturing challenge than pens. The most difficult and costly part of the production involved injection-molding complex plastic cartridges to Gillette's precise design requirements, a job Gillette's Rio factory had always farmed out to vendors in São Paulo at very high cost. The empty cartridges were then shipped to Rio, where the blades were inserted and the completed cartridges and disposable twin-blade razors were packaged for shipment.

Levy conducted a study showing how millions of dollars could be saved by dispensing with the contractors and importing injection-molding equipment duty free from Germany and the United States to a new Gillette plant at Manaus. Moreover, strip steel imported from Europe and Japan was subject to 100 percent duty if landed at Rio but largely exempted from duties if consigned for eventual assembly into cartridges and razors made at Manaus. Levy's plan called for the Rio plant to continue sharpening blades on machinery that could not easily be moved and shipping the blades to the Manaus finishing plant in special nitrogen vacuum containers to protect them from the constant high humidity of the Amazon district.

The Manaus blade plant started operating in 1978 with a work force of 850, mushrooming to 1,700 a few years later, before the combination of new machinery and better-skilled workers made it possible to turn out more products with fewer hands. A major expansion took place in 1988, when a new plastics components factory was built on the site to meet the government rules for more value-added manufacturing to justify continued tax exemptions. By that time about 1,000 people working three shifts daily had transformed the jungle plant from a seemingly crazy gamble into Gillette's third-largest blade factory, after South Boston and London.

"You know the Manaus economics are good when you realize the transportation costs that we have to overcome," said Nei da Silva, the Brazilian manufacturing director based in Rio. Blades sharpened at Rio go by air to Manaus for assembly in cartridges. The finished product for domestic markets goes by barge to Belém and from there, by road two thousand miles to Rio via Brasília. Export products are shipped by barge from Manaus to Belém and then transferred to ocean-going freighters for destinations like Russia.

Gillette veterans like to tell of the computer report that came to the attention of the Australian manager one day that indicated he could buy Atra cartridges from Manaus more cheaply than from Gillette's Melbourne factory an hour away. The logic, expressed in dollars by the computer, was this: Steel from Japan for the blades is shipped duty-free to Rio de Janeiro, where it is processed into blade steel, then shipped up the Atlantic Coast, transferred to a barge, and sent upriver to Manaus, where the plastic molding takes place and the blade steel is mounted into the cartridge. Then the cartridge is barged back down the river to Belém, shipped to Singapore for packaging, and finally sent to the Melbourne warehouse—at a savings over the Melbourne price. Labor costs did not play a significant role. Not long afterward, the Melbourne factory and another blade plant in the Philippines were closed. Global economies can be bizarre.

Levy had to convince the directors he had not lost his senses when he asked their support, given Manaus' primitive conditions in 1975. At that time there was no reliable telephone communication with the rest of the world. As in a war setting, Gillette managers in Manaus contacted the outside via radio until an efficient phone system became reality. The city's reputation as a tropical backwater was so strong that Levy had to devise a generous incentive plan to coax reluctant Brazilian managers from the south to Manaus, paying more extras to a Brazilian to move to another part of his own country than to move to London. In the mid-1970s, the turn-down rate for managers and wives who had been sent to Manaus for a week's look around was 70 percent. It was a struggle to find workers with the needed skills to operate the early-generation production machines. Tuberculosis, syphilis, leprosy, and other diseases that had long since been controlled in developed areas of the world were common.

That changed dramatically over twenty years. Government-industry inoculation programs lowered disease rates to more normal levels. Technical training programs financed by the government with industry support proved to be one of those too-rare examples of government planning that really works. Manaus is not paradise; there are still many shantytown districts and children playing in muddy streets. American shoppers and health inspectors would be appalled at the poor condition of the city's prize fish and produce market perched just above the banks of the river. But landscaped highways from the oversized airport and from the five-star Tropical Hotel en route to the industrial parks pass modern shopping centers, a sports stadium that can seat fifty thousand for football matches, the extensive campus of the state-run university, and many high-rise apartments.

"This was the middle of the jungle in 1975. Since then we have built a modern plant, we have a fine group of workers, and here at Gillette we make a lot of money," said Claudio Augusto da Silva, superintendent director in Manaus, a native of the São Paulo district.

SOUTH BOSTON, BERLIN, AND MANAUS

Gillette directors in 1995 approved a $120 million expansion at Manaus that turned the site into one of the most sophisticated Gillette plants in the world and the only plant, along with South Boston and Berlin, equipped to manufacture the Sensor family of razors and blades, which are by far Gillette's most complex shaving products.

Aluízio Sturzenecker, who is the factory manager, said that the newly industrialized workers of Manaus are up to the job and are more flexible than workers in Russia and India and other parts of the world where he has worked for Gillette. He added that they are "kind to each other and to us," and he senses a "small town feel" to the work force that translates into higher productivity. In the early years, absenteeism was a recurring problem as workers fought the unfamiliar rigidities of a scheduled work week, but they learned to adapt. Gillette helped develop a steady work habit by providing a free shuttle bus to and from work for nearly all production workers, according to Cynthia do Valle Bezerra, manager of the sizable human resources staff. Bezerra is a Manaus native, like the majority of the eight or ten senior managers, all of them Brazilians, who work at Gillette da Amazonia. Gillette is an anomaly in this regard, she said, because most free trade zone companies are heavily staffed with Japanese or other home-country managers.

Bezerra said that in the 1970s and early 1980s Gillette had to import skilled workers from the south, but the government-industry schools and training programs have created a large pool of Manaus men and women with technical and administrative skills. And there will be more, said Bezerra, pointing to a group of women earnestly practicing their English-language skills in a factory office. She said that they were scheduled to go to Boston for further training prior to the start-up of Sensor production.

The Manaus operation is capital intensive, with costly production equipment controlled by computers, now the norm compared to the labor-intensive assembly lines of start-up days at the site. At one time there were nine persons for each machine in the blade factory, but as workers advanced up the learning curve, this total was more than halved.

The industrial jobs at the free trade zone parks have created a relatively prosperous working class at Manaus. Gillette pays a little better than the average industrial wage at Manaus, and makes available company doctors and nurses and medical services for entire families who had been unfamiliar with modern medical practices. Gillette jobs are prized because they are perceived as lifetime work. Benvinida Silva, a small woman in a blue smock, started with the pen assembly operation and twenty years later was still on the job, deftly packing long-handled PrestobarbaMax razors into display cartons. A few benches away, her son Marcos, nineteen, was working in another department. Like the PrestobarbaMax, Marcos is "made at Gillette," her fellow workers joked as Benvinida laughed.

Like many other Gillette managers, Claudio da Silva was doubtful about moving to Manaus when first offered the job, but he became a convert. He said he and his wife prefer steamy Manaus to Rio because there is less crime and violence, and "no need for a bodyguard up here." Several first-rate private schools supplement government schools, with Gillette helping to subsidize the cost for employees who enroll their children. Telephones and satellite television bring in the outside world. There are occasional gala programs in the restored 700-seat opera house. The great tenor Luciano Pavarotti once stopped by the empty opera house, sang a few arias for a handful of friends, and pronounced the house fit for the grandest of grand opera. A few years later the Spanish tenor José Carreras performed to a house filled with dignitaries from all over Latin America.

Brazilian officials liked that recognition but perhaps not as much as Gillette's decision made about the same time to upgrade the Manaus plant to world-class industrial sophistication so that it can be a third factory for the Sensor—a global product if ever there was one. In a sense, it was Yankee Boston rating tropical Manaus as fit to make the best a man can get.

16

A
FOOT ON THE
GROUND

THE "PUTSCH OF FOOLS" in Moscow that shocked the world late
in August 1991 had special meaning for Gillette executives in
Boston, who were making plans for the company's imminent
reentry into the Soviet Union. Unfortunately, in the final stages
the company had dealt with a high Kremlin official who turned
out to be one of the "fools," to borrow a Moscow journalist's
description of the Communist leaders who launched a failed coup
d'état against party leader Mikhail Gorbachev and Soviet president Boris Yeltsin. With the company's sponsor in jail, Gillette's
plans to start making blades in Russia were dead. The incident
required a detour in strategic plans, but the company had accepted
risks many times as the price for moving into markets that were
politically unstable. How Gillette regrouped tells a lot about its
determination to get established in the vast markets long closed
to Gillette by largely political barriers, and where so much of the
company's twenty-first century growth potential lies.

The arithmetic of the foot on the ground strategy is straight-forward. The worldwide blade market, according to Gillette estimates, was nearly 20 billion units by the mid-1990s. Roughly half that market was in North America, Western Europe, Latin America, and parts of the Asia Pacific region where Gillette generally was the market leader in blade sales. The other half of the world blade market lay in the emerging markets of Russia and the former Soviet Union states (FSU), India, China, Turkey, and other parts of Asia, the Middle East, and Africa. In these so-called emerging geographies, to use Gillette's description, the company's share of the blade and razor market generally was minimal when the Cold War ended. Given the scale of the prize, Gillette could well afford to ride out a failed Russian *putsch* to regain entry into the world's third-largest blade market in unit terms (after India and the United States).

PLANNING REENTRY TO RUSSIA

With Chairman Colman Mockler giving his assent, Tony Levy and others at Gillette decided early in 1989 that Gillette should start planning for its reentry into Russia. A few weeks after the Berlin Wall fell in September 1989, the company began the limited export of blades and razors. Moscow soon opened the door to part ownership of a Gillette venture by rescinding a law requiring 51 percent Soviet ownership of businesses operating on Soviet soil.

Gillette announced in February 1990 that it had negotiated a memorandum of intent with a Soviet business partner for a large-scale blade and razor manufacturing project. At the time, the Soviet Union was still intact, and the Communist Party was still nominally in charge, its leaders trying to keep the USSR from disintegrating. The Baltic states and Ukraine were taking the lead in trying to sever ties with Moscow. Soviet leader Mikhail Gorbachev was supporting reform-minded associates who were pushing free market changes opposed by the old Communist elite still powerful at the Kremlin.

At Gillette's invitation, its would-be Soviet partners journeyed frequently during the next year to the London headquarters of

Gillette's AMEE Group. Much time was spent explaining unfamiliar business realities like insurance, profit margins, and advertising. The effort paid off, and in March 1991 Gillette announced that pursuant to the 1990 memorandum of intent, it had signed a joint venture agreement with the Leninets Company of Leningrad to manufacture double-edge blades, disposable razors, and twin-blade razor systems with capacity for up to 850 million units per year.

Leninets is a major Soviet military avionics supplier, research firm, and consumer goods producer. For decades, it was the USSR's second-largest producer of double-edge blades and a major producer of vacuum cleaners and sundry other products. The company headquarters, fronted by a towering statue of Lenin, is a conspicuous sight for travelers driving from the airport into St. Petersburg, as Leningrad was renamed in 1991.

There were some details to be finalized and some papers to be signed at the Kremlin, but the partners were confident. The blade and razor joint venture project had the needed blessing of the USSR Ministry for Radio Industry. The mayor of Leningrad hailed the project as a top priority. Choosing his words carefully, Tony Levy characterized it as a "long-term opportunity in the context of economic realities . . . another step in Gillette's world strategy of expanding its presence in foreign markets with significant growth potential."

In June 1991, Levy was in Moscow with Per Benemar, a Swedish-born naturalized English citizen and veteran Gillette executive in Africa, India, and Eastern Europe, who was to head the joint venture for Gillette. They were trying to get past a final obstacle: Gillette's demand that it receive an assured favorable exchange rate for rubles converted to hard currency. Gillette's rationale was that the joint venture would save the USSR millions of dollars that otherwise would have to be spent on importing blades to meet demand. Attempts to contact Gorbachev fell through. But at last USSR prime minister Valentin S. Pavlov signed off, providing the critical political authority that was needed. To ratify the deal, only one more permission was required—by the Soviet Hard Currency Committee, which was next scheduled to meet in September.

In August, the dramatic events of the failed coup changed

everything. On August 16, Gorbachev was placed under house arrest at his Crimea vacation home by Kremlin turncoats who charged that he and the reformers had sold out the Motherland. Gorbachev refused to budge, and his captors refused to leave without him. On August 19, tanks rolled, troops marched in the streets, and government buildings were shelled. In the memorable climax watched worldwide on television, President Boris Yeltsin clambered onto a hostile army tank in front of the Moscow White House and defied the coup leaders. After three tense days, the coup collapsed. Yeltsin was in charge. A humbled Gorbachev, saved by Yeltsin's defiance, returned to Moscow and promptly disbanded the party leadership and turned over the vast properties of the party to the state, then resigned as party chairman. Valentin Pavlov was arrested and jailed. The breakup of the Soviet Union was underway. Russia, with 148 million citizens (slightly fewer than Brazil), remained the largest and most prosperous piece of Gillette's FSU market.

After a few weeks, Benemar sat down with his Leninets colleagues to assess what could be salvaged. "We knew there would be risks in the political situation and the economy and there was a lot we could never check out with lawyers and market consultants and the like, but we knew we had a great opportunity if we moved in quickly," Benemar said.

The old project had been based on Soviet laws that were suddenly changed. The ruble was made convertible, requiring a new approach to protecting Gillette's investment against currency exchange risks. The original joint venture project that included significant double-edge blade production in a new or renovated factory was dead, but Leninets and Gillette both wanted to revamp and proceed. The two companies agreed to a scaled-down manufacturing start-up limited to the assembly and packaging of twin-blade cartridges and razors in one corner of Leninets' nearly empty vacuum cleaner plant. For the time being, Gillette would stay out of the huge double-edge blade market.

Gillette directors accepted the deal in March 1992. In January 1993, Petersburg Products International (PPI) began operations in a forlorn industrial district several miles from the handsome center of St. Petersburg. Per Benemar and a handpicked staff of expatriates exercised 100 percent management control, and Gillette retained 65 percent ownership. The venture was set up as Gillette's major presence in the FSU. In addition to its razor and blade assembly operation, PPI imported and marketed a full range of Gillette shaving products, including the top of the line Sensor systems and Gillette-brand shaving foams and gels. (Braun, Oral-B, and Stationery Group products are imported into Russia and sold throughout the former Soviet Union under separate arrangements.) PPI grew rapidly, and by 1996, Russian sales of $107 million placed that nation fifteenth among Gillette's twenty largest markets, just behind Australia and well ahead of Colombia.

In 1996, PPI made its coup-delayed entry into the double-edge market by acquiring from Leninets 100 percent ownership of a cash-starved blade maker named Factory for Consumer Products (FCP). Leninets and Gillette had wanted to include FCP in the aborted 1991 deal. FCP made Sputnik blades in an aging plant with capacity for 800 million blades but by 1996 could not afford to buy enough blade steel to support full production runs. By Gillette's reckoning, with this acquisition PPI gained 25 percent of the total former Soviet Union blade and razor market in unit terms and 41 percent in dollar terms, making PPI number two in unit share but number one in dollar share. It seemed only a matter of time before PPI resurrected the pre-coup plan to build a large, modern blade and razor plant from the ground up. The foot on the ground strategy was alive and well in Russia.

Selling to the Russians

Gillette products were largely unknown to Russian consumers when PPI set up shop. Right up to the end of the Cold War, old-fashioned carbon blades held most of the market. Blades were sold at below-production costs, like bread. Disposable razors were largely unknown.

Shut out from making double-edge blades, PPI concentrated on assembly and sales of a twin-blade system named Slalom, which was essentially the Atra/Contour pivoting-head system.

PPI also sold imported products, including disposable razors and the Sensor razor for both men and women. That meant an effective distribution system had to be built up in Russia and in other FSU nations like the Baltic states, Ukraine, and Georgia, a project that consumed a large portion of PPI's time. The old state-run distribution system was grossly inefficient for a private market enterprise and had to be resurrected in bits and pieces. Gillette's experienced Western managers spent countless hours looking for distributors with both the energy and the cash or the borrowing power to bridge the gap between warehouse and retailer. One success was a privatized state distributor that had formerly handled the Soviet Union's perfume trade. Another success for Gillette was a new company formed by several out-of-work geologists. They proved more dynamic than most of the newly privatized distributors, who tended to follow the old way, that is, they put goods in a warehouse and waited for someone to come by and get them.

Gillette plunged in with extensive television advertising from the first days, pushing in particular its Slalom system. Mistakes were made. PPI commercial director David Whitlam, a multilingual British citizen who later moved to a top job in Turkey, recalled the fiasco when he asked the Moscow branch of an American ad agency to develop a local ad linked to Russia's enthusiastic legion of skiers. The idea was to sign up some gifted skier/actors and photograph them as they gracefully schussed down a picturesque mountainside to the sound of upbeat music while a voice-over extolled the Slalom blades. The ad agency, in trying to hold down expenses, recruited well-connected but inept amateurs—a nightclub operator and a lawyer—who skied clumsily down a featureless man-made ski slope that had been built at a Moscow-area recreation center for Party higher-ups. The footage was useless. Gillette learned a lesson and began to closely monitor its ad making.

Gillette had far better luck with slick voice-over ads expressing the universal "Best a Man Can Get" theme. When the words are translated into Russian, with a little deft editing the lyric ends with an emphatic-sounding *nyet*, which rhymes with Gillette.

Sales of the imported Sensor systems for both men and women were well above estimates in the early years, particularly for younger women in Russian cities, who tend to spend more time and money on grooming than women in many other nations where Gillette does business.

Russian consumers are used to shopping in department stores so big that even a Wal-Mart shopper might be intimidated. In St. Petersburg, Gillette products are sold at about twenty separate locations in an aging two-level store on Nevsky Prospekt that is second in size only to Moscow's famed GUM (General Universal Market). Retail advertising focused on television and outdoor signs, including gaudily painted exteriors of transit buses and trains in Moscow and St. Petersburg, but Gillette drew the line at one form of runaway capitalism evident in St. Petersburg that struck Per Benemar as unseemly. PPI declined an opportunity to sell the Gillette name to the city for inclusion on street signs, though several American firms, including Coca-Cola, R. J. Reynolds (Camel cigarettes), and Motorola, jumped at the chance.

Gillette's joint venture broke the rules followed by other foreign companies in some ways. PPI conducts its entire business in rubles, for example, including payroll payments. At first this caused grumbling from workers, who preferred to be paid in dollars, but Gillette made it a better deal by adjusting monthly wages for inflation. Still, the first time Financial Director David Harden went to pick up cash for the weekly payroll, he was surprised when his assistant came out of the vault with two bags she could barely move, filled with the small-denomination bills she assured Harden the workers would expect.

One of the most daunting business challenges for the handful of expatriate Gillette managers at PPI fell to Argentine expatriate Juan Gallo. In the critical early years at PPI, Gallo served as PPI's personnel officer in charge of recruiting staffers for the St. Petersburg headquarters and also for sales jobs spread from the Baltic republics to Vladivostok on Russia's Pacific coast, eleven time zones away. One of many Latin American expatriates, Gallo was first hired by Gillette in Buenos Aires and sent to Boston for two years' management training. Then it was back to Argentina as a human resources officer at Gillette's Argentine company, and next, with wife and baby, it was off to Russia for a couple of years, followed by an assignment to the relatively salubrious climate of southern California, where Gallo was assigned to Gillette's large Stationery Products operation at Santa Monica.

Gallo said that he and his expatriate colleagues approached PPI as a temporary assignment, aiming to smooth a transition to Russian management. "We are here to teach business practices, the Gillette way of doing things, and eventually we'll hand off to the Russians," Gallo said. Gallo noted that recruiting in Russia followed traditional American interviewing and screening processes, with some exceptions. PPI targets almost exclusively young men and women twenty-five to thirty-five. Gallo said that those over thirty-five or forty of necessity had held jobs under the old economic system, and Western consumer goods companies generally found their nontechnical work experience useless, even counterproductive to the needs of a market economy. Some skills Gillette required, as in marketing, simply were not compatible with the old command economy.

There were happy exceptions. One of PPI's best management prospects came not from Juan Gallo's recruiting process but straight from Gillette's Russian partner, the state-run Leninets. Sergey Shipulin, in his mid-thirties, immediately stood out for his entrepreneurial mindset and was assigned to a job in sales management. After a year or so, he was sent to Gillette South Africa for seasoning, then returned to PPI as national sales manager.

Gallo discovered a large pool of well-educated younger people with good English and excellent technical skills. Gallo pointed to a twenty-three-year-old college graduate hired as a financial trainee at the equivalent of $250 a month. If she proved successful, she had the opportunity to move up to the $450–500 average salary for Gillette employees, which was far above the national average salary of $72 in 1995. Production line workers were paid well above the national average figure as Gillette followed its global practice of paying as well as and usually better than competitors, with strong benefits packages, including eligibility to buy Gillette stock through payroll deductions, with the company matching a portion of the set-aside.

A Gillette job is not guaranteed for life, as in the old Soviet system. There is a three-month probation period, and after that it is still possible, though difficult, to fire workers who do not measure up.

THE POLISH EXPERIENCE

Gillette's move into Poland was quick and clean compared with Russia, though not without complications. As many as thirty Polish authorities claimed some role in the privatization of Wizamet Co., the state-run blade maker that Gillette bought after Poland's Ministry of Privatization sought a buyer in the summer of 1992. A team led by Per Benemar and Ken Kames concluded the purchase of 80 percent of the shares of struggling Wizamet late that year. The other 20 percent of the state-owned enterprise was sold to employees at half the price Gillette paid, and under terms of the deal, Gillette agreed to buy out the employee shares later. Kames recalled that a Stanford-educated government official finally sat down with Gillette lawyers in Warsaw and helped to hammer out a definitive deal when negotiations were badly snarled by conflicting claims. Gillette invested about $10 million.

The formerly state-run Wizamet was Poland's leading blade company, indeed the only domestic manufacturer in Eastern Europe's largest nation. Based in the depressed old textile city of Lodz, Wizamet had run up large debts after 1989 in a futile effort to compete with imports, including blades and razors coming in from Gillette. Not the least of the debts was related to a warehouse full of unsalable blades that the Soviet Union had ordered, as in the old days of east bloc trade, but was unable to pay for. Wizamet had also been an important supplier to Iraq before the Gulf War and once had supplied most of Libya's blade market.

Chaotic though it was in Poland's new capitalistic society, there were important differences compared with neighboring Russia. Per Benemar noted that by 1990, Russia had undergone seventy-five years of Communist rule preceded directly by many decades under authoritarian czarist rule, and thus there was virtually no institutional memory of capitalism. Poland and other Eastern

European nations had experienced market conditions to one degree or another prior to 1945, and Gillette products were available throughout Eastern Europe prior to World War II. Moreover, José Ribera, heading up the AMEE Group in London, had made it a priority in the later Cold War years to keep in touch with some of the men who managed state-run trading agencies. These individuals invariably became important decision makers in the privatization process that occurred when party control loosened.

Throughout the Cold War years the Lodz plant produced Polsilver double-edge blades, which were the only domestically made blades in the country, so that the acquisition of Wizamet established Gillette as the clear market leader in Poland. After a year or so, the Lodz plant was re-equipped so that it could assemble and package imported disposables (the equivalent of Good News), which were sold under the familiar Polsilver name. Gillette retained a headquarters office in Warsaw to oversee the marketing and distribution of a full range of Gillette's imported shaving products and embarked on the familiar upgrading strategy of persuading shavers to move up to premium-priced systems products like Atra and Sensor, while at the same time making double-edge blades for the mass market. The Polish operation was headed by an amiable American, Eric Adams, who had great global bloodlines—his father was a Coca-Cola executive in Puerto Rico. After graduating from Georgia Tech, the younger Adams worked for Gillette in Puerto Rico, Colombia (twice), Boston (twice), and Poland, where he was posted with his wife and children in 1993, returning to Boston headquarters in 1996.

The crumbling Wizamet plant in Lodz, a gray and rundown city, was upgraded in part with retooled and refitted Gillette production equipment. But it took more than new production equipment to upgrade the factory complex itself, which was a rundown collection of perhaps two dozen small buildings connected by walkways and alleys. The original plant was built in 1897 to manufacture textile machinery, but in 1945 it became Poland's only blade plant, by Communist Party decree.

Gillette tore down most of the old structures and built a new factory. The exterior was painted blue and silver, and it is perhaps the only building in Lodz that isn't gray or faded brick. "It stuck out like the Taj Mahal in the midst of the dirty, dusty city," recalled Al Zeien, who attended the new plant dedication featuring such capitalistic trappings as a champagne reception and a ceremonial demolition of what was left of the old plant by a local bulldozer operator.

Gillette's director of corporate affairs at Lodz, Zbigniew Glonek, was a holdover from Soviet-era Wizamet. Glonek termed Gillette's purchase of Wizamet a windfall for employees, most of whom were in danger of losing their jobs as the company careened toward bankruptcy. A few years after Gillette's acquisition, nearly half the workforce (mostly older workers) had accepted a retirement buyout package, and many left with a modest nest egg from the sale of their stock at above-market terms. At the same time, Gillette alleviated the overemployment problem it had inherited. The plant employed eight hundred in the late 1980s, with employees paid at a salary level 20 percent below the national average. Less than ten years later, Gillette employed less than half that number but paid its workers at least 20 percent more than the national average. At the end of 1996, the company posted sales of $62 million—Poland was Gillette's twentieth largest market.

GILLETTE ENTERS TURKEY AND PAKISTAN

About the same time that Gillette was re-entering Poland, the company moved vigorously into Turkey, a nation of nearly 60 million people. Gillette had had a minor presence in Turkey for many years, having first opened a sales office in Istanbul in 1919. The Istanbul office did not long survive, and statist policies banned foreign direct investment and restricted imports until the mid-1980s.

Finally, in 1989 Gillette was able to return with a new sales office in Turkey. The company's prime goal was to sell Sensor razors and other premium products to the nation's sizable urban upper-income market. Then in 1991 came the big break. Gillette acquired the dominant domestic blade marker, Permatik Celik

Sanayi AS from its Turkish owners and overnight increased its market share from small numbers to 85 percent in unit terms. This was no rescue operation like the Polish acquisition. Gillette bought a functioning operation that included a large modern factory manufacturing primarily double-edge blades but also disposables and systems under the Permatik name. With substantial further investment in production machinery, including installation of re-tooled Gillette machines to produce coated stainless steel blades, Gillette's Turkish factory soon was producing more than 250 million blades and razors annually. Jose Ribera praised the deal as the capstone of Gillette efforts to reestablish itself in Turkey after decades of being mostly shut out by import restrictions.

Gillette's entry into Pakistan was somewhat similar. Gillette gradually increased its presence in the 1980s as foreign restrictions eased but was unable until 1989 to convince Pakistani authorities to let it set up a joint venture plant to make blades and razors. "We negotiated for something like seven years and had finally put it to one side when suddenly a fax arrived in London saying we could buy 49 percent of a company," Ribera recalled. Gillette pounced on the offer, afterward pushing its ownership stake to 51 percent, and it had its foot on the ground in a nation of 110 million. A few years later, in 1994, Gillette pushed its ownership up to 75 percent and formally changed the name from Interpak Shaving Products to Gillette Pakistan Ltd. Gillette upgraded the factory to assemble disposables and systems, as well as double-edge blades sold under the 7 O'Clock Ejtek brand. Sensor razors and Oral-B's oral care products were introduced the same year, supported by heavy Gillette promotion at important cricket matches. Disposable razors chalked up major sales gains that year, thanks to a radio/ television ditty known locally as "Cha-Cha-Cha-Chan," set to the introductory notes of Beethoven's Fifth Symphony.

THE BIGGEST BLADE MARKET OF ALL

India's 950 million citizens buy almost 3 billion double-edge blades a year, making it the largest blade market in the world in unit terms. The H. L. Malhotra company, a family enterprise with several blade factories in the country, was by a wide margin the leading blade producer, selling to home shavers and the thousands of sidewalk barbers so familiar to travelers. Malhotra is the second-largest blade maker in the world, after Gillette.

Until 1984, Malhotra and smaller domestic blade makers operated without significant foreign competition because Indian laws prevented foreign companies from locating in India and imposed punishing tariff restrictions that made imported goods expensive for consumers. After Prime Minister Indira Gandhi opened the doors partially to foreign investment in 1984, Gillette formed Indian Shaving Products Ltd., taking 24 percent interest, and started production of 200 million blades a year in 1986—a drop in the bucket, given India's market.

In 1991, government restrictions eased somewhat—although Indian laws remained comparatively hostile to outsiders—and Gillette decided to introduce its systems and disposable razors to India. Ownership in Indian Shaving Products Ltd. was increased to 51 percent, and in 1993 the company began to import Gillette-branded male grooming products. In 1995, Gillette acquired another Indian blade maker, Wiltech India Ltd., and by year's end claimed a 30 percent share of the Indian blade and razor market in dollar terms (14 percent in unit sales), with Malhotra carrying most of the remaining 70 percent.

In the late 1980s, Gillette managers had realized that there was more to India than a huge mass market of subsistence-level consumers. There was also a hidden market of some 65 million Indians with income levels far above the national average of $400 a year, who wanted the "Best a Man Can Get" and could afford Gillette's premium shaving products. That hidden market of well-off Indians, marketers pointed out, is greater than the total population of France. The more affluent Indians mostly live in cities, though about three-quarters of Indians live in farms and villages—a high rural population compared with most nations.

Product distribution posed quite a different problem in India than in Russia and China, which are much more urbanized. Russian consumers are used to buying goods in huge department stores, a statist tradition that carried over to the market economy. In Russia and China, Gillette made a policy of moving first into major cities, then next-tier cities, and finally the countryside, where feasible. Most Indians shop in the tiny "mom and pop" stores that dominate retailing, even in cities. India was one country where Wal-Mart had yet to take hold in the mid-1990s—a specific fact that Gillette planners noted because Wal-Mart ranked as Gillette's biggest single trade account in North America and had become a significant retailing presence in Latin America and some other parts of the world.

Gillette strengthened its market leadership in the Indian pen market in 1996, when the company acquired a 50 percent interest in Luxor Pen, a family-owned pen maker and India's leading distributor of writing products. Acquisitions or joint ventures may be the key to the company's long-term goal of leadership in the Indian blade and razor business. Gillette has made no secret of its interest in buying into the Malhotra company and has been involved in ongoing discussions for years. Given Malhotra's seemingly unshakable position in lower-cost blades, a joint venture appeared to represent the surest and surely the fastest means to achieve clear leadership in the world's largest blade market.

Moving into China

Gillette's history in China is not unlike its experience in Russia and India. Gillette opened a branch office in Shanghai in 1919. Cultural and later political hostility to foreign investment and foreign goods minimized the Boston company's impact, though the blades wrapped in blue with the "old man's face" were distributed in parts of the vast country for much of the time right up to the turbulent era of Mao Zedong's revolution. The Communist era that began when Mao banished the Kuomintang to Taiwan in 1949 sealed off the country almost completely to Gillette for decades, with the exception of blades and razors that slipped out of Hong Kong to the mainland in an unofficial but measurable flow.

After Mao's death in 1976 and the ascension to power of reform-minded Marxist leader Deng Xiaoping, the idea of tolerating the "running dogs of capitalism," as Mao called Western companies, began to seem less heretical. Gillette's global instincts were aroused.

In the early spring of 1979, when a mid-level Chinese foreign trade official named Madame Wu made an inquiry about blade-making procedures and cited China's equipment needs, Gillette's London office alerted Walter Hunnewell in Boston. A very short time later, in April 1979, Hunnewell traveled to Beijing, repre-senting the company on a Gillette-sponsored tour of the Boston Symphony Orchestra. He brought up the subject of Madame Wu's inquiry during a visit to the Department of Foreign Trade, which encouraged further response from Gillette.

That was all it took to get Mike Hawley on a plane for Beijing. The group general manager of Australasia (later renamed Asia-Pacific) operations had been waiting eagerly for an opening to the West. Since his days in Hong Kong in 1965, Hawley had felt challenged by the great potential of China, and later, as a senior China-watcher from his post as head of the Australasian group, he sensed the time was right to make a move. With a team of technical people from Boston and senior Australasian managers, Hawley talked on and off for two weeks with a Chinese team headed by another woman, Madame Fu. The idea of a joint ven-ture was broached but seemed to go nowhere, despite another round of meetings and letters back and forth across the Pacific.

One reason may have been that China had almost no experi-ence with industrial joint ventures at the time. With the support of senior management, including Chairman Colman Mockler and Rod Mills, deputy general manager of international operations, Hawley kept on pushing the unfamiliar idea. Hawley said years later that pursuing the difficult joint venture discussions was an example of how Gillette historically has been willing to spend time and take risks with no assurance of success in order to get in on the ground floor of new markets.

After many months and more than a dozen trips to China, a key intervention came when an Asian business consultant whom Hunnewell had met on the Boston Symphony trip raised the possibility of focusing on the northeastern city of Shenyang. Mike Hawley and his team moved in and closed the deal for a Shenyang site, though not before visiting several possible factories under the control of Bo Yang, China's Minister of Light Industry.

Shenyang is a city of four million on a latitudinal line with Montreal. The attraction there was an unoccupied factory awaiting the imminent arrival of the Shenyang Daily Use Metals Products Company, which had been ordered by the Ministry of Light Industry to move in and make blades. Was Gillette interested? Hawley, who had been unable to get permission to build a "greenfield" factory, that is, in Gillette jargon, a new plant from the ground up, decided a "brownfield" factory was better than none at all. After a week of further negotiations, a memorandum of intent was signed in summer 1980.

Hawley and key aides in the Asia-Pacific organization, like the Hong Kong-born, American-educated Philip Hung, struggled to learn who made things happen in China's many-layered bureaucracy. Gillette teams visited the factory, and a Chinese team was invited to visit Gillette factories in the Philippines and Boston. At one point, the project became mired in red tape, and there seemed no obvious way to advance it. Hawley called a meeting of his seven-man team in a Beijing hotel room. Shall we give it up or go ahead? Given all the headaches and the primitive living conditions, is it really worth it? Can it even be done? The management troops agreed it was worth it to soldier on, and late in 1981 definitive papers forming a fifty-fifty joint venture named Shenmei Daily Use Products Ltd. were signed. It took another two years to work out details with local, regional, and national governments, to install Gillette-made equipment, and identify and train middle managers and production workers.

Hawley's break-in team depended on expatriates, mostly overseas Chinese managers living and working elsewhere in Asia for Gillette. Chinese universities had, for all practical purposes, stopped functioning during the long Cultural Revolution, preventing a generation of Chinese men and women from learning the technical and business skills needed in middle management. Political know-how was far more important than an understanding of business practices for the managerial class in the industrialized Shenyang region. The Gillette team spent countless hours with

their Shenyang counterparts going over business taxes, distribution, hiring procedures, insurance, accounting, and other business
functions that were mostly unfamiliar to the Chinese. Gradually,
the factory changed shape as Gillette-made manufacturing equipment replaced or supplemented Chinese equipment. Because of
foreign exchange restrictions, the venture was dependent on Chi-
nese-made equipment for ancillary purposes, and much of the
machinery had to be refurbished on the spot to meet Gillette's
standards.

In spring 1983, pre-production runs started on the Gillette
machinery lines, and the plant was officially commissioned. Gillette's Chinese partners hosted a high-level delegation from Boston that included Colman Mockler, Rod Mills, and Mike Hawley
and their wives Joanna, Liane, and Winnifred, for a five-day visit.
Toasts were exchanged at several fourteen-course banquets.

As Mills told it, Hawley was in a playful mood during a pretrip
briefing for Mockler and made a point of telling him that the
residents of frigid Shenyang enjoyed hearty food. The welcoming
meal, he said, would likely include dog meat and noodles, and
perhaps camel's hump. Mockler predictably grimaced and Mills
said he wanted to "kick Hawley from Boston to China," but
instead he made sure a ten-day supply of American steaks was
aboard the plane. The puckish Mills couldn't resist a bit of fun at
Mockler's expense himself, and his turn came at a ceremonial
dinner when Mockler was seated next to Bo Yang. Mockler had
been warned that the minister, as host, would heap more delicacies
on his plate as soon as it was cleaned off. Forewarned, Mockler
had eaten sparingly and used his chopsticks to poke a serving of
sea slugs underneath a covering of rice. After dinner Mills teased
him, saying, "You know, Colman, you went to a lot of trouble
pushing those sea slugs under the rice. If you'd just let them alone
they would have crawled under themselves."

In August 1983, the first Gillette-made Rhino brand carbon
blades and plastic disposables reached the Chinese market and
Gillette's efforts to penetrate the world's largest national market
had begun. "Whether we will make the proverbial fortune selling
razor blades to a couple of hundred million Chinese men, we don't

know yet, but China is a huge, huge market and at last we are in it," Hung exulted to a reporter from the *International Herald Tribune*.[1]

The Shenyang plant was a modest venture in terms of output, with 40 million annual capacity at the outset, later expanded to more than twice that level with additional shaving products added. By 1992, Shenmei had gained about 10 percent of the Chinese blade market.

Hawley noted in a review of the process a few years later that the nontechnical negotiations after the start-up were especially burdensome. Gillette's expatriate managers resident at Shenyang were worn down with details involving export and domestic prices, worker hiring and firing, and simple matters like being told where they could live. With no modern apartments, expatriates lived for years in rooms at the Russian-built Friendship Hotel and had to fight for amenities, such as private bathrooms. It came as a shock to the local worker councils and local bureaucrats that Gillette insisted on paring down the 240-member workforce to about 80 people and required that job candidates be tested for skills. Gillette paid at least 20 percent more than the prevailing wage rate and installed wage incentives designed to improve quality and rates of output, but it also demanded discipline on the job and the right to fire incompetents, both novel concepts to workers brought up under the Communist social compact. Eng Seng Dieu, a Singaporean expatriate and Shenmei's first general manager, insisted on replacing some politically established managers with young, better-educated Chinese newcomers in their early twenties, but it took him more than a year to get the needed permission. These employees eventually became the solid core of the venture's management as Gillette, consistent in its global management strategy, gradually replaced expatriates with local Chinese managers.

Gillette claimed a modest profit for the joint venture's first full year, in 1984. More important for Gillette's long-term plans, Shenmei's modest foot on the ground provided a learning experience for Gillette both on the scene and in Boston about how to do business in mighty but perplexing China.

The learning curve had to do with more than just the peculiar political economics of China—fundamental things like thin hair, for example. Gillette researchers, who pride themselves on knowing a great deal about human hair and how to remove it, had warned company officials that unlike most Indians and Russians, or most Europeans and Americans, Chinese males generally do not grow heavy beards. Facial hair tends to grow sparsely, with the result that the daily shave routine is less urgent and much less established than in many other nations. Younger office workers in big cities often shaved each morning, but tens of millions of Chinese farmers working small plots from morning to night understandably had no tradition of daily grooming and very little motivation to change. In market terms, there are more male faces in China than in any other nation, but the total consumption of blades is far below the average in most countries. Philip Hung noted in 1984 that he considered it "ridiculous" that the nation's 350 million over-sixteen males averaged just slightly over one blade per year. "If each bought just twenty, even ten, demand would soar," he told an interviewer.

In fact, demand did soar, in Chinese terms: by 1992, annual double-edge blade consumption was up to seven per year, with Gillette aiming to stretch the figure to twelve over time. That compares with about twenty-nine per year for India. In the United States, where twin-blade products predominate, cartridge consumption averages about thirty per year. In the spirit of Hung's excitement about the Chinese market's potential, Gillette global exponents like Mike Hawley and Tony Levy—both having served in Gillette's top international post—pushed for more expansion, building on the Shenyang experience.

Nine years after the Shenmei start-up, Gillette announced in 1992 a second and much larger joint venture in Shanghai to produce double-edge blades, twin-blade cartridges, and pivoting-head razors, with planned capacity for 1.2 billion units. Tony Levy hailed the venture as a major advance in China, and said it added "dramatic momentum" to global expansion. Before long, Gillette's 70 percent-owned Gillette Shanghai Ltd. venture was turning out Flying Eagle and Swordfish blades by the millions, and according to Gillette, the Shanghai plant was Asia's largest blade and razor factory. Gradually, Gillette increased the price of its blades from the giveaway prices of the older order, but the average cost of a blade in 1995 was still only about five cents.

The Shanghai venture was structured to allow the addition of other Gillette lines, such as writing instruments, Oral-B toothbrushes, and Braun products, and within a year or two, these lines were added. Philip Hung, veteran of the Shenmei negotiations and later Gillette's top representative there, became the point man breaking through the red tape and getting Braun off to a start in Shanghai. In addition to importing and selling shavers and appliances, Braun manufactures a line of inexpensive battery-operated electric razors at a Shanghai factory that started production with retooled production equipment from an Irish plant, closed by Braun after the loosening of trade barriers made it expendable.

Eng Seng Dieu, who saw the joint venture through its first two years, became Oral-B's vice president for the Asia-Pacific region and nursed the Oral-B start-up in Shanghai. The 70 percent-owned joint venture started making toothbrushes in a Shanghai factory in 1993 with local resins and packaging materials but imported nylon for the brushes.

Mike Hawley noted that the laborious learning process at Shenyang starting in 1979 had helped make the 1990s major entry into China possible by training a cadre of expatriate managers like Hung and Dieu. These expatriates became experienced in the Chinese manner of doing business and made follow-on ventures much easier to establish—one more payoff of the foot on the ground strategy. It seemed to be working in China, India and Russia. Short of political and social upheaval, these markets were poised to fuel Gillette's double-digit annual earnings growth to which shareholders have become accustomed.

17

THE
RELUCTANT
GLOBAL WARRIOR

BRAUN AG IS Gillette's reluctant global warrior. In 1967, when
the brothers Artur and Erwin Braun sold the family company to
Gillette, it was a very respected, very German maker primarily of
hi-fi sets, cameras and photo equipment, plus electric shavers and
small kitchen appliances. Total sales in U.S. dollars were about $70
million. Braun was number one in Germany in some product
areas, including the electric shaver market, but had never paid
much attention to international markets, apart from a few European nations.

By 1996 Braun was a $1.7 billion business, second only to
blades and razors as a sales and profit contributor to Gillette as a
whole, excluding Duracell. Sales outside Germany accounted for
82 percent of total volume. Prodded by its parent, Braun had
moved from parochialism to globalism in a thirty-year stop and
start process that accelerated in the mid-1980s. It became Gillette's

most conspicuous example of advancing global leadership through acquisition of another company.

World sales were not what Prussian-born Max Braun had in mind in 1921 when he formed Braun AG in Frankfurt. A mechanic and engineer, his first manufactured product was a transmission-belt connector that he had invented. Braun then began production of components for the infant radio industry and, within a few years, began to manufacture radios, phonographs, and radio-phonograph combinations. In 1935 Braun made what the company claimed was the first battery-operated portable radio. Max Braun's small company built a reputation in the 1920s and 1930s for well-designed products aimed at the German market, where attention to detail and design traditionally was prized.

When Adolf Hitler forced German industry to prepare for war in the late 1930s, Braun diverted most of its resources to radio equipment and other military hardware for the Nazi war machine. After 1937, Max Braun devoted what time he could to the development of a new type of electric shaver, reportedly working at odd moments on a prototype he carried about in his pocket. The first electric shavers had begun to show up in Europe in the early 1930s, and Max thought he could build a better product than those he had seen and tried.

Electric shavers had shown up in North America, too. With other competitive entries beginning to appear, Gillette introduced a short-lived line of electric shavers for the 1938 Christmas season, almost simultaneously with its four-for-a-dime cheap blade entry, the Gillette Thin Blade. In 1939, Gillette introduced the Kumpakt, a lower-priced electric shaver whose vaguely Germanic name was lifted from a long-defunct AutoStrop dollar razor set. Any threat dry shaving posed for blades and razors faded as America pulled out of the Great Depression. The new company president, Joe Spang, stopped production of the Kumpakt soon after the World Series radio broadcasts spurred Gillette blade and razor sales. Gillette shifted all its energies to wet shaving products, and electric shavers were ignored for the next quarter century.

During World War II, Braun's factory in Frankfurt was damaged but not destroyed by Allied bombing, and at war's end the company slowly returned to making radios for the consumer market. Max Braun suffered from digestive problems for much of his life, which led him in the late 1940s to develop kitchen blenders and other small kitchen appliances to simplify preparation of the easily digestible foods he needed. These products were the forerunner of the hand blenders, coffeemakers, multifunction food preparation systems, and other small appliances that Braun developed and sold in great numbers in later years. Max Braun's personal interest in electric shavers resulted in a patented Braun shaver in 1949, and in 1950 the company started production of the Braun S-50 electric foil shaver. Max Braun died in 1951, shortly after turning over the business to his sons Erwin and Artur.

The 1950 Braun shaver was technologically different from others on the market. All dry shavers share some characteristics—two blades move against each other, snipping hairs like scissors just below a sieve-like foil that traps the hairs in tiny openings. Other shavers on the market employed a rigid structure, but the Braun shaver featured a flexible foil wrapped around a moving cutter block. With no load-bearing function, Braun foils could be made exceptionally thin, or "microthin" as its publicists preferred to say, resulting in a close shave. When they wear out, typically after many months or years of usage, replacement foils are available, like replacement blades for razors. The many models of Braun shaver that have been developed since 1950 have evolved from and remained faithful to the central idea behind Max Braun's original shaver—its thin, flexible, and replaceable foil.

AN EMPHASIS ON DESIGN

Braun's high visibility, big volume products for most of the 1950s and the next twenty years were its prize-winning audio and photographic equipment lines. They generated the heaviest sales, if not profits, and they were given major attention by Braun's world-famous industrial designers.

Braun's hi-fi (high fidelity) and stereo sound systems evolved from the company's prewar radio-phonograph products. Braun's photographic line that came to include movie cameras and slide projectors started with an electronic flash unit launched in 1952. It was primarily with these products during the 1950s and 1960s that Braun became recognized as a leading exponent of the functional design associated with the Bauhaus movement founded by Germany's Walter Gropius. Bauhaus advocates preached a synthesis of sculpture and architecture and the adaptation of science and technology to structural design. Braun products, including shavers and small kitchen appliances as well as audio systems, began attracting great attention as classics of functional design and won dozens of prestigious international awards. Braun hi-fi sets, cameras, shavers, and toasters were displayed at the Brussels World Fair of 1958 and became part of a permanent display at New York's Museum of Modern Art and at Milan, heartland of Italy's high-style industrial design.

One of Executive Vice President Jacques Lagarde's early jobs at Gillette was at Braun, shortly after the acquisition in 1967. He recalled the reverence in which functional designers were held: "Design was the culture of Braun. The design group worked from the start with R & D, always trying to simplify the product. And there were moral implications. The product had to be honest. It had to be safe. It had to serve the environment. It had to sell itself without support, without claims on what the product could deliver." In 1989 a much-traveled Lagarde returned to a much different Braun as chairman, but he noted that much that was best about the Braun design culture remained.

Dieter Rams, Braun's director of corporate identity affairs, for almost forty years the company's chief designer and a bridge from the old days, had done a lot to spread the Braun design gospel to other parts of the Gillette world. He had helped design an early Paper Mate pen shortly after the acquisition, and many years later Rams was asked by John Symons to help design the handle of the Sensor razor, winning kind words from the perfectionist Symons for his contribution.

Norbert Gehrke, the long-time personnel specialist on Braun's board of management, was another Braun executive steeped in the design mystique. Seated with Rams in a spare, functionally designed conference room at Braun's Kronberg headquarters during the summer of 1995, the two men recalled the dedication of pre-Gillette Braun to the sanctity of functional design and the carryover of this belief after Gillette took over the company.

"We followed one idea for four decades and that is that the usefulness of a product should be put first," Rams said. In Braun terms, he said, usefulness is a quality that exceeds its basic function—for example, to chop vegetables, brew coffee, or shave facial hair. Usefulness encompasses such values as how easily the product can be understood, its reliability, and its longevity. Braun products have both an economic and ecological dimension, he said, never giving in to purely decorative goals. In his early days at Braun, along with his colleague Hans Gugelot, Rams designed the stark black and white "Snow White's Coffin" radio set, which won the admiration of designers for its combination of wood and clear plastic.

Rams worked closely with the brothers Braun when they directed the company in the 1950s and 1960s. He characterized Artur as chiefly interested in technology, whereas Erwin was the company leader and family philosopher who was fond of extolling the importance of good design. "Erwin used to say that our role should be that of a good English butler: our products should be there when needed, in the background blending with the environment, not disturbing, not spectacular . . ." Rams recalled.

Gehrke said that the company's commitment to functional design went beyond the shape and feel of products and the work environment. "It was and is a consistent value system, a statement of the company's principles of integrity and order." Gillette, he said, understood the commitment and did not interfere.

GILLETTE WAKES UP TO THE THREAT OF DRY SHAVING

Gillette had awakened in the mid-1960s to the growing threat dry shaving posed to wet shaving, especially in Europe and Japan. Gillette's managers led by CEO Vincent Ziegler had two choices if they chose to fight back: acquire an electric shaver company and get off to a running start or make the huge investment in time and resources to start from scratch and develop a Gillette electric shaver in-house.

All Ziegler had to do was look at the figures. In 1957 Gillette claimed 40 percent of a total European shaving market that was split 77 percent wet and 23 percent dry. Ten years later, Gillette's share of the total European shaving market had dropped to about 30 percent, largely because electric shavers had grabbed 44 percent of the total, and Gillette had no product.

One theory for the popularity of dry shaving in Europe held that after the devastation of World War II, low-cost electricity was more common than bathrooms with hot running water, hence dry shaving was more convenient and certainly more comfortable than cold water shaving. Dry shaving caught on first and remained most popular in Scandinavia and Finland and through the low countries south to Germany, a climatic region where shavers were seldom bothered by humidity that made their faces sticky. Moreover, these northern shavers had less motivation for the refreshing aspect of wet shaving than their neighbors in hot-weather nations like Spain and Italy. Whatever the reasons, it had become distressingly obvious that dry shaving had evolved to more than just the nuisance factor it had once been, especially in Europe and Japan. For that matter, figures in the United States were not reassuring; although down from a temporary peak in the 1950s before stainless steel blades were launched, almost 25 percent of American males regularly used electric shavers. But Europe was the crisis point.

At the September 1967 board of director's meeting, the vice president for business development, Robert S. Perry, put it plainly: "It is obvious that if we are to retain or improve our true position in the shaving products business in Europe we must enter the electric shaver market in that area." With that, he urged the directors to approve a large sum of money that would give Gillette negotiators a free hand to beat rival bidders for Braun and ensure for Gillette the instant presence it needed to compete in the electric shaver market. Gillette officials had first made contact with Erwin and Artur Braun in 1965, and this was the time to strike, Perry and Ziegler explained.

The Braun brothers had gone public in 1962 in order to raise money for their growing enterprise, having learned that it takes more than prestige to be successful, but by 1967 they were still short of capital and looking for a partner. There were plenty of suitors. The huge Dutch firm Philips, a major worldwide consumer electronics company whose Norelco brand shavers led the U.S. market, was high on a list that also included Canon of Japan, Siemens of Germany, and American companies, among them Sunbeam, Westinghouse, IBM, and ITT—this was, after all, the era of conglomerates.

Making what Ziegler termed a "shock offer," Gillette proposed an outright purchase of Braun for $50 million. That appealed to Erwin, who thought a Gillette deal provided the best chance of "staying independent and keeping Dad's business intact," the words recalled decades later by Wolfgang Krohn, a German lawyer who worked with Braun during the acquisition negotiations and came to work full time for Braun in 1971. By the end of the year, the deal was approved, and Gillette had achieved its goal of protecting its leading role in the European shaving market—and in the process acquiring a parochial German company with a distinct culture and a broad range of consumer products, from toasters to stereos.

An antitrust suit brought by the U.S. Department of Justice restricted Gillette's ability to influence Braun's shaver business in the United States, though there were no restrictions on the other Braun products. The antitrust suit required Gillette to enter a "hold separate" arrangement that stipulated Gillette had to run Braun's shaver line as a separate operation. Gillette was not allowed to consolidate, merge, or transfer to itself the assets or goodwill of Braun's shaver business. The long-running antitrust suit was settled by a consent decree in 1975 that called for Gillette to establish a new company to market Braun-made shavers in the United States and then sell it off. Cambridge Shaver Imports Inc. was formed and sold Braun shavers under the Eltron trademark. It soon was sold to Becker & Becker Inc. of Westport, Connecticut.

Not until 1984, at the end of an exclusive supply deal with Cambridge Shavers, was Gillette at last free to start selling Braun shavers under the Braun name in the United States.

The U.S. government's antitrust zeal was not the only reason Braun was a nonfactor for many years in global shaver markets outside continental Europe and Japan. The Braun brothers had entered a license agreement in 1954 with the Ronson Company of the United States, maker of the Ronson electric shaver. The agreement granted Ronson exclusive rights to Braun shaver sales in North and South America, the United Kingdom, and the nations of the British Commonwealth. In return, Ronson agreed to stay out of Braun's European backyard. It was an onerous restriction to Gillette internationalists, who wanted Braun to expand and become a global presence in electric shaving. The Ronson agreement finally was canceled in 1974, and Braun was free to sell its shavers throughout the United Kingdom and its old dominions and in the Americas, including Canada, though not the United States, where antitrust restrictions prevailed.

Ronson never did much with its Braun franchise in the United States or elsewhere. By the time Gillette was finally allowed to sell Braun shavers directly in the United States, Braun sales were far behind Philips (Norelco) and, to a lesser degree, competitors like Remington and Sunbeam.

Braun tried to overcome its late start in non-European dry shaving markets by pushing its leading edge technology in thin foil shavers. In 1984, Braun introduced System 1-2-3, a line of rechargeable and cord models that automatically adjusted to any voltage in the world, even twelve-volt batteries in cars and boats. It was an example of a universal product for a global market and also showed off the company's expertise in small battery technology applicable to any number of portable appliances. The company's rechargeable shavers consistently won "*sehr gut*" ratings from the German Institute for Product Testing, and this was a source of great pride at Kronberg. The first pivoting-head, twin-foil model was introduced in Europe in 1990 and in the United States in 1992. Flex Control was followed by the Flex Integral shaver, which combined the features of its predecessor with a free-floating integrated cutter and twin foils.

Braun proved particularly successful at selling electric shavers in Japan, the single largest dry shaving market in the world. When Jacques Lagarde moved to Braun shortly after the acquisition, he began a long, slow push to move Braun shavers into a Japanese market that was dominated by domestic brands. Many years later, when Lagarde had returned to Braun, this time as chairman, the German company was primed to make its most powerful move into Japan with Flex Control, and by 1992 Braun had raced past such Japanese competitors as Hitachi and Sanyo and had displaced the long-time leader Matsushita, gaining about 40 percent of the electric shaver market in value terms.

The company's advertising campaign in Japan, TV's "Braun Morning Report," stimulated sales of shavers that commanded a premium price of up to $144. The ad featured commuters who are persuaded to stop en route to work and try a Braun shaver even though they had shaved with another brand an hour earlier. Right there on the street or in the subway station, they shaved again. Without fail, they were surprised and appreciative and bowed to the announcer when the shaver head was opened and numerous hairs were dumped on a white cloth, as visual evidence that Braun shaves closer than Brand X.

Lagarde noted that the German heritage of Braun products plays well in Japan, where Braun shavers are marketed with the red, yellow, and black colors of the German flag to make sure that the national origin is recognized by the consumer. With dry shaving holding a 70 percent share of the total market in Japan in the mid-1990s, there was no better place for Braun to hold a lead. It also was number one in Germany, where dry shavers accounted for 54 percent of the total market (down several percentage points since unification with wet-shaving East Germany). About one-quarter of the American and British shaving markets remained dry, and 21 percent in Italy, whereas the big markets of Russia, India, and Latin America have hardly been touched by electric shavers.

Dry shaver sales accounted for about 35 percent of Braun's total 1996 volume of $1.7 billion. For Gillette as a whole, Braun's shaver sales of course cannibalize Gillette's wet shaver sales, and vice versa, but there is virtually no impact on Gillette's bottom line. Studies by the company show that men and women buying Braun shavers essentially generate the same very high level of profits as wet shavers. It makes no difference to Gillette profits whether a customer shaves dry or wet so long as he or she chooses the premium-priced Gillette shaving systems and/or the higher-priced Braun shavers.

Although Braun had become the world's leading seller of electric shavers, it still trailed entrenched Philips in the United States in the mid-1990s, demonstrating in a bitter way the wisdom of Gillette's own foot-on-the-ground strategy of moving into a market early and hanging on. Philip's three-headed Norelco shavers gained a head start in the United States, even before Gillette bought Braun, and increased its lead during the years when Braun was shut out by antitrust regulations. With the help of its long-running Christmas ad featuring a laughing Santa sliding down a slope on his Norelco sled, and more controversial ads making disputed claims about the effectiveness of Norelco versus an un-named blade and razor product that looked suspiciously like SensorExcel, Philips proved difficult to overtake.

A Melding of Styles

Dieter Rams gives Vincent Ziegler high marks for easing the fears of Braun staffers who had read and seen enough of the stereotypical "Ugly American" corporate profiteer to be nervous about their

---

OUCH!—THE HORSE-POWERED BEARD MILL

Happily for eighteenth-century men, a shaving machine described in a 1754 patent application as a "horse-drawn beard mill" apparently never was constructed. Vaguely reminiscent of a benign and horizontal guillotine, the beard mill was designed as a carousel-like cylinder with several circular holes in which bearded men were to stick their faces. A horse would walk around the beard mill, providing the horsepower to draw a large, sharp blade around the cylinder, which automatically scraped hair off one exposed chin after another. Whether the beards were to be wet or dry as the blade shaved each face is not recorded.

futures. "He said he wouldn't destroy us and he seemed sensitive to our differences. He spoke German to us," Rams recalled.

The company was practically a shrine among German industrialists and the German press because of its prestigious reputation for designing prize-winning products. The possibly apocryphal headline over the acquisition story in a German newspaper caught the mood: "Mein Gott, Nicht Braun!" (My God, Not Braun!) Ziegler understandably was reluctant to Americanize the company and damage morale, not to mention destroy consumer rapport in Germany, where Braun did so much of its business.

Then there was the matter of dealing with labor unions and other nonshareholder public interests, which held far more power in German corporations than in American companies, where shareholders have ultimate power over management. German law mandated that union and work council members hold half of the seats on supervisory boards, which look over the shoulder of the *vorstand*, or board of management, in publicly owned companies.

At the outset, many Braun managers resented having to learn English to work in Gillette's world, but Gehrke said that this resistance had disappeared by 1980, by which time managers down to third-level ranks understood and accepted the need to be bilingual. On the other hand, Braun's legal language is German, and routine contacts with outside supervisory board members were in German, so expatriate senior managers assigned to Braun had to speak German to get along in everyday operations.

Germans retained the company's chairmanship for several years. After 1975, expatriates were appointed to the job, starting with Al Zeien, who had spent several years as a senior executive at Braun. Zeien was succeeded in 1978 by Paul G. Stern, a talented American technologist and operations manager who soon left Gillette and eventually became the CEO of Burroughs and then of Northern Telecom. Stern was followed by Americans Lorne Waxlax and Robert Murray, French-born Jacques Lagarde, and Canadian Archie Livis—all of whom spoke German acquired or improved while working for Gillette.

There were bound to be clashes between the relatively freewheeling managers sent from Gillette and the by-the-numbers German managers; in the early years, an American complained, it was impossible to contact anyone on business after 4:30 P.M. because the written rules said that was when the business day ended, and that was that. Older Braun managers, including several Luftwaffe comrades that Erwin had recruited to Braun, did not take well to suggestions that management should communicate more directly and more often with employees. "We have written rules to let employees know what they must do," a senior Braun manager explained to a Gillette personnel specialist sent from Canada to evaluate Braun's personnel practices. Gillette officials took note and kept to Ziegler's prudent policy of integrating the two companies at a gradual pace.

The patience eventually paid off as Braun adapted to the faster-moving Gillette culture. According to Braun personnel chief Gehrke, such benefits as the company-wide employees' savings plan persuaded many of Gillette's good intentions and proved helpful to long-term stability. "Headhunters can't attract our best people because our people want to keep their options," he explained.

THE GLOBALIZATION OF BRAUN

Gillette approached its new acquisition with a determination to expand the entire business globally. The first contact most Braun operating managers had with Gillette after the acquisition was with Zeien. His orders were to move to Germany as the ranking American and to take hold of the many-headed dragon. Make sure the electric shaver business flourished in Europe and expand it to other markets, Zeien was told, but also get a handle on Braun's complex business structure, streamline its marketing, cut out overlaps, do what you can to change Braun's Euro-Germanic mindset to a more global outlook. It was a tall order.

The first thing Zeien did was to separate the non-German businesses from the company's five operating divisions and consolidate them in one international division. A few years later, following a brief return to Boston, Zeien was sent back to Kronberg, where he restructured the company's domestic business in the face of more than a half year's unprecedented red ink caused by the sudden withdrawal of German government price supports.

When he was named Braun chairman, Zeien developed a matrix management organization that later became the model for the 1988 reorganization of the entire Gillette company. (See Chapter 14.) The idea of his Braun matrix, Zeien said, was to disturb any entrenched hierarchy by making sure there were always two people responsible for making decisions, such as how to price shavers in Spain or where to manufacture hair dryers. The Braun matrix consisted of one business management structure responsible for the strategic direction of a given product line and another geographic business structure with a manager responsible for a given country's results. Managers of the two groups crossed in each country, ensuring what Zeien termed "dynamic conflict."

On his way to becoming executive vice president of the international division, Rod Mills spent part of the early 1970s at Braun prodding his reluctant German colleagues to look outward. By 1973, more than half the company's volume was outside Germany, compared with only one-third at the time of acquisition. To Dieter Rams, that was logical, because German functional design, he argued, was more transferable to world markets than, say, Italian or Scandinavian designs, which he considered more stylish and fleeting. In later years, when Braun had become a leader in important markets like Japan and opened a major kitchen appliance plant in Mexico and built plants in Asia, the earlier parochialism that Mills experienced was difficult to imagine.

The hi-fi headache that Gillette inherited with its 1967 acquisition kept Braun off balance for fifteen years. The handsome audio and camera products that the company kept turning out produced good sales but little or no profit. Braun North America, the U.S. distributor of Braun's nonshaving products, had no better luck than other Braun distributors. No amount of profits from shavers could make Braun consistently profitable under these conditions. Wolfgang Krohn, the lawyer who was close to Erwin Braun, said many years later that he thought Ziegler and later Colman Mockler overprotected Braun in their desire not to upset the Braun organization and the German public. Krohn said Ziegler's failure to get rid of the hi-fi and photography-related businesses within months of the 1967 acquisition surprised, among others, Erwin Braun, who had considered selling off those product groups before Gillette bought his company.

It became more clear each year that Braun's elegantly designed audio and camera products were ill-matched in the world marketplace against the stream of well-made, attractively priced, and above all technically advanced products from Japanese manufacturers like Sony. When pressures to abandon the product lines arose, managers and their allies on the supervisory board argued that these prize-winning products were so identified with Braun that dropping them would hurt other product lines, too.

When he became Braun chairman in 1981, Lorne Waxlax, with the endorsement of Joe Turley, Gillette's newly elected president, faced the inevitable and started a two-year process of phasing out the money-losing lines. "It had to be done but you cannot imagine the turmoil, the emotions at Braun," Norbert Gehrke recalled. Yet he noted that once the bloodbath was over and Braun was focused on its shaver and small appliance products, profits started to climb, and Braun's future as a valued part of Gillette was assured. Gradually, the calls from institutional investors demanding the divestiture of Braun tailed off and were heard no more by the late 1980s, when Braun emerged as a steady and sometimes spectacular profitmaker.

With hi-fi's and cameras gone and shavers doing well, Waxlax focused on turning out new appliances that had advanced features but were not so high tech that they confused consumers. He tried to get marketing personnel talking on the same wavelength with the company's powerful design team by promoting more beer parties and other informal events that are important in German corporate lifestyle. Above all, he made it clear that Braun's strategy was to use its manufacturing skills as a competitive edge. At the time, most competitors, like Black & Decker and Sunbeam, were scouting the world for cheap vendors, buying decent-quality products from Asian suppliers and basically turning themselves from manufacturers into marketers of Asian-made products stamped with their brand names. Braun's strategy was risky because it required heavy capital investment and depended on a flow of new products that would sell strongly in many geographic markets. There were skeptics who argued that Braun should stick to electric shavers and forget the rest, but the strategy of making value-added small appliances that were sold at premium prices drew consistent support from Colman Mockler.

The company invested in integrated production techniques and proprietary automated manufacturing systems. New types of coffeemakers and travel alarms and hair dryers and dozens of other new products started to appear that became market leaders based on innovations that consumers could recognize. Rid of the hi-fi burden, the company moved more aggressively into global markets. Simultaneous strength in several major world markets became a Braun hallmark, compared to competitors who tended to be strong in European appliance markets, or American markets, or Japanese, but not in all three. The aim was to offer products that retained an understated and distinctive "Braun look" that set them apart from others. Former Braun chairman Bob Murray summed up the formula: "We existed on the cachet of Braun design and Braun gestalt in a terribly overcrowded industry [small household appliances] that became commoditized."

It was a gradual process. By 1990, Braun still was clearly the worldwide leader in only one small market—hand blenders, which accounted for 6 percent of its sales. But six years later, Braun claimed world leadership for products making up 82 percent of its sales: Braun had finally displaced Philips as global leader (though not in the United States) in electric shaving dollar sales and was the world leader in oral care appliances (the Braun Oral-B plaque remover), epilators, hair dryers, and hand-held blenders.

Braun's Synthesis with Oral-B

Braun conducted a minor business in electric toothbrushes for a number of years, using skills in gearing miniaturized motors learned while making shavers. Its best success was in Scandinavian markets. Then in the mid-1980s a small American company, Dental Research Corporation, introduced a new type of electric brush named Interplak. Interplak was positioned as a plaque remover and sold for $99, which was three times the price of an ordinary electric toothbrush. That caught Braun's attention.

From his post as president of Oral-B in California, Jacques Lagarde had taken note too and, in fact, had tried to buy Interplak, figuring it was a perfect match for Oral-B, the leading manual toothbrush maker. Clinical tests seemed to prove the claims for the new oral appliance: the plaque remover was more efficient in cleaning teeth than manual toothbrushes, and Lagarde wanted the best of both worlds. But Bausch & Lomb acquired Interplak in 1988 by paying $133 million, which was considerably more than Gillette was willing to bid.

It turned out to be one of the best acquisitions Gillette never made. Bausch & Lomb struggled without great success to develop a substantial plaque remover business, but it finally gave up and sold the Interplak line to Conair in 1996, taking an after-tax loss of $6.3 million. While Bausch was struggling, Gillette had enjoyed great success with its own line of plaque removers by combining the resources of Braun and Oral-B.

When he moved to Germany in 1989 to take over as Braun chairman, Lagarde had a plan. He would marry Oral-B's expertise in bristle technology with Braun's skills in small motors, rechargeable batteries, and product design. By the time he arrived, Braun researchers had already started to develop a plaque remover featuring a replaceable bristle head geared to oscillate efficiently between teeth to destroy plaque in hard-to-reach spaces.

Lagarde put the Oral-B bristle specialists together with Braun engineers to fashion a superior bristle head. Braun completed its work on the motorized handle, especially the gearing for the separate head, and had a product ready for market. But how to sell it? Braun's name was not well known in the key U.S. oral products market; most dentists had never heard of the company. Those same dentists knew Oral-B well and had become a prime force behind the success of the company's manual brushes by making patients familiar with Oral-B's line and becoming unofficial agents for the company. The unorthodox solution Gillette decided on was to call the new product the Braun Oral-B Plaque

Remover, breaking a rule of thumb in marketing decreeing that two brand names on a single product confused customers. This was the exception to the rule, Lagarde figured. Braun was a respected name in shavers and appliances, connoting superior design and reliability. Oral-B was a respected brand name in toothbrushes, known to dentists and to health-conscious consumers, who had always been willing to pay a little more for Oral-B's high-quality manual brushes. The name would provide double value.

Having with some difficulty sold Braun and Oral-B management on the shared brand concept, Lagarde went a step further and decided to have the two companies share distribution. Braun distributes the plaque remover to retailers handling electric appliances and to mass merchandisers that carry all types of Braun products. Oral-B distributes the product through its established channels that include pharmacies, food markets, and the like, and provides thousands of plaque removers to dentists for sampling and, it is hoped, their endorsement to patients.

It was not the first time Lagarde had practiced a bit of synergy with Oral-B and Braun. While in California he had enlisted the help of Braun to help redesign the handles of Oral-B manual toothbrushes and had been pleased with the results. Another time, he asked Braun designers to redesign the packaging of Gillette's Jafra cosmetics line, the idea being to give a higher quality look to products sold at Jafra home "parties."

The cooperatively designed Braun Oral-B plaque remover in short order sold widely. Braun chairman Archie Livis noted that a few years' market experience showed that steady users replaced bristle heads four times a year, producing a repeat sales business that had provided stronger results than expected. Sales of Braun oral care appliances advanced more than 20 percent a year in the early 1990s and by 1996, accounted for $335 million in world sales.

In 1995, Braun entered a new market for Gillette—personal home diagnostics—with the acquisition of San Diego-based Thermoscan Inc., the leading marketer of electronic infrared ear thermometers used to measure human temperatures. The ink was not yet dry on the deal before Braun announced plans to extend distribution of the thermometers beyond North America to Europe and the Far East. The noninvasive thermometers are well suited for the home diagnostic market that Gillette sees as a global growth industry in the face of the rising costs of medical care in hospitals and doctors' offices. And not least, the thermometers feature disposable tips, ensuring still another steady replacement market.

King Camp Gillette would have liked that. And he would have enjoyed listening to Archie Livis at his Kronberg office talk about how Braun, a company once reluctant to venture outside its home market, had just built a factory in China for battery-operated shavers, had started new factories in Latin America, and was about to establish new marketing operations in India and the Philippines. Geographic expansion was the key to Braun's growth, Livis noted, sounding a lot like Gillette and Thomas Pelham and Vincent Ziegler and Colman Mockler and Al Zeien and so many others who, each in their way, positioned Gillette to take on the world.

Epilogue

AS GILLETTE'S SENIOR executives flew back to Boston from London in the fall of 1996, after winning the support of company directors to complete the Duracell acquisition, they were buoyed by the nearly universal praise for the "sixth leg" deal from media analysts and those on Wall Street. In particular the analysts agreed that Gillette's existing distribution and marketing strengths would lead to greatly increased sales of Duracell products outside Europe and North America in potentially higher-growth markets including China, India, and Russia.

That these markets have the "potential" for higher growth is worth a cautionary note. China could turn hostile to Western companies and free market nostrums, Russia and other nations of the former Soviet Union might grow weary of the austerity needed to wean their economies from communism and could retreat to old policies hostile to Western companies, and India could turn inward once again. Free market reforms anywhere around the globe could falter if other nations perceive them as synonymous with American domination, or, for that matter, if a populist wave causes the United States to renege on free trade commitments, setting off a global retreat to protectionism. Along with world growth has come a troubling and widening gap between haves and have-nots that could endanger free-market policies from skittish Europe to Latin America. There are many more "ifs and buts" that could slow down or derail the post-Cold War global economy that is so well suited to Gillette's grand strategy, but past experience shows that Gillette can handle geopolitical bumps in the road. The company has weathered external setbacks caused by wars, revolutions, and various forms of nationalistic or anti-business movements inimical to its aim of selling blades, shavers, pens, shampoos, and other quality goods to consumers around the world. Since its inception nearly 100 years ago, Gillette has consistently moved faster than its competitors into new geographic markets, sometimes at great risk, and has invested heavily in the development of world-class products as well as in the development of managers with global skills. It has remained doggedly internationalist in its outlook.

As a result, at the turn of the twenty-first century Gillette appears uncommonly in tune with the fast-moving global economy that has emerged in the 1990s. According to the International Monetary Fund, the world's economies averaged annual increases in gross domestic product of only 2 percent for the twenty years preceding 1993, then started a steady climb to the 4-percent range through 1996. The WEFA Group of Eddystone, Pa., long-term forecasters, expect 4-percent average world growth to continue for the next twenty years.

Gillette is well positioned to benefit from this growth. Al Zeien cites India as an example. After decades of success, Gillette was effectively thrown out in 1959 as the Indian government sought to protect domestic blade makers in the world's largest blade market. But as noted in Chapter 16, when India gradually began to re-open its markets to foreigners in the 1980s, Gillette plunged in via a joint venture with an Indian partner. When it became possible, Gillette sought an outright acquisition. With quality products to sell and a distribution system in place, the company expects to realize extraordinary growth in the subcontinent and in other fast-growing areas whose economies will continue to catch up with those of the more developed regions of the world in the decades ahead.

Zeien cautioned that the company has much more work ahead if it is to maintain its global momentum. An important factor will be Gillette's ability to expand its corps of global managers to handle the anticipated world growth; Zeien warned this will take time. He said the company must choose its priorities wisely and must smarten up and invest in the right people and the right projects. He is satisfied that the corporate culture has adjusted to his credo that a quickly growing global company must operate with speed and a sense of urgency moving products to market; it cannot afford complacency or gradualism—both of which almost cost Gillette its independence in fierce takeover battles less than a dozen years ago.

At the core of Gillette's global success today is its expanding menu of universal products—always beginning with blades—that are of the same quality wherever they are sold. Al Zeien: "I said the other day [to a group of securities analysts] that I would not trade our product portfolio with anybody, and they said, 'including Coke?' and I said, including Coke."

With the completion of the Duracell acquisition at the end of 1996, Gillette achieved one of the goals of its 1991 mission statement: "To achieve or enhance clear leadership, worldwide, in the existing or new core categories in which we choose to compete." In all, over 80 percent of the combined Gillette/Duracell sales of roughly $10 billion come from thirteen product categories in which Gillette holds a world leadership position.

It is worth noting that a post-Duracell round of senior promotions at Gillette early in 1997 resulted in the selection of three men of different nationalities for the three posts of executive vice president—fast-track jobs often leading to the top. Bob King, an American, was made executive vice president of the Gillette North Atlantic Group; Jorgen Wedel, a Dane, was made executive vice president of Gillette's International Group; and Jacques Lagarde, born in France, kept his job of executive vice president of Gillette's Diversified Group. At the same time Philip Hung, the Hong Kong native who was integral in Gillette's start-up ventures in China, was named to the top Braun job outside of Germany.

Globalism has arrived with full force in the Boston executive suites of Gillette. This seems yet another sign of an unstoppable momentum towards global business leadership envisioned by founder King C. Gillette almost a century ago.

ACKNOWLEDGMENTS

————

THIS BOOK FOCUSES on events of the modern era of Gillette, and so the major source of information is from interviews with men and women who have played a role in these matters since about 1975. I was fortunate to talk with some company veterans who were active at Gillette during the postwar years, including retired president Stephen J. Griffin and former Latin American and international executive vice president Walter Hunnewell. I was also fortunate to be able to speak with other retirees who played major roles in the 1960s and early 1970s. I am especially grateful to them for supplying much-needed "institutional memory" for the decades after World War II until the mid-1970s, when the main narrative of this book picks up. The Gillette Company encouraged its people, active and retired, to talk openly with me and helped arrange interviews with individuals outside the company who were linked with the company's modern history. These men and women are cited throughout the text by name when appropriate. Listed below is everyone I interviewed at length, whether or not they are cited in the text. Without exception, their patient cooperation was helpful.

As it became clearer to me that Gillette's relentless move toward globalism was at the heart of the company's history, I spent much time with Gillette people overseas and with Boston executives involved with global management, which is to say practically all Gillette senior executives. Many thanks to the good people at Gillette outposts in England, Germany, Poland, Russia, Brazil, and Argentina who showed me around their parts of the Gillette world.

Lisa J. Barstow of the Gillette public relations staff worked tirelessly as my cheerful and able associate, and her imprint is in every phase of this book. Her research work included interviewing and reporting in several chapters, especially those pages dealing with women's products. She read and critiqued my work with a critical eye that I valued greatly. Lisa left Gillette before the book's completion to join the public affairs staff at Massachusetts Hospital Association, but even after she left the company, she extricated me from a nearly terminal computer glitch one eventful weekend. Earlier, her expertise with the mysteries of the Apple computer system averted various disasters of my own making. Nikki Sabin at Harvard Business School Press read and red-penciled the manuscript, and I thank her and colleague Sarah Merrigan for numerous good suggestions.

Joan M. Gallagher and Danielle M. Frizzi from Gillette's public relations staff took over where Lisa left off and saw *Cutting Edge* through its final months. My long-time friend from early days together at *Business Week* magazine, Gillette public relations vice president David A. Fausch, invited me to write the book and was a calm and effective advocate throughout the process. And a special word of thanks to retired vice president for planning Paul N. Fruitt, for editorial direction and insights. At Gillette's public relations department, Matthew M. Miller, Patricia H. Klarfeld, Steve Brayton, and Jason T. A. Hogue provided timely help.

My wife Peggy was a constant source of enthusiasm tempered with good sense. She was a wonderful travel companion to some of Gillette's global outposts, and she asked insightful questions that helped a lot. I thank her, and all my family, for encouraging me in this project. Special thanks to my son, Bill McKibben, for reading an early draft with his writer's eye and suggesting some nifty and workable changes.

Among those at Gillette who provided data and insights on

short notice were Bruce Farmer and Marianne McLaughlin in the planning department, William Mostyn and James P. Connolly in the legal department, and Rita Shanahan, Paul Demers, Marianne Smith, Jill C. Richardson, John MacKenzie, and Susan Flinn.

Interviews were conducted in the United States with the following Gillette people, active and retired: Alfred M. Zeien, Joseph P. Mullaney, Thomas F. Skelly, Michael C. Hawley, Jacques Lagarde, Robert G. King, Joel P. Davis, Robert E. DiCenso, Edward F. DeGraan, Everett R. Howe, William J. McMorrow, Kenneth F. Kames, Lloyd B. Swaim, Milton L. Glass, Joseph F. Turley, Gian Camuzzi, Sharon A. Keith, John M. Darman, Jill Shurtleff, William D. Donovan, Peter K. Hoffman, Tim Schramm, Norman Roberts, Derwyn F. Phillips, Rodney S. Mills, Walter Hunnewell, Stephen J. Griffin, Gaston R. Levy, Robert W. Hinman, Robert J. Giovacchini, Robert E. Ray, Leonard A. Spalding, Robert J. Murray, Edward E. Pomfret, and Gregg Dwyer.

Gillette directors: Warren E. Buffett, Joseph J. Sisco, and Lawrence E. Fouraker.

Gillette executives or retirees in London, England: John Symons, José Luis Ribera, and Robert G. L. Forrester; Braun AG, Kronberg, Germany: Archie P. Livis, Dieter Rams, Norbert J. Gehrke, and Wolfgang Krohn; Lodz, Poland: Eric Adams and Zbigniew Glonek; St. Petersburg, Russia: Per Benemar, David Harden, David Whitlam, and Juan Gallo; Buenos Aires, Argentina: Jorge E. Micozzi, Augustin Merello, Carlos Ruiz Echazu, and Carlos Rotondo; Rio de Janeiro and Manaus, Brazil: Claudio Enrique Daireaux, R. M. Guia, Nei Eduardo da Silva, Claudio A. da Silva, Cynthia do Valle Bezerra, and Aluízio Sturzenecker.

Also, Robert Mockler, Eric Gleacher, Augustus Oliver, Joseph Flom, John Newman, Patrick F. McCartan, Samuel Hayes, Philip Dusenberry, and Ted Sann.

NOTES

Chapter 1

1. Robert W. Sampson, "Double, Stubble, Toil & Trouble: Innocence in the Art of Pogonotomy Is No Excuse," *Esquire,* July 1956, 57.

2. Howard Mansfield, "The Razor King; King Camp Gillette Created a Revolution in Shaving. He Tried to Create a Revolution in Society—But No One Cared," *American Heritage of Invention & Technology,* Spring 1992, 40–46.

3. Ovid's Poem on ms. pg. 17.

Chapter 2

1. *All Out of Step: A Personal Chronicle* (New York: Doubleday, 1956). Lambert wrote three other books before his personal chronicle, including a sailing mystery titled, "Murder in Newport," but gave up fiction writing when publisher Charles Scribner, an old friend, told him a second thriller was unpublishable.

Chapter 3

1. "500 Largest U.S. Industrial Corporations," *Fortune,* July 1962.

2. Much of the account of Gillette's foray into Iran is spelled out in a thick "Iran file" that was kept by retired Gillette executive Robert W. Hinman, who graciously made it available to the author and added his comments during an interview.

Chapter 4

1. Neil Ulman, "Gillette Chairman Takes a Long View in Program to Brighten Profit Picture," *The Wall Street Journal,* 28 June 1977.

---

2. Eleanor Roberts, "They're Born Again," *The Boston Herald American,* 23 January 1977.

3. Susan Trausch, "Mockler's Quiet Takeover at Gillette; All Along the Line—A Sigh of Relief," *The Boston Evening Globe,* 28 July 1974.

4. While published accounts say that the "Cricket" was born with that name, it seems possible that the first French-only lighter was named "Criquet," the French word for grasshopper, which rhymes precisely with "briquet," meaning lighter, and "Criquet" later was anglicized to "Cricket."

Chapter 6

1. "NLJ TOP 250 DATABASE," *National Law Journal,* © 1996, New York Law Publishing Company.

Chapter 7

1. Robert J. Cole, "High-Stakes Drama at Revlon," *The New York Times,* 11 November 1985.

2. George Anders, "Boesky Fund Sold Big Blocks of Securities; Sales of $440 Million Made Before Friday's Report of Trading Violations," *The Wall Street Journal,* 20 November 1986.

3. David Wessel and Michael W. Miller, "Gillette Appears to Have Little Chance of Staying Independent After Revlon Bid," *The Wall Street Journal,* 17 November 1986.

4. Ibid.

5. Daniel Hertzberg and James B. Stewart, "SEC Is Probing Drexel on 'Junk Bonds,' Ties to Boesky as Sources Identify More Prominent Figures in Inquiry; Trader Wired During Talks; Subpoenas Said to Name at Least 10 Other People," *The Wall Street Journal,* 18 November 1986.

6. Geoffrey Smith, "Revlon Boss Unloads on Gillette Brass," *The Boston Herald,* 20 November 1986.

7. Marvin R. Shanken, "Ron Perelman: Q&A Interview," *Cigar Aficionado,* Spring 1995.

Chapter 8

1. Alex Beam, "For Gillette, Life Not Same After Arrival of Perelman," *The Boston Globe,* 19 June 1987.

2. Robert Guenther, "Gillette Is Severing Ties with Citibank over Bank's Role in Hostile Revlon Plan," *The Wall Street Journal,* 14 August 1987.

3. Ibid.

4. "Irwin Jacobs Confirms He Owns 'Substantial' Gillette Stake," *Dow Jones News Service*, 19 June 1987.

5. Alison Leigh Cowan, "Revlon Asks to Bid for Gillette; Proposed Offer of $47 a Share Turned Down," *The New York Times*, Early NY Edition, 18 August 1987.

6. John King, "Takeover Battles Heating Up; Perelman Keeps Pushing, Makes 3d Offer for Gillette," *The Boston Globe*, 18 August 1987.

Chapter 9

1. Milton Moskowitz, "Viewpoints; The Selling of America; Takeovers by Foreign Firms Were Temporarily Slowed by Crash—Now They're Back in Full Swing," *Los Angeles Times*, 24 January 1988.

2. Randall Smith, "Top Raider Coniston to Disband; Colder Environment for Debt Financing Caused the Decision," *The Wall Street Journal*, 22 June 1990.

3. David Callaway, "Investor Trio Parlayed $3 Million into $600 Million," *The Boston Herald*, 18 February 1988.

4. Stephen Taub, "Strop Tease," *Financial World*, 20 September 1988, 12.

Chapter 11

1. Anthony Ramirez, "Gillette Challenge to the Disposables," *The New York Times*, 4 October 1989.

2. "Chairman of Gillette Dies at Work," *The Boston Globe*, 26 January 1991.

Chapter 12

1. "Gillette's Takeover Plan OK'd; Court Allows Company to Bid on Parker Pen;" *The Boston Globe*, City Edition, 24 March 1993. No author cited; however, it is noted that *The Associated Press* contributed to this story.

2. Barbara Carton, "Thank Carl Klumpp for the Swell Smell of Right Guard; Gillette Co.'s Chief Perfumer Comes Up with Fragrances with World-Wide Appeal," *The Wall Street Journal*, 11 May 1995.

Chapter 13

1. William M. Bulkeley, "Duracell Pact Gives Gillette an Added Source of Power; Purchase of Battery Maker for $7.3 Billion Promises Distribution Advantages," *The Wall Street Journal*, 13 September 1996.

Chapter 14

1. Mitchell Zuckoff, "Taking a Profit, and Inflicting a Cost; U.S. Firms

Seeking Riches Among the Foreign Poor; Foul Trade; First of Three Parts," *The Boston Globe,* 10 July 1994.

2. Louis Uchitelle, "Gillette's World View: One Blade Fits All," *The New York Times,* 3 January 1994.

Chapter 16

1. Michael Parks, "Gillette Carves Out Piece of China's 'Huge' Razor-Blade Market," *International Herald Tribune,* 11–12 August 1984.

Chapter 17

1. No trace of this newspaper could be found at the Braun offices in Kronberg, but this story is firmly entrenched in Gillette lore.

NOTES ABOUT SOURCES

Chapters 1–3

Much of the material in these chapters that provides an overview of King C. Gillette's life and the Gillette corporate history from 1901 to 1975 was first published in *King C. Gillette: The Man and His Wonderful Shaving Device* by Russell B. Adams, Jr. (Boston: Little, Brown, 1978). I have added or embellished some material from the same company archives that Adams plumbed so well for his book, which emphasizes the life and times of King Gillette, and looks at the duality of his life as inventor-businessman and social utopian. In this book, there is new material on the early era; for example, references in Chapter 2 to the magnetized blade-compass Gillette built for World War II spies is from a book by Lloyd R. Shoemaker (*The Escape Factory*, St. Martin's Press, New York, 1990) and a telephone interview with retired Gillette employee André Doucet of Paris, who related how Gillette hid its blade-making machines from the occupying Nazi forces during World War II. The account of Gillette's ill-fated Iranian joint venture is largely from correspondence preserved by retired Gillette executive Robert Hinman and from his recollections, along with those of retired president Stephen Griffin. New material regarding the development of the Trac II razor is from an unpublished memo by Dr. Norman Welsh and interviews with Trac II co-inventor Edward Pomfret. *Once over Lightly* by Charles de Zemler (New York: Chas. de Zemler, 1939) is an anecdotal and entertaining tale of barbering from the earliest times that includes numerous illustrations of male hair and beard styles. Gillette's wonderfully readable house organ of the prewar days, the *Blade,* while hardly a neutral source, is filled with rich anecdotal and factual material, especially in the mid-1920s.

Chapters 4–5

The information about Liquid Paper history before its sale to Gillette is from the April 1980 issue of *Letter Perfect,* a magazine published by Liquid Paper Corp.

Special thanks to Robert Mockler for tracing his family history, and for his professional comments on the business career of his older brother, Colman Mockler.

Chapters 6–8

The account of the takeover period is mostly from dozens of interviews from those involved in this time of crisis for Gillette. This information is supplemented by numerous articles in the *Wall Street Journal, New York Times, Boston Globe* and a large array of magazines including *Business Week* and *Fortune.*

Patrick McCartan and Jack Newman, with a lot of help from associate Nancy Adamczyk, guided me through the voluminous Revlon and Coniston courtroom and legal documents stored in the Cleveland law offices of Jones Day, and helped put human flesh on the legal bones. Leonard Spalding gave me similarly insightful help in steering through legal documents stored in Boston.

Ronald O. Perelman did not respond to requests for an interview. Interesting references to Perelman, Ivan F. Boesky, and Drexel Burnham Lambert, some of them specific to the Gillette takeover attempts, can be found in several books, including *The Predators' Ball,* by Connie Bruck (New York: American Lawyer/Simon & Schuster, 1988); *Going for Broke,* by John Rothchild (New York: Simon and Schuster, 1991); *April Fools,* by Dan G. Stone (New York: Donald I. Fine, 1990); *Nightmare on Wall Street,* by Martin Mayer (New York: Simon and Schuster, 1993); and *Den of Thieves,* by James Stewart (New York: Simon and Schuster, 1991). Academic accounts, many critical of Gillette's efforts to remain independent at the cost of short-term gains to shareholders, were numerous during this period, when the issue of greenmail was being debated. Harvard Business School professor Joseph Auerbach and Boston University School of Management professor Allen Michael were among the many academic critics of Gillette's buyback of Perelman's shares.

Chapters 9–11

A long, and unflattering article about the Coniston Partners and their relationship to Tito Tettamanti ("Silent Partner," by Joe Queenan) was published by *Barron's* on August 15, 1988. During a phone interview, Augustus "Gus" Oliver, speaking for the Coniston Partners, challenged the article's accuracy and alleged repetition of unproven innuendo.

Videotapes, which fill several floor-to-ceiling cases at Gillette, started to supplement or replace written documents as historical accounts at about this time; for example, the video of the climactic 1988 annual meeting provides a good sense of that dramatic event, and videos of product introductions like the Sensor launch tell more about the length the company will go to introduce new shaving systems than any amount of words. It seems likely that corporate historians in the twenty-first century will spend nearly as much time watching videos as reading documents.

Buffett, by Roger Lowenstein (New York: Random House, 1995), is a well documented and entertaining account of Warren Buffett's personal life and business dealings.

Chapters 12–13

The Mallorys of Mystic: Six Generations in American Maritime Enterprise, by James P. Baughman (Middletown, Conn.: Wesleyan University Press, 1972), tells of the Mallory family's shipping empire and the early days of Philip R. Mallory, the first Mallory to leave the family business to strike out on his own. His firm, P. R. Mallory Company, was the parent of the enterprise that became Duracell International Inc. A Duracell publication, *The Story of Packaged Power,* traces the key role of inventor Samuel Ruben in Duracell's history and is a rich source of information about electrochemical cells that store energy for release when a switch is flipped on—in other words, batteries.

Chapters 14–17

Most material is from interviews and observations at several Gillette sites in Latin America and Europe, and from interviews with Boston executives experienced in all parts of the world. Among the many documents and books that were helpful are *World Class: Thriving Locally in the Global Economy,* by Rosabeth Moss Kanter (New York: Simon and Schuster, 1995) and *If Everyone Bought One Shoe: American Capitalism in Communist China,* by Graeme Browning (New York: Hill and Wang, 1989).

INDEX

ABOUT THE AUTHOR

———

Gordon McKibben has spent 40 years as a business writer and editor. During his career, he has worked for *The Wall Street Journal* in California, and for *Business Week* in Los Angeles, Toronto, and Boston. He also spent 15 years at *The Boston Globe* as business editor, European correspondent, and ombudsman. He holds a bachelor's degree in journalism from Stanford University and a master's degree in political science from the University of Washington. He is married and lives with his wife Peggy in Lexington, Massachusetts.